Heeren, Arnold Hermann Ludwig

Historical researches into asiatic nations, scythians, indians, appendixes

Heeren, Arnold Hermann Ludwig

Historical researches into asiatic nations, scythians, indians, appendixes

Inktank publishing, 2018

www.inktank-publishing.com

ISBN/EAN: 9783747769027

HISTORICAL RESEARCHES

INTO THE

POLITICS, INTERCOURSE, AND TRADE OF THE PRINCIPAL NATIONS OF ANTIQUITY.

BY A. H. L. HEEREN,

KNIGHT OF THE NORTH STAR AND GUELPHIC ORDER; AULIC COUNSELLOR AND PROFESSOR OF HISTORY IN THE UNIVERSITY OF GOETTINGEN; AND MEMBER OF SEVERAL OTHER LEARNED SOCIETIES.

TRANSLATED FROM THE GERMAN.

VOL. II.

ASIATIC NATIONS. SCYTHIANS, INDIANS, APPENDIXES.

LONDON:
HENRY G. BOHN, YORK STREET, COVENT GARDEN.
MDCCCXLVI.

CONTENTS

OF

THE SECOND VOLUME.

SCYTHIANS.

INDIANS.

APPENDIX.

SCYTHIANS.

SCYTHIANS.

CHAPTER I.

Geographical Survey of the Scythian Tribes.

GOMER, AND ALL HIS BANDS; THE HOUSE OF TOGARMAH OF THE NORTH QUARTERS, AND ALL HIS BANDS: AND MANY PEOPLE WITH THEE.

EZEKIEL, xxxviii. 6.

The aspect of Central Asia, or the wild countries between the Taurus and Altai chain of mountains, have not, it must be confessed, the same attractions as the southern parts of this quarter of the globe. Those boundless plains, without wood or arable land, and covered only with pasture for cattle, present to the eye as little variety as the encampments of the wandering tribes who travel through them with their herds. But the great influence which these people have exercised on the fortunes of the human race would render it unpardonable to pass them over in silence, even if the period of the Persian empire did not supply us with more ample materials for the investigation than we might otherwise expect.

The name of Scythians is quite as vague in ancient geography, as those of Tartars and Monguls are at present. We sometimes find the name applied to a particular people, and sometimes to all the nomad tribes who were settled throughout that immense tract of country extending from the north of the Black and Caspian Seas, into the heart of Asia. The same uncertainty prevails in the use of a name for the country, the term Scythia being sometimes applied to the region inhabited by Scythians properly so called, and sometimes employed as an indefinite appellation for modern Mongolia and Tartary. We shall use the names Scythia and Scythians in this latter extended sense, a liberty which will be permitted in a general survey, although the Scythi-

B 2

ans may have already formed a distinct people, at the era to which our researches apply.

We cannot be surprised that nations who have never had any fixed place of abode, but have always led an unsettled life, should leave their country on the slightest occasion, and wander about from one to another. Moreover, these changes of habitation make it necessary to take one particular point of time when we are delineating such countries; for otherwise, it is evident from the nature of the case, the several parts of our sketch will not be in keeping with each other; perhaps they will even be at variance with truth. This necessity becomes much more urgent when we are taking a general survey of the nomad tribes of Central Asia. From the earliest times we have noticed periodical emigrations of these nations from east to west; their extensive country seems to have been, as it were, the magazine of our race. The farther back we go into the history of the first ages of the world, the more probable does it appear that the whole of western Europe received its population from thence; and it is a case of common notoriety, that these regions have been the focus of important revolutions at a more modern epoch. It would, therefore, be a great error to found our observations on Pomponius Mela, or Ptolemy, or to intermix the picture set before us by these geographers, with the more credible delineations of earlier writers.[1] Herodotus,[2] then, a contemporary author, will be our only

[1] An investigation concerning the ancient northern tribes is, according to Ptolemy, one of the most difficult in history. This chaos was first reduced to something like order by Gatterer, in his inquiry into the origin of the Finni, Letti, and Slavi, in the *Commentat. Soc. Götting.* (Vol. XI. XII.) His first treatise particularly, *de Sarmatica Letticorum populorum origine*, belongs to our subject. Many illustrations on this point have been given in Mannert's Ancient Geography, and in Rennel's Geography of Herodotus.

[2] Herodotus did not confine his travels to Olbia, but saw also a part of the country of the Scythians, (iv. 81,) and obtained as much information about them, as he did relative to the Greeks of Pontus. It is certain that he examined these countries with great care, and faithfully related whatever he had seen and heard. I rely therefore implicitly on him for measures and distances. We have no means of deciding whether those he gives are correct or not, and risk much more in departing from, than we do in following him. The different accounts of Darius's Scythian expedition rested upon traditions which were collected here; and on this point I acknowledge with the excellent biographer of Herodotus, DAHLMANN, *Forschungen aus der Geschichte*, (Historical Researches,) II. p. 159, that these people have gone into much exaggeration on the subject, when they assert that Darius advanced as far as the Wolga, and raised some forts on that river. But we must not forget

guide, who has devoted the fourth book of his work to a description of the immense steppes which unite Europe to Asia. This great historian seems here to be perfectly familiar with his subject; he is acquainted with the rivers, the country, and the people; their manners and way of life no less than their parentage. The wilds of the Ukraine and Astracan are geographically described by him; and it is in his work that the ancestors of the Letti, Finns, Turks, Germans, and Calmucks first occupy a place in history; he has mentioned the Ural and Altai chain, though without a fixed appellation; and we even read of traditions concerning Siberia, which, though they at first appeared unworthy of credit, have been subsequently verified.

Herodotus begins his description with the European countries on this side of the Don or Tanais, or new Ukraine, and for the sake of method, it will be necessary to follow him in the same order. The division which he has adopted, is that formed by the rivers, and is indeed the best way of settling the boundaries of districts inhabited by wandering tribes who have no fixed residence. The principal rivers mentioned by the historian are undoubtedly correct; but two, which flow across the steppes, are uncertain, and he seems to have considered them larger than they are in reality.[3]

Conformable to his exactness in fixing localities, is the distinction which he establishes between different tribes, enumerating eight of Scythians, properly so called: who-

that the Persian army contained an abundance of light cavalry, which could and must have advanced in all directions as the Scythians retired before them. To what distances do not the Cossacks at this day remove before the regular armies of the Russians? I would not, however, maintain that the vanguard of the Persian army advanced as far as the Wolga, or found upon the traditions a distinction which they do not make; but could only give the point of view in which we ought, in my opinion, to look upon the subject.

[3] The principal of these rivers are, the Ister or Danube, the Tyras or Dniester, (still called Tyral, near its mouth,) the Hypamis or Bog, which unites with the Borysthenes or Dnieper, before it empties itself into the Black Sea. Between this last and the Tanais or Don, which flows into the sea of Azof, Herodotus has placed three secondary rivers, the Pantikapes, the Hypakyris, and the Gerrus, of which the last is uncertain, and the two others are not to be found, at least according to his description. (See MANNERT, *Geography*, iv. p. 31. RENNEL, p. 57.) These uncertainties, however, only affect the line of demarcation of some Scythian tribes between the Dnieper and Don, and have nothing to do with other nations settled beyond the Don, and farther towards the north.

ever were not included in these did not belong to the Scythian stock. The settlements which he assigns to the Scythians proper extend from the Danube to the Tanais, or Don,[4] around which several other tribes had their residence. The Scythians, or Skolots, as they were called in their own language, had not always inhabited this tract of country, but were reported, by historical tradition preserved among themselves, to have come from the East. Being pressed by another people, the Massagetæ, they crossed the river Araxes, expelled the Cimmerians,[5] and took possession of their settlements, which they still retained in the age of our historian. From time to time they made irruptions into the south of Asia; and in a great expedition undertaken by the whole nation against the remains of the Cimmerians, they even conquered the Medes about seventy years before Cyrus, kept the whole of Asia Minor in subjection to them for eight and twenty years, and extended their excursions to the borders of Egypt, whose king Psammetichus was obliged to buy them off.[6]

I shall now make the reader acquainted with each of the tribes comprehended under the general name of Scythians. My plan will be to present them in the order of their relation to each other, and to fix their settlements by rivers; which, I flatter myself, will prevent our falling into any considerable mistakes. As long as we are confined to the shores of the Black Sea the subject will be clear and with-

[4] The boundaries which Herodotus assigns to Syria are as follows: on the south, the coast of the Black Sea, from the mouth of the Danube to the Palus Mæotis (called by him Mæetis); on the east, the Persian Gulf and the Don, or Tanais, to its rise out of the lake Ivan, which Herodotus was acquainted with; on the north, a line drawn from this lake to that out of which the Tyras (or Dniester) flows, that is, to the northern arm of the last lake in the circle of Sombrov in Galizia, towards the 49th degree of latitude; for Herodotus makes this lake the frontier between the Scythians and Neuri, whose settlements began about the 50th degree. HEROD. iv. 55. Lastly, the western boundary was a line from thence to the Danube. Thus the figure of Scythia is that of an irregular oblong, which Herodotus ascribes to it, iv. 101, 102.

[5] HEROD. iv. 11, 12. I forbear to notice the other fabulous traditions concerning the Scythians. In this passage, we are, in my opinion, to understand the river Wolga for the Araxes. I have already remarked, that this name does not always mean the same river, in Herodotus, but is also applied to different streams on the eastern side of the Caspian Sea; it was probably a general denomination for any river.

[6] HEROD. i. 103—106. This is the famous Scythian invasion, which Michaelis and Schlözer have shown to be identified with that of the Chaldeans.

out difficulty: it is first involved in obscurity, and we cannot be surprised, when it regards the remote countries of the North.

The northern coast of the Black Sea was occupied by Greek colonies, of which the most considerable was Olbia on the Borysthenes, whose name it sometimes bore. With respect to these, it has been already observed,[7] that they had all one common origin from the city of Miletus. They were situated at the mouths of the large rivers; and beyond them the Greeks had formed many other settlements; viz. in the Crimea at Panticapæum, and on the farther shore of the sea of Azof, at the mouth of the river Tanais,[8] where Milesian merchants had established themselves.

In their vicinity, the Tauri occupied the greatest part of the Crimea, to which they gave their own name. They figure in Greek mythology as a people of barbarous customs and manners, being even addicted to human sacrifices, which were practised among them in the days of Herodotus.[9] "They gain their livelihood," says this historian, "by war and plunder." Their origin is not known, but they were probably a remnant of the Cimmerians,[10] whom the Scythians dispossessed of their settlements; for the most ferocious conquerors are seldom found to exterminate a people utterly; and as we find no further traces of them in their former country, our conjecture may be considered very probable, at least in the absence of any express testimony.

Next to these, the Scythian tribes first occur along both sides of the river Dnieper; and to the west, on the banks of this river, above the city of Olbia, the Callipidæ, a mixed people of Greeks and Scythians,[11] who had fixed habitations, and applied to agriculture as well as their neighbours, the Alazones, whose ancient abodes must be sought where the Dnieper and Bog approach the nearest to each other. The

[7] See above, p. 70, sq.

[8] A new light has been diffused over these cities, and principally over Olbia, by the controversies which have been lately entered into. See Raoul Rochette, *Antiquités Grecques de Bosphore Cimmerien*, Paris, 1822; Peter Von Koppen, *Alterthümer am Gestad des Pontus*, (Antiquities of the coast of Pontus,) Vienna, 1823; and Von Kolu, *Zwei Aufschriften Von Olbia*, (two inscriptions from Olbia,) Petersburg, 1822. I shall make use of these different works in speaking of the Greek colonies. It would as yet be too soon, while we are engaged with the inland nations.

[9] Herod. iv. 103. [10] Gatterer, l. c. p. 140. [11] Herod. iv. 17.

tribes which were settled above these, comprehended under the general name of agricultural Scythians, followed the same way of life.[12] They cultivated the land, however, less for the sake of enjoying its produce themselves than on account of the trade which they carried on in corn.

These last, it is true, extended far towards the west, but the principal tribes were only settled on the eastern side of the Dnieper, between this river and the Don or Tanais. "Having crossed the Borysthenes," says Herodotus, "a woody region first presents itself, after which we come to the agricultural Scythians, whom the Greeks name Borysthenites, but they call themselves Olbiopolites."

It is uncertain whether there remain any traces of that woody region. Some old maps present the name of the Black Forest in the very same place; and this may have had a much wider extent in earlier times. From the communications of several travellers, however, it appears, that there is no wood there now, although the fact of its having once existed, is preserved in the popular traditions of the country; nor does the woody country occur until we come to the banks of the river Don.[13] Modern travellers assert, that these districts, which at the present day are occupied by colonies of Germans, Greeks, and others, afford a soil very favourable to the pursuit of agriculture. Rich meadow land, which can easily be converted into arable, is their general character; from the Don to the Danube, from Poland to the sea of Azof, the soil is deep and fruitful, and well adapted to every kind of produce.[14]

According to Herodotus, the settlements of those agricultural Scythians extended three days' journey to the east from Olbia, as far as the river Pantikapes, which empties itself into the Dnieper, and flows through the woody country to the north, eleven days' navigation up the Borysthenes. If we follow Gatterer in considering the Pantikapes to be the same as the Desna, we must make the woody country

[12] Herod. l. c.

[13] The forest commences near Tcherkask, on the banks of the Don, and extends to the Dnieper near Tchernigov, in 52° 30′ of north latitude, having the appearance of a long black line on the horizon; it is here succeeded by a steppe, which continues to the Black Sea, and presents a considerable number of monumental mounds.

[14] *New Russia*, by Miss Holderness, Lond. 1823.

reach as far as Kiev; in this case, the country of the agricultural Scythians would begin at the confluence of the Desna and Dnieper, and extend northward to Mohilow on the Dnieper, 54° N. L.[15] But it is not easy to believe, that the Pantikapes is the same river as the Desna; as we are not authorized by the expression of Herodotus to suppose that the woody country extended so far north; and the distance between the Dnieper and the Desna is not equal to three days' journey. I would therefore take the Pantikapes for one of the more southern rivers which fall into the Dnieper, either the Sula or the Psol. Under this view, the limit of the country inhabited by the agricultural Scythians, will be fixed near Kiev, 51° N. L. The importance of settling the locality of these tribes will be readily acknowledged; but we shall pursue the investigation no farther, as it is amply sufficient for all the purposes of a general survey, to know that the district in question lies between the Don and the Dnieper, and that the agricultural Scythians occupied the western part of it. On the other side of the Pantikapes, we enter upon the country of the nomad Scythians, who neither plough nor sow. It is a steppe destitute of wood, and comprehending a space of fourteen days' journey in an eastern direction as far as the river Gerrus, and the region which bears the same name, where are the tombs of the Scythian kings.[16] Beyond this river the ruling horde of the Scythians, who were named royal, first appear; their country is bounded on the south by the lake Mæotis and

[15] M. v. Koppen, l. c. p. 12, note 2, thinks I am mistaken in making the Scythia of Herodotus extend so far north as Mohilow; he adds, that it was terminated by the southern *tumuli* in the government of Kursk, where, owing to peculiar circumstances, we discover quite a different race of men, inasmuch as the southern and northern Russians differ from each other, both in language and in manners. It is, however, doubtful whether these *tumuli* should be considered to decide the question; at the same time it seemed reasonable to fix the limit at Mohilow, on account of our uncertainty respecting the course of the Pantikapes, as well as the mention of eleven days' navigation on the Dnieper. If, as I think, the river Psol is the ancient Pantikapes, the opinion of M. Köppen with respect to the north-western limit of Scythia, coincides with mine: but I hold, from the express declaration of Herodotus, that its north-eastern frontier extended as far as 54 or 55° N. L.

[16] Herod. iv. 19. The region of Gerrus must have been at a considerable distance up the Dnieper, as we are told that forty days' navigation on that river were required before they came to it (iv. 52). But we cannot form any estimation of these days' navigation against the stream. We are acquainted with no vestige of the tombs of the Scythian kings.

the city Cremni, and on the east by the river Don, which here terminates the whole of Scythia.

Herodotus speaks of some other nations on this side of the river Don, who bordered on the Scythians to the west and north, but were not of a similar extraction with them. These, with the addition of the Tauri and Greeks, whom I mentioned before, as being settled on the south of Scythia, were the Agathyrsi, the Neuri, the Anthropophagi, and the Melanchlæni. Among these, the Agathyrsi were farthest towards the west; they lived, according to the express words of our historian, on the Maris,[17] (Marosch,) which falls into the Danube, and occupies a part of Transylvania and Temeswarian Banat. They were a very rich people, having an abundance of gold, probably obtained from the Carpathian mountains, which they employed for the fabrication of their utensils. We are not to suppose that they were at the trouble of working gold mines, as the metal was probably found in the sand washed down by their rivers. In the centre of the region which now comprises Poland and Lithuania, Herodotus places the Neuri,[18] bounded on one side by the Carpathian mountains, and the lake out of which the Dniester rises;[19] and on the other, by the Dnieper. They had been once obliged to leave their country, on account of a quantity of serpents, with which it was infested, and had taken refuge with the Budini on the eastern side of the Don; but they afterwards returned.[20]

[17] Herod. iv. 48, 100, 104. This helps to determine the settlements of the other tribes. It is surprising how well Herodotus was acquainted with the inferior rivers which flow into the lower Danube (i. 48, 49). For this accurate information he must have been indebted to intimate commercial relations between the Greeks of Pontus and the inhabitants of the Carpathian mountains.

[18] Herod. iv. 17.

[19] Herod. iv. 51. This author was acquainted with the entire course of all the rivers from the Danube to the Don, the Dnieper alone excepted, respecting which he avows his ignorance, iv. 53.

[20] So Gatterer explains the passage, Herod. iv. 105, translating ἐς ὅ πιεζόμενοι, "so long as they were molested," which was formerly rendered by "while they were thus molested:" this does away with all apparent contradictions in Herodotus to the passage in iv. 21, as well as puts an end to all discussion relative to the country of the Neuri and Budini. (See the commentators on Herodotus and Mannert.) Schweighæuser ad h. l. translates ἐς ὅ, *ad extremum*, because Herodotus never uses these words in the sense of *quamdiu*. He adds, however, that the Neuri returned to their country when it was no longer infested by the serpents. Whatever interpretation may be adopted, it will not affect the limits which have been assigned to the Neuri, Herod. iv. 51.

Scythia was bounded on the west by the country of these two nations; and on the north, by that of the Anthropophagi, (cannibals,) and Melanchlæni, (black clothed,) from whom it was, however, separated by a desert.[21] The former of these were settled in the modern government of Smolensk, and the latter in the vicinity of Moscow; and their names were not the peculiar appellation of the tribes to which they belonged; but rather were derived from their customs and dress. Herodotus says expressly, that they were not of Scythian extraction; and we learn at a later period that their true name was Bastarnæ.[22] These were a branch from the German stock, which probably first occupied the Scythian country, and were expelled from it by the inroads of other wandering tribes. Thus Herodotus is the first author who has made us acquainted with the ancestors of the modern Germans, such as they were in these remote ages, when they clothed themselves with the skins of animals and fed on human flesh.

The Tanais or Don formed the eastern boundary of Scythia. On the other side of this river we meet with a new race, that is to say, the Sarmatians,[23] whose name is no less celebrated than that of the Scythians. "On crossing the Tanais we come to no more Scythians, but enter into a country inhabited by the Sarmatians, who extend to a distance of five days' journey towards the north from the Palus Mæotis. The district which they possess is equally destitute of wild and of cultivated trees." It is clear from this passage of the historian, that they occupied the steppe, which is now appropriated to the Cossacks of the Don; and perhaps a part of that of Astracan besides. As fifteen days' journey are equivalent to about seventy-five German miles, (about three hundred English,) their country must have extended to the 48th degree of north latitude, or to the point where the Don and the Wolga approach the nearest to each other. The language, however, of the Sarmatians was a dialect of the Scythian; and according to the fabulous tra-

[21] HEROD. iv. 18, 20.

[22] GATTERER, l. c. p. 148. From a comparison of Herodotus with Strabo. It is plain that the appellations of Anthropophagi and Melanchlæni were derived from the Greeks.

[23] HEROD. iv. 21. He calls them Σαυρομάται.

dition, their nation owed its origin to an intermixture of the Scythians with the Amazons.

Another very remarkable people were settled above the Sarmatians, viz. the Budini.[24] "They inhabited a country full of thick woods. They were very numerous, and had blue eyes and red hair. In their country there was a city, whose walls, houses, and temples were of wood; and each of its sides were thirty stades (about three miles) long. The inhabitants of the city, however, the Geloni, were originally Greeks who had retired thither from the commercial towns; and they spoke a mixed dialect of Greek and Scythian. The Budini, on the contrary, had a language and way of life peculiar to themselves; they were nomads, and lived by hunting, while the Geloni cultivated the soil, and supported themselves by its produce. They likewise differed from each other in complexion. It is true that the Greeks used to apply the name of Geloni to the Budini; but it is very incorrect to confound these two nations."

According to this, the settlements of the Budini began where those of the Sarmatian steppe ended, viz. in the government of Saratov; but Herodotus does not inform us how far they extended to the north or east; his calling them, however, a great and powerful nation is sufficient to convince us that their territory must have been considerable. If we admit that it was equal in extent to that of the Sarmatians, it will have comprised the present governments of Pensa, Simbirsk, Kasan, with a part of that of Perm, and terminate in the vicinity of the southern branch of the Ural mountains. We know that at this day these provinces abound in woods of oak, the magazines for Russian naval architecture; which perfectly agrees with the account of Herodotus, that the Budini inhabited thick forests; as they were not then so enlightened as at present. We cannot now discover the lake mentioned by Herodotus; but it is to be observed that he describes it as a morass, and we shall remark hereafter that the same place where we should expect to find it, is occupied by marshy grounds, which at certain periods turn the land into a vast lake; and this will also afford me an opportunity to express my opinion re-

[24] Herod. iv. 108.

specting the colonies of Greeks which were established here, and their motives for forming such settlements.

"Beyond the Budini[25] on the north, there is a desert, seven days' journey in length. Having crossed this, and turned eastward, we come to the Thyssagetæ, a large and independent nation, who live by hunting. In the same country, and adjoining them, we come to another people, the Iurcæ, who follow the same way of life. They climb trees, where they watch for the deer; and hunt with horses and dogs; their horses are taught to lie down on their belly in order to appear smaller. To the east of these are to be found a colony of emigrants from Scythia, (Scythæ exules,) who came from the country of the royal Scythians."

Thus we fix the northern boundary of the Budini, in 54° N. L., and adding to the account the desert of seven days' journey, or five and thirty miles, (about one hundred and forty, English measure,) we shall come to the government of Wiatka, towards the 56th degree of latitude. Here we must turn towards the east, in order to arrive in the country of the Thyssagetæ, and Iurcæ; and this can be no other than the government of Perm, near the Ural mountains. Herodotus assures us that the Thyssagetæ were very numerous; whence we are authorized to suppose that they would occupy the whole of the government of Perm, and even extend beyond it on the north. With respect to the Iurcæ, who, as it has been remarked, inhabited the same country, it would appear, forming our calculation from the order adopted by Herodotus, that they occupied the eastern part, that they reached nearly to the Ural chain, and were even to be found in the interior of these mountains. In the succeeding chapter we shall return to the Iurcæ, and endeavour to throw some light upon them, as well as upon the Scythian emigrants.

Herodotus continues thus:[26] "Leaving the habitations of these Scythians, the country, which was before plain and open, now becomes unequal and mountainous." Taking this passage as our guide, we shall seek for the ancient abodes of these tribes on the western side of the Ural chain; but as they are said to have extended to the foot of these

[25] Herod. iv. 22. [26] Ibid. iv. 23.

mountains, and even into their interior, we shall conclude that they touched upon the frontiers of Siberia.[27]

Hence we can have no difficulty in deciding the stony and mountainous country which follows, to be the Ural chain, reaching from the northern side of the Caspian to the icy sea.

"Having[28] proceeded a considerable way through this stony region, we come to the people named Argippæi, settled at the foot of high mountains. The women as well as the men of this nation are bald from their youth; they have flat noses and large jaw bones; their costume is Scythian; but their language peculiar to themselves." From the physical account of this people, with which our author has furnished us, we can have no hesitation in identifying them with the Calmucks, a principal branch of the Monguls. "Their diet," says Herodotus, "partly consists in the fruit of a tree named Ponticum, about the size of a fig tree. The fruit which it produces resembles a bean in the pod. When this is ripe, they put it in bags for filtration, and a thick black juice issues out, which is called Aschy; this becomes a part of their food, either by itself, or mixed with milk. The mass of the fruit remaining after this process is formed into cakes, which are baked and eaten by them. They have few sheep, as their pastures are but indifferent." The fruit in question is probably the bird's cherry, (Pennus Padus, Linn.,) which at this day the Calmucks eat in almost the same manner; they dress the berries with milk, then press them in a sieve, and afterwards form them into a thick mass, which is called *moisun chat;* a small piece of which, mixed with water, makes a nutricious and palatable soup.[29] This people made their tents as at present, of black felt, but they were not yet acquainted with the method of supporting them artificially like the moderns.[30] They each of them hung their canvass on a tree[31] for their winter abode; in

[27] GATTERER, l. c. p. 128, derives the name of Iurcæ from the river Irgis, which flows on the eastern side of the Ural chain, and empties itself into the lake Acsacal.

[28] HEROD. l. c.

[29] NEUNICH, *Polyglot Dictionary of Natural History*, s. v. *Prunus Padus* L. According to Wassili Michailow, (Riga, 1804,) an intoxicating beverage is made from this fruit.

[30] PALLAS, l. c. i. p. 111.

[31] This must be a misunderstanding which has arisen from the supporters

summer, when they lived in the open air, it was folded up. The horde of which Herodotus speaks does not appear to have been one of the most wealthy; we collect, however, from him, that they roved about in the same country which is inhabited by the modern Calmucks.

"We are now arrived," continues Herodotus, "into the most distant country which we can become acquainted with, as this terminates the journeys undertaken by the Scythian and Greek caravans from the commercial cities of Pontus. No one can give any account of that region which is beyond the Argippæi, because this people are separated from the remote districts in question by inaccessible mountains, which have never been passed. The Argippæi, it is true, assert that men are to be found there with goats' feet, and that at a great distance the country is inhabited by men who sleep six months in the year. But these stories are fabulous, and quite unworthy of credit."

The inaccessible mountains which terminate the region possessed by the Argippæi, are evidently the Altai chain bounding southern Siberia, which in this passage first occurs in history, though without a name, like the Ural mountains. The tradition concerning men who had goats' feet is one of those stories which are so often indulged in with regard to distant countries, and particularly Siberia. In the other tradition of men who sleep six months in the year, we can perceive a ray of truth, inasmuch as we know that the polar regions continue for six months, more or less, without having the light of the sun; their darkness being only relieved by the moon and the aurora borealis. This was unknown to the ancients, and their ignorance of it justifies the caution of Herodotus.

"The country to the east of the Argippæi," continues the historian,[32] "we know to be inhabited by the Issedones. These people have a custom, when any one loses his father, for the relations to kill a certain number of sheep, whose flesh they hash up together with that of the dead person, and feast upon it.[33] But the dead man's skull is cleansed

of their tents being of the shape of trees, which were not to be found in the desert.

[32] Herod. iv. 25.

[33] Incredible as this custom may appear, it nevertheless exists amongst the

and gilded, and becomes a sort of idol, to which they offer sacrifices every year. In other respects they are said to be a civilized nation, and women amongst them are eligible to the sovereignty as well as men."

Although the Greek writer has not given us any positive account of the country of this nomad people, it is not difficult to determine the point. They began in the interior of Great Mongolia, the present residence of the Sungares, and were terminated by ancient Serica, whose inhabitants appear to have been derived from them.[34] The Greeks were acquainted with the name of this people long before the time of Herodotus, from an epic poem, attributed to Aristeus of Proconnesus.[35]

"To the north of the Issedones[36] we find, according to this people themselves, men with only one eye, called in the Scythian language Arimaspi, and griffins, who watch over the gold. The Scythians learned this circumstance from the Issedones, and we ourselves from the Scythians."

We have already spoken of the fabulous country of the griffins, and have proved that it was situated more to the south of the mountains bordering on Little Bucharia. But since the gold mountains of Eastern Asia extend as much to the north as to the south, it is probable that the tradition prevailed in both these directions; moreover, this fabulous story of the Arimaspi, and the griffins who watched over

Battas of Sumatra. The inhabitants of that land related to Dr. Leyden that they frequently eat their nearest relations when they are become old and infirm; and this less to gratify their appetite, than in obedience to a precept of religion. When a man gets old and perceives his strength fail him, he himself engages his relations to eat him, at the season when salt is the cheapest. He then ascends a tree, and his children, with his nearest kinsmen, dispose themselves around it; they shake the tree, singing these words: "The fruit is ripe, and must be shaken down." After which, the old man descends from the tree, and is killed and eaten by his relations at a solemn repast. In other respects, the Battas as well as the Issedones are described as a civilized people. LEYDEN in *Asiat. Research.* ix. p. 202. It is remarkable that Herodotus has the same story concerning an Indian people named Padæi, iii. 99.

[34] Ptolemy places the Issedones in Serica.

[35] This poem, entitled 'Αριμάσπεια, contained the most ancient traditions concerning the east and north of the ancient world. The poet pretended to have travelled into the country of the Issedones, and related a multitude of fables respecting them. (HEROD. iv. 13—15.) He lived about two hundred years before Herodotus; and we see by that historian's account of the poet, to what high antiquity the commerce of the Greek colonies of the Pontus Euxinus with Eastern Asia must be referred.

[36] HEROD. iv. 27.

the gold, tends to confirm the opinion which we have given in the introduction, that the gold mines of Southern Asia were known from the most remote antiquity.

We shall now follow our historian along the eastern side of the Caspian Sea, and the lake Aral, where his geographical knowledge will excite our admiration quite as much as it did in the north. No subsequent ancient writer, nor even any modern geographer, has collected equally exact accounts of these regions. The greatest part of the tribes were settled in Great Bucharia; yet any attempt to fix the residence of each of them would be fruitless, as that must have changed frequently in the vicissitudes of their wandering life; but there will not be much danger of confounding them with each other, because we know them already from the list of nations tributary to Darius, and have seen them exhibited with their arms and accoutrements in the immense army of Xerxes.

The vast plains of Great Bucharia, or Tartary, to the east of the Caspian Sea, have been at all times the favourite abode of nomad tribes. Some have been attracted to these seats of commerce, the staples for southern Asiatic productions, by their wants; while the commodities in which they abounded have afforded others an inducement to piracy. On the whole, the nations in question do not appear to have been ever more numerous than they were in the age of the Persian empire, in the service of which they were for the most part engaged.[37]

The tribes of the Caspii, Pausicæ, Pantimathi, and Daritæ, wandered along the shores of the Caspian Sea, between it and the lake Aral. The Caspii figure in the army of Xerxes with costumes of fur, their arms being sabres, and bows made of a sort of reed.

The other nations which we have just named did not appear in the army of Xerxes, but were included in the tributaries of Persia, as may be seen by the catalogue made under Darius, where they are placed by the side of the Caspii. The name of the last has undergone no alteration; at a later period, however, they are found on the west and north of the Caspian Sea.

[37] FROEMMICHEN, *Asiæ Herodoteæ difficiliora*, with the notes of Gatterer: this treatise gained a prize from the academy of Göttingen in the year 1794.

To the south of these tribes, in the vast plains of Khiva, the habitations of the Chorasmii and Thamanæi were dispersed. The name of Chorasmii constantly appears in history. According to Herodotus, they were settled on the Aces, that is to say, the Oxus,[38] and in the army of Xerxes had the Median arms with the Bactrian costume. The Thamanæi lived on the banks of the same river, and are only found in the list of tributaries.[39] Their neighbours were the Mycians[40] and Utii, who are probably identical with the modern Uzes, known as the ancestors of the Turks. These two nations were principally clothed with fur cloaks, and applied to agriculture like the Chorasmii, though at a later epoch they are enumerated amongst nomad tribes.

To the north of these last, on the lower Jaxartes, lived the Paricanii and Orthocorybantii. The Paricanii[41] were clothed with fur like the preceding, and armed with bows made in their own country. We have already seen in Herodotus another people bearing this name, and cited in the list of tributaries with the Asiatic Ethiopians,[42] which will authorize a conjecture that they extended much farther to the south than the people of whom we are speaking here. With regard to the Orthocorybantii, they do not appear in the expedition of Xerxes, being only mentioned in the catalogue of satrapies.[43]

In the interior of Great Bucharia, and on the east, these are succeeded by the Gandarii, Aparytæ, Dadicæ, and Sattagydæ. The Gandarii and Dadicæ imitated the Bactrians[44] in their method of arming themselves; the two other people were included in the list of tributaries, though not in the army of Xerxes.[45]

Such are the ancient nomad tribes which Herodotus was acquainted with, and has faithfully described. After his time the greater number of them do not appear any longer in history, though some, as the Caspii and Utii, are found more recently in other districts to the west of the Caspian Sea; and by this remarkable change of situation, confirm the ob-

[38] It has been frequently asserted, that the Aces is the Ochus of the moderns, but the opinion of Gatterer, who takes it for the Oxus, appears to me the most probable. GATTERER, l. c. p. 17, in the notes.

[39] HEROD. iii. 93. [40] Ibid. iii. 93; vii. 68. [41] Ibid. vii. 68; iii. 92.

[42] Ibid. iii. 94. [43] Ibid. iii. 92. [44] Ibid. vii. 66.

[45] Ibid. iii. 91.

servation already made, that these nomad hordes have moved from east to west. If we reflect, however, on the uninterrupted expeditions of the powerful nomad nations of Great Tartary, there will be no room to doubt that the hordes mentioned in Herodotus were detached branches of them. These hordes, whose country was beyond the borders of the Persian empire, that is, on the other side of the Jaxartes, were confounded by the Persians under the general name of Sacæ, an appellation as indefinite perhaps with them, as that of Scythians with the Greeks, or that of Tartars with us. "The people named Scythians by the Greeks," says Herodotus,[46] "are called Sacæ by the Persians." We may add that these tribes followed the Persians in all their expeditions, in the capacity of mercenaries, and formed the greater part of the armies of the great king.

Besides this general information, Herodotus has given a detailed account, equally instructing and interesting, of a nation beyond the Jaxartes, bearing the name of Massagetæ, against whom Cyrus undertook the expedition which occasioned his death.[47] "Some assert," says the historian, "that they are a warlike nation established on the eastern side of the river Araxes, and near the Issedones; others, that they inhabited an immense plain to the east of the Caspian Sea, and were related to the Scythians. The Massagetæ do, in fact, resemble the Scythians in their costume and manner of life. They fight on foot as well as on horseback, being equally skilled in both. They make use of bows and lances, and are accustomed to the battle-axe. Their lances and clubs are of brass; their helmets and girdles ornamented with gold. The harness of their horses is of brass; though the bit is gold as well as the ornaments of the bridle. They are not acquainted either with iron or silver, their country being entirely destitute of these metals, while it affords gold and brass in abundance."

The exactness of the geographical data here furnished us, renders it impossible to mistake the situation of this people. The Araxes can be no other than the Jaxartes, as we are referred to a large river on the east of the Caspian Sea. It is true, that this designation would equally apply to the Oxus;

[46] Herod. vii. 64. [47] Ibid. i. 201, 204, 215, 216.

but the name of Araxes cannot be given to the latter, because Herodotus calls it the Aces, and because it flows in Bucharia; for the Massagetæ were not inhabitants of this country, but rather were fixed more to the east or to the north, and near the Issedones. To which it may be added, that they were not tributaries of the Persians, or mercenary soldiers in their armies, like all the other nations of Great Bucharia; that the gold and brass with which their country abounded were not found in Great Bucharia, but in the Altai mountains; and that the immense plain to the east of the Caspian Sea is that steppe land, which at this day includes Sungaria and Mongolia, touches on the frontier of Eygur, and extends to the Altaic chain.

It appears, then, that the Massagetæ were neighbours of the Issedones, and that these two nations had a common origin, being both, as well as the Argippæi, of Mongol extraction. With these, our historian concludes his survey, his geographical knowledge not extending beyond their country; for he does not seem to have been acquainted with the name of Seres, who have since become so famous in the west; and yet they were, as we have already proved, a branch of the Issedones. We may supply his place by the Chinese annalists, who take up the thread of narration where he quitted it; but here we shall only remark, from what they relate[48] of the Hiongnu, (according to all appearance, the ancestors of the Huns,) that this people, to the east, bordered on the Issedones and Massagetæ, of whom they probably formed a part; and we do not intend to pursue our inquiries so far as to touch upon nations, which, being extremely remote from all parts of the world known to the ancients, cannot furnish us with facts of much importance to the present investigation into the commerce and manufactures of antiquity.

[48] De Guignes, *Histoire des Huns*, ii. p. 13, etc.

SCYTHIANS.

CHAPTER II.

Commerce and Intercourse of the Nations of Central Asia.

JAVAN, TUBAL, AND MESECH, THEY WERE THY MERCHANTS; THEY TRADED THE PERSONS OF MEN AND VESSELS OF BRASS IN THY MARKET. THEY OF THE HOUSE OF TOGARMAH TRADED IN THY FAIRS WITH HORSES AND HORSEMEN AND MULES. EZEKIEL, xxvii. 13, 14.

If it be true, as our preceding pages evince, that the interior of Asia was better known in the times of the Persian empire than it is now, the knowledge of this fact ought to make us entertain a very high idea of the relations of every kind which in these remote ages existed between the different nations of Asia; it ought to enlarge the picture which we have undertaken to portray of ancient commerce, and enrich it with an additional group in the back ground, which will be more attractive from the contrast which it forms with the rest.

In this task we are not reduced to content ourselves with simple conjectures. History has fortunately preserved a sufficient number of positive accounts to enable us to attain to correctness in our general view of the subject, though some of its details may be liable to exception.

The Greek cities on the coasts of the Black Sea infused life and activity into the tribes of the north; their bold and enterprising genius opened to them a connexion with the most remote countries of the East; and perhaps they even introduced into their own country the commodities of India, conveying them over the immense steppes of Asia.

We have remarked already, that all these cities were colonies from Miletus; Olbia, situated at the mouth of the Borysthenes, on the site of the modern Cherson, being the most considerable. The second rank was distinguished by

Panticapæum, in the Tauric peninsula; Phanagoria and Tanais, at the extremity of the sea of Azof; Dioscurias, near the mouth of the Phasis; and lastly, Heraclea, Sinope, and Amisus on the shores of Asia Minor, which were washed by the Pontus Euxinus. These cities, the greater part of which were founded seven hundred years before the Christian era, and consequently existed before the Persian dominion, appropriated to themselves the navigation and commerce of the Black Sea; they saw in profusion in their own markets, the productions of all the countries bordering on this sea, which found here a sale as advantageous as it was prompt; and their industry increasing with their wealth, they at length monopolized all the productions of the North and East. We shall now proceed to trace their commerce through its different branches.

All the cities in question, and especially Dioscurias, Panticapæum and Phanagoria, had formerly the most considerable and famous slave markets. The countries situated on the north and east of the Black Sea were inexhaustible magazines for this shameful and inhuman traffic: hence the name of Scythian was frequently used as synonymous with the word slave.

In the continual wars which the nations of Mount Caucasus waged against each other, all the prisoners were sold as slaves; for slavery was generally prevalent amongst the Scythians, as amongst other nomad tribes;[1] and the slave markets of Panticapæum and Dioscurias were, even in the time of Strabo, a great attraction to these barbarous nations.[2]

But a much more advantageous commerce for them was that which consisted in corn. We have already seen in our quotations from Herodotus, that several Scythian tribes had attained to the knowledge of agriculture, and that the Ukrain, amongst others, on the two banks of the Dnieper, produced a considerable quantity of corn. The cultivated part of this district reached to the modern government of Kiev. We have likewise remarked in the same historian, that the inhabitants cultivated the soil not for the purpose

[1] Herod. iv. 2, 3.

[2] Strab. p. 757, 761. According to the testimony of this author, there were more than seventy tribes collected together in the great markets of Panticapæum.

of consuming its productions themselves, but to find their account in it by the profits of commerce.[3] Thus the Ukrain was, in the Persian era, as it still is in our time, very productive in corn, and the city of Olbia served as an emporium for this branch of traffic. The same city maintained especially an intercourse[4] with Athens, whose territory did not produce enough of this necessary commodity to supply the wants of its inhabitants.

The commerce which was carried on with fur put it in the power of the Greeks to penetrate still deeper into the heart of this country. We have already observed in another place, that this commerce could not have been so considerable in ancient times as it has become recently; but it was not of less importance. The climate of the regions bordering on the Black Sea, as that of many others on the same degrees of latitude, was more inclement than at present; and warm garments were more necessary.[5] Accordingly the use of furs was nearly general among the nations of Thrace, and all the Asiatic tribes settled in countries above the 40th degree of north latitude. The Thracians wore caps of fox skin and boots of fur;[6] the Scythians and Melanchlæni used cloaks of the same material. Similar habiliments were common to other people on the east of the Caspian Sea; and we shall show afterwards that fine furs were of equal estimation in Southern Asia.

But the adventurous and enterprising spirit of the Greeks on the shores of the Euxine Sea did not confine itself to this commerce with the nations of the North; they penetrated into the East, and made way for themselves even into Great Mongolia. Herodotus is still our authority on this subject.

"As far as the Argippæi,[7] (the modern Calmucks,) the country is very well known; and also that of the other nations whom we have mentioned before. For it is often visited, either by the Scythians, who readily communicate what they have learned respecting it, or by the Greeks of Olbia and its neighbourhood. The Scythians who go into these districts usually carry on their affairs in seven different

[3] HEROD. iv. 17. [4] DEMOSTH. *in Lept.* p. 254. ed. WOLF.

[5] This inclemency of the climate is a fact of which we may assure ourselves from Herodotus, (iv. 28,) if we are inclined to consider the complaints of Ovid exaggerated.

[6] HEROD. vii. 75. [7] Ibid. iv. 24.

languages, by the assistance of the same number of interpreters."

This remarkable passage of our historian evidently describes a commerce by caravans, which, having crossed the Ural mountains, travelled northward round the Caspian Sea, and thence advanced into the interior of Great Mongolia. This commerce was jointly carried on by the Greeks of Pontus and by Scythians; and when we once know its route, it will be easy to explain its organization; as the Scythians were accustomed to travel with immense herds, and were possessed of many beasts of burden, they were probably the best conductors of merchandise; and we must therefore conclude, that they in a great measure formed the caravans which travelled into Eastern Asia.

Hence we can entertain no doubt as to the place of setting out, or the termination of their journey. It began at Olbia, near the mouth of the river Borysthenes, and ended beyond the Ural mountains, in the country of the Argippæi (the Calmucks). This people belonged to the great Mongolian family, and formed the most western branch of it. Their tents being made of felt proves in some degree their relation with the Mongols or Calmucks; while the Scythians, by living, according to Herodotus, on their waggons,[8] showed their Tartar origin. All we know of the country of the Argippæi is, that we must seek them in the western part of Great Mongolia, and probably in the present canton of the Kirghis:[9] we must not however conclude from this that the region was of moderate extent; for it might have reached to the Jaxartes on the south, that is, to the confines of the tribes of Great Tartary and Mongolia; and on the east, to the territory of the Issedones. Our acquaintance with their neighbours on two sides seems very important, as it tends to prove that the commerce of the Greeks with the Argippæi could open to them a communication with the different countries situated on the east and north of Asia.

We shall now examine the routes of this commerce.

The latter part of the route which crossed the steppes beyond the Ural mountains, was the same as that at present traversed by caravans from Orenburg towards Bokhara, or

[8] Herod. iv. 46.
[9] The Kirghis emigrated very late from Siberia to their present country.

Khiva, or from these latter cities to Orenburg. The commercial expeditions of the Russians, particularly that in the year 1820, have thrown considerable light on these countries and their roads; and we have obliged the reader with the information which has been communicated to us in writing.[10]

According to these accounts, there is no high road between Orenburg and Bokhara. From Orenburg to the Sir-Darja we find no beaten way; we only meet occasionally some paths made by camels.

The Russian caravan, which, as it was accompanied by a strong escort, could without danger take the most frequented road, doubled the north-eastern extremity of the lake Aral;[11] passed the two arms of the Sir-Darja, on the north and south, and then proceeded along the desert of Kisil-Koum, in northern Bucharia. But for several reasons, caravans are not always able to travel on the same road: sometimes on account of the insecurity occasioned by the predatory hordes, which are roving about; at others they are prevented by the want of forage and water for camels, which it is not safe to pasture any where, except on the territory of friendly hordes. The Khivans have four routes of communication with Russia. The first passes between the lake of Aral and the Caspian Sea across the steppe of the Kirghis. This is safe only in times of peace, and when an intelligence is maintained with these tribes, which has been difficult for some years. The second road is by way of Saruchek, along the frontiers of Russia, and ends likewise at Orenburg. By this circuitous route the Khivans seek to avoid the insults of the Kirguis. The third road goes from Saruchek to Astracan, from whence merchandise is transported to Novgorod by the Wolga. The fourth road sets out from Khiva and leads to Karagan,[12] and from thence by the Caspian Sea to Astracan. Of these four roads the second and third are most frequented.

[10] Vol. i. p. 168, (note [41].)

[11] It went to Bokhara, and not to Khiva; if the latter city had been its destination, the road between the Caspian Sea and the lake of Aral would have been the shortest.

[12] Karagan is the most westerly cape of the eastern shore of the Caspian Sea, towards the 44th degree of north latitude, and at the shortest distance from Astracan.

We shall show how far these data will apply to Scythian commerce, after having explored the commercial route of the cities on the Black Sea, from the shores of that sea to the Uralian mountains.

Although Herodotus has not accurately determined this road, it is not difficult to trace it from the indications he has left. According to him, the commercial Scythians and Greeks were obliged to traverse countries inhabited by seven different tribes, and speaking seven different dialects, and consequently under the necessity of employing the assistance of seven interpreters, in order to make themselves understood. These cannot be the same which Herodotus himself has mentioned:[13] the Tauri, the Sarmatians, the Budini, the Geloni, the Thyssagetæ, the Jurcæ, and the Argippæi.[14]

Thus if, with Herodotus, we consider Olbia to have been the emporium in whose neighbourhood the caravans assembled, their route must have passed along the Hylæan or wood country, and have coasted the sea of Azof, as far as the mouth of the Tanais. It was here that the Tauri[15] inhabited, whose settlements extend far beyond the peninsula to which they have given their name. Having passed the Tanais, the caravans entered into the steppe of Astracan, whence they took a northern direction across the country of the Sarmatians, reached the territory of the Budini, and arrived in the wooden city of the Geloni. Hence they turned to the north-east, and after seven days' journey through a desert, they reached the country of the Thyssagetæ and Jurcæ, on the frontiers of Siberia. After passing the Ural chain they came into the steppes of the Kirghis and Calmucks, which terminated their journey.

[13] This is proved incontestably by the context.

[14] I pass over in silence the Scythian exiles or emigrants; in their intercourse with whom the caravans had no need of interpreters, as they still preserved their own language. If, however, we were desirous to substitute them in this passage for the Tauri, there could be no reason to oppose this disposition. Herodotus does not fix their settlements positively; he only says that they were formerly established on the east of the Jurcæ, without explaining the cause of their emigration. It would seem that this was a voluntary emigration, (as we should understand by the expression ἀποστάντες,) and that the object of this people in changing their country was to be fixed on the great commercial road.

[15] Herod. iv. 99.

It is evident that this was not the shortest way from Olbia to the country of the Argippæi. It was necessary to turn to the left, make a circuit in the northern direction, and proceed as far up as the frontiers of Siberia, if not pass beyond them; for the account of Herodotus will not permit us to assign a more southern position to the regions traversed by the caravans. Perhaps this circuitous route was necessary, on account of the predatory hordes which infested the more direct way. It appears, however, from the text of Herodotus, that it was rather enjoined by the demands of commerce than any other necessity; and what proves this to a demonstration is the fact, that the caravans were obliged to use interpreters, whom they could have dispensed with, if it had not been their purpose to traffic with different nations. With respect to the nature of this traffic, Herodotus himself has taken care to inform us that this road of the Scythian caravans had been frequented from time immemorial by merchants who traded in furs.

According to the testimony of Herodotus, the Budini, Thyssagetæ, and Jurcæ, were all hunting people, who lived in the midst of the woods; they watched for the animals from the top of trees, and killed them with their arrows; sometimes also they hunted with horses and dogs. The deserts which separated their territories formed, as it were, parks filled with all kinds of animals; and the object which they had in view when they hunted these animals, like the modern Siberians, was to possess themselves of their valuable furs. This is, moreover, confirmed by the following passage from Herodotus. "In the country of the Budini, there is a lake and a marsh full of rushes, where they catch otters, beavers, and other animals of the same kind, whose skins serve for the decoration of garments."[16]

The wooden city, of which we have spoken above, was situated in the country of the Budini, and was surrounded

[16] HEROD. iv. 109. The authenticity of this passage, doubted by some authors, has been justly defended by Schweighæuser, ad h. l. Let naturalists explain, if they can, what is meant by square-headed animals. As to myself, I at first believed that sables were intended, although I have quitted this opinion, since the fact has come to my knowledge, that sea-dogs (phocæ vitulinæ) inhabit the lakes of Siberia. I have no doubt of these being the animals which Herodotus had in view, because they are amphibious, like those which he has mentioned first in this passage; and the surprising size of their head justifies the expression he has employed in defining them.

by a wooden enclosure, each side of which was thirty stades long. This establishment, founded by the Greeks of the commercial cities of Pontus, contained buildings and temples for their use.[17] There can be no doubt as to their object in founding this *slobode.* It could only be designed as a staple for the fur trade. And this fact explains why the Greek caravans, instead of taking the direct way to the end of their journey, did not reach it till after a long circuitous route to the north. For the wooden city was a great market, where they not only disposed of the fruits of their own industry, but received other commodities in exchange, which they carried away for the purpose of traffic with remote nations.

A German scholar,[18] who, alas! died much too soon for the interests of science, a short time ago succeeded in throwing a brighter ray of light on these countries, hitherto involved in such obscurity. He has proved from original documents, that the country which has been sought for a long time on the north-west of Russia, is that into which we have just arrived with the caravans whose route Herodotus has described. This country comprehended the vast territory on both sides of the Ural chain, the government of Perm, and the western part of that of Tobolsk, to the banks of the Obi. Its inhabitants, the Jugrians, are the same who at this day live near the Obi, under the name of Voguls and Ostiacks. The district in question, one fourth larger than Germany, contains sixteen thousand square miles, from the 56th to the 67th degree of north latitude. It has been always celebrated for animals whose furs are held in estimation, found in the greatest numbers on the east of the Ural mountains, which were passed three different ways. The soil of this country is in a great measure marshy, and becomes more and more so as we advance towards the north: which explains the passage of Herodotus, where he

[17] HEROD. iv. 108.

[18] *Untersuchungen zur Erläuterung der ältern Geschichte Ruszlands,* (Researches relative to the illustration of ancient Russian history,) by A. C. LEHRBERG; published by the Royal Academy of Sciences, under the superintendence of Ph. Krug. St. Petersburg, 1816; with an introductory biographical sketch, extremely interesting. This admirable man found after his death an equally admirable friend in the publisher of his work. The first treatise belongs to our subject; entitled, *On the geographical position and history of Jugria.*

mentions a large lake, or rather a marsh, of rushes. Here also were found the best sort of beavers, those, namely, who built near the water: and those animals which supply the finest furs, as sables, squirrels, and foxes, of every description.[19] During the long period of the middle ages, Jugria was in possession of this commerce. But after the eleventh century, this trade fell into the hands of the inhabitants of Novgorod, who soon reduced it into a province of their republic; nor did the ruin of this state, as Lehrberg has proved, interrupt the commerce in question.[20] Finally, the caravans of Bokhara came to these districts in the sixteenth century, and conveyed thither the commodities of their own country and of India.[21]

We refrain as much as possible from founding our opinions on a mere resemblance of proper names. But if it is established that the Jurcæ inhabited the same country where at a later period we find the Jugrians, and that this country extended into the interior of the Ural mountains, are we not authorized in supposing that the Jugrians and Jurcæ are the same people; and the commerce which subsisted amongst them until the fifteenth century of our era had flourished perhaps for several thousand years before? We find in these cold regions a city resembling that of the Budini; the *spotted herd*,[22] so named from the piebald horses which they give to the Indians in exchange for their commodities; and lastly, we even hear of the fabulous traditions mentioned by Herodotus; for the story of men sleeping six months in the year is incontestably a Siberian tradition,[23] which would naturally prevail in a region where, with the exception of man, the whole of nature, animated and inanimated, sleeps during the winter.

The caravans, leaving behind them these countries of skins and these hunting tribes, turned to the east of the Thyssagetæ, and passed the Ural mountains, whose most southern branch, under the name of Auro-Uruk, reaches to the shores of the lake Aral. It would be difficult to determine the point at which they passed this chain; but it is probable that after having gone so far north, they did not effect the passage lower than Orenburg, in 52 degrees of

[19] Lehrberg, l. c. p. 31. [20] Ibid. p. 32. [21] Ibid. p. 37, 38. [22] Ibid. p. 41. [23] Ibid. p. 44.

north latitude; and the road which they followed from this point must have been one of those we have already described, conducting them from Orenburg to the steppes of the Kirghis; and, according to Herodotus, there was still a great distance to the country of the Argippæi: we must, therefore, seek the ancient abodes of this people in the eastern part of the steppes of the Kirghis; and perhaps they extended in a southern direction to the Jaxartes or the Sir-Darja, like the habitations of the Kirghis.

But it may now be asked, whether they could expect amongst the Argippæi a favourable market for their principal commodity, which were furs. In order to reply to this question, we must recollect an observation made in the introduction[24] to this work, that furs have been at all times not only an object of necessity, but also of luxury; as they have been used for personal decoration in general: hence they have been by no means confined to the northern countries, but have always found a market amongst the nations of Southern Asia. Captain Cook had no difficulty in disposing of the otter skins which he had obtained from Nutka Sound, in the market of Canton, a city of Southern China. Going farther back into antiquity, we learn from Herodotus, that there were several tribes on the shores of the Caspian Sea who wore cloaks of fur; and that they were also worn in Babylon, being considered a necessary to wealth, rank, and beauty. We have already observed furs among the presents of the governors, represented on the great relief of Persepolis;[25] and in the sequel of our researches, we shall prove that this object of luxury was in great estimation amongst the Indians from the most ancient times. The Scythians and Greeks, therefore, could have been under no difficulty in selling their furs to the Argippæi, any more than the Russians of modern days who exchange them at Kiachta for the merchandise of China. This will be set in a clearer light by the following observations.

Herodotus, it is true, says that the Scythian and Greek merchants of the Euxine Sea did not go beyond the country of the Argippæi, but he does not say that this was the termination of their commerce. All we learn is, that the

[24] Vol. i. p. 42. [25] Vol. i. p. 108.

caravans of the East and West assembled amongst the Argippæi, and that they here found markets in which they exchanged their merchandise.

And in fact, although the journey of the Greeks ended in the country of the Argippæi, they were not ignorant of the existence of more remote tribes, such as the Issedones and Massagetæ. Whoever has studied the history of ancient commerce, will easily discover from the account of Herodotus, what it was which attracted the Greeks into those remote countries. However important the traffic in skins may have been, it could not have been sufficient to induce them to undertake such long and perilous journeys; in addition to this, they furnished themselves with horses, camels, and other beasts of burden from these pastoral tribes. They also procured various metals, for all these nations had much brass, and some of them a great abundance of gold.[26]

Settled just on the frontiers of the mountainous districts of Asia, they maintained a relation with these countries; and their communication was facilitated by a long concatenation of various tribes which succeeded each other without interruption from these frontiers to Bactra and Maracanda, the two principal marts for Indian merchandise. This it must be confessed is only a presumption, but a presumption which approaches to certainty; for how could Herodotus have been so well acquainted with the nations on the eastern side of the Caspian Sea, if these districts had not been traversed by commercial roads? With respect to the object of this commerce, that is to say, gold, or the merchandise of India; here, as before, the historical inquirer has ample matter for admiration, as well as for the most serious reflection. And this surprise will considerably increase, when he reads in Herodotus that there existed at the same time

[26] The same abundance of gold is attributed to the nations which frequented the market of Jugria in the middle ages. LEHRBERG, l. c. p. 42.

[The information for which we are indebted to Herodotus on the subject of the riches of the Ural mountains, has been latterly confirmed by the discoveries of the Russians. The Ural chain is at this day the object of the most accurate scientific investigations. We know by the public papers, that gold is found there at such a very slight depth, that no expensive mining operations are necessary in order to obtain it. This sufficiently explains how the nomad tribes, such as they were described by Herodotus, were able to procure this metal without much trouble. *Inedited note of the author.*]

an organized navigation on the Caspian Sea. Herodotus is far from falling into a similar error with some more recent authors, who have supposed this sea to be a branch of the Northern Ocean; he is acquainted with the circumstance of its being an inland sea, and even gives an estimate of its length and breadth in days' navigation.[27]

Whence could he have obtained his knowledge if this navigation had not been really established? In the Macedonian period, the productions of India and Bactria were carried down the Oxus to the Caspian Sea; then over this sea to the mouths of the Araxes and Cyrus; after that by land to the Phasis, where they were again conveyed by water to the different Greek cities on the coasts of the Euxine Sea.[28] There is no positive historical evidence for this route which we have just traced; but one conjecture will naturally arise from other circumstances which we know for certain respecting the traffic in its neighbourhood.

These conjectures seem to be strengthened by the picture which Herodotus has drawn of the character and manners of the principal nations of Central Asia. He describes the Massagetæ as a warlike people, and the Argippæi and Issedones as devoted to peaceful possessions; which would almost make us suppose that there existed distinct castes amongst these nations. "The Argippæi," says he, "are never injured by any one, for they are regarded as a sacred and holy people. They carry no arms, and reconcile the differences of their neighbours. And when a man takes refuge with them, he is not disturbed."[29] Their territory was, therefore, a sanctuary, as well as the emporium of an extensive commerce. The name of holy people which was given them, shows plainly that there was a religious character attached to them, and that they filled the same office amongst the Mongols, as the sacerdotal order amongst other nations. The circumstance of their being bald, which is added by Herodotus, proves our assertion, for the priests of the Calmucks, that is to say, the Lamas, are bald-headed. When he says of them that they reconciled their neigh-

[27] Herod. i. 203.

[28] See my treatise, *de Græcorum cum Indis commerciis, in Commentat. Soc. Goett.* p. xi. 76.

[29] Herod. iv. 23.

bours who were at variance with each other; this can imply nothing else than that they acted as mediators in the differences which occurred between the merchants who had come to so great a distance from their own country, and were such entire strangers to each other. We thus discover the connecting link so often in antiquity uniting religion to commerce, which we have already observed in some nations, and shall have occasion to remark again as we proceed in our subject. Here, however, it differs a little from that which has been the subject of our previous observations, as it is appropriated to a particular place, and conformable to the ideas of a people who were not acquainted with either temples or any permanent sacred edifice, but at the utmost had only a tent set apart for religious purposes, like their descendants the modern Calmucks. As the Massagetæ, who were neighbours of the Argippæi on the south, and descended from the same stock, are represented in Herodotus as a warlike people, and accustomed to the use of arms, we may suppose that they formed a caste of soldiers. But this was not the case with the Issedones, who were neighbours of the Argippæans, and related to them like the Massagetæ, but were not devoted to arms; on the contrary, they were described under the honourable name of a just people, that is, civilized, and were not hostile to any other nation.[30] This nation, in particular, were those from whom any information concerning the most remote districts of the east and north of Asia was obtained; for the Scythians had their intelligence from the Issedones, and the Greeks from the Scythians. They thus appear as the commercial people, who extended their relations even to Greece. If we add to this, what has been remarked before, that the Seres were a branch of this nation, a still clearer light is thrown on the fact of the propagation of the woven stuffs of the Seres having been their principal employment; and the most ancient path of the silk trade is thus discovered amongst them.

Thus also it is explained, how the frontiers of their settle-

[30] Herod. iv. 26. Compare Gatterer's first treatise, *de Hunnis*, in Commentat. Soc. Goett. vol. xiv. p. 19, etc. In the second, he has placed the Budini and their neighbours on the east of the Sarmatians, instead of the north, quite contrary to the opinion of Herodotus.

ments became the principal seat of trade, and terminated the journey of the caravans which travelled thither from the shores of the Black Sea in order to traffic for those productions which the Issedones imported from Western Asia. But here history is lost in complete darkness. We shall not, however, give up all hopes of throwing some light upon this obscurity, particularly with regard to Eastern Asia, when we shall have entered upon our investigation relative to the Indians, in the succeeding part of this work.

INDIANS.

ADVERTISEMENT.

In preparing the following translation of Professor Heeren's work on India, the translator has been furnished with some additional matter from the author himself, which will be found in two of the Appendixes at the end of the volume. The first contains a brief sketch of the works connected with Sanscrit literature, which have appeared since the last edition of the " Researches," in Germany, together with a confirmed statement of the author's method of determining the several ages of Sanscrit classical compositions. The second comprises an interesting discussion relative to the island of Ceylon, which the Professor satisfactorily shows to have been the principal emporium of Oriental commerce for upwards of two thousand years.

The translator has also examined the French version of M. Suckau, with the view of incorporating such of his notes as appeared likely to throw some further light on the subject; and has at the same time added a few remarks of his own, in the humble attempt to explain, and sometimes to modify, the assertions of the author; for these, he has only to request the reader's favourable consideration.

With regard to the orthography of the Sanscrit names occurring in the body of the work, it was at first apprehended that any attempt to correct the vicious mode of spelling adopted by some writers, from whom Heeren quotes, would unavoidably impede the reader in verifying the references made to them; but upon second thoughts, and particularly as there is no sort of reason why an erroneous custom should usurp the rank and authority of a legal precedent, the translator has uniformly endeavoured to ascertain the genuine orthography by an immediate reference to the Sanscrit originals. This, however, was a task of considerable difficulty, because, in quoting from English writers, who have adopted one mode of spelling proper names, the writers of the continent employ, as might be expected, another, peculiar to themselves; so that, after a few successive alterations of this kind, by the time the words in question find their way back again to England, it is frequently no easy matter to say precisely what they stand for. In some cases, indeed, the complete restoration of the true form was altogether impracticable; as, for example, in the review of the great epic poem, the Mahabharat, which Heeren derived solely from the accounts contained in the Ayin Acbari, and of course has followed the corrupt spelling peculiar to the Persian writers upon India, who have disfigured the proper names of Sanscrit origin quite as much as their own were, formerly, by the Greeks. And as the translator was unable to procure a copy of the Mahabharat, he has therefore been obliged to leave the barbarous spelling of the Ayin Acbari, with a few exceptions, just as he found it, in which it would certainly puzzle Ganesa himself to discover any thing like a resemblance to Sanscrit orthography. The same reproach of misspelling applies also in full force to most of the Sanscrit words noticed in Polier's Mythology of the Hindus. As to the manner of representing Oriental names in European letters, the system first proposed by Sir W. Jones, and recommended by the practice of almost every subsequent writer in this department of literature, has been followed as the most convenient and simple, and at the same time of universal application, as it enables the scholars of the continent to comprehend, at a glance, the proper way of pronouncing an Eastern word, even when occurring in English writers, whose general pronunciation has scarcely any thing in common with that of the rest of Europe. According to this system, the vowels will be pronounced after the Italian method, while the consonants, with the exception of certain aspirated forms, such as *th* and *ph*, etc., (to be pronounced as in the words *nut-hook, hap-hazard*, etc.,) retain their English sounds unaltered. The translator has to apologize for a few casual deviations from the above system; but there is no occasion to detain the reader any longer with the trifling minutiæ of verbal criticism, which it is probable (supposing the translator to have bestowed as much care upon sentences as upon words) he may willingly choose to overlook, for objects of much greater importance, and infinitely more worthy his attention.

With regard to the particular merits of the work here presented in an English dress, the public will be the most appropriate judges; and the reputation of the author is too well established to be affected by any thing that might be offered in this place; which, besides its liability to be considered as nothing more than an attempt to bias the reader, would, together with observations of another kind, be more suitably exhibited in the pages of a Review.

PREFACE

TO THE FOURTH EDITION.

As the following Researches are almost wholly derived from native Indian sources, which the recent study of Sanscrit literature in Europe has just opened to us, it will be requisite to give the reader a brief notice of the works I have been enabled to consult in this inquiry; more particularly as at the time of my first edition, the state of continental blockade prevented me from having recourse to many valuable works which could only be procured in England. They are as follows:—

The Ramayana of Valmiki, in the original Sanscrit, with a prose translation and explanatory notes, by William Carey and Joshua Marshman. Vol. i. containing the first book, Serampore, 1806, 4to, pp. 656. Vol. iii. containing the latter part of the second book, Serampore, 1810, pp. 493.

Of the seven books which compose the entire poem, the two first are all that has appeared; but unfortunately the copies of the second volume were lost in their passage to Europe, and no others, I believe, are now to be found even in England, certainly not in the libraries of the continent. It is with great regret, therefore, that I have been obliged to confine myself to the first and third volumes only; for it is unquestionable, that next to the Mahabharat, the Ramayana is the purest and most fertile source for the elucidation of Hindu antiquities. In preparing the first edition of my work, it was by mere chance that I was able to procure even the first volume of this poem.

Nalus, carmen Sanscritum e Mahabharatâ, edidit, latine vertit, et adnotationibus illustravit Franciscus Bopp. Londini, 1819, 8vo, pp. 216.

Bhagavad-gita; id est, Θεσπέσιον μέλος, *sive almi Krishnæ et Arjunæ Colloquium de rebus divinis, Bharateæ Episodium. Po-*

etam recensuit, adnotationes criticas et interpretationem Latinam adjecit Aug. Gul. a Schlegel. Bonnæ, 1823, 8vo, pp. 189. .

The Megha-duta, or Cloud-Messenger, a poem in the Sanscrit language, by Calidasa, translated into English verse, with notes and illustrations, by Horace Hayman Wilson. Calcutta, 4to, pp. 120.

Gita-govinda, by Jayadeva, in Sir W. Jones's Works, vol. i.

Sacontala, or The Fatal Ring, by Calidasa, in Sir W. Jones's Works, vol. vi.

Hitopadesa of Vishnusarman, in Sir W. Jones's Works, vol. vi.

Institutes of Hindu Law, or the Ordinances of Menu; verbally translated from the original Sanscrit, with a preface, by Sir W. Jones. Calcutta, 1796, 8vo.

A Digest of Hindu law, on Contracts and Successions, with a Commentary by Jagannatha Tercapanchanana; translated from the original Sanscrit by H. T. Colebrooke, in three volumes. London, 1801, 8vo.

Upnekhat, studio Anquetil du Perron. Paris, 1801, 2 vols. 4to.

Bhagavadam, ou doctrine divine, ouvrage Indienne canonique, par Obsouville. Paris, 1788, 8vo.

A Grammar of the Sanscrit Language, by Charles Wilkins. London, 1804, 4to.

Cosha, or a Dictionary of the Sanscrit Language, by Amara Singha, with an English interpretation, by Colebrooke. Serampore, 1821, 4to.

Amara-Singha, sectio prima de cœlo a P. Paulino a Sto. Bartolomæo. Romæ, 1798.

Ejusdem, Vyacarana seu Samscrdamicæ Linguæ Institutio. Romæ, 1804.

Ejusdem, Systema Brahmanicum. Romæ, 1802.

Ejusdem, Grammatica Samscrdamica. Romæ, 1790.

Chrestomathia Sanscrita, quam ex codd. Manuscriptis, edidit Othmarus Frank. Monachii, 1820, vol. i. ii.

Asiatic Researches, or Transactions of the Society instituted in Bengal, vol. i.—xiv. The last volume is only known to me by partial extracts.

Annals of Oriental Literature, part i. ii. iii. London, 1821.

Indische Bibliothek, von A. W. von Schlegel, Heft. I. II.

With regard to separate treatises on India, travels, copper-plate representations of ancient monuments, etc., it is unnecessary to mention them here, as they will be found quoted in their proper places.

The above list, I believe, contains all the works of any importance relating to Sanscrit literature, which have hitherto been procurable in Europe. The writings of Father Paulino are included, less on account of any use I have made of them, than merely to complete the enumeration. The Grammars of Carey and Wilkins, notwithstanding their acknowledged merit, were but little applicable to my purpose. In the use of translations I have strictly confined myself to such as were generally allowed to be correct by Sanscrit scholars themselves; rejecting, on the other hand, all poetical versions, or at least imitations, similar to those of Sir William Jones, which it is obvious cannot safely be depended on. Should it nevertheless be objected to me that an acquaintance with the Sanscrit is indispensable to a writer on Sanscrit literature, I answer, that my inquiries do not so much concern language as matters of fact; in proof of which, I can only appeal to the work itself.

It may be as well, however, to enter somewhat more into detail with regard to the particular subjects discussed in the first chapter of the ensuing Researches. My object was to furnish a critical view of Hindu Archæology, whether consisting in ancient works of art, or the writings of native authors. This chapter, therefore, was intended to supply such a body of useful preliminary information as, in addition to a knowledge of the language, would enable the student to prosecute his inquiries into the literature and antiquities of India. That some such introduction to the study would not only be serviceable, but even necessary, can hardly admit of doubt.

When the present essay was first published, in the year 1814, there was absolutely no similar compilation then in existence; and the very favourable reception awarded to my undertaking, inspired me with well-grounded hopes that I had not laboured in vain, and had even materially contributed to introduce the study of Sanscrit literature among the scholars of Germany. Since that period, however, I have not yet been able to meet with any work completely satisfactory on the subject, and calculated to supply all the deficiencies of our existing information relative to India.

Under these circumstances, it can scarcely be expected that I should furnish the reader with a general account of Hindu antiquities, except in so far as they are connected with the particular object of the present work. I can promise no learned disquisitions on the mythological, philosophical, or religious systems of the ancient Hindus; and least of all is it my purpose to institute a comparison between them and other nations in any of these points, or to investigate the probable manner in which such systems may have been communicated to other countries. An undertaking of this nature, besides being extremely hazardous, would altogether exceed the legitimate province of history. I shall therefore be satisfied with merely introducing the reader to the threshold, if I may so call it, of Hindu Archæology; well aware that even such a step will not be deemed superfluous, if he would penetrate the recesses of the interior.

The study and elucidation of Indian antiquities from native sources, is, in my opinion, one of the most important additions that have been made to the literature of the present day, and will, it is hoped, enlarge its circle of acquirements to a much greater extent hereafter. It is not merely the æsthetic merit of Sanscrit literature, great as that is, which renders it so valuable in our estimation; the same merit also attaches to it in an historical point of view. We must, indeed, allow, that we are not yet enabled to attempt any composition resembling a consecutive critico-chronological history of ancient India; the means at our present disposal are far too inadequate to effect such a laborious undertaking; and probably they will continue to be so. At the same time, however, while it carries us back into remote ages, and among a distant people, who have attained a high and peculiar degree of civilization, the ancient literature of the Hindus discloses to our sight a new world, which is so much the more captivating, as it is entirely different from our own. I would ask, is the addition thereby made to the general history of mankind of no more value than a series of chronological tables, containing only a dry nomenclature of princes and dates? or should we be willing to receive them in exchange for the Ramayana and Mahabharat of the Hindus, or the Iliad and Odyssey of the Greeks?

Our present knowledge of Sanscrit literature may be said to

stand nearly on the same footing as that of the Greek did in Italy towards the end of the fifteenth century. The inestimable benefits which the study of the latter has conferred upon the whole Western world, are too well known; and though it were presumptuous, perhaps, to expect the same important consequences from the study of the Sanscrit, yet we are not without the wish and the expectation, that it may also flourish and produce its own peculiar fruits.

July 27, 1824.

INDIANS.

CHAPTER I.

A Critical View of the Antiquities and Literature of India.

THE ACCOUNTS WE RECEIVE OF INDIA REQUIRE AN IMPARTIAL AND UNPREJUDICED CONSIDERATION, FOR IT IS SITUATE AT A VERY REMOTE DISTANCE FROM US, AND BUT FEW OF OUR COUNTRYMEN HAVE EXAMINED IT WITH ATTENTION; AND THOSE EVEN WHO HAVE TRAVELLED THITHER, HAVE SEEN ONLY PARTS OF IT, AND WHAT THEY RELATE IS MOSTLY FROM HEARSAY. STRABO, LIB. XV. INIT.

THE historians who have inquired into the religion and learning of the East, have almost always been obliged to revert to India for information in their researches. That distant country, however, has at no former period attracted the attention of Europeans, in these particulars, so much as at the present day. From the time that it became subject to the English, it has excited their regard, not more by its productions than by its arts and literature: and the learned of Great Britain now flatter themselves, that they have at length discovered the sources from which, not only the rest of Asia, but the whole Western World derived their knowledge and their religion. They have accordingly endeavoured to render these sources accessible to Europe, through the medium of learned dissertations on the most important points of Hindu mythology and civilization, as well as by translations of native works.[1] These inquiries have given

[1] Sir W. Jones, the first president of the Asiatic Society founded at Calcutta, in 1784, has undoubtedly the credit of having originated these studies, and by his own exertions contributed to render them worthy the notice and favourable consideration of the European world. What other scholar indeed but himself could have brought to the task such multifarious acquirements, such a profound knowledge of languages, such extensive views of history, so rich a vein of poetic feeling, and, in a word, such a predominant taste for every thing Oriental? And if occasionally his amiable enthusiasm hurries him beyond the limits of true criticism, we can easily excuse it in one who was the means of exciting the same spirit equally in others, and thus giving

rise to corresponding ones in Germany; the number of students in this department of letters has greatly increased; the sacred language of India, together with its literature and poetry, have been introduced to our acquaintance; and editions of Sanscrit works printed in the original character have issued from the German press, as well as from those on the banks of the Ganges and the Thames.

Were it possible clearly to define and characterize in all its extent, the influence which this most cultivated people of the East has exercised upon the rest of the world, we could scarcely then doubt the probability of our being able to supply one of the most important chasms in the present history of the civilization of mankind. The Hindus, however, have been always too much occupied with themselves to pay much attention to other nations, except when obliged by invasion and conquest; they have therefore, as it would seem, preserved no information for us on the subject; and the conclusions which might be drawn from a comparison of their knowledge and institutions with those of other countries, however probable, are yet by no means certain; and even supposing they were, we shall still have to reply to such questions as the following: What do we really know of the ancient learning of this people? of their religion, their poetry, their arts, their political institutions, or of their commerce, and their influence upon other nations? From what sources do we derive this knowledge? And to what extent are these sources themselves clear and authentic, or the reverse? We must satisfy ourselves upon all these points, before we can even pronounce upon our ability to compose an historical sketch of that olden time when the Hindus, as yet their own masters, and not bowed down under the yoke of a foreign conqueror, had free and unfettered liberty of developing the national character.

Such an inquiry as this, however, is one of the most difficult for many reasons. First of all, the very abundance of

due effect to the important axiom, that Hindu Antiquities can only be satisfactorily explored in the country itself.

Of the writings of the above Society contained in the Asiatic Researches, I have only consulted the first twelve vols., (i.—iv. of the 4to edit. and v.—xii. of the 8vo,) not having been able to procure the thirteenth, which was all then published. The essays of Sir W. Jones may be found also in his Works, vol. i.—vi. 4to edit.

materials itself is one obstacle. And again, notwithstanding the vast accumulation of facts, we are perpetually meeting with great and important chasms. Add to this the still greater number of difficulties naturally inherent in the subject, which impede the progress of investigation, and which can only be removed by an intimate acquaintance with the spirit and ways of thinking peculiar to Eastern nations; it is by such means alone that we can hope to arrive at more ample and satisfactory conclusions.

It is true we have one great advantage here which does not assist our researches into most other nations of antiquity —it is the fact that the Hindus still exist as a people. Completely separate by their customs and religion from the rest of the world, and disdaining to make converts, they have thereby preserved their national existence. Even the foreigners who have settled among them, and what is still more surprising, their very conquerors, remain altogether as distinct and isolated as they would be in their own native land. It is this exclusive character which renders communication with them so difficult, and checks all our inquiries. And though it is very probable they would not under all circumstances maintain the same reserve towards a foreigner, who knew how to insinuate himself into their confidence, yet travellers too often bring with them preconceived opinions, or are deficient in that kind of knowledge which will enable them to profit by the information they may obtain: and moreover, instances are by no means rare of the fact, that a desire of flattering strangers will often induce a cunning Hindu to furnish them with statements either absolutely false, or at least so artfully mixed up with what is true as not to be worthy of confidence.[2]

The Hindu passes as it were a kind of spiritual existence in ages long since gone by. The present is to him an age of profound corruption, and according to his legendary notions a still more deeply corrupted era is to ensue, until the restoration of a former happy state shall introduce a new and better order of things. But this present age, truly so

[2] Wilford, (*Asiat. Res.* vol. viii. p. 250, etc.,) with noble frankness, admits this to have been the case with respect to his essay on Egypt and the Nile. (*Asiat. Res.* vol. iii.) His Hindu teacher had falsified the names of places occurring in the MSS. from which he borrowed his materials.

named by us, is no other than what a European writer would generally term "The Age of History." The Brahman, however, looks down upon it with a glance of indifference, if not of actual contempt. His soul discovers more abundant nourishment in the contemplation of those far distant periods of time when the mighty Vishnu, disguised as Rama, made war on the Demons, or when, in the character of Krishna, he became the restorer of a better order of things. What could induce him to condescend to the survey of this present age of misery? What could reconcile him to such studies as those to which we are indebted for our critical history of his countrymen? To no purpose should we search for a native of this description, and yet, nevertheless, to the Hindu, such as he is, does the European apply for information. The grand object, therefore, of a writer who would describe this singular people, would be to make himself a Hindu among Hindus, without at the same time divesting himself of the character of a European. Whoever has satisfied himself of the difficulty of fulfilling these requisites, must necessarily, in proportion as he distrusts his own abilities, be obliged to make larger claims upon the impartial judgment of his readers. Even though he had in person visited the banks of the Jumna and the Ganges, and received instruction at the feet of the most learned pundits of Benares, yet he must still allow the impossibility of fully complying with the pre-requisites to his task. How then must the difficulties be increased to one who, living under a dreary northern sky, has never beheld the gorgeous magnificence of an Indian climate; who, out of all its rich literature, is acquainted with but a few detached fragments; and who, in order to obtain even this scanty knowledge, must content himself with translations, themselves probably imperfect and incorrect!

We have however (thanks to the preparatory labours of English scholars) arrived sufficiently far on our way, to be able to fix on some certain point of view from which we can take a comprehensive survey of the whole field of Indian antiquities and literature, though many portions of it still remain enveloped in mist and obscurity. It will therefore be our principal task to determine the correctness and extent of our sphere of vision, as well as to ascertain the degree of clearness with which the several objects strike our view. It is indeed always a considerable point gained, when we are able to distinguish what we know from that which we are ignorant of. The day perhaps may come when the mists which now intercept our observation will be dissipated; should that ever be the case, some later artist may then fill up this imperfect outline with a more sure and successful hand. Incomplete and defective as it now is, it will nevertheless, till that time, have a certain value, and will perhaps suffer but little in the estimation of my successor, even should he pass a correct and impartial judgment on its merits.

Since, then, the object of our inquiries has been thus determined, it follows, of course, that we have here nothing to do with laying down systems of Hindu religion and philosophy by themselves, nor with starting hypotheses, as for example, touching the earliest connexion of India with Egypt, or the transmission of Hindu civilization into the Western World, etc. (although probably we shall have occasion now and then to advert to these subjects): as little do we propose to contradict those learned men who have written upon these topics. Our end will be attained when we have discovered a fixed standard, by reference to which we can examine and set a just value upon their researches.

The general opinion of ancient as well as of modern times is unanimous in considering the Hindus as one of the earliest, if not in fact the oldest, civilized nation in the world. The critical inquirer however has an undoubted right to demand upon what foundation this universal opinion of the high antiquity of the Hindus rests; and whether the bare assertion of the natives themselves be equivalent to an absolute verification of the fact? Or, have not we also good reasons for being incredulous in an equal ratio to their own exaggerated accounts of their antiquity, particularly as it appears more and more evident that India is the last place to look to for any thing like authentic systems of chronology? To this question however we shall only be able to furnish a decisive answer in the sequel of our inquiry. In the mean time, it will merely be necessary at the outset to define with somewhat more precision the rather vague acceptation of the words "high antiquity." Allowing as we do the Hindus to be a most ancient people, we are not therefore obliged to appeal to their chronological series of years reckoned by the million, nor indeed, with several English writers, need we go so far back even as the deluge, at which period, according to their calculations, the fourth age of the Hindus, the age of corruption, began. Under the title of high antiquity we generally comprehend that space of time which extends to the tenth century before the Christian era. The historic records of no other people, if we except the Jews, reaches beyond this point. All that goes further back is concealed beneath the cloak of tradition and hieroglyphics, and as long as we can draw no broad line of demarcation in the case, the definition just laid down will generally be found sufficient for our purpose. Whether the civilization of India reaches back to one thousand years before the Christian era, as is pretty certain, or even to two, which is not improbable, can never be a question altogether devoid of interest. But it is equally certain, that at the precise point where the thread of history and the connexion of its details is broken off, the interest attached to accurate chronological data ends likewise; and all judicious readers must be unanimous in allowing that it is much better to confess ignorance, than boldly to substitute conjecture in the place of knowledge: at the same time however a writer must have free permission to advance probabilities, and even, occasionally, conjectures, *as such*.

Our knowledge of Indian antiquities is derived partly from Grecian sources, and partly from the accounts of the natives themselves. The first of these authorities has already, in great measure, been weighed and examined in our work on Persian India, and the writers themselves are too well known to require any critical notice in this place. I shall content myself therefore with repeating the general conclusion deduced from their histories, that, at the period of the Macedonian invasion, nearly three hundred and fifty years before the commencement of our era, the Hindus already appeared to have reached the same degree of refinement and civilization, both in public and private life, which they subsequently maintained: we are therefore fully authorized in the conclusion, that this civilized state must then have been several hundred years in existence, and even extend as far back as that "high antiquity" above defined. The present inquiry then will be limited solely to a consideration of Indian sources of information: these are of a twofold description; Monuments and Writings. Each kind will therefore require a separate examination.

The monuments still remaining of Indian architecture, considered with a view towards furthering our knowledge of the people, are scarcely less important than those on the banks of the Nile are for a similar purpose with respect to the Egyptians. Who has not, even though he may be ignorant of all else, at least heard something of those stupendous erections to be seen in the islands of Salsette and Elephanta? These serve to confirm the remark, that the more India is examined, the greater variety of illustrative subject-matter, in this point of view, presents itself to the inquirer. But before we can regard Hindu monuments as authentic sources of information on the antiquities of India, we ought previously to ascertain the extent of our acquaintance with them;—how far in connexion with this object they have already been examined—to what degree they are capable of further illustration? And moreover, what are the conclusions, particularly with respect to the antiquity of the nation, which we are enabled to deduce from our present knowledge of them? Our first endeavour then will be to furnish a satisfactory reply to each of these questions.

We are indebted for almost all that we know of Indian monuments to the labours of Englishmen. Neither the Portuguese nor the Dutch, nor yet the French, have employed their minds on the subject, if we except a few occasional remarks occurring in books of Travels. But partial notices, and even descriptions in detail, explain but little when unaccompanied with accurate engravings. The English have presented us with several magnificent works on India, but they have for the most part considered the subject in a very different light. It was rather their aim to represent Indian nature in general as it now appears, than to give a description of the Hindus of antiquity. The great work of Hodges is composed with this design.[3] The two

[3] *Views of Hindostan*, vol. i. ii. Other works, such as PENNANT'S *Views of*

volumes of copper-plate illustrations contain only two pages descriptive of ancient Hindu temples, the pagodas, namely, of Deogur and Tanjore. In a work indeed of this kind every thing is calculated more for effect than to give a true and correct representation; and moreover the whole manner of Hodges is very little adapted to convey an adequate idea of Hindu architecture, as he gives nothing but sketches and views.

As far as I am aware, before any thing of importance towards illustrating these monuments appeared in England, a native of Germany had already gained the credit of leading the way, and had given a description of the rock excavations at Elephanta.[4] The name of Niebuhr is a sufficient guarantee for the correctness of his copies, and we are indebted to that enterprising traveller for a ground-plan of the rock temple, a design of one of the pillars with its dimensions, and seven plates representing the bas-reliefs on the walls. His drawings of Elephanta are even now the most accurate that we have, though he describes only a few of the bas-reliefs, sufficient however to give us some notion of Hindu sculpture. A large field still remains open to future draughtsmen.

Nevertheless Niebuhr's attempt was so much the more meritorious, in that it appears to have given the first impulse to British zeal and activity. A few years afterwards there appeared in London a work under the title of "The Ancient Monuments of India, by R. Gough."[5] In this production, however, we meet with evident proofs of the low state in which Indian archæology still continued in England. It contains merely a notice of the writers who have spoken about Salsette and Elephanta; Niebuhr is translated word for word, and the accompanying plates are all copied from his designs: only one new engraving is added, containing ground-plans of the rock temples of Salsette and some others, together with a view of that island, and two or three inscriptions. Our knowledge of Indian monuments is not therefore much increased by this meagre compilation. We are

Hindostan, which contain no designs of ancient monuments, I shall pass over in silence.

[4] NIEBUHR's *Travels*, vol. ii. 1778, plates iii.—xi.

[5] *A Comparative View of the Ancient Monuments of India, by* R. GOUGH, London, 1785.

indebted for a more accurate acquaintance with the temples of Salsette to Lord Valentia.

The foundation of the Asiatic Society at Calcutta about this time, under the auspices of Sir William Jones, led us to expect fresh information respecting the monuments of India. Such subjects, it is true, were not excluded from the researches of the Society, but their principal attention was directed to languages, literature, and science; and what notices they have given of Hindu monuments are confined to the description of certain pagodas, chiefly those of Ellora and Mavalipuram, and some pillars charged with inscriptions. Thankfully as we acknowledge even these, our gratitude would have been much greater had we been favoured with more drawings, and on a larger scale.

Although since the appearance of Gough's work, designs of monuments had been given in various books of Travels and other writings;[6] yet the splendid work of the Daniells[7] was the first exclusively devoted to the monuments of Hindu architecture. Their plan comprised the whole extent of Indian antiquities, and even the buildings of modern time, particularly those of the Mogul period. But even this work, if I may be allowed to judge from what I have seen of it, appears more calculated to charm the eye than inform the understanding. The employment of colours is scarcely capable of giving an accurate idea of architecture, because it unintentionally embellishes too much, and that this latter is even sometimes done with design a modern traveller is obliged to confess.[8] How often, indeed, does suspicion force itself upon the mind of the beholder that these paintings are too beautiful to be true! Besides, the editors of this publication were artists and not scholars; neither are the monuments there designed classed according to time and nation; and we feel the want of a learned commentary to give us the previous instructions under what era to arrange them. It is impossible therefore with no better materials than these to compose a history of Hindu architecture.

[6] As in MAURICE's *History of Hindostan*, 1794, etc., CRAWFURD's *Sketches of Hindostan*, and others.

[7] *Antiquities of India, from the Drawings of* THOMAS DANIELL, *engraved by himself and William Daniell, taken in the years* 1790, 1793.

[8] LORD VALENTIA's *Travels*, vol. i. p. 357.

The work of Mons. Langlès,[9] finished but a short time before his death, presents, it is true, only designs of monuments already known, after the original drawings of the Daniells and others; but it is nevertheless of great merit, because he has incorporated a variety of information dispersed abroad in costly and scarce collections, and has thereby materially abridged the labours of the student. With reference, however, to the accuracy of the monuments of Elephanta designed by them both, it appears to me upon comparison that the preference is due to Niebuhr. The scale too of the designs, I think, is not sufficiently large to convey a just idea of the original. The great in architecture can only be represented by corresponding greatness in the delineation. At the same time the work above mentioned proves, in a striking manner, that we have as yet scarcely passed even the threshold of a perfect acquaintance with Hindu monuments. The learned Orientalist has not even ventured to classify the buildings according to their age, style, and the particular architects; but has followed rather a geographical plan, in proceeding from south to north.

Among modern travellers, Lord Valentia has distinguished himself above all others by presenting us with correct drawings[10] of particular ancient monuments, with which we were previously altogether, or at least but imperfectly, acquainted. Since this period, a considerable number of Travels and other publications connected with India have made their appearance; but I have not been able to meet with any remarkable illustrations, or descriptions of monuments, contained therein.

Fortunate indeed would it have been for our labours, had these interesting relics employed the hand and exercised the ingenuity of a Wood or a Stuart! Every opinion delivered upon architectural remains, must always be hazardous and uncertain when we have no plans on an accurate and extensive scale to guide our judgment. But nevertheless, we cannot still be said to grope our way in perfect darkness. The works above mentioned have contributed a good deal towards showing the path, and have led to conclusions

[9] *Monumens Anciens et Modernes de l'Inde en* 150 *Planches, par* L. Langlès, Paris, 1813.

[10] See the copper-plate engravings attached to his *Travels.*

which are of the greatest importance to a correct knowledge of Indian antiquities.

The monuments of Hindu architecture naturally divide themselves into three classes; the first, comprises subterraneous temples hewn out of the rock; the second, contains those temples which have been similarly formed upon the surface, but have also portions of the structure under ground; the third, includes buildings, properly so called. They have all a common connexion with religious purposes, being dedicated as well to the worship of Vishnu and Siva or Mahadeva, whose followers exist to this day, as also to Buddha, whose sect, long since expelled this part of India, still subsists universally in Ceylon and the Ultra-Gangetic continent. I enumerate the above three classes in the order which appears to agree also with the date of their construction. If this be but a conjecture, there certainly is every appearance of probability in its favour, for it can scarcely be maintained that a people, who had already been accustomed to build in the open air, should subsequently begin to lodge their divinities in under-ground temples; on the contrary, it appears more natural on the very face of things that excavation of the rock should have preceded its exterior embellishment. Whichever be the real state of the case, we must necessarily divide them into three classes, of each of which we will now attempt to give a correct view in succession.

The rock temples of the first kind are found in various parts of India, and are probably not all known to us even at the present day. Although in the plains of Bengal and the Punjab, the nature of the ground does not admit of their construction, yet, on the other hand, the whole of the peninsula on this side of the Ganges is traversed by a rocky chain of Ghauts, at present in great measure unexplored. The nature of this country itself would seem to suggest the convenience of under-ground habitations, where neither the vertical rays of the sun nor the impetuous torrents of the rainy season could penetrate. The natives of many other portions of the globe have adopted similar contrivances; and in proportion to the more extensive scope allowed by them to the introduction of science, so will it appear less wonderful that a people in such a situation, and not deficient in tools, should exercise their ingenuity in this way.[11] The same kind of habitation which a man would construct for himself, he would also appropriate to his gods. It was a religious feeling which transformed a hut into a temple. But an excavation of the rock would seem just so much the more obvious to him, as it favoured his design of rendering these monuments of his religion imperishable. A design which is apparent in the monuments themselves; and which is exhibited still more strongly among all nations in proportion as we go further back into their antiquity. But the extent of these buildings in India, the vastness of the plan, the care displayed in the execution, the richness of the ornaments which adorn the walls, often indeed fantastic, yet still finished with great taste, all conspire together in exciting the admiration and surprise of the observant traveller; and immediately suggest to his mind the propriety of a remark which one has so often occasion to make, when contemplating the gigantic works of remote antiquity, that such stupendous edifices could hardly have been the production of one generation, but must have required the peaceable and uninterrupted labour of upwards of a century to bring them to completion. We shall now proceed to detail in regular order the accounts of those monuments which are already made known to us.

The rock temple in the small island of Elephanta,[12] near Bombay, has been the most frequently visited of any. This, together with the adjacent buildings, is hewn solely out of the rock, and forms consequently a perfect grotto. The temple itself, exclusive of the apartments and chapels attached, is about one hundred and thirty feet in length, and the same in breadth. In front of the principal entrance facing the north, and therefore sheltered from the sun, is an artificial terrace, from which there is an extensive prospect of the ocean, and on each side is an additional opening to

[11] Even the naked Hottentots are in the habit of sketching rude designs on the walls of their huts. But what a wide interval is there between an African kraal and a Hindu rock temple! and yet the refined artifice observable in the latter, must have previously traced the intermediate steps between the two extremes. An authentic account of the rise and progress of grotto architecture, (were sufficient materials at hand,) would doubtless lead to new and interesting conclusions respecting the general history of mankind.

[12] So called by Europeans from a colossal figure of an elephant hewn out of the stone; the head and neck are now fallen off, and the whole statue threatens approaching ruin. Langlès, vol. ii. p. 148.

admit the fresh breeze. The rock which serves for a roof to this grotto is supported by twenty-six pillars and sixteen pilasters: the latter occupy half of each side, and are left by the architect in the original unhewn state of the material. The chambers or chapels adjoining are not quite so high, but are finished in precisely the same manner. The walls, without inscriptions, but formerly covered with a beautiful stucco, are still ornamented with reliefs, some of which are so highly prominent that the figures are merely attached to the rock by their backs; there is no doubt therefore that they are as old as the temple itself. Similar carving is observable on the walls of other rock temples, and the same figures present themselves: the whole are consequently borrowed from the same mythology. The question is, whether from that of the modern Hindus, and whether these monuments belong to the same people, or are they the production of an earlier race which has now disappeared, together with its religion? Although it is not the object of the present work to furnish a detailed history of these sculptures, of which by the way we have only a few partial drawings, yet they require a more particular examination, in order that we may offer some reply to the foregoing question. I shall endeavour, therefore, in following the order of Niebuhr's drawings, to give some illustration of the subject; premising, however, that where any thing is doubtful I shall choose rather to confess my own ignorance than advance idle conjecture.

The first of Niebuhr's seven plates[13] is the easiest to explain. We here see directly in the entrance of the temple a colossal bust, thirteen feet high, with three heads and four arms. It represents, as he has rightly observed, the Hindu Trinity,[14] Brahma, Vishnu, and Siva or Mahadeva, the three Devas, or personifications of the godhead. The middle one is Brahma, that on the right Vishnu, the left with a serpent and mustachios is Siva. The same mythological idea still remains perfectly unaltered among the modern Hindus. There is an accurate representation of these three figures,

[13] Plates to NIEBUHR's *Travels*, vol. ii. plate v. LANGLÈS, plate lxxiii. vol. ii.

[14] Called Trimurti by the Hindus, from the Sanscrit *tri*, three, and *murti*, form. PAULINO, *Systema Brahmanicum*, p. 109.

with their proper attributes, to be seen in an idol of bronze in the Borgian museum, which has already been copied and described by Father Paulino.[15] It is uncertain what characters the large human figures represent which are on each side of the bust; probably they are chobdars, or attendants, usually assigned to divinities and great men as part of their retinue. The one on the right hand, supported by a dwarf, bears on his left shoulder a cord, which is the usual distinction of a Brahman, but in many of the reliefs is as often applied to a godhead. In either case we cannot but consider these personages as of a higher rank than simple attendants, a supposition which is confirmed by their stature, the Brahmanical thread, and the additional circumstance of their being supported by inferiors.

The representation contained in the following plate (tab. vi.) is very remarkable. It portrays Siva or Mahadeva,[16] as an hermaphrodite with one breast, a circumstance which has sometimes caused the figure to be mistaken for an Amazon. He is however recognised by his insignia—in one of his four hands he holds a snake, in the other a timbrel, in the third a whip, and with the fourth he supports himself on the bull *Nundi*, his usual mode of conveyance.[17] Father Paulino has already observed,[18] that it is very common to represent Siva, as well as the two other great deities, under the form of an hermaphrodite, an emblem which no doubt contains some deep and mysterious meaning. On his left stand two female figures, one holding a fly-flap, the other an unknown instrument; both therefore evidently in a menial character. On the right Siva himself again appears as a man, with his usual attribute, a trident, the symbol of his dominion over the upper, middle, and nether world. Behind, or rather above him, is an intended representation of Brahma, with four heads, of which however only three are visible; but the four accompanying swans (the bird that carries him through the heavens) leave no doubt of the real number. On the other side, opposite to Brahma, is Kartikeya, the son of Siva and Parvati, the god of war, with

[15] *Syst. Brahm.* p. 105, sqq. tab. xv. *a.*

[16] Mahadeva, "The Great God," is only one of the many surnames of Siva.

[17] See PAULINO, *Systema Brahmanicum*, pp. 88, 89.

[18] PAULINO, *Syst. Brahm.* p. 86. It is from this that he is called "Arthanari," (*Arddhanarisa,*) the lord, half female.

sword in hand, sitting upon his conquered enemy, the giant Kaymughusura. Next to Brahma is Ganèsa, the god of wisdom, holding in his hand a style: another attribute of his is an elephant's head, which the god himself often bears.[19] On another part of the wall is represented the fable of his origin, (which Niebuhr has recounted, without however subjoining any illustration,[20]) and from which also is evident that he must have formed part of the suite of Siva. The figures hovering above them in the attitude of adoration, are a choir of Devas and Devanis, (male and female genii,) who compose Siva's court in his palace of Kailasa.

In the next plate (tab. vii.) Siva again appears as the principal figure, recognisable by his attribute, the snake, in one of his four hands. He is adorned with the Brahmanical thread, and is supported on a dwarf, who carries a fly-flap. At his side stands his consort Parvati, supported also on a dwarf. The stature and attributes of the four-headed Brahma, Ganèsa, and Kartikeya, are similar to those of Siva; and we see also here the accompanying choir of Devas and Devanis. The principal figure in the lower part of tab. viii., in human form, and in a sitting posture, is difficult to determine, because the four arms being broken off, the attributes have disappeared likewise. It should, as the similarity of the head ornaments, the four arms, and the Brahmanical thread make sufficiently probable, be another representation of Siva. Under this supposition the female figure sitting near him would also be his wife. The two chobdars on each side, both ornamented with the Brahman's thread, denote in either case the presence of two great deities, upon whom they are attendant. Their inferiority of condition is expressed in this, as well as in the foregoing plates, by the smallness of their stature. Of these two figures, both of which are female, one carries a fly-flap, the other an infant, indicative of Lakshmi,[21] the consort of Vishnu. If this explanation be correct, the figures before us become very re-

[19] In Niebuhr, owing to a mistake, the head only of an elephant is represented, without adding thereto the image of Ganèsa; the god himself appears in LANGLÈS, vol. ii. plate lxxv., and also in the following plate of Niebuhr's book itself.

[20] NIEBUHR's *Travels*, vol. ii. p. 39.

[21] See F. PAULINO's description of the bronze statue in the Borgian Museum, *Syst. Brahm.* tab. xii.

markable, inasmuch as the wife of Vishnu is here represented in the capacity of a menial attendant upon Siva. However, I consider it more likely to be a female servant carrying the son of Parvati, that is, Kartikeya, the god of war.

The figure of a man with two arms, in the upper part of the same plate, is without any attributes, unless we suppose what he is represented to be sitting upon is a lotus flower. But this peculiarity is so common to many other Hindu deities, that we can draw no certain conclusion from the fact supposing it be true. I cannot possibly agree with Langlès,[22] in imagining it to be Buddha, for that personage has no business here, nor is there the slightest trace of his worship to be found in any part of this temple.

The representation given in the following plate (tab. ix.) is one of the most remarkable. In the human figure which occurs here also, though three arms with the accompanying attributes are lost, there can be no mistaking the presence of Siva. Every thing favours the conclusion, that the subject before us represents a passage taken from the history of that god—it is in short Siva, receiving his consort Parvati from the hands of Kamadeva, the god of love, into his paradise of Kailasa. The tedious hinderances which had opposed this union, so necessary to the welfare of the universe, were at length happily surmounted. This adventure is here portrayed in all that simplicity of style which seems so peculiar to the ancient Hindu mythology. Other deities, among whom the four-headed Brahma is conspicuous, assist at the ceremony; an attendant is bringing in a covered dish, probably in allusion to the marriage feast; a numerous band of Devas and Devanis are employed in keeping holy day. If any one wishes to see an example of the manner in which this Hindu fable, so simple in its origin, has been spun out by the poets, let him compare the recital communicated to a modern antiquary by one of their learned pundits.[23]

The frightful object represented in plate x. is easy enough to comprehend. It is Siva again, but as the Avenger and Destroyer; he is therefore armed with all the attributes of terror—the sword, the infant marked out for slaughter, the serpent, and the timbrel: instead of the Brah-

[22] Langlès, vol. ii. p. 161.
[23] Polier, *Mythologie des Indous*, tom. i. p. 204, etc.

manical thread he wears a collar of skulls. The same subject, but furnished with a greater number of attributes, is observable in a painting in the Borgian museum, described by Father Paulino.[24]

My intention in offering the above remarks being less to give a circumstantial account of these pieces of sculpture than to note down the prevailing idea in each representation, I shall therefore omit the last plate in Niebuhr's book, of which I need only observe in passing, that it appears to describe some scenes in the history of Siva. Nothing further is necessary to enable us to draw certain legitimate conclusions, of no small importance to a correct knowledge of Hindu monuments.

First, then, the representations to be seen in the island of Elephanta are borrowed from the Hindu mythology still in existence, and are therefore capable of being illustrated in a general way by referring to that source; though at the same time, the particular details must still remain inexplicable, owing to the extent of a very complicated mythology, and our limited and imperfect acquaintance with its allusions. And even supposing that the Brahmans of the present day were themselves unable to explain a great portion of the subjects here represented, yet this circumstance would furnish additional proof of the high antiquity of these monuments. It is however actually demonstrable, that the people who excavated the temple and designed the sculptures, must have possessed the same religious worship, and the same mythological system, though probably more circumscribed than the present.

Secondly: It is no less certain that the grotto of Elephanta is dedicated to Siva. All the ornamental designs represented on the walls either exhibit him in person, or have a manifest allusion to his history; the prevailing idea is to describe him seated on a throne in his palace of Kailasa, surrounded by his court of Devas and Devanis.—Were there, indeed, any doubt of the person intended, it would be removed by the gross obscenity of the figures which are observed on the walls, though Niebuhr has omitted to mention this circumstance. The chief symbol of Siva is the

[24] *Syst. Brahm.*, pp. 88, 89, tab. x.

Lingam, or Phallus, the organ of generation, which is represented in all the modern temples dedicated to him; and is itself an object of religious veneration. It is also found here, in the back-ground of the principal temple.[25] The obscenity displayed on the walls surpasses every thing that the most depraved European fancy could possibly imagine.[26] It has however been remarked by many writers, that no conclusion can properly be drawn from this peculiarity, respecting the morals of the nation itself.

Thirdly: It is also sufficiently clear that the worship of Siva and the sect of his followers, were already in high repute in India at the early period when these rock temples were excavated. Of Vishnu and his worshippers, however, to the best of my knowledge, I can find no trace whatever. Yet under all circumstances it would be too precipitate, to infer that his sect was not at that time in existence. That of Siva certainly appears to have been predominant—and the probability that it is also the most ancient, derives material confirmation from the fact.

And fourthly, If it be asked to what era must we assign the formation of these grottos, and with what reason is that high antiquity so commonly attributed to them? We can only plead the want of accurate chronological data, for suggesting a satisfactory answer. The Hindus themselves confess their perfect ignorance upon this point,[27] and where then shall we seek any other historic testimony? The Greeks, it is true, under Alexander and his followers, became acquainted with India, but they saw only the northern parts of it, the plains lying between the Indus and the Ganges, where structures of the above description are not to be found. To the best of our knowledge, the first certain trace of the existence of Hindu grotto temples that we meet with in ancient authors, is found in a fragment of Porphyry's treatise on the Styx, preserved to us by Stobæus.[28] The colossal statue of a god with two sexes there

[25] Gough's *Monuments, etc.*, p. 14.

[26] I judge so at least, from an engraving published in London, and which was communicated to me.

[27] Niebuhr's *Travels*, vol. ii. p. 41.

[28] Stob. *Eclog. Phys.* vol. i. p. 144 of my own edition. "The Indian messengers," says Bardesanes, a contemporary of Heliogabalus, "report that there is in India a large grotto under a lofty hill, in which is to be seen an image

mentioned, evidently alludes to the figure of Siva already described. Though at the same time no one can venture to affirm that the account given by the Indian Bardesanes directly refers to the pagoda of Elephanta, yet it is nevertheless quite plain, that he must be speaking of some temple precisely similar, and also adorned with sculptures, in which he reports, that at certain times the Brahmans were there wont to assemble and keep holy day, and where also the judicial trials or ordeals, of which there were many kinds among the Indians, used to take place.[29]

It is therefore only from the monuments themselves that we can draw any conclusions respecting their antiquity, and in them indeed every thing concurs to render the fact certain. Their vast extent and perfect execution of detail, as well as the nature of the undertaking itself, sufficiently show that it must have required a great number of years to bring them to completion. The rock out of which they are hewn is a clay-porphyry, one of the very hardest kinds of stone;[30] and in all probability could only be worked by the help of that celebrated Indian steel called *Wudz*, which even in ancient times was famous for its excellent temper. Is it credible that all recollection of such a laborious enterprise as this should have been totally lost, were it not dated from very remote antiquity? Even nature itself has impressed the marks of venerable age upon them, and many of the sculptured representations on the walls are so dissolved by the operation of the atmosphere that they can with difficulty be recognised. How many hundred years must have been necessary to produce such an effect upon a rock so hard! In fine, the style itself also of these ingenious works would seem to attest their extreme age; characterized as they are by great simplicity, united with consummate perfection. The figures of the gods appear all of them naked, but at the same time carefully furnished with their respective ornaments, their head-dress, necklaces,

from ten to twelve ells high, with the arms folded across, and the right side that of a man, the left a woman, etc.

[29] There is a curious dissertation on this subject, in the *Asiat. Res.* vol. i. p. 389. In this grotto was performed the ordeal by water. STOB. vol. i. p. 148.

[30] I can attest the truth of this myself, as I have by me a specimen of the stone from the collection of M. Blumenbach, together with a penknife made of *Wudz*, the first instrument of that material manufactured at London.

earrings, girdles, together with their proper attributes. There is here no appearance of that excessive surcharge of apparel with which the modern Hindus disfigure their idols.

Grotto temples of a similar description but of larger size are found in the neighbouring island of Salsette, which is also opposite to Bombay. Of these we possess a description, with a ground-plan and a view, but of the sculptures by no means such correct drawings as those of Elephanta, for Niebuhr did not visit Salsette. We are indebted to Gemelli Carreri,[31] an Italian, for the first account of these monuments. Anquetil du Perron, in the preface to his edition of the Zend-Avesta,[32] has given a more accurate description, but the subjoined ground-plan is not very intelligible. A more particular notice and an exterior view have been furnished by Lord Valentia;[33] and it is only a few years since we have been presented with a new ground-plan of the temple, and some drawings of the bas-reliefs, by Mr. Salt.[34] These, with the accounts given in the Calcutta Journal, have already been made use of by Langlès.[35] The above publications are sufficient to convey some general idea of the monuments, but of the numerous sculptures they give only a few specimens.

In point of size and number, the temples of Salsette[36] are much superior to those at Elephanta. The lofty mountain, which this island contains, is also composed of a species of rock equally hard, but which nevertheless is excavated in every direction. The grand pagoda is vaulted, and extends over an area of forty paces in breadth and one hundred in length: exclusive of the four columns at the entrance, thirty are enumerated inside, of which eighteen have their capitals formed of elephants; the rest are merely of an hexagonal shape, which would induce a supposition that they still re-

[31] GEMELLI CARRERI, *Voyage autour du Monde*, tom. iii. p. 36, etc. It contains merely a description without either plan or drawing.

[32] This is translated, and the plan copied by GOUGH, *Ancient Monuments*, etc., p. 38, sq.

[33] VALENTIA, *Travels*, vol. ii. p. 195, plate x.

[34] In the *Transactions of the Bombay Literary Society*, vol. i.

[35] LANGLÈS, *Monumens de Hindostan*, tom. ii. p. 181—208, and pl. lxxvii.—lxxxii.

[36] This island is called by the Portuguese, Canaria. From thence the great temple has its name of "The Pagoda of Kennery;" the others are called "Monpeser" and "Jegvasary."

main unfinished. At the end of the pagoda, which terminates in a circular form, is a kind of cupola, which, as well as the other portions of the structure, are all hewn out of the living stone.

The Great Pagoda is only so termed by way of distinction, for there are two others scarcely inferior in size, which are even furnished with several stories, one over the other; and between and round about these there is an innumerable quantity of smaller chapels. Every part is ornamented with sculpture, and the apartments, tanks, open courts, are all hewn out of the rock.

The architecture of these monuments so nearly resembles that of Elephanta as to preclude all doubt of their belonging to the same people and the same age, though the excavations at Salsette must have occupied a considerably longer time in execution. The effects of the weather on the sculptures here, too, give striking evidence of the many hundred years that must have elapsed in order to reduce them to their present state of decay.

But a distinguishing feature in the temple grottos of Salsette are the inscriptions, which we meet with on the walls. Of these Anquetil du Perron has enumerated twenty-two, specimens of which he has subjoined.[37] The alphabet in which they are composed has no resemblance to any one among the great number that are still used in the peninsula, nor has any one hitherto been able to decipher their meaning.

But the large temple of Kennery is distinguished from that at Elephanta principally by the circumstance of being consecrated to Buddha. We here see manifold representations of this god, who is easy to be known by his woolly hair, long ears, and sitting cross-legged.[38] His principal statue is surrounded with small reliefs, describing, probably, some scenes taken from his mythological history, in one of which is represented the fore-part of a vessel filled with strangers; but these sculptures are, in general, too diminutive in size to enable us to offer any illustrations of their meaning.

On the other hand there is no doubt that of the smaller temples, the one called Monpeser is dedicated to Siva, as

[37] They are also copied by Gough, vid. supra.

[38] LANGLÈS, plate lxxx. This proves it to be the statue of a god, and not a devotee, though the woolly hair is also attributed sometimes to the latter.

that of Jegvasary is to Indra. In the first we meet with a colossal statue of Siva surrounded with all his court, receiving his consort Parvati, as before observed in the reliefs at Elephanta taken by Niebuhr.[39] In the other we see Indra with his wife in the same position as represented in the plate already explained.[40] It follows, therefore, that in the same small island, and near to each other, formerly prevailed the two hostile sects of Buddha and of Siva, unless we might take it for granted that the sculptures are anterior to the expulsion of the Buddhists by the followers of Siva. It is also worthy of remark, that they contain no allusion to the history of Vishnu: on the contrary, according to the testimony of Lord Valentia, Vishnu is in one place represented as the servant of Buddha, being employed in fanning him.[41] "Not only the great number of these grottoes," continues the same traveller, "but also the tanks, the terraces, the flights of stairs leading from one to the other, all clearly show what must have been the population of these arid rocks in former times, where all now is silent except the casual footstep of the inquisitive traveller. The plains once so highly cultivated are become an impenetrable jungle, the lair of ferocious wild beasts, and the abode of desolation and noxious miasmata."[42]

Another rock monument of the same kind, and to the best of my knowledge first described and delineated by Lord Valentia, is the temple grotto of Carli,[43] situate about half way between Bombay and Poonah, the capital of the Mahrattas. The drawings we have of this piece of antiquity are much superior to those of any other. Considered with regard to the complete finish of its details, the temple of Carli appears to occupy the first place of all, though in point of extent it is inferior to that of Salsette. The principal grotto is one hundred and twenty-six feet long, and

[39] Langlès, plate lxxxii. [40] Langlès, plate lxxxi.

[41] The relation of superiors and inferiors, as Gemelli Carreri remarks, is here also represented by a difference in stature.

[42] Valentia, *Travels*, vol. ii. p. 198.

[43] Valentia, *Travels*, vol. ii. p. 162, sq. Plate viii. an interior view of the grotto. Plate ix. plan of the same. There are many grottos at Carli, of which the largest only has been delineated. The interior appears altogether like that of Salsette. The pillars are supported by elephants, on which male and female figures are sitting. Underneath the vaulted roof is an arcade of timber, no doubt of modern construction.

sixty-four in breadth; the roof is also vaulted and supported by pillars, and moreover terminates in a circular chapel, surmounted with a cupola. There are no sculptures in the interior, but only on the walls of the portico, partly representing elephants, and partly figures of men with two sexes. The statue of Buddha is observable in many parts, sometimes in a sitting posture, after the Indian fashion, at others in an upright position, and always surrounded with worshippers. Here also we meet with numerous inscriptions, and all in the same unknown character which is found in the seven pagodas at Mavalipuram.[44] It appears, therefore, that this temple also was dedicated to Buddha; but as the drawings of the several figures, and the inscriptions, left to the Literary Society at Bombay by Lord Valentia, still remain unpublished, we can offer no further opinion on the subject: there is, however, less reason for doubt, because the Brahmans ascribe its erection to the agency of Rakshasas, or evil genii; and all religious services therein are peremptorily forbidden.

As far as our knowledge extends, Ceylon is the only other Indian island besides Salsette and Elephanta, in which there are temple grottoes; and it is not many years since we became acquainted with this island after its possession by the British, through the medium of Davy's Travels in the interior. The largest structure of this description is found in the southern part of the island, in about 7° N. Lat., near to Damboulou, and in a south-easterly direction from the capital town of Candy.[45] These rock temples, according to Davy's opinion, are the largest, the most perfect and ancient, as well as the best preserved, in the whole island. They are contained in a grotto, much less indebted to art than to nature for its formation, before which a wall extends of four hundred feet in length. The dimensions of the largest temple are one hundred and ninety feet by ninety, and forty-five in height. The smaller one is ninety feet long and seventy broad; the third is seventy-five feet in length and only twenty-one in breadth. They are all dedicated to Buddha, whose religion is still preserved exclusively in

[44] VALENTIA, *Travels*, vol. ii. p. 163. All these inscriptions have been copied by Lord Valentia.

[45] JOHN DAVY, *Account of the Interior of Ceylon*, London, 1821, p. 232.

Ceylon, and perhaps there in its greatest purity. The principal temple contains a recumbent statue of Buddha, thirty feet long, of colossal size, as he is generally represented; we also meet with numerous smaller statues of this god, or his worshippers, in different attitudes; of which fifty-three have been counted, representing probably persons of his suite. It is however in the heart of India, and in the midst of the Ghaut-Range, that buildings of the above description are found, which far surpass all those hitherto enumerated. These are the celebrated grottoes of Ellora, in the neighbourhood of Dewgur and Aurengabad.[46] The first, I believe, who gave any account of them, though a very superficial one, was Thevenot;[47] a more correct description, especially of the sculptures, is furnished by Anquetil du Perron.[48] The latter visited the grottoes in person, accompanied by two Brahmans, on whose veracity must depend the correctness of the explanations given of the sculptures, of which however he has subjoined no engravings. Du Perron has certainly the merit of having supplied a tolerably detailed account of these monuments, most of which he appears to have seen, and noted down the observations of the Brahmans on the subject: nevertheless, without presuming to question the fidelity of these latter, few descriptions, accurate as they may be, are alone capable of conveying any just idea of the subject.

This deficiency was in some measure remedied by an Englishman of the name of Malet, to whom we owe a description of Ellora, accompanied with some designs and a ground-plan of the principal temple.[49] He states, however, that bad health prevented him from visiting every one of the numerous grottoes in person; and moreover that, his draughtsman being sick also, he could neither guarantee the correctness of the designs made by the latter, in which, too,

[46] In Lat. 20° North, and Long. 76° East. It might be owing to chance, but it is worthy of remark, that Ellora is situate exactly in the middle between the northern boundary of India and Cape Comorin. Its distance from the coast is somewhat greater on the east than on the west side. The expression, nevertheless, that it is in the centre of India, is sufficiently correct, whether that was the effect of design or mere chance.

[47] THEVENOT, *Voyage des Indes*, pp. 220—223.

[48] *Zend-Avesta, Diss. Prelim.* p. ccxxxiii.—ccl., and copied by GOUGH, *Monuments, etc.*, p. 60, sq.

[49] *Asiatic Researches*, vol. vi. p. 382, sq.

we are sometimes at a loss to discover the true expression of Indian character.

A great deal more certainly was effected by the Daniells, from whose splendid work Langlès has copied his illustrations in thirty-four plates on a reduced scale. In the above we are presented with a ground-plan, as well as an exterior and interior view, of twelve of these rock temples; but only a few designs, and those already known, of the many bas-reliefs.[50] Our acquaintance, therefore, with these works of Hindu sculpture still remains very imperfect; it is sufficient, however, to give some idea of the whole, and to enable our deducing certain legitimate and irrefragable conclusions.

Let the reader imagine to himself a chain of rocky mountains consisting principally of very hard red granite, and in a semicircular or rather horse-shoe form, with a distance of nearly five miles between the extreme points. In this range is found a series of grotto temples, some of two and even three stories in height, partly in juxta-position with each other, and partly separated by intervals, which in their turn are filled with a number of smaller temples; and the whole ornamented with innumerable reliefs, many of which have suffered from the effects of time, and not a few from the hands of wanton violence. It is difficult to determine precisely which is the principal temple of all these, but the largest, and that of which we possess a ground-plan and the greatest number of views, is called the temple of Kailasa, i. e. the palace of Siva or Mahadeva.[51] All that is great, splendid, and ornamental, in architecture above ground, is here seen also beneath the earth; peristyles, staircases, bridges, chapels, columns, porticos, obelisks, colossal statues,

[50] The ground-plan and views of the temple of Jagannatha, (Juggernaut,) are given in plate xxxv.; of Parasu Rama, in plate xxxvi.; of Indra, in plates xxxvii.—xlii.; of Dumar-Leyna, in plates xliii.—xlv.; of Jenussa, in plates xliv.—xlvi.; of Ramishur, in plates xlviii., xlix.; of Kailasa, in plates l.—lv.; Dasavatara, in plate lvi.; of Ravana, in plates lvii., lviii.; of Tintodi, in plates lix., lx.; of Dautali, in plates lxi., lxii; of Visvakarma, in plates lxiii.—lxv.; of Dherwara, in plate lxvi.; and general views of the country about Ellora, in plates lxvii.—lxix. The vignette title page of this volume contains a view of Jagannatha, after plate xxxv.

[51] According to the dimensions given of this temple, the vestibule is eighty-eight feet deep by one hundred and thirty-eight in breadth; the temple itself from the door of the portico to the inmost wall is one hundred and three feet in length by sixty-one broad, exclusive of the platform behind the temple, which makes the whole length one hundred and forty-two feet: so that in point of extent it might bear a comparison with several of our Gothic churches.

and reliefs sculptured on almost all the walls, representing, as we have already noticed, Hindu deities and their fabulous history: nor must we omit to mention the imposing effect produced by a row of enormous elephants, who seem to bear up the superincumbent weight of the temple.[52]

In an open court, to which we arrive through the grand entrance, stands within the grotto itself a second temple; the whole mass of the rock which has been suffered to remain having been hewn into a pyramidal form as a pagoda. Of this wonderful structure, the variety, richness, and skill displayed in the ornaments surpass all description.[53] There are also many other temple grottoes here, which are little if indeed any thing inferior to that of Kailasa; that of Indra and his consort Indrani contains in like manner a pagoda of the form just described, and in point of richness of architecture and decoration is fully equal to it. The two divinities, both surrounded with worshippers, are represented as sitting, Indra on a recumbent elephant, Indrani on a lion: all these figures are of colossal dimensions. The grotto known by the name of Dumar-Leyna, and consecrated to Siva and his wife Parvati, is not a whit less remarkable and surprising. The sculptures on the walls describe among other subjects the marriage of Siva and Parvati, and are therefore confirmatory of the explanations already given of a similar scene in the grotto of Elephanta.[54] According to Anquetil du Perron, one of the intermediate pagodas was dedicated to Vishnu, and several of the adjacent ones to his wives and followers, particularly to his architect Visvakarma, who constructed the palace which the god occupies in his celestial abode of Vaicuntha;[55] another pagoda is consecrated to Rama, his wife, and various persons in their suite, etc. Among all the Hindu divinities, in whose honour temples have been erected, there is hardly one who does not appear to have possessed at some time or other his respective sanctuary at Ellora; and in fact we might justly consider the gallery in rear of the great temple of Kailasa, as a perfect specimen of an Hindu Pantheon. The names of not

[52] Langlès, vol. i. plate lii.

[53] *Asiatic Res.* vol. iii. p. 405.

[54] See above, p. 60.

[55] *Asiatic Res.* vol. vi. p. 421. The grotto here given is vaulted like that of Carli, but the arcades are of stone.

less than forty-three deities of one sort or other have been there enumerated by Malet.

The age of the grottoes at Ellora is as difficult to determine on just historical principles as those at Elephanta. If we believe the reports of the Brahmans communicated to Malet, they must have been constructed as much as seven thousand eight hundred and ninety-four years ago, by one Rajah Ilu![56] consequently long anterior to the commencement of the Cali Yug, i. e. the present age according to Hindu computation, and therefore also in the fabulous period. On the other hand, a certain Mahomedan professes to have heard from some learned pundit, whose name by the way he has forgotten, that these temples, together with the fortress of Deogur, now called Dawlatabad, were the work of one Rajah Il, who reigned above nine hundred years ago. Such testimony as this, however, which rests on no certain foundation, must appear in the eyes of a critical inquirer, as little satisfactory and convincing as the former. Indeed, the single circumstance that all these stupendous buildings could have been completed by one rajah involves an absolute contradiction; it is very possible the fortress might have been built at the time specified, and this supposition would at least furnish some ground for the general report. It follows, therefore, that in the present state of the question, we can only ascertain the age of the monuments at Ellora, by considering them either separately or in comparison with others already described; and in conducting this examination, I believe I can fairly secure certain conclusions which are too important to be withheld from the reader.

In the first place, Every thing in these grotto buildings wears an Indian character, no foreign admixture whether of mythology or art is perceptible. They must therefore belong to a period of time when the people, freely left to themselves, and under no foreign yoke, were able to lead what sort of life they pleased, and were their own masters in every thing. There is, nevertheless, in their architecture, a certain gradation which it is impossible to mistake; while at Salsette and Elephanta all is simplicity in the extreme, and the art of sculpture appears yet in its infancy; so on the

[56] *Asiatic Res.* vol. vi. page 385.

other hand, in the principal temple at Ellora, the richness and variety of the designs, and the completeness of execution observable in the details, both of architecture and sculpture, exemplify the most flourishing period of Hindu art. The completion of these surprising works must, according to our calculations, have required some hundreds of years; but we must also allow a space of time nearly equal in duration to that epoch, in which Ellora, situate in the middle of India, and near to Deogur, (i. e. the Divine Mount,) continued to be the central point of the Hindu religion: and although it might be impossible to determine this period with chronological exactness, yet every thing concurs to prove that the temple grottoes of Ellora are posterior in construction to those of Salsette and Elephanta.

2. In the rock temples of Salsette and Elephanta, as well as Carli, the prevailing creed appears to have been that of Siva or Mahadeva, and next to this, even that of Buddha. They must consequently be prior in point of time to the expulsion of the latter from India. On the other hand, the temples of Ellora betray not the slightest symptom of any connexion with the worship of Buddha: whether it directly follows, therefore, that at the period of their excavation, the Buddhists were already driven from the Indian continent, I cannot certainly venture to determine: this however seems unquestionable, that at the above period the two still existing sects of Siva and Vishnu were then already separate, and flourishing in the neighbourhood of each other, a fact which an examination of the grottoes at Elephanta and Salsette still permitted us to doubt, and which also furnishes us with additional presumptive evidence of the more modern antiquity of Ellora.

3. It appears highly probable that, at the time when these temples, or at least those of Ellora, were constructed, the Hindu system of mythology had already attained its full and perfect state of development; as on the walls of these grottoes we find not merely the several deities by themselves, but represented also with their companions, relations, and attendants in general, and indeed to much greater extent and perfection at Ellora than any where else; from which we may safely argue for a more recent foundation in the case of the latter temples, independent of the great increase

of probability which the argument derives from the following very remarkable circumstance. We observe on the walls of Ellora sculptured representations of great epic subjects, which appear beyond a doubt to have been furnished by those famous Hindu heroic poems the Ramayana and the Mahabharata, of which we shall have occasion to speak hereafter. In the large temple of Kailasa, on the right side, is represented the engagement between Rama and Ravana, in which Hanuman the king of the monkeys plays a chief part.[57] This forms the principal subject of the Ramayana. On the left side, directly opposite to the former, is observed the battle of Keyso Pandos taken from the Mahabharata.[58] The armies engaged consist mostly of foot soldiers; some are riding upon elephants, others in chariots, but none on horses. The principal weapons appear to be bows and arrows, though we may occasionally remark the use of maces and straight swords.[59] In another grotto at Ellora, called the three-storied temple, (*Teen Tal,*) is seen a representation of the five brothers of the family of Pandu, all of whom are principal characters in the Mahabharata.

4. The plan upon which these great temple grottoes are constructed is usually simple, but at the same time always grand in conception. The first entrance is through a vestibule, supported by several rows of pillars; this leads frequently by a series of steps into the grand portico, which is covered in some instances with a flat roof; in others it is vaulted.[60] For the most part this is of a rectangular form, yet terminating in a circular end, and furnished with two rows of columns, by which the nave of the temple is divided through its whole length into three portions. This plan

[57] *Asiatic Res.* vol. vi. p. 406. This last circumstance shows clearly that the representation on the walls is copied without variation from the Ramayana.

[58] *Asiatic Res.* vol. vi. p. 407.

[59] The Hindu painting in the Borgian Museum described by Father Paulino in his *Syst. Brah.* tab. xvii. and xviii., represents the battle between Rama and Ravana in perfect conformity with what is noticed above, and is most likely a direct, or at least a second-hand copy of the reliefs at Ellora.

[60] It is therefore quite clear, that the architect of these subterranean temples was no stranger to the principles of vaulting, though it does not at all follow that he knew how to apply them to buildings above ground. Lord Valentia's conjecture, (vol. ii. page 189,) that the temples dedicated to Buddha only were vaulted, appears to be groundless, from the fact that a building of this description is found at Ellora consecrated to Visvakarma, an attendant of Vishnu. *Asiatic Res.* vol. vi. p. 420.

however is not always observed. There is one grotto at Elephanta which is supported by three rows of pillars; and another at Salsette has as many as six. The sanctuary of these temples, which is frequently nothing more than a chapel furnished with a Lingam, is generally found at the extremity: in the large grottoes at Ellora it is a perfect temple of itself, hewn out of a portion of the solid rock which has been suffered to remain for that purpose. On the right and left are chambers cut out of the rock, apparently designed for the reception of priests belonging to the sanctuary; and in some cases a gallery, supported on pillars, runs round the whole extent, the walls of which are ornamented with exquisite taste and skill.

5. The number and extent of these structures, particularly at Ellora, appear to show sufficiently the object contemplated in their erection. They must have been designed as a sanctuary and habitation, not only for the principal deity, but also for his family and attendant worshippers. Hence arose the necessity of providing for them also, and erecting for each his separate place of worship. The vast number of smaller grottoes, though without doubt partly intended for the accommodation of the priests, were yet however in a much greater degree adapted to receive the many thousand pilgrims and penitents who flocked to the temples, as they still do to the celebrated pagodas of modern India.

6. The idea of employing colonnades in the cases before us, arose from the obvious necessity of leaving pillars to support the roof of the excavated rock, and of course their form would not in the nature of things be so slender as the Grecian column. There is, however, in several instances, an evident desire to produce the utmost degree of attenuation and delicacy of shape which the enormous weight they had to sustain would allow.[61] And what ravages the hand of time has been able to effect in other parts of these venerable structures, the colonnades and pillars seem generally to have escaped. It is not without an involuntary shudder that we pass the threshold of these spacious grottoes, and compare the weight of the ponderous roof with the apparent slenderness and inadequacy of its support; an admirable and in-

[61] See GOUGH, tab. i.; NIEBUHR, tab. iv.; and VALENTIA, vol. ii. tab. viii.—x.

genious effect, which must have required no ordinary share of abilities in the architect to calculate and determine! In the general form and mode of decorating these columns, judging by the few designs we have of them, we meet with great variety, although the pillars in the same grotto have always the same form and dimensions. The length of the shaft, in comparison with its diameter, is also subject to considerable variation; in some cases, as for instance, in the temple of Kennery at Salsette, the pillars are furnished with capitals apparently suffered to remain in order to confer additional strength. These capitals, agreeably to the purposes for which they are designed, would not therefore admit of that delicacy of shape which is observed in the buildings above ground; the design and general form of the capital itself appears to be copied from certain plants, particularly the lotus. But an accurate and characteristic description of these details, which however would be scarcely intelligible without illustrative designs, we must leave to the study of professed architects: yet after mentioning the colonnades and pillars, we ought not to omit noticing the obelisks, which to the best of our knowledge are only met with in the grottoes of Ellora. The single one which up to this time has been copied and designed, and is of a circular form,[62] certainly favours the supposition that it was intended to represent a Phallus: nevertheless, Malet expressly remarks, that two others are found of a square figure.[63]

7. The Hindu sculpture, like that of the Egyptians, appears to have proceeded from relief, but owing to the small number of designed specimens at present in our possession, it is impossible to deliver any correct opinion of its rise and progress. The art of sculpturing in very low relief seems to have remained foreign to the usual practice of Hindu artists; probably because in these temples they were obliged to make their calculations with reference to the general effect which could be produced by the whole, when viewed from a certain distance. Their sculpture however appears, even from the commencement, to have usually developed itself in

[62] *Asiatic Res.* vol. vi. p. 392. In the drawing of LANGLÈS, plate xxxvii., copied from the work of the Daniells, this monument has almost entirely lost the form of an obelisk.

[63] *Asiatic Res.* vol. vi. p. 405.

a colossal form; as almost all the statues of gods are from ten to twelve feet high: it has also been already observed, that the relation of inferiority is here expressed by a corresponding diminution of stature, extending even down to that of dwarfs.[64] The walls of these grottoes, at least those at Ellora, were overlaid with a kind of stucco, called Chunam, (Churna,) that progressively hardens by length of time.[65] Now the employment of colours would naturally serve to enliven the sculpture; we accordingly find, that the Hindus like the Egyptians used to paint their reliefs. The climate of India, which is not so dry as that of Egypt, would appear to be less favourable to the preservation of fresco paintings; we nevertheless find in the temples at Ellora universal proof of the contrary. From working in relief, the art of sculpture would insensibly proceed to statuary; several of the reliefs themselves having been formed in such high prominence that they are merely attached to the walls by a portion of their backs. A colossal character was also applied to their statues, not merely when they represented divinities, but likewise, and indeed in an especial manner, to animals, such as elephants, bulls, lions, etc., which was partly necessary perhaps in order to preserve the general keeping of the whole, and partly was agreeable to the sense of Hindu mythology. These numerous colossal figures of animals, according to the testimony of an eye-witness, contribute to enliven as it were the general appearance of the temples, and seem to give the whole a species of animation. Even fabulous beasts were not excluded from this mythology: though we still want accurate designs for enabling us to compare them with those of the Persians and other nations.

Lastly, the grottoes of Ellora contain also certain inscriptions, two or three of which have been made out in San-

[64] What is most striking in these figures, at least at Elephanta, besides their diminutive height, is the peculiar fashion of their hair, partly resembling the largest full-bottomed wigs of our ecclesiastics; and as this head-dress is confined to a few only of the attendants, they must therefore belong to a particular class by themselves. Is it probable that they are professional story-tellers? According to Hindu mythology, the rajah Vicramaditya used to have forty-two of these little creatures standing round his throne. POLIER, vol. i. p. 90. Sir Stamford Raffles was informed at Java, that similar head-dresses were worn by native hermits. *History of Java*, vol. ii. p. 10.

[65] *Asiatic Res.* vol. vi. pp. 397, 408, 409.

scrit, by Wilford, with the help of a book professing to be an explanatory key to several ancient Hindu alphabets, and communicated to him by some pundits, provided they are to be relied on.[66] According to this explanation, the inscriptions refer in part to the subjects taken from the Mahabharat, and represented in sculpture on the walls, and the conjecture is certainly not improbable that they may be real quotations from that poem. The last of these inscriptions mentions the name of the sculptor who executed the work.[67] They are, however, less remarkable for their contents than for the peculiar idiom in which they are written, as it tends to prove that the Sanscrit, though in a form which is now obsolete, was still the prevailing dialect when these grottoes were excavated; a circumstance which must furnish additional proof of their antiquity.[68]

The range of Hindu architecture, however, was not limited to the construction of this first, and probably most ancient

[66] *Asiatic Res.* vol. v. p. 135, sq.

[67] His name is Sakya Padamrita. Ibid. p. 138.

[68] Langlès, in his seventh number, admits the probability of the beforementioned report of a learned Mussulman, viz. that the grottoes of Ellora were excavated nine hundred years ago, by one Rajah Il; and that in his time Deogur, the capital of the Deccan, was the metropolis of a great empire: and further, that architects from Ethiopia might have constructed these temples upon Ethiopian or Egyptian models. For my part I must confess, that excepting a few partial resemblances, I am unable to detect any traces of general imitation in these works, which are so perfectly Indian in their whole character, and indeed were so pronounced to be at the first inspection by Malet. *Asiatic Res.* vol. vi. p. 383. How unreasonable is it to suppose that any foreign artists could at once bring into existence such a peculiar kind of architecture as the Hindu, and at the same time leave only indistinct and altogether uncertain traces of their own! As to the report above alluded to, we have already remarked on what slender ground it rests, while the Mussulman himself could adduce no authority in confirmation of it; to say nothing of the utter improbability that one prince's reign could suffice for the completion of such vast and laborious undertakings. At the same time, however, I am perfectly willing to allow, that a portion of these grottoes, consecrated to the religious services of modern sects, as the Sevras or Jats, may be of later origin (an opinion already advanced by English writers, *Asiatic Res.* vol. vi. p. 384); but this is no argument whatever against the antiquity of the rest. We have not, to my knowledge, any true historical notice of this Rajah Il, beyond the mere opinion of the Mohammedan above mentioned, who supposes him to have been a contemporary of Shah Momim-Arif, who reigned some nine hundred years ago in Persia. There might possibly have existed such a person as Rajah Il of Deogur, but he could scarcely possess a very extensive territory; since, according to the very few fragments of Indian history still remaining to us, the whole country, previous to the Mohammedan invasion in 1002, was parcelled out into a number of petty principalities, (Dow's *History of Hindostan*, vol. i. p. 32,) and consequently would contain no one prince at all capable of erecting such stupendous monuments.

class of buildings; nor did it remain satisfied with excavating temples and habitations in the heart of rocky mountains; but it also elaborately fashioned the outside of the rocks themselves into the form of an architectural monument, and thereby produced effects still more great and surprising than in those temple grottoes we have just now described, although even these latter are not wanting to increase the magnificence of the other kind.

India contains one specimen of this new class which is so pre-eminently distinguished above all the rest, that a particular description of it alone will be sufficient. Such are the "Seven Pagodas," or ancient monuments so called, at Mavalipuram on the Coromandel coast,[69] of which extraordinary buildings it will hardly be too much to assert, that they occupy a most distinguished place in the scale of human skill and ingenuity. But we must in this case also, before we can offer any remarks on their style of architecture, previously ascertain the extent of our acquaintance with them.

This, in truth, is at present but very imperfect. Those travellers who have visited them, appear to have seen little more than the parts immediately adjacent to the coast; few indeed would venture to penetrate into the interior, over rugged barriers of rock, and through jungles infested with tigers and noxious reptiles, and certainly no single individual could possibly make the attempt with safety. The first account of these buildings was communicated in the Asiatic Researches, by Mr. Campbell;[70] but only from recollection of a visit made eight years before. He was followed (in the same collection) by Mr. Goldingham;[71] and a few years subsequently by Mr. Haafner.[72] Neither of these travellers, however, have given any illustrative designs; and in the large work of the Daniells, only two plates are devoted to the subject, which were afterwards copied by

[69] Situate in 12° 30″ North Lat., one day's journey south of Madras. They are called "The Seven Pagodas," because there appears to be a greater number of temples when seen from the sea; some of these project into the water, and others are actually submerged.

[70] *Asiatic Res.* vol. i. p. 145.

[71] Ibid. vol. v. p. 69, sq.

[72] Haafner, *Reise längst der Küste von Coromandel*, vol. ii. p. 192, sq. He is the only one who pretends to have made his way into the interior of these pagodas, though it must be confessed, the account of his travelling adventures frequently savours rather too much of the marvellous.

Langlès.[73] From these and some other detached accounts, arose the instructive description of these ruins compiled by the late Mr. Ehrmann, and inserted in the Geographical Ephemerides.[74] This in its turn produced a valuable dissertation by the late Baron Dalberg,[75] communicated in the same periodical work. These essays, however, even at best, serve only to show how limited and imperfect our knowledge is, the whole extent of which may be comprised in the following statement.

The ruins of Mavalipuram do not merely consist of a few subterranean temples, but the whole has an appearance of a royal town, almost completely hewn out of the rock. A large, and probably the most considerable portion, appears to have been swallowed up by the sea; but a few miles inland are seen, on the summits of a rocky hill, a vast collection of grottoes, halls, apartments, and other buildings, all worked in the solid stone: not all of these, however, are temples; for among other structures, we meet with one supported by two or three rows of pillars, which seems to have been a choultry, or place of accommodation for travellers: in another part of the hill is a kind of couch formed out of the rock, and which some imagine to represent a king's throne. Besides these excavations, there are other remnants of architectural works, properly so called; these consist of massy walls formed of hewn stone, immense blocks of which are piled one above the other, similar to those buildings termed Cyclopean: and, again, the whole of the top of the hill is strewed with bricks. This is the sum total of our acquaintance with the ruins of Mavalipuram. The two drawings, to be found in the work of the Daniells, are merely exterior views, one of them representing the entrance of a grotto, the walls of which are ornamented with sculpture—the other, two temples excavated in the rock, the style and workmanship of which is peculiarly striking, and might almost be compared with some of our Gothic churches. The sides of the rocky hill are here also in every direction covered with reliefs in sculpture, which the Daniells have but imperfectly designed, or rather only sketched, if we except a few more elaborate specimens of

[73] *Monumens de l'Inde*, plates xxiii. xxiv.

[74] *Allgem. Geograph. Ephemeriden*, 1809, Sept. [75] Ibid. 1810, May.

colossal figures, such as elephants and lions : we must therefore confine ourselves here to the brief accounts which Mr. Goldingham has given of these sculptures. According to him, then, they represent for the most part statues of Hindu deities, with four or more arms, and furnished with their various attributes, as the Brahmanical thread, and different animals consecrated to their service, etc., all which points of resemblance leave no room to doubt the fact of these divinities being borrowed from the same system of mythology as those in the rock temples already described ; indeed Mr. Goldingham had previously come to the same conclusion, after comparing the sculpture of Mavalipuram with that of Elephanta, and particularly the double statue of an hermaphrodite, and the dwarfs. These circumstances, as well as the representation of the Lingam, are quite sufficient to prove that the worship of Siva prevailed here also, conjointly with that of Vishnu, in so far as the latter is said to have appeared on earth in the character of Krishna. And, according to the same authority, similar figures of men and animals are found here also, and even whole scenes taken from the Mahabharat, representing among other subjects, the fable of Krishna's sojourn among the Gopis or shepherdesses; we therefore know where to find a key to the interpretation of these sculptures: but this desirable object can only be attained by the traveller who is enabled to investigate these ruins with the Mahabharat in his hand. Even the inscriptions over the several statues, and which have been copied by Mr. Goldingham, do not, however, furnish us with any explanations, because the character has not yet been deciphered, and consequently we know nothing of the language in which they are composed. If this peculiar alphabet really were identified with that in which the inscriptions at Kennery are written, it would prove the same character to have been in common use on both sides of the peninsula.[76]

[76] LANGLÈS, *Monumens de l'Inde*, p. 50, has remarked a similarity between the characters used at Mavalipuram and those at Kanara (without doubt he means Kennery). But for my part I can discover no resemblance between the drawings made of the former by Goldingham, and those of the latter copied by Gough. On the other hand, I fancy they are more like those found at Ellora, communicated by WILFORD in the *Asiatic Res.* vol. v. p. 141. At all events there is a general resemblance in the form of the character, though the individual letters are not exactly the same.

The buildings at Mavalipuram are partly in an unfinished state, and furnish evident proofs of having been interrupted by some terrible convulsion of nature, such as an earthquake, which has rent the solid rock, and perhaps ingulfed a considerable portion of the town in the sea, under which the ruins are still seen, extending a great way out. But all recollection of the time when this catastrophe happened is completely lost; which is another probable ground of the high antiquity of these structures, on which moreover the finger of Time has imprinted other strong marks of age, in the defacement and obliteration apparent in many of the sculptures. Nevertheless, imperfect as our knowledge of these interesting monuments certainly is, I still conceive myself entitled to make the following observations.

1. Mavalipuram was at the same time the chief seat of religion, the residence of kings, and in all probability a town of considerable commercial importance. The monuments still remaining, attest the certainty of its having been at some former period a place of very great extent; and supply us also with additional evidence of the intimate connexion that subsisted in these countries between religion and commerce.

2. Hindu tradition itself assigns a very high antiquity to these buildings, in attributing their erection to the kings Yudhishthira, of the family of Pandu, and Bali (both of them related to Krishna, and principal characters in his mythological history);[77] their age therefore extends back to the fabulous period, which is of course independent of all accurate chronological determination. But upon comparing these monuments with one another, it appears highly probable that they do not themselves all belong to one and the same period, but were constructed at long intervals of time, both on account of their great extent, and particularly the variation observable in their style of architecture. Two of these rock pagodas appear to have, as it were, a vaulted roof, but terminating in a sharp angle, similar to a Gothic arch.[78] Near to these are observed others constructed

[77] Polier, *Mythologie des Indous*, vol. i. p. 122, 338.

[78] Chambers, in the *Asiatic Res.* vol. i. p. 151. See the drawing in Langlès, plate xxiii. Goldingham, in the *Asiatic Res.* vol. v. p. 74, quotes a

merely with blocks of stone laid across one another in a pyramidal form, like the oldest specimens of architecture above ground. Does not this variety of structure, which a more intimate acquaintance with these ruins, and a greater number of well executed drawings, would doubtless increase, tend to prove that the monuments of Mavalipuram are of very different degrees of antiquity; and likewise that the city itself must have had a duration of several hundred years?

3. The sculptures at Mavalipuram have reference as well to the religious worship of Siva as of Vishnu, principally however to that of Vishnu. On the other hand, as far as our present knowledge extends, we find not the least trace of the service of Buddha. This circumstance, together with the high state of perfection in which the sculptures are finished, must necessarily lead us to infer that these monuments, though of great antiquity, are yet however by no means the oldest in India.

4. But they are also very remarkable for the close relation in which they stand to the great epic poem of the Mahabharat. The sculptured representations on the walls, are for the most part borrowed from the fabulous legends therein recounted; and, according to the testimony of the Brahmans, the very name of the place is mentioned in that poem, under its Sanscrit appellation of Mahabalipura, "The city of the great Bali."[79] This fact, if true, together with that of the inscriptions having become unintelligible, would seem fresh evidence in favour of its high antiquity. We must not, however, confound Mavalipuram with the wonderful city Dwarka,[80] celebrated in the Ramayana, which was situate in the middle of the ocean, not on the coast: and in

traditionary report, according to which it would appear that, about a thousand years since, a certain northern prince wished to execute some splendid work of architecture, but could not agree with the Hindu architects about the price; and that the latter, being in number upwards of five thousand, fled away in consequence, and in the short space of five or six years completed these superb monuments, after which the above-mentioned prince recalled them. BARON DALBERG, in the *Allgem. Geograph. Ephemerid.* vol. xxxii. p. 7, has repeated this tradition, but, through inadvertence no doubt, has omitted the word Hindu. I remark this expressly, lest it should be inferred, in consequence of the omission, that a certain kind of architecture had been introduced into India from the north.

[79] CHAMBERS, in *Asiatic Res.* vol. i. p. 146, 155.

[80] The conjecture of BARON DALBERG, *Ephem. Geogr.* vol. xxxii. p. 12.

the Hindu legend, Vishnu is represented as marching from Dwarka to Mavalipuram.[81]

5. In the same country where we now discover the ruins of Mavalipuram, Ptolemy places the situation of a town called Maliarpha.[82] He mentions it as a commercial resort, (emporium,) and according to his account there were several others on the same coast of India. The situation and resemblance of name concur in making it very probable that this town can be no other than Mavalipuram; admitting which to be correct, we have consequently an historical proof that it existed in the time of Ptolemy, and was also a place of considerable commercial importance. This, however, is no sort of argument against the supposition that these monuments are of much higher antiquity, especially if we consider Ptolemy to have derived his information from sources long anterior to the times in which he wrote.

Such are the most considerable of the rock monuments that have hitherto been discovered in India:[83] and from the brief examination we have been able to give them, it must by this time be sufficiently evident, that the natives of that country, surrounded as they are with every natural inducement for the undertaking, have carried the art of constructing and ornamenting excavated grottoes to a much higher degree of perfection than any other people; though it does not at all equally follow that the Hindus were accustomed to employ grottoes and caves in general for the purposes of domestic habitation. The structures we have just been considering are only met with in certain portions of the country, and even then not as the common receptacles of the living or the dead, but solely as places of abode for the divinities and their attendant worshippers. Every thing, therefore, concurs to establish the fact, that an all-powerful

[81] *Asiatic Res.* vol. i. p. 156. [82] PTOLEMY, vii. cap. 1.

[83] [See an animated description of the ancient temples and ruins of Barolli, in Rajpootana, in the second volume of COL. TOD'S *Annals of Rajasthan*. The grand temple is dedicated to Siva, and stands in an area of about two hundred and fifty yards square, enclosed by a wall of unshaped stones without cement; and contains unrivalled specimens of sculpture, some parts of which, especially the heads, in the language of an eye-witness, would be no disgrace to Canova himself. The whole is in wonderful preservation, being chiseled out of the close-grained quartz, though some of the figures have suffered from Moslem bigotry. "In short," says Col. Tod, "it would require the labour of several artists for six months to do any thing like justice to the wonders of Barolli." TRANSL.]

priesthood must have formed them, in order to serve as indestructible sanctuaries and central points of religious attraction, and not improbably also with a view of securing political influence. When we consider indeed, as will appear still more evident in the sequel of this inquiry, the very intimate connexion that formerly subsisted in India between religion and politics, what more effectual method, we would ask, could be adopted for working upon the feelings of the multitude through the medium of religion, than by erecting such stupendous fabrics, where the pomp and splendour of art might co-operate with the awful solemnities of religious worship? Dead, as it were, and unmeaning as they must appear when considered abstractedly and by themselves, they receive in the eyes of the historian a kind of reflected animation and significance, when he views them in connexion with the religion and mythology of the people, as preserved to us in their epic poetry: the conviction immediately flashes across his mind, that the one must have given birth to the other; and while he hears the voice of their religion speaking in the language of remote antiquity, he scruples not, therefore, in the absence of all accurate chronological testimony, and as long as no direct proof of their more modern origin has been given, to assign these time-honoured works of art to the same age that produced the former.

After having treated of rock monuments, whether subterraneous or above ground, there still remains a third and most numerous class of buildings to examine, which are altogether the production of human art. These are of different kinds. But as we are engaged only with ancient structures, we shall not stop to inquire into the disputed age of a few mountain fortresses, which are the only other monuments exclusive of the rock temples that prefer any claim to antiquity; we must therefore confine our researches to those temples that have been called by Europeans, Pagodas,[114]

[114] *Vihara* in Sanscrit, Langlès, p. 4. [Vihara properly means a Bauddha or Jaina temple: see Wilson's Dict. *in voc.* The word pagoda is a corruption of *Bhagavati*, "holy house," one of the several names by which Hindu temples are known. Others have derived it from the Persian *Putkedeh*, "House of Idols;" which, as it appears to involve a term of contempt, is not at all probable. They are also called in Sanscrit, *Sabha*, "a house;" *Prasrda*, "palace;" or *Devalaya*, "abode of the gods." See Bohlen's *Alte Indien*, vol. ii. p. 82. Transl.]

an appellation previously unknown even to the Hindus themselves.

Many of these buildings have been copied in the works already so often alluded to. But whoever wishes to regard them as authentic sources of information in the study of India antiquities, will soon find reason to employ great circumspection and cautious mistrust when he would determine their age with even the semblance of probability. The grand desideratum of a perfect historical account of Hindu architecture, becomes immediately evident.[81] And unless he chooses blindly to follow the accounts given by the Brahmans, who perhaps make a merit of deceiving him, he will be obliged to stop short at every question involving the antiquity of any particular edifice. This is a chasm in history which no one can reasonably expect to be filled up by the present investigation. A professed architect alone could possibly supply the deficiency; but even he I am persuaded would derive very little assistance from consulting the copper-plate illustrations we possess; it is only by a personal inspection of the places themselves, and after long and repeated observation in several parts of India, that he would be enabled at last to furnish the required history. And yet, notwithstanding the imperfect state of our knowledge of this subject, I cannot avoid submitting a few remarks to the judgment of my learned readers.

The Architecture of India, as the excavated rock temples sufficiently inform us, was the daughter of Religion; and continued to remain so even in the case of structures raised above ground. This character was completely developed only in pagodas, and other buildings connected with them: not however in private dwellings. What, properly speaking, are the Hindu cities of the present day? What is the Black Town (so called) of Calcutta, Madras, and other places, any more than a collection of huts such as the climate requires, formed of bamboo and similar materials, and surrounding a pagoda? But while their architecture was inseparably connected with religion, the one remained as imperishable as the other. Without doubt certain periods might be named, in which the erection of splendid architec-

[81] See CAPT. M'KENZIE's remarks on this subject in *Asiatic Res.* vol. vi. p. 443.

tural works became more rare and uncommon; as, for instance, during the subjection of India to foreign power; but even then the religious zeal of the Hindus was only repressed, not at all extinguished. Temples have been constructed at all times throughout India, and continue to be so still; we should therefore be cautious in attributing a high antiquity to pagodas in general, though it is very likely that in several instances a particular pagoda may have just claims to that title.

Supposing, then, that we have now satisfactorily proved the existence of a sacred architecture in India from the earliest periods, it still remains for us to ascertain, how far it continued free and independent of external influence; or otherwise, to what extent did its foreign masters succeed in altering its distinctive character? Previous to the Mohammedan invasion, which took place about the commencement of the eleventh century, we have no certain information whether any foreign invaders ever permanently established themselves, and became naturalized in India: though it is probable that a portion of the country might have been occasionally subject to the neighbouring governments of Persia or Arabia. And notwithstanding there is equal probability that distinct Arabian colonies might have been settled at an earlier period on the coasts of the peninsula, yet up to the present time no traces, I believe, of Arabian architecture have been discovered in India, similar to those still found in many parts of Spain. But since the establishment of the Mongols in the country, and the erection of their splendid empire, the study and practice of architecture flourished among them also, and an infinite number of palaces and mausolea, particularly on the banks of the Ganges, still remain as proofs of their ingenuity and taste. The progress of architecture among that people in India, would no doubt furnish subject-matter for a most highly interesting chapter in a general history of this art in the East; but I feel myself incompetent to undertake such a task. In the mean time, though I certainly cannot dispute the reciprocal influence which Hindu and Mongol architecture may have exercised upon each other, yet, nevertheless, to me it appears much more probable that the Mongols borrowed something from the Hindus, than that this latter people were indebted to the former: and even admitting the willingness of the Hindus to copy foreign models, would their religious principles have allowed them to do so? The Mongols profaned and overthrew their sacred edifices, and is it likely that the Hindus would reconstruct them in the architectural style of their enemies? I am much more inclined to believe, that Indian architecture in all its principal traits has preserved its character pure and uncontaminated by foreign admixture; while at the same time I allow, that in the subordinate details, particularly in the ornamental part of their buildings, the Hindus may very possibly have adopted some hints and improvements from their conquerors. Hence, therefore, arises the very natural question as to wherein consists the peculiar characteristics of Hindu architecture? To this, it is believed, the following remarks will furnish an appropriate solution.

1. The architecture of the Hindus originated with the pyramid, in which form the oldest pagodas are built. This is the principal feature which distinguishes the buildings of India Proper from those of the Ultra-Gangetic continent, and probably also the greatest portion of the rest of Asia; where the architectural character betrays evident marks of having been borrowed from the form of a tent.[85] It is obvious to remark how this difference of origin must have respectively influenced the general character of both architectures, as well as their particular details.

2. The pyramidal form essentially excludes the notion of an arch, and by consequence the employment of vaulted roofs. It is certainly true from the description above given of the temple grottoes, that the Hindu architects were no strangers to the idea of vaulted roofs; but, as we have before remarked, it does not at all follow therefore, that they either did in fact, or even knew how to apply this principle in the construction of buildings properly so called. Some modern writers indeed directly question their ability to form an arch;[86] whereas in the drawings we have of their oldest specimens of architecture, a considerable number are ob-

[85] Let the reader compare, especially for the opposite continent, Ava, Pegu, etc., the drawings of Birmese temples and monasteries, represented in SYMES's *Travels*.

[86] See particularly LANGLÈS, p. 54.

served to terminate in a cupola;[87] does not this circumstance therefore imply their being able to construct a vaulted roof; or are these cupolas only modern additions to the original fabric? The designs given us of these buildings, however, as we shall soon have occasion to remark, do not even agree among themselves; we must consequently leave this question for architects, and persons supplied with more accurate sources of information than ourselves, to discuss.

3. This pyramidal architecture, moreover, renders the employment of columns and pilasters altogether unnecessary; and yet, nevertheless, they were already well known from their use in subterranean structures; and as they could not be applied to buildings constructed on the principle of a pyramid, they consequently found a suitable place in those of another description; and even in the latter case they evidently appear to be copied from the models already furnished by the grottoes themselves. In the proportions and ornaments of their pillars, the Hindus remained very far behind the Egyptians and the Greeks, but in the richness of decoration bestowed on their pilasters, and, among other things, in their execution of statues resembling caryatides, but not used for support, they far surpass both those nations.[88]

4. As the pagodas were the resort of many thousand pilgrims, the necessity became obvious of constructing edifices of another class in the neighbourhood, in the number of which, the choultries, or houses of accommodation, ought first to be reckoned. These might be termed caravanserais, were no false idea of a similar destination likely to arise from the similarity of name. The Hindus regard the erection of such buildings in the light of a religious duty, or at least place it in the number of good works; we shall therefore be less surprised at meeting with such a vast quantity of them, or at their being usually most numerous in the vicinity of a celebrated pagoda. It is in the construction and ornament of these choultries, where religion has prescribed no definite plan to be followed, that Hindu architecture seems to have exercised itself in all its perfec-

[87] As, for instance, in the pagoda of Tanjore.

[88] Compare the specimen of a richly ornamented pilaster given in LANGLÈS, plate vii.

tion and freedom of restraint.[89] It is here also that pillars and pilasters find their most appropriate situation: as to vaulted choultries, I have not been able to meet with any such specimens in the drawings of Hindu monuments at present known: whether this fact entitles us to infer that the art of vaulting, without being altogether unknown to the Hindus, was yet employed but in a few instances, and probably in forming cupolas only, I shall leave to professional judges to determine. A tank or reservoir of masonry, filled with water, is always in the neighbourhood of a choultry.

5. In the construction of pyramidal pagodas, we may, I think, easily remark the various degrees of progressive improvement made in the art. The most ancient specimens appear to be those which are built after the manner of structures called Cyclopean, with naked blocks of hewn stone piled one over the other in the form of a pyramid, and destitute of all ornament. The next step taken, appears to have been exterior embellishment, and the introduction of various kinds of architectural decoration. The art subsequently proceeded to represent the figures of gods and animals in sculptured relief on the outer walls, and soon after, whole scenes from the great epic poems were added. The interior of these pyramidal temples is usually awful and gloomy; the light of day is excluded, and only a single lamp serves to make the darkness visible, and show the several objects under a doubtful light. In progress of time the architecture appears to have successively laid aside its massive and unwieldy form; the pagodas assumed a lighter aspect, and concluded their improvements with the addition of grand entrances or portals in the interior of the sanctuary. The whole extent of this portion of the pagoda was furnished with one, two, or even more enclosures; within which other buildings and necessary works were erected, such as large halls with a flat roof, supported in the Egyptian manner by several rows of pillars; edifices appropriated to the reception of colossal images of holy animals, and other apartments containing the necessary furniture for processions with the statues of the gods from one sanctuary to an-

[89] See the magnificent choultry of Madura represented in LANGLÈS, plate vi.

other, together with tanks of holy water for the purposes of ablution, etc. If we possessed an authentic history of these pagodas, we should probably find that in the first instance the sanctuary was isolated and stood by itself, as is proved beyond a doubt in those of Egypt, until devout individuals erected the adjacent buildings, which in point of splendour and decoration frequently eclipse the pagoda itself.

Before I proceed to mention the particular pagodas which are distinguished for their antiquity, I ought to premise an observation of no gratifying import to the historian of Hindu architecture. In that portion of the country, which must ever be considered as the cradle of Indian religion and civilization, the ancient monuments have for the most part been destroyed by the fanatical bigotry of the Mohammedans. Bengal Proper contains the fewest remains of antiquity of any; more are discoverable in Behar, and especially in the holy city of Benares. On the other hand, Coromandel, being much less exposed to similar devastation, presents us with the greatest number of celebrated religious structures, both on the coast and in the interior of the peninsula. "Here," says Lord Valentia,[90] "almost every village has its respective pagoda, adorned with a lofty portal of stone, and by no means contemptible in point of architectural merit, where the Brahmans reside either at their own private expense or supported by the liberality of government. The high roads leading to these holy places are thickly studded with choultries for the reception of crowds of pilgrims; and which are also taken care of by the Brahmans." Thus in India we meet with the direct reverse of what has happened in Egypt; whereas in the latter country that portion of it which had been the cradle of its greatness, I mean the upper part, still presents the most considerable remains of architectural skill, while lower Egypt is proportionably deficient: on the contrary, in upper India, where it is probable they were first erected, these monuments have mostly disappeared; and whatever may be the age of particular structures which the peninsula still preserves to us, we may rightly conjecture they are not the oldest India has ever possessed.

[90] VALENTIA, *Travels*, vol. i. p. 355.

In the number of those pagodas, which, according to their style of architecture and the testimony of the natives themselves, appear to be the most ancient, we must first reckon Deogur or Dowlatabad, in the vicinity of Ellora. This is formed, similar to those at Mavalipuram, of a group of three pagodas, and is built in a pyramidal form of blocks of hewn stone laid one over another, without any sculptures.[91] On the summit of each of them is raised the trident of Mahadeva, a certain proof that they were dedicated to that god. The Hindus themselves are unable to determine their age any further than they reckon them among the most ancient, an opinion which appears to be confirmed by their position and style of building. Is there not indeed the highest probability that they must have had some connexion with the neighbouring rock excavations already described, and that they may belong to the period, when, as we have before observed, Ellora was most likely the central point of Hindu religion and civilization? We shall have another occasion of reverting to this subject hereafter.

The celebrated pagoda of Tanjore presents a perfectly similar specimen of architecture: it is also constructed of hewn stone piled in large blocks one above another, without any exterior decoration, and without a cupola.[92] The pyramid is two hundred feet high, and according to the opinion of Lord Valentia, is the most beautiful work of this kind in India. The interior contains a hall only lighted with lamps, and which is a place of assembly for the Brahmans. All determinate accounts of the time of its construction are wanting, and this circumstance, coupled with the peculiar style of architecture, warrant us in referring it to a period of high antiquity. The presence of the Lingam denotes its consecration to Siva, and this is confirmed by a colossal statue of his bull, *Nundi*, which appears in an adjacent

[91] They are represented in HODGES, plate xxiii.; and in MAURICE's *History of Hindostan*, vol. vi.

[92] The engraving of this pagoda, given in MAURICE's *History of Hindostan*, vol. i. plate iii., after a drawing by Hodges, essentially differs from that given by LANGLÈS, plates ix. x., after the Daniells. In the latter, the pyramid is adorned on the outside with false windows, almost like the obelisk at Axum, (VALENTIA, *Travels*, vol. iii. plate vii.,) and terminates in a small cupola. But Valentia himself confesses (vol. i. p. 305) that the Daniells have embellished too much. I therefore follow the engravings given by Maurice.

building supported by pillars in the true Indian style.[93] The statue is formed of an entire block of brown porphyry, sixteen feet in length, by twelve feet high; and although much inferior in size to the colossal statues of Egypt, is nevertheless a proof that the Hindus were acquainted with the method of transporting unwieldy masses. This bull is, no less than the god himself, an object of religious veneration; and it was amid the din of cymbals and flutes in the vicinity of his apartment, as well as the pagoda, that those solemnities were observed which involuntarily recall to our minds the Bacchanalian orgies of the ancients.

The pagodas of Ramiseram are remarkable for their situation on an island between the continent and Ceylon, from whence Rama made his celebrated expedition against Ravana, which forms the subject of the Ramayana. They consist of a group of pagodas, of which Lord Valentia has given a description but no drawings.[94] The largest is dedicated to Rama, the second to his consort Sita, and a third, which is the smallest, to Mahadeva. They are still regarded as the most ancient sanctuaries of the nation, and no foreigner is allowed to enter their precincts. The statues of the gods must be washed only with water from the Ganges, which is brought for that purpose by pilgrims and fakirs. The whole is surrounded with an enclosure, the principal gate of which is forty feet high; a grand entrance, constructed in the form of a truncated pyramid, leads to the principal pagoda, and reminded Lord Valentia of the ancient monuments of Egypt. It is here that we recognise all the characters of primitive architecture, which consists in piling up rough hewn blocks of stone one above another, first perpendicularly and then in a horizontal direction. The exterior of the pagoda is painted red, and adorned with a surprising number of sculptures. The interior is here also lighted with lamps, "but the whole building," says the same noble traveller, "presents a magnificent appearance, which we might in vain seek adequate language to describe."

Among the number of those pagodas which are remark-

[93] In LANGLÈS, plate x. But here also, according to Lord Valentia, the drawing made by the Daniells is incorrect.
[94] VALENTIA, *Travels*, vol. i. p. 340.

able for their antiquity, that of Madura, under all circumstances, appears to deserve mention. It is like the others, of a pyramidal form,[95] and the exterior is adorned with architectural embellishments, such as pillars and false windows. But at the same time it may serve to show how cautious we should be in pronouncing upon the antiquity of these structures; the buildings which surround the pagoda, especially the choultry, are altogether of modern origin; the latter, for instance, was constructed in the year 1623. It is nevertheless highly remarkable as furnishing a specimen of Hindu architecture at that period, and as a proof that, although probably in the subordinate details somewhat may have been borrowed from the Mohammedans, yet the general character of the whole, as well as the ornaments, appear to be truly Indian.[96]

One of the oldest, and at the same time most holy pagodas of India, is that of Jaganatha, or as it is more commonly pronounced, Juggernaut, a surname of Krishna, to whom it is dedicated. It is situate almost at the northern extremity of the Coromandel coast, and is known to Europeans by the name of the "Black Pagoda," because its dark colour being relieved by the sandy shore makes it a conspicuous object to mariners a great distance off.[97] This structure is also of a pyramidal form, and a number of smaller pagodas are found in its vicinity, the largest of which is one hundred and twenty feet high;[98] with respect to its age, opinions are very much divided. The Brahmans reckon it among the most ancient of their holy places;[99] on the contrary, Langlès will have its antiquity extend no further back than from seven hundred to eight hundred years.[100] It is, however, highly remarkable as it concerns the religious history of the Hindus, if the assertion be correct, that at the epoch

[95] See LANGLÈS, plate v. p. 3, copied from the Daniells.

[96] See a drawing of this magnificent choultry in LANGLÈS, plate vi.

[97] VALENTIA, *Travels*, vol. i. p. 55.

[98] LANGLÈS, plates i. xxv. xxvii., gives the best illustration of this pagoda that I know of, together with a ground-plan, after a design which had been communicated to him.

[99] POLIER, vol. ii. p. 162, reports the legendary account of its foundation by Rajah Ainderdon, in the time of Krishna's sojourn upon earth.

[100] LANGLÈS, *Notice Geographique*, vol. i. p. 120, etc. His reasons for this opinion appear to be very weak, as is almost always the case when he chooses to support mere conjecture.

of its foundation the distinctions of caste were abolished, and superiors might eat in company with their inferiors without incurring pollution.[1]

We have already remarked above, that although Indian architecture remained constant to its primitive forms in the construction of temples, yet, nevertheless, its progressive improvement in the sculptures with which they were adorned, as well as in the style of the adjacent buildings, and particularly the enclosures surrounding the consecrated precincts, was very conspicuously developed. In the first instance, for example, an additional number of pagodas were built in the immediate vicinity of each other; a practice which evidently had its rise (as in the case of the temple grottoes) in the wish to provide, near the habitation of the god, a similar place of abode for his wife or his companions: subsequently other buildings were erected, and in particular those flat-roofed halls, formed like the Egyptian specimens of blocks of hewn stone, and supported by several rows of pillars. The next step made was to surround the whole sacred enclosure with a wall of hewn stone, which frequently comprehended a space of very considerable extent, and for this reason again required entrance gateways on a large and magnificent scale. As it is obviously inconsistent with my present purpose to give a detailed account of every one of these pagodas, I shall therefore confine myself in this place to a description merely of those of Siringam with its sevenfold enclosure;[2] of Kanjeveram,[3] dedicated to Siva and his consort Parvati; and above all, to that of Chalambron,[4] in the district of Tanjore, which may with great propriety be considered the model of all the others. A twofold enclosure surrounds the sanctuary of this pagoda,[5] the outer one

[1] According to POLIER, vol. ii. p. 167, this custom subsists even at the present day.

[2] LANGLÈS, p. 25. The outermost enclosure comprehends the space of a square league. The four sides exactly correspond with the cardinal points, and each of the four grand entrances is surmounted with a pyramid richly adorned with sculpture.

[3] See a drawing of this pagoda in LORD VALENTIA'S *Travels*, plate xii.; and in LANGLÈS, plate xxviii.; it is particularly remarkable for presenting a row of statues of animals, which seem, as it were, to officiate as guards of the temple.

[4] This pagoda is situate two leagues from the coast, and nine in a southern direction from Pondichery.

[5] See a detailed description given in LANGLÈS, p. 26, sq., together with a ground-plan in plate xv.

forms a complete rectangle, two hundred and twenty fathoms in length, by one hundred and sixty broad, is exactly opposite to the four cardinal points, and is composed of bricks, faced however with stone; the second enclosure is built wholly of the latter material. Each side is furnished with a magnificent gateway, formed of large blocks of stone, and decorated with pilasters thirty-two feet high, surmounted moreover with a pyramid of one hundred and fifty feet in height, the architecture of which evidently resembles that of the pagodas, though it is of a lighter character, and is ornamented from top to bottom with sculptures representing gods and animals.[6] Within this second enclosure, are the holy buildings and offices, and a portion of the area is occupied by a third enclosure, round the interior of which runs a colonnade; this contains three chapels, one consecrated to the Lingam, another to Vishnu, the third is without any religious symbol. A large tank, appropriated to the purposes of ablution, occupies the centre of the area; this is also adorned with a colonnade and steps of stone, by which the pilgrims descend into the holy water, there to employ themselves in religious contemplation. On the right side is the principal temple, dedicated to Parvati, whose statue stands immediately facing the entrance: this building also has its separate enclosure, which is surrounded with an interior colonnade; and a peristyle, supported on six rows of columns, leads to the temple, the sanctuary of which is lighted by numerous lamps, and before the entrance is seen a statue of the bull *Nundi*. The pilasters which form this entrance are bound together at the top by a chain of stone, the links of which are very ingeniously formed of a single piece. Both colonnades and pillars are decorated from top to bottom with sculpture. Adjoining the temple towards the south, is a large hall with a flat roof, supported by one hundred columns; and on the north is a perfectly similar building, only of smaller dimensions. But the most wonderful structure of all is on the other side of the large tank; this is a sanctuary or chapel in the middle of an enormous hall, three hundred and sixty feet long, by two hundred and sixty in breadth, and supported by upwards of one thousand

[6] See the drawing in LANGLÈS, plate xvi.

pillars,[7] each thirty feet high, and disposed in regular order; the roof is flat, and like the Egyptian temples is formed of immense blocks of stone laid horizontally. Every part of it is ornamented with sculpture representing scenes taken from the Mahabharata, and other general subjects of Hindu theogony. These different halls, together with their chapels, were destined to receive the statues of the gods, when conveyed to them on huge cars at the celebration of the annual festivals. Not less than three thousand Brahmans were employed in the religious services of this sanctuary; and how prodigious therefore must have been the influx of pilgrims, whose pious liberality was sufficient to maintain such a number of priests, as the temple possesses no landed property itself!

I have considered it necessary to give a somewhat more particular account of this temple, in order that the reader might be furnished with a kind of scale, by which he might judge of other similar specimens of Hindu architecture; and at the same time, with a view of confirming the remark previously made, as to the different periods of time in which the large Indian monuments were erected, and the degree of caution which is necessary in determining their respective ages. With regard to the origin of the sanctuary above described, the Brahmans adduce positive testimony from Sidambara Purana,[8] (or history of this temple,) according to which it was built by the three monarchs, Durjohn, Choren, and Pandu, and finished about the year 400 of the Cali Yug, or 617 before the Christian era.[9] The names of these rajahs belong to the mythological period celebrated in the Mahabharata,[10] and therefore we should receive with mistrust any chronological testimony which places them within the sphere of historical record; to say nothing of the very great uncertainty we are in respecting the genuineness and even the contents of the Sidambara Purana itself. There

[7] Although the number of these pillars may not, perhaps, amount exactly to one thousand, yet it cannot be far short of that sum, as is probable from comparing the hall with one hundred, which latter number has been actually ascertained. Before the entrance are erected lofty standards with colours flying.

[8] Sidambara is a name of Parvati, to whom the pagoda is dedicated.

[9] According to the usual calculation. See LANGLÈS, pp. 36, 37.

[10] For an account of Durjohn [Duryodhana], who lived in the time of the war between the Pandus and Corus, see POLIER, vol. ii. p. 140, sq.

is sufficient evidence, however, that the Hindus themselves regard this pagoda as one of the most ancient. It would indeed be difficult to find another where the gradual rise and progressive increase of the adjacent buildings is more strikingly exhibited, according to the remark of an eye-witness;[11] and it is very probable that this pagoda, together with its appendages, would alone be sufficient to give a sketch, as it were, of Hindu architecture throughout the most distant periods of time. One of the large entrance gateways, according to the report of Lord Valentia, was not many years ago rebuilt by a pious widow, at an expense of not less than 40,000 pagodas; (almost equal to £16,000;) and even at the time of his visit to the place they were still employed on one of the colonnades, which was not yet roofed in.[12] On the other hand, the principal pagoda, according to the same traveller, bears such evident marks of the oldest style of architecture, that he scruples not to place it even anterior to those of Tanjore and Ramiseram. It is, however, scarcely possible that the rich sculpture of the colonnades, representing for the most part subjects taken from the Mahabharata, could be the production of an infant state of the art; and whoever attentively examines the drawings made of those elegant and profusely decorated pyramids over the principal entrance, together with the rich pilasters, and the ornamental chains of stone that so tastefully connect them, will hardly be able to persuade himself that the art could have commenced with such works as these.

It would be unnecessary to enter into further detail here respecting the other pagodas,[13] as the object I proposed has been sufficiently answered already; which was to show, by a comparison of the accounts that we possess of these monuments, incomplete as they are, the evident marks of progressive improvement which Hindu architecture presents to our view. Let us expect that some artist and critic (for a

[11] VALENTIA, *Travels*, vol. i. p. 370: according to whom, the principal temple appears to be the most ancient: an opinion which the inscriptions there found, in an unknown character, would seem to confirm.

[12] VALENTIA, *Travels*, see above, l. c.

[13] I ought, however, to mention the pagoda of Trichinopoly, which, deviating from the pyramidal form, is reported to be of square construction, and to contain traces of the worship of Buddha; LANGLÈS, p. 22, plates xii. xiii. But the accounts, as well as the drawings of this temple, are too unsatisfactory for enabling us to deduce any further conclusions from them.

union of these two qualities is indispensable) will ere long complete these researches in the country itself, and fill up the deficiencies while he rectifies the mistakes of this brief and imperfect outline. We can then only hope to arrive at more accurate conclusions respecting the comparative age of the monuments themselves.

But our knowledge of Indian antiquities and architecture has been greatly enriched since the last edition of this work, by the discoveries made in Java, by the late Sir Stamford Raffles, who distinguished himself no less as a zealous antiquary than as the governor of that island. His administration, which lasted only five years, has served to make us more intimately acquainted with Java than even the two hundred years' possession of it by the Dutch. In the course of his travels he penetrated into the interior of the island, and discovered the greatest portion of those remains of antiquity, which he has devoted a separate chapter of his valuable work to describe.[14] The interior of Java, especially the south-east part, abounds in monuments of Indian architecture and sculpture; which not only prove these arts to have once flourished here, but also in as high a degree of perfection almost as on the continent itself. All these monuments, however, belong to the class of buildings properly so called; for, to the best of our present knowledge, no such structures as grotto temples have yet been discovered in Java. The largest edifices are those in the neighbourhood of Branbanan, almost in the centre of the island; these consist of five parallelograms contained one within the other, and comprising a number of no less than two hundred and ninety-six small temples or chapels; the principal one is in the form of a pyramid, and before the entrance stand several human figures of colossal size, appearing to act as guardians of the temple. The whole is without doubt consecrated to the purposes of Brahmanical worship, and from its interior arrangements reminds us of the above-mentioned pagoda of Siringam, with its seven-fold enclosure.[15] Whether indeed any certain proofs of the worship of Buddha are to be found in the island, particularly at Boro-Bodo, is still a matter of doubt.[16] The buildings are partly constructed of hewn

[14] RAFFLES's *History of Java*, vol. ii. pp. 1—65. [15] See above, p. 94.
[16] RAFFLES, vol. ii. pp. 10, 29. The Brahman who accompanied Sir Stam-

stone, and partly of brick; the latter kind are of course less ancient than the former; though the age of none of them extends so far back as those found on the main land. According to Sir Stamford none of them are anterior to our era, while for the most part the largest of them appear to have been erected between the sixth and ninth centuries. They consequently belong to the middle ages, and are not indeed for that reason less worthy the attention of the inquirer, as tending in all probability to throw some light on a period of Indian history hitherto so perfectly obscure and unintelligible. In other respects Java is the only one of the great Indian islands where, to the best of our present knowledge, any monuments are discovered which exhibit traces of the formerly prevailing Brahmanical worship; nothing of this sort has yet been found either in Sumatra or Celebes.[17] We must, however, be cautious in pronouncing decisively on the subject, as these islands are by no means sufficiently explored, and there may possibly exist monuments in the heart of impenetrable forests, which the rank and luxuriant vegetation of those climes would often conceal from the eye of a traveller, though almost in their immediate vicinity: who, indeed, would venture to determine what may be contained in the interior of Borneo, the largest island on the globe, and which is altogether unexplored? Might we not expect the most important results, were that spirit of discovery so peculiar to our times, and which undauntedly explores barren and desolate wastes, to direct its attention with the same activity and zeal to this most mysterious, and probably the richest of all nature's domains.[18]

Although, however, up to the present day, we are often

ford, maintained the negative side of the question, alleging that the artificial head-dress of woolly hair, which in other cases is one of the insignia peculiar to Buddha, is also common to devotees on certain expiatory occasions. However this may be, the whole plan of construction, and the sculptured representations at Boro-Bodo, so nearly resemble those in Ceylon, that, under all the circumstances, I cannot help considering the former to be a Buddhist temple.

[17] RAFFLES's account of Celebes, vol. ii. in the Appendix, p. 281.

[18] [A late traveller in this island observes, that "in the very inmost recesses of the mountains, as well as over the face of the country, the remains of temples and pagodas are to be seen similar to those found on the continent of India, bearing all the traits of Hindu mythology; and that in the country of Waahoo, at least four hundred miles from the coast, there are several of very superior workmanship, with all the emblematical figures so common in Hindu places of worship." See DALTON's account of the Diaks of Borneo, *Asiatic Journal*, N. S. vol. vii. p. 153. TRANSL.]

H 2

left in uncertainty respecting the age of Hindu temples, yet there are other monuments which speak with more clearness and precision on this point, and which therefore cannot be passed over in silence. These are the inscribed pillars, or tablets, for an interpretation of which we are indebted to British sagacity and skill. It was the ancient custom in India to transmit the memory of any important event to posterity by means of inscriptions written on pillars,[19] as well as to engrave on metal or stone tablets, royal grants of land, by way of title deed, and as a security to the possessor. Of those which have been hitherto deciphered, and containing also chronological dates, the most ancient is a conveyance of land, engraved on a plate of copper, found at Monghir in Bengal, and according to Wilkins, bearing date the twenty-third year before the birth of Christ.[20] It only mentions indeed the thirty-third *samvat* or year; we must therefore infer that the calculation here used is to be understood of the era of Vicramaditya, which commenced with the death of that prince, fifty-six years before Christ.[21] The particular object of this inscription is to record the liberality of a certain renowned conqueror named Deb Pal Deb, who overran all India, from the sources of the Ganges to Rama's bridge at Ceylon, which is celebrated in the Ramayana.

Of the same age, probably, is another inscription, found on a pillar at Buddal in Bengal, and also deciphered by Wilkins;[22] which is destined to convey to posterity the names of Gurava Misra, who erected it, and those of his ancestors. It however contains no date, but the characters strikingly resemble those of the preceding inscription;[23] it also makes mention of a king Pal Deb, probably the same person as already mentioned, and is like the other in Sanscrit, and not only mentions several mythological heroes of the Mahabharata and Ramayana, but also the name of the poet Valmiki, who composed the latter.

Of not much later date, I imagine, than the 67th year of the Christian era, is a third inscription, found on an obelisk[24]

[19] *Asiatic Res.* vol. iii. pp. 46, 47. [20] Ibid. vol. i. p. 123.
[21] Ibid. vol. i. p. 142: see the note of Sir W. Jones. [22] Ibid. vol. i. p. 131.
[23] Compare the specimens of character used in both inscriptions, given in the *Asiatic Researches*.
[24] According to Col. Polier, *Asiatic Res.* vol. i. p. 379, this obelisk contains five inscriptions in Sanscrit; the first in honour of Visala Deva, bears

erected over a monument commonly attributed to Firozshah, who reigned at Delhi between the years 1351 and 1388; although another, which professes to be a more correct copy of the inscription, maintains the date to have been mistaken in the first instance, and that instead of the abovementioned year, A. D. 67, we must read A. D. 1164, which makes it comparatively modern. The inscription itself is in honour of the rajah Visala, or Vigraha Deva, whose victorious arms were extended as far as the snowy mountains in the north *(Himadri)*.

The most ancient inscription of any that he had yet examined, Wilkins considered to be one found in an artificial grotto, with a vaulted roof, at Gya (the modern Nagarjeni) in Behar;[25] it is without any date, and written in a character essentially different from the preceding ones, but which Wilkins conceived to be the oldest of all that he had seen: the language, however, is pure Sanscrit, and purports to be an invocation addressed to the goddess Durga, or Parvati, the wife of Siva, to whose temple a devout prince named Ananta Varma had made a grant of land.

Of a fifth inscription, remarkable for its date and contents, Wilkins has furnished a translation, without however subjoining any specimen of the character, or any observations of his own:[26] it was found engraven on stone, at a place

date 1230. The second, of which we are now speaking, is dated 123 of the era of Vicramaditya (i. e. 67 after Christ). It is expressly added, (*Asiatic Res.* vol. i. p. 480,) "The date is here perfectly clear, at least it is clear that only the three figures are written, without even room for a cipher after them." After such positive testimony who could doubt the truth of the fact? and yet in the same work, vol. vii. p. 175 of Colebrooke's essay, we read, "The date instead of being 123 of the era Vicramaditya, or A. D. 67, as appeared from the former copy of Col. Polier, was clearly ascertained from the present, (made by Capt. Hoare,) to be 1220 of the above era, or A. D. 1164." Here, then, we see two authorities directly opposed to each other: Polier, however, had procured not merely a copy, but, to use his own words, (vol. i. p. 379,) "exact impressions," of the inscription: our readers, therefore, must decide which of these two accounts is most worthy of credit. The circumstance of the first inscription being dated 1230 might possibly give rise to some doubt on the matter, as both that and the second are in honour of one and the same prince: but Polier expressly remarks that this date also may be read 123, as the double circle, which stands for the cipher 0, may be nothing more than an ornamental flourish or termination; in which case both inscriptions are of the same date, that is, A. D. 67.

[In deciding between Polier and Colebrooke we must recollect that the former was not acquainted with Sanscrit. FRENCH TRANSL.]

[25] *Asiatic Res.* vol. i. p. 279.

[26] Ibid. vol. i. p. 284. He does not mention the author of the inscription. For the two following, see vol. i. p. 357; vol. iii. p. 39.

called Buddha Gaya, in a wild and solitary part of Behar; where once upon a time Amara Deva, during his twelve years' penance, had a vision of Buddha when he appeared on earth at the commencement of the Cali Yug. This Amara Deva was one of the nine jewels, as they were called, or wise men, who adorned the court of the celebrated king Vicramaditya, whose prime minister he also was. The inscription testifies him to have erected a temple or sanctuary to Buddha, in the year of the era Vicramaditya 1005, that is, A. D. 949.

Another inscription in Sanscrit, and translated by a learned Hindu, contains a grant of land made to certain holy pilgrims by the rajah Arikesari Deva, whose ancestors and their heroic exploits are here celebrated in a poetic strain. It is dated in the year 939 after the death of king Saca, that is, 1018 A. D. The subjoined specimens of the character are very much like that of the first inscription mentioned above, as answering to the date of A. D. 23; several of the letters are exactly similar; the language also is pure Sanscrit.

Another inscription of an age still more modern contains, in like manner, a grant of land made by rajah Krishnaraya, who pretended to be sprung from Buddha, and bears date 1448 of the same era, called *Sacabda*, which answers to 1526 of ours. Two or three others without date we shall pass over in silence.[27] The inscriptions published and explained in the ninth volume of the Asiatic Researches, are as usual engraved on copper-plates, nine in number; and represent, like the preceding, documentary conveyances of land, or proprietary rights. They are written in Sanscrit with the Devanagari character, and the oldest is of a date corresponding to A. D. 1173. The introductory formula contains a panegyric on the person who makes the grant; and as it sometimes recapitulates his genealogical descent, (as in the case of an inscription without date published in the twelfth volume,) this circumstance might probably throw some light on the succession of the several families who reigned in India during the middle ages.

The inscriptions, therefore, that have been hitherto explained, (supposing this explanation to be correct,) extend

[27] *Asiatic Res.* vol. ii. p. 167; vol. v. p. 132.

but a few years beyond the commencement of our era; while on the other hand they reach down even to the termination of the middle ages. They can consequently furnish no sort of conclusions respecting the earlier Indian antiquities; but, nevertheless, exclusive of information on other separate points of history which are irrelevant to our present purpose, they lead to some important consequences respecting the language, the peculiar characters used in writing it, and the chronological system of the ancient Hindus.

The inscriptions that have been deciphered are all of them composed in Sanscrit, and that generally pure and uncorrupt; whence it follows, that, although the Sanscrit might not have been at that period the vernacular tongue of the whole of India, yet, that in the neighbourhood of the Ganges, especially in Behar, it certainly was the written, and most probably the spoken language of the people. We further learn from these inscriptions, that two kinds of chronological computation were in common use; one reckoned from the death of rajah Vicramaditya, the other from the death of rajah Saca; these modes were, however, in all probability confined to different parts or provinces of India. The commencement of both these eras is sufficiently ascertained, that of Vicramaditya begins fifty-six years before, and that of Saca about seventy-eight years after the birth of Christ: and according to the inscriptions both methods were still in use, the former until the middle of the tenth, and the other as long as the sixteenth century. The objections brought forward by Bentley, in the Asiatic Researches,[28] relative to the age of Vicramaditya, do not so properly concern his era, as the question, whether the above-mentioned nine wise men, or poets, particularly Amara Sinha, Calidas, and Varaha Mihira, flourished at the court of an earlier, or a more modern prince, named Vicramaditya? A subject to which we shall soon have another occasion to refer.

The alphabetical character in which the above inscriptions are written, is either that sacred species known by the name of Devanagari, (writing of the gods,) or one so nearly

[28] *Asiatic Res.* vol. viii. p. 243.

connected therewith, as to be easily deciphered by an acquaintance with the former. The successful inquiries of learned Englishmen have, therefore, incontrovertibly demonstrated that the use of this character extends even beyond the commencement of our era, and has been perpetuated down to the present day; but we are still as far as ever from possessing a general key to all the Hindu alphabets. The inscriptions discovered in the grottoes and rock excavations at Salsette, Mavalipuram, and other places, are not at all capable of being interpreted by any modes of Hindu writing at present known, whether ancient or modern, not even excepting the Devanagari itself. They, moreover, appear to be very different from each other, which would make it probable that, even in the earliest times, a variety of alphabets were in common use throughout India. But since notwithstanding, as we have previously remarked,[29] a key to the alphabets used in the inscriptions at Ellora has actually been discovered, and they are proved to be written in Sanscrit and not in any unknown language, what should prevent us from indulging the reasonable expectation that the others also are capable of being deciphered with equal success? The task indeed would be comparatively easy, did we but possess an accurate inquiry into the connexions subsisting between the various alphabets of India, considered with reference to their age and probable origin.

There is, perhaps, no country throughout Asia, where the art of writing has been in such general use as in India, as indeed there is none other that possesses such a vast number and variety of alphabets. But on this point the opinions of learned men differ so much, that they are not unfrequently in direct opposition to each other; let any one, for example, compare the assertions of Sir W. Jones with those of Father Paulino: according to the former the Devanagari is the alphabet originally employed to write the several Hindu dialects, and which is still in universal use from the borders of Cashgar to Ceylon, and from the Indus to Ava, and is even the original source from whence the alphabets of Western Asia were derived.[30] On the contrary, says Father Paulino, "whoever made such an assertion could never

[29] See above, p. 77.

[30] *Asiatic Res.* vol. i. p. 423.

have seen the other Indian alphabets, or at least, never have compared them attentively with the Devanagari."[31] He then goes on to enumerate four different alphabets in which Sanscrit is commonly written, the Devanagari, used at Patna and in the neighbouring country; a second employed by the Brahmans in their schools at Benares; a third called the Telinga character, common to Orissa and the interior of the peninsula as far as Golconda; and fourthly, the Malabar Sanscrit alphabet, which is exclusively used in that country, as well as on the Coromandel coast, to write Sanscrit. This contradiction, however, is more apparent than real, for Sir W. Jones was so perfectly well acquainted with those different alphabets, that even in his very first essay on the subject, he expressly distinguishes the Devanagari from that used by the Brahmans of Bengal.[32] The Devanagari, (which is by no means confined exclusively to the expression of Sanscrit, but is as common to other languages of India as the use of Roman characters is with regard to those of modern Europe,) is found in the same essay explained in the order of the several letters; and since we have been possessed of the grammars and profound researches of Carey, Wilkins, Bopp, and Frank, an additional and sufficient degree of light has been thrown over the elementary characters of this alphabet. It presents us with sixteen marks to denote vowels, as the long and short are separately distinguished, and thirty-four to represent consonants; although, according to Wilkins, these fifty characters may be reduced to twenty-eight simple articulations, that is to say, five vowels and twenty-three consonants.[33] The Devanagari is, then, the character still most generally adopted for expressing the Sanscrit: and carefully executed copies of the ancient inscriptions have not only proved that it was commonly used in very distant times for the same purpose, but also, that the forms of its letters have subsequently undergone considerable modification and change; by no means, however, such a complete transformation as not to admit of being deciphered by means of study, and a critical acquaintance with the language, together with a comparison of the ancient with the modern Devanagari.

[31] *Gramm. Samscrd.* pp. 6, 7. [32] *Asiatic Res.* vol. i. p. 9.
[33] WILKINS, *Gram.* pp. 2, 3.

Nevertheless, as long as the history and relative connexion of the Hindu alphabets still remain to be further examined and elucidated in the country itself, we must confine ourselves here also to certain general remarks, which a comparison of them appears to suggest.

1. All the inscriptions hitherto discovered in India, even the most ancient, which are not yet deciphered, consist universally of literal characters, without the least appearance of hieroglyphics. Again, the small number of alphabetical signs, which are therefore continually recurring, prove beyond a doubt that the writing in question is not syllabic like that of the Chinese. Moreover, the reading of the Vedas, which is enjoined as the most sacred duty of a Brahman, presupposes the use of literal characters, which in their turn must necessarily be anterior to Hindu civilization itself, as the latter is mainly grounded on the art of writing.

2. The inscriptions hitherto deciphered are read from left to right, which, according to Wilkins, is the general rule for all languages of the Hindu class;[34] they also contain separate marks to represent the vowels as well as the consonants.[35]

3. The alphabets of India which have come to our knowledge, as well as the inscriptions found in excavated temples, could never have been immediately designed, as is the case with the cuneiform letters of Western Asia, for the purposes of engraving on stone, or for inscriptions exclusively. The traces of these letters are generally of a circular character, and are for that reason less convenient to engrave; while the quantity of minute flourishes peculiar to their form, renders that operation still more difficult. We observe, therefore, that although the Hindu monuments are not universally without inscriptions, yet these latter are only seldom used; and when met with, are always very short. The whole character, indeed, of these alphabets, seems rather to imply their being invented, and usually employed, only for the purposes of writing, properly so called. India moreover supplies a vast quantity of suitable materials, such as

[34] WILKINS, *Gram.* p. 2.

[35] SIR W. JONES had before expressly asserted both these facts (*Works*, p. 116). And herein, therefore, the Indian alphabets essentially differ from the Semitic family, while at the same time they coincide with those of a cuneiform character.

the palm leaf for instance, and although we cannot exactly ascertain the period when this came into use, it is, however, perfectly certain that it must have been employed from very remote antiquity.[36] Again, to say nothing of the popular report attributing the Devanagari, as the name itself implies, to the invention of the gods, Hindu religion and civilization are mainly founded on the holy books; the size and contents of which are a sufficient proof that no other than literal characters could have been used in their composition.

The course of our inquiries into the mode of writing peculiar to the ancient Hindus, naturally leads us to an examination of their languages, in so far as they still exist in works of literature, and particularly the Sanscrit.

Supposing, then, that India was originally inhabited by one people speaking one and the same language, yet, nevertheless, when we consider the vast extent and diversified nature of the country, it must inevitably follow, that in course of time this one language would be divided into a great number of dialects; so different probably from each other that only a remote resemblance could be traced. Upon recollecting, however, the many foreign immigrations that have occurred, principally too of conquerors retaining their own native language, we shall find less reason to be astonished at the variety of dialects which prevail in India: at the same time the difference between the original and foreign idioms is so strongly marked, that it is impossible to confound the two; and this diversity of character appears, not only in the case of those dialects which still subsist, but also in those which are no longer spoken.—To the former class belong the Bengali, current in the neighbourhood of the Ganges, the Mahratta, the Telinga, used in the interior of the peninsula, the Tamul spoken on the Malabar, and the Hindustani on the Coromandel coast: to the latter are confined principally the Sanscrit and the Pracrit.[37]

[36] See the inquiries of Father PAULINO on this subject, in his *Samscrdamicæ Linguæ Institutio*, p. 327, sq., where it is also proved that the use of cotton paper in India extends beyond the commencement of our era.

[37] See on this subject especially, Colebrooke's treatise on the Sanscrit and Pracrit languages, inserted in the *Asiat. Res.* vol. vii. p. 199. I adopt throughout the orthography of this learned scholar in spelling the word Sanscrit, of which he gives the derivation at page 200. According to him Sanscrit signifies *polished* (language), in contradistinction to Pracrit, which means *vulgar*.

None of the other ancient languages of Asia have in our days attracted such general attention as the Sanscrit; though it is only within the last fifteen years that its study may be said to have taken firm root on the continent. The credit of having given the first impulse, is perhaps justly due to Father Paulino,[38] formerly a missionary in India, however unfavourable in other respects have been the opinions pronounced on his merits.[39] The state of war and continental blockade effectually prevented all access to the Grammars and other works on Sanscrit, published in .Bengal and England, in which latter country a professorship had already been founded at Hertford, with the express purpose of teaching the languages of India; nor was it until the re-establishment of peace in Europe, that we at last became acquainted with these and other valuable works on the subject.[40] In the mean time, however, the philological zeal of Germany was excited; and two young scholars, Bopp[41] and Frank,[42] supported by the liberality of the Bavarian government, made a successful voyage to England, with a view of consulting the fountain-head of Sanscrit literature. They were closely followed in these studies by the Schlegels and others; and we can now no longer doubt that the seed thus sown, and already budding forth, will, at no distant period, grow to maturity, and produce an abundant harvest.

The grammatical treatises of the above-mentioned scholars,

[38] Or, as he styles himself, Frater Paulinus a S. Bartholomeo, Carmelita excalceatus Malabariæ Missionarius.

[39] *Grammatica Samscrdamica*, Romæ, 1790. The same writer also noticed the similarity existing between the Sanscrit, Persian, and German languages, in his treatise, De Antiquitate et Affinitate Linguæ Samscrdamicæ, Zendicæ, et Germanicæ, Romæ, 1798. Subsequently appeared his Vyacarana, seu locupletissima Samscrdamicæ Linguæ Institutio, Romæ, 1804, containing a Sanscrit Grammar and Lexicon.

[40] A Grammar of the Sungscrit Language, composed from the works of the most esteemed grammarians, to which are added examples for the use of the student, and complete lists of the Dhatoos or Roots, by William Carey, D. D., teacher of the Sungscrit, Bengalee, and Mahratta languages, in the College of Fort William, (price eight guineas,) 1808. Judging from its high price, this should be a work of considerable extent, though I have not yet seen it. A Grammar of the Sanskrita Language, by Charles Wilkins, L. L. D., London, 1808; the work that I have principally consulted.

[41] Bopp, On the Conjugation-system of the Sanscrit, as compared with the Greek, Persian, Latin, and German, together with Episodes translated from the Ramayana and Mahabharata. See *Annals of Orient. Lit.* P. i. pp. 1—65.

[42] Chrestomathia Sanscrita, quam ex Codd. MSS. adhuc ineditis, Londini exscripsit, et in usum tyronum, versione, expositione, etc., illustratam edidit Othmarus Frank, Monachii, 1820.

in conjunction with the assistance furnished by translations, although still limited and imperfect, are nevertheless sufficient for enabling us to give some general opinion on the subject. And even admitting that the claims of Sanscrit upon our admiration have been sometimes enthusiastically overrated, yet it is hardly possible to avoid considering it as one of the richest, most harmonious, and refined languages in the world. With respect to its character for harmony, the vowels are almost all pure, there being only two diphthongs in the whole alphabet; and the thirty-eight consonants, as well simple as compounded, are for the most part labials and linguals:[43] it would indeed be difficult to instance another language exhibiting so just a proportion between the vowels and the consonants, in which it is not even exceeded by the Spanish; beyond this point we can scarcely speak with confidence, so long as we have no other guide to our judgment than the sound of a dead letter. At the same time we can safely assert it to be one of the richest and most refined of any. Poetry, in all its various forms, whether epic, lyric, or dramatic, appears to have been the peculiar appanage of Sanscrit, as is sufficiently evinced by the many excellent poets of either class, who for so many ages have made it the vehicle of their compositions: it also admits the employment of rhyme, without however being fettered by its restrictions, nor is it unacquainted even with alliteration, while it seems to have appropriated all the most delicate species of metre for which the Indian ear is susceptible.[44] And though perhaps it may not possess the charms of rhetorical composition, (which the temper of Indian governments would not admit,) it is nevertheless abundantly

[43] [This appears to be a misapprehension, as there are but thirty-four consonants at most; and these are distributed into five classes, viz., gutturals, palatals, cerebrals (or linguals), dentals, and labials. The diphthongs, properly speaking, are four, *e* and *o*, as well as *ai* and *au*, being usually reckoned among the number; though to be sure the two first differ not in sound from the simple vowels in the words *there* and *stone*; but as the author had previously restricted the vowels to five, viz. *a*, *i*, *u*, *ri*, and *lri*, (see p. 105,) we must necessarily include *e* and *o* under the diphthongs. TRANSL.]

[44] On the metrical art of the Hindus, we now possess the learned Essay of Colebrooke, On Sanscrit and Pracrit Poetry, inserted in the *Asiatic Researches*, vol. x. p. 389, etc., and which is exclusively devoted to this subject. Sanscrit literature contains several copious works on Prosody, as that of Pinjala and others. The most common metre is that of the slokas, or stanzas consisting of four verses of eight syllables each.

recompensed with a poetic prose,[45] which the best writers were perpetually endeavouring to embellish and refine: it has moreover reached a high degree of scientific cultivation, and the richness of its philosophy is no way inferior to its poetic beauties, as it presents us with an abundance of technical terms to express the most abstract ideas. It appears to have received its grammatical structure at a very remote period of antiquity, as the Hindus carry their oldest grammarians far back into the fabulous ages,[46] while at the same time the study of grammar seems to have furnished their learned men with a never-ending source of occupation and amusement. The inflection of nouns in Sanscrit is different, according as the word terminates with a vowel or consonant; the declensions are eight in number, and completely designate each case by a variation of the terminating syllables; among these occurs a triple ablative.[47] The numbers are singular, dual, and plural. The three genders, masculine, feminine, and neuter, are also distinguished by the termination; but there appears to be no common gender, as in our Occidental languages.[48] The inflection of verbs, also, is accomplished by means of different terminations; they are divided into ten classes or conjugations, and admit in addition to the active, passive, and deponent, an imperative and optative form: the tenses also are variously modified by the employment of three preterites, and two futures, together with several participles, and like the nouns they admit the distinction of singular, dual, and plural num-

[45] [See Colebrooke's Essay on this subject, p. 449. In this kind of prose compound words are principally used, which are considered a great beauty. Mr. Colebrooke mentions four kinds of prose; viz. 1. Simple prose, admitting no compound terms. 2. Prose in which compound terms are sparingly admitted. 3. Prose abounding in compound words, some of the inordinate length of one hundred syllables; and, 4. Modulated prose, frequently exhibiting portions of verse. TRANSL.]

[46] For instance, Panini, whose Grammar serves as the text, on which later grammarians have commented. An excellent review of the History of Hindu writers on Grammar, is inserted in the seventh volume of the *Asiatic Researches*, p. 202, etc., by Colebrooke.

[47] [This is incorrect; the author seems to have confounded the instrumental and locative cases with the ablative, from which, however, they are perfectly distinct, as well as from each other. TRANSL.]

[48] [In remarking on this passage the French translator observes, "There are actually more nouns of common gender in the Sanscrit than in any other known language;" and indeed, WILKINS, in his *Grammar*, p. 614, sq., gives copious lists of nouns which are of any two genders respectively, and even of all three together. TRANSL.]

bers.[49] In all these points the attentive observer will remark a striking resemblance to the construction of Western languages; while in its extraordinary capabilities of forming compound expressions, the Sanscrit evidently has the advantage; for by the elision of certain letters it can unite a number of words together, almost to an indefinite extent, a licence which, especially in reading the poets, often serves to retard the progress of the learner, but to the experienced eye of a native presents no obstacle whatever.[50]

The Sanscrit, according to the Hindus, is the language of the gods;[51] in it are composed for the most part their religious books, and the writings which form their classic literature; it is not therefore without reason that it has been called a holy tongue. At present it is a dead language, understood only by the pundits, who themselves have been obliged to make it their previous attentive study. This circumstance has induced some writers to question the fact of its ever having been a living or vernacular tongue, and to suppose, on the contrary, that it was a mere invention of the Brahmans, having for its object the interest and preservation of their religion.[52]

This is, however, a gratuitous supposition, which the present state of our acquaintance with the Sanscrit will furnish ample and satisfactory means to contradict; besides, it is not very easy to define what is precisely meant by the expression of inventing a language: and indeed admitting that such an invention were even possible, yet still its further development could only be accomplished through the medium of vernacular speech: for how can we imagine it at all likely that a literature, which is one of the richest both in poetry and prose, should have been formed in an unspoken language, or how could the works contained in it have been, I will not say preserved merely, but even have acquired their high degree of classical reputation through-

[49] All this is borrowed from Wilkins's Grammar, compared with that of Bopp.

[50] These prodigious compounds, some of them extending to one hundred and fifty-two syllables, (see *Asiat. Res.* vol. i. p. 360,) seem rather an artificial embellishment, peculiar to the written style, than to have had any influence on the spoken language. [See also *Asiat. Res.* vol. vii. p. 202; Colebrooke on the Sanscrit and Pracrit Languages. TRANSL.]

[51] *Asiatic Res.* vol. vii. p. 199.

[52] Ibid. p. 201.

out the country? A language which was once spoken is still capable of being preserved in its literature, as is the case with the Latin and the Greek; but this very literature could only have been produced when the respective languages were vernacular.

Asia supplies us with several examples of languages that have been formerly spoken but are now dead, still subsisting in their literary compositions; we need only mention the old Persian dialects, although none of these, in point of richness and extent, deserves even a remote comparison with the literature comprised in the Sanscrit. Where the religious opinions of any people are founded in holy books, the language also in which these are written, however in progress of time it may be corrupted, and even become actually obsolete, will yet never be altogether forgotten; especially when a privileged caste of priests are made the sole depositaries of their contents, together with the particular forms of worship enjoined in them. We ought moreover to recollect, that among the Eastern nations, the connexion between literature and religion is usually very close, in some instances indissoluble; and this is in a high degree the case with the Hindus; consequently when the Sanscrit ceased to be any longer a vernacular language, its literature still found a never-failing support in the religion of the country.

The question whether the Sanscrit was an aboriginal Indian language, has been variously answered. Sir W. Jones is of opinion that the principal Asiatic nations and dialects were derived from Persia; and also that conquerors from the latter country invaded India and brought with them their own language,[53] to which cause he attributes the striking resemblance between the Sanscrit and the Zend, one of the most ancient Persian dialects. Father Paulino, who is so fond of contradicting Jones in every thing else, is on this point, however, unanimous with him.[54] The name of a later antiquary, Dr. Leyden, to whom I shall soon have another occasion to refer, would certainly add much weight to this

[53] *Works*, vol. i. p. 26, etc. And with respect to the Zend especially, pp. 82, 83, in his Discourse on the Persians; "I was not a little surprised," says Sir W., "to find that out of ten words in Du Perron's Zend Dictionary, six or seven were pure Sanscrit."

[54] In his treatise, De Affinitate Linguæ Samscrdamicæ et Persicæ.

opinion, provided we were sure that the extent of his philological acquirements embraced a sufficient knowledge of the Zend also. But so long as all our acquaintance with the Zend is merely derived from one imperfect vocabulary, and beyond which the learning of the above-mentioned orientalists themselves did not extend, we may be allowed to defer pronouncing any opinion on the subject till we are in possession of further information. Whether the Sanscrit was introduced into India by foreign invaders, is a question which we are equally unable to determine upon any certain historical principles, because the date of the supposed occurrence is too far beyond the range of authentic history; neither indeed does its solution appear to be of any great practical importance. Those writers even who assume the fact, must at the same time be obliged to confess that the Sanscrit could only have acquired its exquisite refinement in India itself, and among the people who inhabited it. Now it is unquestionable that the proper country of any language is that where it was cultivated and refined, not the one from whence it was originally brought. So in the case of the German, which modern philologists, with every appearance of probability, have derived from the Persian; yet no one will therefore be disposed to question the fact of the German language having been formed in Germany alone: it is probable, indeed, that the resemblance between the Sanscrit and the Zend, owing to the neighbourhood of Persia, may be much greater than that between the German and the Persian; but still, according to all our notions on the subject, the Sanscrit could only have been perfectly developed and refined in India, just as the German only in Germany; and all the writers and poets who have contributed to the refinement of Sanscrit belong to India, with the same propriety as those of Germany do to the latter country.

Although, however, it is impossible to doubt the fact of the Sanscrit having been formerly a living language, yet it still remains for us to determine whether this was the case all over India, or whether it was only spoken in particular districts, and where? as also, how it came to be the language of literature, and what was the period of its most perfect development? and further, when, and from what causes, did it cease to exist as the medium of vernacular intercourse? These, it is true, are questions to which we can then only expect to furnish a full and satisfactory solution, when we have a critical history of the nation itself; in the absence of which, therefore, we must be obliged to content ourselves with conjectural probabilities, instead of absolute historical facts.

In asserting the Sanscrit to have been once a living language, we are far from concluding, therefore, that it was ever spoken in one single part of India, much less over the whole country, with the same degree of refinement and purity as we now find exhibited in the classical works of Hindu literature: we only maintain the literary Sanscrit to have been formed on the basis of a highly polished and improved colloquial idiom. That in this sense of the word, at least, the Sanscrit was formerly vernacular to a great portion of India, may be inferred with the highest probability from a comparison of the other still existing Indian dialects, and the various degrees of relation in which they stand to the Sanscrit. According to some learned English writers, who were not likely to be mistaken on such a point, there is at present a language spoken in Cashmir so nearly resembling the Sanscrit, that it is impossible to avoid deriving it from that source. Colebrooke affirms that the Bengali contains few words which are not evidently borrowed from the Sanscrit.[55] And, according to the same writer, the present dialect of the Punjab is nothing more than a corruption of the Pracrit; which in its turn is a peculiar dialect of the Sanscrit, and next to that language most successfully cultivated by the poets. Do not all these circumstances, then, unite in authorizing the probable conclusion, that in the northern parts of India, especially on the banks of the Ganges and in Behar, the scene of so many of the oldest Hindu poems, the Sanscrit was at one time the vernacular language of the people? We have, besides, already proved, from an examination of the inscriptions, that it was used in this very country for the purpose of inscribing on public monuments. Mr. Colebrooke further conceives himself to be fully borne out in asserting the Hindustani, which is spoken in certain parts of the interior, to be a veritable de-

[55] *Asiatic Res.* vol. vii. p. 224.

scendant of the Sanscrit.[56] On the other hand, it appears uncertain whether a similar origin can be justly attributed to the Mahratta, as well as the dialects prevailing on the coast, such as the Telinga, spoken on the banks of the Krishna and Godavery, and the Tamul on the Malabar coast; and, although we are informed that many words in these languages are derived from the Sanscrit,[57] yet this will not prove their whole structure to be so likewise.

But the researches of the learned Dr. Leyden, in whose death the interests of Hindu philology received a severe blow, have satisfactorily proved the Sanscrit to have extended much further, and that it must have been prevalent in the Ultra-Gangetic continent. This country, over which is spread the religion of Buddha, though perhaps considerably modified, is also in possession of a sacred language, called Bali, or Pali, in which the holy books are written. According to the investigations of the above-mentioned scholar, who lived a long time in that part of the world, and to whom we are indebted for the most accurate accounts of the nature, analogy, and derivation of the several dialects prevailing in those countries, there is every reason to believe that the Bali is a legitimate daughter of the Sanscrit, as well in its terms as in its grammatical inflection.[58] Dr. Leyden, indeed, considers it, together with the Zend, as the very oldest offspring of the parent tongue; and asserts it to be the predominant language of religion from Malacca to China. It would therefore follow that the Bali was propagated in these countries at the same time with the worship of Buddha, but whether as an independent language, or merely a corruption of Sanscrit, consequent among nations situate at a distance and using different idioms, cannot certainly be determined.

Admitting, then, the above-mentioned dialects to be really derived from the Sanscrit, and as moreover the oldest works of Hindu literature are composed in that language,

[56] *Asiatic Res.* vol. vii. p. 221. [57] Ibid. p. 228.

[58] On the Language and the Literature of the Indu Chinese Nations, by J. Leyden, M. D. in the *Asiatic Res.* vol. x. pp. 158—288. In this essay the author enumerates thirteen dialects current in India beyond the Ganges, of which he points out the nature and analogy; and finishes with an account of the Bali, the sacred language of those countries. [Consult also with respect to the Bali the researches of Messrs. Burnouf and Lassen. French Transl.]

I 2

it follows, therefore, that in one sense at least its high antiquity has been proved, simply because we know of no other language in India more ancient than the Sanscrit. But it still remains to inquire at what time it received its full and perfect development; and when, and from what causes, did it cease to be a living language? To the first of these questions, the ensuing remarks on Hindu literature in general will furnish an appropriate answer. With respect to the second, we can only adduce conjectures more or less capable of proof.

The inquiries of Sir W. Jones and his literary friends brought them to the conclusion, that the century immediately preceding the commencement of our era must be considered, if not as the earliest, yet at least one of the most brilliant periods of Hindu literature;[59] for it was at this time, according to native tradition, and in the court of the rajah Vicramaditya,[60] (whose era commences with his death, fifty-six years before Christ,) that nine of the most celebrated Hindu poets flourished, particularly Calidasa, who wrote the Sacontala, and Amara Sinha, the author of a dictionary called the Amara Cosha. An English critic, already mentioned, of the name of Bentley, contends against this opinion, and endeavours to prove that Vicramaditya and the nine gems of his court belong to a much later age, that is to say, to the twelfth century of the Christian era; and that he succeeded one rajah Bhojah, who died in the year 1182, after a reign of one hundred years.[61] This chronological statement, however, which assigns such a modern prince of the name of Vicramaditya, at whose court those nine poets are supposed to have flourished, is founded solely and entirely upon the bare assertion of a learned Hindu, which Bentley eagerly took up because it confirmed his doubts respecting the age of the poet Varaha, which he objected upon astronomical grounds to place so early as the reign of an elder Vicramaditya, as is commonly supposed. But this report of a Brahman who produces no authority, and may very possibly have forged it in order to meet Bentley's views,

[59] Jones's *Works*, vol. i. pp. 310, 311.

[60] Dow, in his History of Hindostan, and Polier write this name Bickermagit. [The indistinct pronunciation of the vulgar. Transl.]

[61] *Asiatic Res.* vol. viii. p. 243.

is so much the less calculated to bias an unprejudiced reader as it is indirectly refuted by history itself: for the supposed age of the later Vicramaditya is that in which the conqueror Mohammed Ghauri overthrew the dynasty of the Ghaznavide sultans, who reigned in Northern India.[62] Is it at all likely that at such an epoch a number of poets flourished at the court of an Indian prince, and obtained a classical reputation throughout the country, while the very name of this prince is not even mentioned in history? Moreover, the hundred years' reign attributed to his predecessor rajah Bhojah, seems to have originated in a mistake, as it is not the predecessor but the successor of the elder Vicramaditya, called also rajah Bhojah in Indian history, who having come to the throne after the disturbances that ensued upon the death of the latter, is said to have reigned not a hundred, but fifty years;[63] and the coincidence of the two names must appear no less extraordinary and improbable than the pretended long reign.

But, whatever may be the opinions respecting the true age in which these nine poets flourished, it is impossible to regard that alone as the most ancient epoch of classical Sanscrit poetry. The great epic poems had already been composed many years previous, and what we shall soon have occasion to say respecting the influence which these works have exercised upon the civilization of India, will it is hoped be sufficient to prove, that the classical period of Sanscrit literature must be referred to a much higher antiquity than the reign of Vicramaditya. The strongest general evidence in favour of this supposition may be drawn from the advanced state of cultivation exhibited in the language and literature itself, which could only have been produced by the successive labours of many generations; and also from the additional circumstance of the Vedas, which are the indispensable requisite of the Brahman caste, being all composed in Sanscrit, and consequently furnishing a decisive proof that the language must be as old as the establishment of that caste.

But the question is, whether, from being once a living language, the Sanscrit has gradually degenerated in the

[62] In the year 1183, A. D.
[63] Dow's *History of Hindostan*, vol. i. pp. 26, 27.

mouth of the people who spoke it, or has its disuse been owing to the same causes which contributed to the decay of the Latin in Europe, and which now only survives in the cognate tongues? These, however, are points of inquiry, which, considering the perfect chasm that appears in Indian history during nearly the whole first ten centuries of our era, it would be impossible to determine satisfactorily. It is indeed probable that a more accurate knowledge of Sanscrit literature in general, may succeed in clearing up some of our difficulties; but till then we must be content with adducing merely a few dates, which at best scarcely serve to throw a partial ray of light amidst the universal darkness in which the subject is involved.

The proper country of the Sanscrit, according to our notion, that is, the northern parts of India, is exactly that portion of the country which has been most exposed to invasion by foreign conquerors, from the time of Alexander down to Nadir Shah. This circumstance would naturally enough, we might suppose, have some influence upon the language; but since no conquerors ever permanently settled themselves in the country, at least before the time of the Mohammedan invasion, this does not appear to have been the case. Unfortunately the Greeks have left us no sort of information respecting the languages of India, either at or subsequent to the time of Alexander; nevertheless the inscriptions we have already examined, sufficiently attest the fact of Sanscrit being throughout that whole interval the exclusively written language of the country. The first accounts we have of the popular dialect of India, date no higher than the commencement of the eleventh century, at which period the Mohammedan invasion took place. At this time, we are informed, the Bhasha, which is nothing more than a colloquial variation of the Sanscrit, was commonly spoken in Bengal.[64] "The term Bhasha," says Colebrooke,[65] "is employed by all the Indian philologists, from Panini downwards, to denote a popular dialect of the Sanscrit, in opposition to the obsolete language of the Vedas; and is further used in common acceptation to designate any modern dialect of India, particularly if it be corrupted from

[64] JONES's *Works*, vol. i. p. 25. [65] *Asiatic Res.* vol. vii. p. 225.

the Sanscrit." From this account it would follow that the corruption of the Sanscrit as a popular dialect must be long anterior to the invasion of India by the Mohammedans. But since, however, the oldest Hindu grammarian, Panini, distinguishes the Bhasha or colloquial speech from the written language, does not this lead us to conclude that such distinction must have existed from time immemorial; and further, that we cannot with so much probability regard the colloquial form as a corruption of the written Sanscrit, as that this last is rather a polished and improved variation of the popular language? It is certainly very possible that the colloquial dialect may have been considerably altered since the period of the Mohammedan invasion; but from what we have already observed respecting the modern Bengali, and its striking resemblance to the Sanscrit, it would appear in all probability to be that identical Bhasha reported to have been spoken when the Mohammedans first invaded India, subject only to the natural corruptions introduced by foreigners. As to the rest, Mr. Colebrooke[67] makes a very important observation, which is, the fact that the ancient dialect, Vraja Bhasha, formerly spoken in the country of Mathura, where Krishna made his appearance, is still used in great purity over a considerable portion of the Duab, and on the banks of the Jumna and Ganges; and that the amorous adventures of that god with the Gopis, usually form the subject of the national songs composed in this dialect. Indeed the nearer we approach the north, the more frequent traces do we find of Sanscrit preserved in the common language of the people.

The remarks, hitherto made, will serve in some sort to pave the way to our inquiries into the second grand source of Hindu archæology, viz. the literature of India. Here also we must premise the usual questions, as to the extent of our acquaintance with this subject, our ability to form any decisive opinion, and what general conclusion we may be allowed to draw from a comprehensive survey of the whole.

The expression, however, Hindu literature, appears to be rather vague and indefinite: with us the denomination will chiefly comprise the literary productions written in Sans-

[66] *Asiatic Res.* vol. vii. p. 231.

crit, considering the high degree of interest which this language has excited in Europe, though it is by no means the only one which the Hindus have cultivated and refined as a written language. The same distinction has been enjoyed by several other dialects, some of them no longer spoken, such as the Pracrit,[67] which may be considered a more soft though less polished variation of the Sanscrit; and even those which still exist are not at all deficient in works of prose, and especially poetry, which are even in some degree considered classical by the nation. But on account of the decided pre-eminence of Sanscrit literature over all the rest, this appellation has been more exclusively applied to the compositions written in that language: it is besides regarded by the Hindus as a holy tongue; their most ancient books on religion, the Vedas, and all that has any reference to the same subject, are uniformly composed in Sanscrit, which is also the language of their oldest and most celebrated epic poems. The reunion of all these qualities, therefore, concurs to direct our attention with more particular respect to that part of Hindu literature which is comprised in the Sanscrit.

The sum of our acquaintance with these productions is no longer confined to a mere knowledge of their titles;[68] but includes also translations, and copious extracts, together with impressions of the original text. From them we learn how rich the Sanscrit is in works of poetry and prose, and yet a more accurate examination of the particular details will but show our knowledge of the whole extent of this literature, notwithstanding our acquisitions, to be still limited and imperfect.

[67] JONES's *Works*, vol. vi. p. 206. The Pracrit, which is little more than the language of the Brahmans, melted down by a delicate articulation to the softness of the Italian.

[68] As far as these are concerned the most important information has been contributed by Messrs. Hamilton and Langlès, in their Catalogue des Manuscrits Sanscrits, de la Bibliothèque Impériale, avec des notices sur la plûpart de ces écrits, etc., à Paris, 1807. This list contains the titles, and partial extracts of one hundred and seventy-eight works in Sanscrit, and fourteen in Bengali. To these we must not omit adding, Catalogus Librorum Sanscritanorum, quos Bibliothecæ Universitatis Havniensis vel dedit vel paravit Nathanael Wallich, M.D. Horti Botanici Calcuttensis præfectus. Scripsit Erasmus Nyerup, Bibliothecarius Universitatis. Hafniæ, 1821. This valuable collection comprises the titles of almost all the Sanscrit works printed in Bengal, accompanied with short though interesting literary remarks by the editor.

The Vedas are reputed to be not only the most ancient composition in Sanscrit, but in the whole circle of Indian literature; and even in a certain sense as the real source from whence the latter was derived. On every occasion they are mentioned as the holy books, which it is the especial duty of a Brahman to study, as the fountains of religion, and in short as the gracious communication of Brahma himself.[69] The first question therefore we have to discuss will be, what is our knowledge of the Vedas, and of their contents?

Europe possesses one copy of the Vedas in the original Sanscrit, which is probably complete, and is preserved in the British Museum.[70] But they have not yet been translated; indeed their vast extent will scarcely perhaps admit of this being ever perfectly done. Some of the hymns have been rendered by Sir W. Jones in English verse,[71] and Bopp has furnished us with translations of several other passages;[72] the former however are not so properly to be called translations, as poetical imitations; we are nevertheless indebted to that learned Orientalist for more exact information in his essay on the literature of the Hindus.[73]

These, however, and some other scattered notices or fragments, alone, would be far from enabling us to pronounce even a general opinion on the subject of the Vedas, had we not also the assistance of Mr. Colebrooke's essay,[74] who was the first that undertook a critical examination of these holy books, and yet nevertheless was obliged to pass over without notice several important sections, owing to the very great difficulty of procuring a complete copy of the Vedas even in India itself.

The collection of sacred writings, which we call the Vedas, though forming one perfect whole, is however divided

[69] See the essay translated from the Sanscrit, On Indian Literature, in the *Asiatic Res.* vol. i. p. 340; with the commentary.

[70] This manuscript, contained in eleven very large volumes, was brought from India and deposited in the Museum by Col. Polier, the same gentleman to whom we are indebted for an account of the Mythology of the Hindus, of which we shall have occasion to speak hereafter. See *Asiatic Res.* vol. i. p. 347.

[71] JONES'S *Works*, vol. vi. p. 313, sq.

[72] Subjoined to his Conjugation-system of the Sanscrit.

[73] JONES'S *Works*, vol. i. p. 349.

[74] In the *Asiatic Res.* vol. viii. pp. 377, 497: On the Vedas, or Sacred Writings of the Hindus. I follow Mr. Colebrooke in writing Vedas, not Vedams, Veds, or Beds, as the word is sometimes spelt.

into four parts, each of which is considered a separate Veda, and is further distinguished by a particular name. These are the Richveda, the Yajurveda, which is again subdivided into the white and black, the Samaveda, and the Atharvaveda.[75] The last is generally regarded by critics as of later origin than the others, but nevertheless, without wishing to maintain the authenticity of the whole, it seems highly probable that a portion at least of the fourth Veda is as ancient as any of the rest.[76] The reason why it has not been so frequently mentioned as the three former, is perhaps owing less to its supposed difference in point of age than to the nature of its contents. The names of the three former Vedas are descriptive of the different nature and destination of the several prayers which they respectively contain, and which are wont to be recited on solemn festal occasions. The term Rich, therefore, denotes their being in verse; Yajus is applied to prose; and Saman to the purposes of chanting. The fourth Veda also contains prayers, but they are not employed in the same festal ceremonies as the others, it is consequently of a distinct character by itself.

Each Veda consists of two parts, viz. prayers (Mantras), and precepts (Brahmanas). The whole collection of hymns, prayers, and invocations, which appertain to a Veda, is termed its Sanhita. All the rest belongs to the Brahmanas, comprising certain precepts which inculcate religious duties, together with maxims explanatory of those precepts, and arguments which relate to theology; the latter are called Upanishads. The above classification, however, of the contents of the Vedas, is not always strictly followed. Some Upanishads are portions of the Brahmanas, properly so called; others are found only in a detached form; and one is a part of a Sanhita itself.[77]

The Vedas, then, consist principally of hymns and pray-

[75] In Persian they are called Rig, Yagir, Sam, and Atherbam. See the *Ayin Acbari*, vol. ii. p. 408. The Ezour Vedam, ou ancien commentaire de Vedam, traduit par un Brame du Sanscritam, published by Voltaire in 1778, and so long considered one of the genuine sources of Hindu wisdom, is nothing more than a modern forgery, as Mr. Ellis has lately proved in his Account of a Discovery of a modern imitation of the Vedas. *Asiatic Res.* vol. xiv. p. 1. The name Ezour is corrupted from Yajus, or Yajur.

[76] Colebrooke, l. c. p. 381. It is certainly of very great age, for even the oldest epic poems make mention of four Vedas as already existing.

[77] Colebrooke, l. c. pp. 387, 388.

ers; those of the first are chiefly panegyrical, and are comprised in ten thousand verses, or rather stanzas, of various measures; they are put in the mouth of holy men, (Rishis,) who are therein mentioned, along with the divinities, to whom the prayers are addressed. The composers are very frequently Rishis themselves,[78] and count among their number Brahmans, and sometimes even royal personages. The same Veda contains, also, invocations and gratulatory poems in honour of certain princes who had liberally rewarded the authors. The hymns and prayers of the second Veda, written partly in verse and partly in metrical prose, form but a small portion of its contents compared with the first. The hymns refer chiefly to certain sacrifices, during which they were to be recited, especially at the solemn one of a horse: the prayers are to be employed at the inauguration of kings, and are attributed some to Rishis, others to various gods.[79] The hymns and prayers of both this and the preceding Veda are intended for recitation, but only according to certain invariable prescript forms: on the other hand, the hymns of the third Veda, composed altogether in verse, are destined exclusively for chanting. The fourth Veda, in fine, contains upward of seven hundred and sixty hymns and prayers, which are for the most part of an imprecatory character. The divinities, however, to whom they are addressed are by no means those who subsequently make such a brilliant appearance in the Hindu heroic mythology, but consist rather of personified natural objects, such as the firmament, fire, the sun, the moon, water, air, atmosphere, the earth, etc., designated under various appellations.[80] The peculiar sacrifices to be offered them, the incense and holy drink, made of the juice of *Soma* or moonplant,[81] afford abundant matter for the numerous prayers which are to be recited during each ceremony; and of which, according to a singular principle laid down by the Brahmans, it is not at all necessary

[78] COLEBROOKE, l. c. p. 392. What follows, is borrowed from the same writer.

[79] Several of these prayers are translated in Mr. Colebrooke's three important essays, On the Religious Ceremonies of the Hindus, and of the Brahmans especially, inserted in the fifth and seventh volumes of the *Asiatic Researches*.

[80] See particularly COLEBROOKE, *Asiatic Res.* vol. viii. p. 398, and compare the specimen of a translation given by Bopp.

[81] Asclepias acida, or Cynanchum viminale.

to comprehend the sense! The only requisite, they say, is to know what holy person is speaking, the divinity whom he addresses, the particular event which is the occasion of the hymn, the syllabic measure or rhythm, and the different modes of recitation, whether word for word, or alternately backwards and forwards, to which latter method some occult virtue is usually attributed.[82]

The second part of each Veda consists of Brahmanas and Upanishads. All those portions which do not belong to the Sanhita, are collectively termed Brahmanas, of which the Upanishads constitute the major part: the latter appellation does not signify mysteries, as it has often been translated, but the knowledge of God, and that indeed in a twofold sense, as describing not only the knowledge itself, but also those writings in which it is explained and taught.[83] The Upanishads are consequently the true foundation of Hindu theology, as they contain special inquiries into the being of God himself, the world, and the nature of the soul, etc. Each Veda, we must allow, contains also Upanishads, but in the first two they form only a small proportion; whereas the Samaveda comprises the most detailed and abstract researches of the above description; and even in the fourth, or Atharvaveda, they occupy more than half of the whole book.[84] These Upanishads are composed in various forms, ordinarily in dialogues between the divinities, Rishis, and the elements, etc.; frequently, however, they assume a didactic character, and as they very often diverge into a precative form, it is evident that we cannot always draw an exact line of distinction between them and the Mantras: some of these pieces have been translated by Sir W. Jones,[85] but it is to Anquetil du Perron, the learned Orientalist, who brought the Zendavesta to Europe, that we are indebted, if not for a complete translation, yet at least for extracts so very considerable as to occupy no less than two quarto volumes of his Upnekhat.[86] With such assistance as this, one might be led to suppose that very little was further wanting to complete our knowledge of Hindu theology. In

[82] Colebrooke, l. c. p. 389, 390.
[83] Ibid. l. c. p. 472.
[84] Ibid. pp. 461, 471.
[85] Jones's *Works*, vol. vi. Extracts from the Vedas.
[86] *Upnekhat studio* Anquetil du Perron, Paris, 1801. Upnekhat is the Persian form of the word Upanishad.

the first place, however, this Upnekhat is nothing more than a Persian abridgement, and the translation is made from the latter tongue instead of the original, and how can we guarantee the fidelity of the Persian translator? Besides, had the editor even intended that his book should be completely unserviceable to nine-tenths of his readers, he could scarcely have adopted a more convenient plan for the purpose than the disorderly arrangement he has observed. The Upnekhat contains, it is true, selections from all the four Vedas, but they seem to be made at random, sometimes from one and sometimes from another; by far the greatest part are taken from the fourth: the consequence is, that there can be nothing like a systematic and complete view of the whole. Again, the extracts are rendered into such literal and therefore unintelligible Latin, that he has very frequently been obliged to subjoin in a parenthesis an additional version somewhat more explanatory than the one made word for word. Now let any one conceive the difficulty of wading in this way through a subject which of itself is sufficiently abstract and obscure, and he would not be at all surprised to find that, with the exception of the author and his printer, no person had yet been able to read through the whole of Du Perron's Upnekhat: and supposing any one actually has had the patience to achieve a complete perusal, I would then ask him whether he understood it? For my part, I must confess my own repeated attempts have proved unsuccessful, and I must, therefore, leave to the inquirers into religious history the difficult task of elucidating its obscurities.[87]

These discussions, however, will serve to furnish a general reply to the question, as to the contents of the Vedas? It is indeed no small advantage to know what these books comprise in the whole of their subject, as well as in their constituent parts, (though each of the latter still require a separate and particular examination,) for even our present

[87] [There is a notice of this work in the *Edinburgh Review*, vol. i. p. 412. The critic therein does full justice to M. du Perron's knowledge of the Persian, but questions his knowledge of the Sanscrit, or rather, announces his total ignorance of that language. Ritter also remarks that the Upnekhat contains so many mistakes and false interpretations as to be quite useless in a work of investigation. See *Geschichte der Philosophie*, vol. i. p. 75. A milder sentence is pronounced by the Count Lanjuinais in the *Mag. Encycl.* tom. iii. TRANSL.]

imperfect acquaintance with these sacred writings is, nevertheless, of itself sufficient for enabling us to draw certain weighty conclusions.

First, then, the Vedas are, for the most part, collections of small detached pieces by different authors, whose names are frequently therein cited, as is the case with the hymns.[88] They cannot, therefore, be all of the same age, and although, for reasons which shall appear in the sequel, we must necessarily refer them to a remote period, yet it must have required a long interval of time to produce and unite them together in one collection as they now appear. And as they consist principally of hymns and prayers, it would seem highly probable, even independent of such being the actual report, that at first they were preserved by means of oral tradition, until the assistance of letters enabled them to be transmitted with greater certainty to future ages.[89]

2. In order to give them their present arrangement and connexion, the Vedas must evidently have required the labours of some compiler who incorporated the detached pieces into one work. And in effect Hindu tradition has assigned the task to Vyasa, whose age goes far back into the fabulous periods. Vyasa, however, is nothing more than a common term applicable to any compiler in general;[90] we are therefore still in the dark. Mr. Colebrooke attributes the surname in question to Dwaipayana, whom he supposes to have compiled the Vedas. But even of this latter personage we know nothing further, and Mr. Colebrooke himself confesses[91] the total absence of any chronological data for ascertaining the exact period when they were either composed or set in order. There is, however, the less reason to be surprised at this uncertainty, the case is the same with the books of Moses and the Zendavesta.

[88] Each Veda, for instance, is furnished with an index of "unquestionable authenticity," which describes the contents of the several pieces, and adds also the names of the composers. *Asiatic Res.* vol. viii. p. 392; where Colebrooke mentions the most important. Among the royal authors noticed in this list, we meet with none that are found in that of SIR W. JONES, *Works*, vol. i. p. 296, sq.

[89] *Asiatic Res.* vol. viii. p. 378. The Greeks who accompanied Alexander, had already remarked the Indian custom of reciting these hymns; and it was in singing one to the praise of the gods that the Brahman Calanus so readily mounted the funeral pile. ARRIAN, *Op.* p. 147. Is it possible to doubt the fact of their being taken from the Vedas?

[90] *Asiatic Res.* vol. viii. pp. 378, 392, 488.

[91] Ibid. p. 489.

They have been preserved to our times, but the true account of their origin is involved in the deepest obscurity.

3. With respect to the age of the Vedas, we are in possession of several weighty reasons for referring it to very remote antiquity. They are without doubt the oldest work composed in Sanscrit; as is sufficiently attested by the obsolete idiom in which they are written, and which interposes such frequent and serious obstacles in the way of translating and explaining them. Another proof is derived from the circumstance that all, even the most ancient Sanscrit writings, allude to the Vedas as already in existence, and cite numerous passages from them almost at every page.[92] What a considerable portion, indeed, of Hindu literature is principally founded upon them, we shall soon have occasion to observe. And lastly, to each Veda is subjoined a treatise explanatory of the regulations of the calendar, which defines the exact time appropriated to certain religious ceremonies. It is adapted to the comparison of solar and lunar time with the vulgar or civil year; and was evidently composed in the infancy of astronomical science.[93]

4. But the strongest proof of the antiquity of the Vedas, in my opinion, is the fact that they exhibit no traces whatever of the present existing sects of Siva and Krishna; which is expressly remarked by Colebrooke.[94] "In no part of the Vedas," says he, "excepting only the latter sections of the Atharvaveda, which must therefore be regarded as spurious, have I been able to discover the slightest vestige of the worship of Rama and Krishma, considered as incarnations of Vishnu." Does not this entitle us to infer that the Vedas must be long anterior to the origin of those sects, which are themselves, however, of remote antiquity, as we have already shown in our examination of the monuments of Hindu architecture. At the same time, moreover, the above

[92] *Asiatic Res.* vol. viii. p. 482.

[93] *Asiatic Res.* vol. viii. p. 489. This calendar is termed Jyotish, and the cycle, (Yuga,) therein employed, extends only to five years; the months are all lunar; but in the middle and end of the period, an intercalation is effected by doubling one of them. Colebrooke (p. 493) quotes a passage from the calendar of the second Veda, which contains a determination of the solstitial point at that time, and which coincides with the fourteenth century previous to the commencement of our era. These inquiries, however, more properly belong to the province of astronomy.

[94] Ibid. p. 494.

remark serves to explain the reason why the different sects of India do, nevertheless, regard the Vedas as the authentic source of their respective dogmas; just in the same way as the various denominations of Christian believers do, all of them, severally uphold the authority of Scripture.

5. Admitting, however, the Vedas to be of very great antiquity, is it not probable that during the lapse of ages, and since they were committed to writing, several important changes and interpolations may have crept into the original text? What appears to confirm such a supposition, is the fact that, according to Hindu report, Vyasa had numerous disciples, each of whom again had their own respective scholars, who successively instructed others in their turn; insomuch, that at length the vast number of alterations made in the text, and variations in the manner of reading and reciting it, gave rise to no less than one thousand one hundred different schools of scriptural knowledge.[95]

Now, without estimating such a report at more than its real value, we are fully authorized in suspecting the existence of considerable interpolation; though our conjecture, it is true, can only be ascertained by a comparison of several copies of the Vedas. In the first place, however, these alterations, for the most part, would only concern the outward form of pronunciation, which is so much the more likely, as that appears, from what has gone before, to have been the principal object in making them. And secondly, these very alterations can hardly be of modern date, but must have existed for centuries; or in other words, the text of the Vedas, whatever changes and modifications it may formerly have experienced, has continued in its present state from very remote antiquity. This is proved, both by the numerous quotations occurring in the oldest writings, and which perfectly agree with the modern copies of the Vedas, and also from the circumstance of their being furnished with ancient scholia; which, as the learned natives of India pretend, is the only security against falsification, owing to the scholiast's taking care to explain every word, and comment on the sense of every passage.[96] And lastly, the strict rules prescribed for reading or chanting the Vedas

[95] *Asiatic Res.* vol. viii. p. 382.

[96] Ibid. p. 480, sq.

in a certain defined rhythm or tone, would render every attempt at interpolation very difficult, if not impossible, as it must be immediately detected.

6. As the Vedas, like the Zend-Avesta, are for the most part conversant about ceremonial laws, they imply consequently the existence of a certain form of religious worship; which being obliged to the observance of peculiar rites and invocations, would of course be confided to a sacerdotal caste. Now the worship in question concerns a religious system, which, according to the unanimous opinion of all those who have studied the subject, has for its foundation the belief in one God.[97] This divinity however was manifested in the grand phenomena of nature, which were themselves again separately invoked as deities under various denominations; we might, therefore, in this sense, consider the religion of the Vedas as a kind of natural religion. But at the same time, and this constitutes its national peculiarity, it is interwoven with a tissue of the most refined speculations, which particularly abound in the Upanishads. In those abstruse and mysterious disquisitions, on the infinite, on the origin and nature of things, on the emanation and absorption of beings into the Godhead, the Hindus, naturally addicted to profound contemplation, would discover abundant food for the intellect, and frequent opportunities of indulging their taste for abstract reverie to the wildest extent. That portion of the Vedas which is contained in the Upanishads is not we must confess very easy to understand; but still a moderate degree of application and study, would no doubt succeed in illustrating the principal traits in the intellectual character of this remarkable people, and their proneness to abstract speculation.

7. The Vedas were consequently the real source of the religion, it is true, but certainly not of the mythological system of the Hindus. The origin of the latter, as will be shown in the sequel, was the Indian epic poetry. The divinities, to whom are addressed the invocations contained in the Vedas, though many in number, are yet only personifications of natural objects, and according to the commen-

[97] *Asiatic Res.* vol. viii. p. 396. Sir W. Jones, Father Paulino, and the reports of the Danish missionaries, all agree on this point; which is further confirmed by numerous passages in the Upanishads.

tators may be reduced to three,[98] viz. Fire, Air, and the Sun; and these again in their turn are to be considered nothing more than particular manifestations of the one original Being. In some passages, indeed, we occasionally meet with the groundwork of certain fables, subsequently expanded by the poets, but no trace whatever of the favourite legends peculiar to those sects who adore Krishna, or the Lingam;[99] whence it necessarily follows, that the religion of the priests was always distinct from that of the common people; though it cannot be denied that both stood in some mutual degree of relation and connexion one with the other; to explain which will be the special business of an inquirer into the religious opinions of India.[100]

The Vedas, then, which are the sources of the sacerdotal religion, can by no means be considered as such with regard to the popular system of belief: the common people are not even once permitted to read these books; whereas it is the duty, as well as the exclusive privilege of a Brahman, to study and explain them; and the reputation of being versed therein is considered an honourable title of renown. The caste next in immediate order is only allowed to hear them read, or at most barely to read them; while the inferior, comprehending the general mass of the people, are absolutely forbidden both: so that the Brahmans appear to have always had it in their power to communicate as much or as little of the Vedas to the other castes as they thought proper. But is it possible that such abstruse dogmas as those contained in the Upanishads could have been adapted to the purposes of popular instruction, even supposing the willingness of the Brahmans to make them so? Is it not rather

[98] COLEBROOKE (*Asiatic Res.* vol. viii. p. 396) has given the passages in the original, together with a translation. Compare the first of his three treatises On the Religious Ceremonies of the Hindus, *Asiatic Res.* vol. v.; which contains the daily prayers and exercises of a Brahman. These are addressed to the Sun, Fire, and Water, etc., and not to Vishnu or Siva, etc., though the names of the latter occur two or three times. But much more frequently is Brahma mentioned as the first and unchangeable; "Brahma is truth, the one immutable being," etc., p. 362. It was only after the establishment of the sects of Siva and Vishnu that the worship of those deities superseded that of Brahma; the last is of a purely spiritual character; the two former are altogether sensual.

[99] COLEBROOKE, p. 389, note.

[100] The treatise of Colebrooke just mentioned, though it does not absolutely distinguish the two religions, contains nevertheless the most important evidence for establishing the fact.

agreeable to the common order of things, that, in a nation whose priesthood was in the exclusive possession of the holy books, a natural distinction should exist between the sacerdotal and popular forms of religion? The truth and importance of this remark will derive additional illustration from the results of our inquiries into the religious system of ancient Egypt.

8. It is, however, far from probable, that the ancient dogmas and form of religion peculiar to the Vedas, should have been preserved even among the Brahmans in all their original purity. How indeed were this possible, when the obscure and obsolete idiom in which they are written, especially the three first, renders their study extremely difficult even to Brahmans themselves,[1] to say nothing of the small number of copies to be found in the country? Mr. Colebrooke observes,[2] "A very great proportion of what the Vedas teach has already become obsolete; other religious precepts and ceremonies have been substituted in its stead; a ritual founded on the Puranas, and customs borrowed from the impure source of the Tantras, have in great measure antiquated the liturgy of the Vedas. The worship of Rama and Krishna has replaced that of the elements and planets." This remark will, therefore, serve to throw some light on the origin of religious sects among the Hindus: a variation in the manner of reading and explaining the Vedas would naturally produce a variety of different schools, and we have already noticed[3] the great number which were established by the Brahmans in consequence; but the same cause will not account for the different sects which have arisen among the common people. The latter have reference to the worship of certain divinities, not to be found in the Vedas, but derived solely from the Indian epic poems. It was long ago remarked by the Father of Grecian history, that Homer and Hesiod furnished the deities of popular mythology; and in the same manner the great epic poets of India have in great measure supplied the numerous gods which fill the Indian Pantheon. We must not, however, forget to observe, that these poets themselves belonged to the Brahman caste; a circumstance which might explain not only, in general, the intimate connexion always subsisting between the religion

[1] *Asiatic Res.* vol. viii. p. 497. [2] Ibid. vol. viii. pp. 495, 496.
[3] See above, page 128.

of the priests and that of the common people, but also more particularly the reason why, upon the corruption of the old Vedantic system among the Brahmans, the two forms became confounded, and as it were assimilated together.

With respect to the origin of the several Hindu sects, we are not at all in a condition of giving any correct historical account of them, or of assigning the respective dates to each. Those of Siva and Vishnu are at present the most generally prevailing ones, but they are not alone: by their side flourish that of Ganesa and many others.[4] The intrinsic character and objects of worship peculiar to the sect of Siva, which adores the Lingam, afford a reasonable presumption in favour of its being the most ancient, and probably the original creed of the common people: whereas that of Vishnu, on the contrary, worshipped under the name of Krishna, owes its origin merely to a reformation, undertaken for the purpose of refining the grossly sensual worship of the former. The sect of Krishna, however, stands in such intimate connexion with the epic poem, which has for its principal subject the history of the incarnation of Vishnu under the character of Krishna, that we may correctly term it a poetical religion, as will appear still more evident when we come to examine the subject of Hindu epic poetry in general. The attempts of Sir W. Jones to fix the origin of the last-mentioned sect, one thousand two hundred years before the Christian era, repose upon no more solid grounds than his argument for placing the appearance of Buddha two centuries later, both one and the other being founded solely on the traditionary reports of certain natives of Cashmire.[5] All that we know with certainty of Buddha is, that he was the founder of a sect, which must formerly have prevailed over a considerable part of India, but whose tenets and forms of worship were in direct opposition to those of the Brahmans, and engendered a deadly hate between the two parties, which terminated in the expulsion of the Buddhists from the country. One may easily conceive, therefore, how many questions of great historical importance still remain to be solved in the course of our inquiries into this subject, in addition to our ignorance respecting the time

[4] See especially on this point Colebrooke in the *Asiatic Res.* vol. vii. p. 279, sq.

[5] JONES's *Works*, vol. i. p. 29.

when the sect was first established. Notwithstanding the various conjectures which have been advanced by learned men on this point, Mr. Colebrooke, who cannot be supposed inferior to any Sanscrit scholar living, nevertheless only ventures to surmise that the Buddhists, though certainly of more modern origin than the Vedas, are yet, however, anterior to the sects of Siva and Krishna.[6] That they must be of considerable antiquity is, I imagine, quite apparent, from the fact that a great number of the oldest rock temples, as we have already remarked, were dedicated to Buddha. But what is a still more important proof in support of their age is, that the Buddhists are actually mentioned in the Ramayana, (though we believe only in one passage,[7]) and are there classed along with atheists, that is, the opponents of Brahma who reject the doctrine of the Vedas. It would follow, therefore, that at the time when the Ramayana was composed, the Buddhists were not merely in existence as a religious sect, but were considered also the adversaries of the Brahmans. What relation, however, there might have subsisted between the respective dogmas of these two sects, together with the history of the persecution and expulsion of the Buddhists from India, is at present involved in impenetrable obscurity. Mr. Colebrooke would make the difference between the two consist in the Buddhists wishing to do away with animal sacrifices, or at least, to diminish the frequency of their occurrence: by which the Brahmans would lose their perquisite of the flesh of the victims.[8] But without presuming to question the correctness of this opinion, there is a still more important point, I

[6] *Asiatic Res.* vol. viii. p. 495. His reasons for attributing a greater age to the Vedas are again brought forward in his Observations on the Jains, ibid. vol. ix. p. 293, etc.

[7] *Ramayana*, Part iii. § 76, p. 452. "As an atheist fallen from the path of rectitude! as a thief, so is a Buddhist!" The whole of this section, in which the Brahman Javali is represented under the assumed character of an atheist and a Buddhist, in conversation with Rama, is very interesting. What principally excites the abhorrence of the Brahmans is the rejection of funeral sacrifices to be offered by surviving children, and by consequence, the depreciation of matrimony.

[The passage of the Ramayana just quoted, is one of a great many in which the translators through improvident haste have misconstrued the sense: moreover, it is not at all improbable that the whole is an interpolation. Vide SCHLEGEL's Preface to his edition of the *Ramayana*, tom. i. p. 55. FRENCH TRANSL.]

[8] COLEBROOKE, l. c.

think, to which we ought rather to direct our attention. The religion of Buddha yet prevails throughout Ceylon, over the whole of India beyond the Ganges, (except the countries where Islam has been introduced, as for example the Malayan peninsula,) in Tibet, and even in China, where the religion of Fo, which is the popular creed, is reported to be synonymous with that of Buddha.[9] These assertions, it is true, require the support of more accurate inquiries and comparisons than have hitherto been instituted into the subject, but supposing them to be founded on fact, we have an immediate and striking proof of the difference between the Brahmans and the Buddhists.

In all the countries above mentioned the distinction of castes is perfectly unknown; is it because probably rejected by the doctrine of Buddha? With regard to the higher castes, particularly that of the Brahmans, the fact is clear; the inferior ones are not of so much importance. This, then, sufficiently explains the hatred of the Brahmans towards the Buddhists. There is, however, an additional circumstance, no less remarkable, to be observed: wherever the Buddhist creed prevails, the sacerdotal caste of the Brahmans has been replaced by a monastic order of priests, established throughout the respective countries under various denominations, being called Talapoins in Ava and Pegu, and Gylongs in Tibet. In the latter country these monks possess the sovereign power; in some others, as in Ava, (the Birmese Empire,) and in Ceylon, they either have or had formerly considerable political influence. But as this monastic corporation preserves its existence, not by the enjoyment of hereditary rights, but solely by the accession of fresh members, they must consequently be obliged to the observance of perpetual celibacy, and be immured in a cloister all their lives.[10] The Brahman, on the contrary, is not only permitted but absolutely enjoined by his religion to marry, and he must be the father of a family before he can be allowed to offer sacrifice, or be admitted to the privileges of holy expiation. The hope of leaving children

[9] Jones's *Works*, vol. i. p. 104.

[10] Two monasteries of this description are reported to exist in Ceylon, viz. those of Malvathe and Asgiri; Davy, p. 47. With regard to those of Birmah and Tibet, see the accounts given by Symes and Turner in their respective Travels.

behind him is the very point on which all his happiness depends, not merely in reference to this life, but to the next also, on account of the funeral sacrifices which his children are religiously obliged to offer, and which involve the eternal welfare of the soul of the deceased. Under such circumstances as these, what violent disputes must necessarily have arisen when the Buddhists first began to propagate their obnoxious doctrines!—disputes probably more outrageous than those occasioned by the introduction of celibacy into the Christian priesthood. We have, as yet, no accounts of the persecution and expulsion of the Buddhists from India, and this circumstance of itself would allow us to infer, with great probability, that those events must have taken place at a very remote period of antiquity. And though some modern writers bring the date of these occurrences as low down as the first and second centuries of our era,[11] their opinions seem to have no better foundation than mere conjecture. It is, however, very true that some traces of them are supposed to have been found in India, which are as late as the middle ages;[12] but they are, nevertheless, of very doubtful authority: and even should we admit the probability that a feeble remnant of this sect might still be discovered to exist in some one part of the country, yet the admission would not be at all conclusive against the fact of the Buddhist persecution and consequent expulsion having taken place at a much earlier date.

The Vedas are regarded by the Hindus as the source not only of their legislation, but of all their scientific knowledge. The intimate connexion, indeed, which usually subsists among Oriental nations, between religion, laws, and science, especially where these form the exclusive appanage of a sacerdotal caste, has already been demonstrated in our work on the Persians; and will receive additional proof from the

[11] [See a learned discussion of this subject in WILSON'S preface to his *Dictionary*, pp. 15, etc., and 33. Mr. W. considers it probable that an utter extirpation of the Buddhists was effected between the twelfth and sixteenth centuries, and that the Jains performed an important part in their expulsion. With regard to the peculiar doctrines of the Buddhists, see MR. HODGSON'S Memoir, in *the Transactions of the Royal Asiatic Society*, tom. ii. pp. 225, 257. TRANSL.]

[12] Partly in the inscriptions above explained, see p. 100, and partly in the accounts of two Arabian travellers through India in the ninth century, translated by RENAUDOT, p. 109.

result of our inquiries into the Egyptians. Before, however, we can attempt to illustrate this question, we must examine how far we are in possession of the requisite data which will enable us to pronounce an opinion in the case.

It was the legislative system of India which first attracted the attention of its English conquerors, and justly too, in preference to any thing else. For though by no means in itself an uninteresting subject to them as antiquarians, yet considered with reference to their political situation it was essentially necessary for them to become acquainted with the laws of a people whom they wished to govern. Now as the Hindus themselves attribute a very high antiquity to their laws, so a particular examination of this subject must necessarily involve an inquiry into a very principal branch of Sanscrit literature. The learned founder of the Asiatic Society made it the favourite object of his studies, and published the Institutes of Hindu Law, accompanied with a preface.[13] This was followed soon after by a work of much greater extent, from the pen of Mr. Colebrooke, and entitled A Digest of Hindu Law.[14] We are scrupulous to preserve the respective titles of these two works, as Sir W. Jones has already made use of them to express their comparative relation.[15] The first, however, on account of the high antiquity assigned it, is more important for our purpose of giving a general outline of Hindu legislation than the Digest, of which only the titles of contracts and the right of succession have hitherto been published.

The Laws of Menu comprise in twelve chapters the principles both of public and private right. In ascribing their composition to Menu, the first of the mythological kings, the grandson of Brahma and father of Bhrigu, nothing

[13] Institutes of Hindu Law, or the Ordinances of Menu, according to the gloss of Culluca, containing the Indian System of Duties, religious and civil, verbally translated from the original Sanskrit; with a preface by Sir W. Jones, Calcutta, 1796.

[14] A Digest of Hindu Law on Contracts and Successions, with a Commentary by Jagannatha Tercapanchanana, translated from the original Sanscrit, by H. T. Colebrooke, Esq., in three volumes, London, 1801. In this work we are presented, first, with the text of the ancient Hindu jurists, Menu, Sankha, Vrihaspati, and others; then follow the interpretations of the commentators. That part which treats of the law of succession is particularly important, as it contains also the laws of family relations, of man and wife, parents and children, etc.

[15] *Institutes, etc.*, preface, p. iv.

more is meant, according to Hindu expression, than that they are of Divine origin, and the most ancient code of law belonging to the nation. They were communicated by Bhrigu to the Rishis, or sages, who consulted him for that purpose.[16] These laws are so closely allied to the Vedas, particularly the first three, which are quoted almost at every page, that we may with great propriety refer them to that source, and consider the Vedas to be the parent stock of Hindu legislation in general.[17] The Institutes of Menu are consequently posterior to the sacred books just mentioned; nevertheless it will be very easy to persuade ourselves in reading them, that they cannot be all the work of one person, scarcely indeed of one generation, but that they must have been some considerable time in practical use before they were collected together and committed to writing. They form a strange medley of barbarism and civilization, and although several portions of the code, especially the penal laws, betray the infancy of political science, yet upon the whole it exhibits remarkable proofs of a very advanced state of society for an Asiatic nation. The distinction of castes appears to have been already organized, the ceremonial laws of religion in full practice conformably to the doctrine of the Vedas, and the dominion of the Brahmans perfectly established, although the sovereigns were not yet chosen from that caste. The various relations of proprietary right are already very numerous and complicated, and money is considered as the usual medium of exchange, with reference to which most of the penal laws are determined. This is, by no means, such a system of legislation as would be supposed coeval with the nation itself.

On the other side, however, we are in possession of considerable evidence, both internal and external, for attributing a high degree of antiquity to the Code of Menu. Several proofs already adduced in support of the age of the Vedas, will apply with the same force to the laws in question. And first with respect to the language in which they are written; this is metrical Sanscrit, and in an obsolete idiom,

[16] *Institutes, etc.*, preface, p. viii.

[17] Ibid. p. xviii. The Vedas are the foundation of law, which in itself, and notwithstanding it was given by Menu, is nevertheless entirely explained in the Vedas.

similar to that of the Vedas, though not so ancient. According to Sir W. Jones, when compared with the language of the classic poets, it is analogous to the Latin of the Twelve Tables as compared with that of Lucretius.[18] Further, the laws of Menu are exactly conformable to the Vedas in all that concerns religion and its ordinances; we find the same divinities, always excepting those celebrated by the poets. Thirdly, we meet with no traces of the sects already alluded to, into which the Hindus were subsequently divided. And in conclusion, the long list of commentators and scholiasts who have endeavoured to explain these laws, would alone serve to prove their great age, and justify the common opinion of the Hindus in regarding them as the most ancient code they possess.[19]

Notwithstanding this general evidence, however, in favour of the antiquity of the laws of Menu, we have no positive testimony with regard to the precise time when they were collected and embodied in their present shape. Sir. W. Jones endeavoured to prove that they might have been compiled about eight hundred and eighty years before the commencement of our era; and that, at most, their age cannot exceed one thousand two hundred and eighty years before that period. In order to arrive at this conclusion, he supposes that the Yajur-Veda, according to the list therein given of masters and scholars, in connexion with certain astronomical data, relative to the determination of the solstitial point, may be referred to the year 1580 before the birth of Christ.[20] He observes further, that judging by analogy from the alterations which have taken place in the Latin language, as evidenced by a comparison of the fragments we possess of the laws of Numa with those of the Twelve Tables, it must have required upwards of three cen-

[18] Preface, p. vi.

[19] The whole collection of these glosses and commentaries by the ancient Munis, or sages, on the Laws of Menu, is called the Dherma Sastra, or System of Law. One of the most celebrated of these sages is Culluca, whose commentary has been published together with the text, etc.

[The original text of Menu with the commentary was first printed by Babu Ram, at Calcutta, in 1813. The splendid and accurate edition of Mr. Haughton followed at London, in 1825. This was in great measure the basis of a third lately published at Paris by M. Loiseleur Deslongchamps; and, lastly, a fourth edition has just appeared at Calcutta, under the authority of the Committee of Public Instruction. TRANSL.]

[20] *Institutes, etc.*, preface, pp. v. vii.

turies to produce similar modifications in the style of the Vedas, so as to become what it is in the Code of Menu; and by consequence he places the latter one thousand two hundred and eighty years before the Christian era. Although we cannot, for obvious reasons, enter into a particular examination of this hypothesis, requiring as it does not merely an acquaintance with astronomy, but a critical knowledge of Sanscrit as spoken at the most distant periods, yet our readers will easily perceive upon what vague and uncertain grounds it rests; and without taking into consideration the supposed analogy existing between the intervals of time required to produce the respective changes in the Sanscrit and Latin, it is evident that these very changes, owing to the most different causes, are sometimes quick and at others slow in their operation; a striking example of which is afforded in the history of the German language.

With regard to the question how far the Hindus have pursued the study of philosophy, it would be impossible to furnish a complete answer with the aid of their writings on this subject alone; and indeed could we do so, the task is more properly within the province of the writers upon philosophy in general. All that we know of the Hindu philosophical Sastras, is confined to a few extracts, for none of them have yet been completely translated. The only one of these treatises which Sir W. Jones studied in the original, and which is commonly ascribed to Vyasa, is short and very obscure, though consisting of some beautifully modulated sentences.[21] The most accurate information on this subject is given in the Ayin Acbari, which treats of nine different schools, and quotes the several writings on which they are respectively founded.[22] The work however itself will only possess a secondary authority in the eyes of an antiquarian who wishes to consult the first and most authentic sources, though it may nevertheless serve to furnish a general notion of Hindu philosophy; and particularly to determine the question whether it be distinct, or derived from the religion of the Brahmans. Now it is scarcely possible to doubt after a perusal of the Ayin Acbari, that the bond of union between Hindu philosophy and religion was as close as the

[20] *Institutes, etc.*, preface, pp. v. vii. [21] Jones's *Works*, vol. i. p. 103.
[22] *Ayin Acbari*, vol. ii. p. 406, etc.

peculiar interests of an exclusive priesthood would allow us to expect, and that consequently the Vedas were as much the real source of the one as they certainly were of the other. This is further proved by the circumstance of the principal school of Hindu philosophy being referred to Vyasa, the compiler of the Vedas and the preceptor of Jaimini, whose work, entitled Vedanta, both in its appellation and contents, gives evident proof of being derived from those holy books.[23] The Upanishads by their mysticism and obscurity afforded exuberant subject-matter for the display of abstract speculation, and of course gave rise to a variety of opinions, which subsequently produced the various sects enumerated in the Ayin Acbari. It is here that the character of the Hindus for profound and subtile investigation, so closely allied to their fondness for a contemplative life, is exhibited in the most conspicuous manner. But this indissoluble connexion subsisting between Hindu philosophy and religion, must at once forewarn us not to expect the same free development of philosophical spirit among the natives of India as among those of the West.[24] The philosophy of the Hindus appears to have taken the same course as the scholastic of the middle ages; it is quite as subtile, and like it attaches a preference to the study of dialectics; while the various schools seem to be founded on distinctions equally minute and refined with those which divided the schoolmen of Europe. The Hindus, nevertheless, have cultivated practical philosophy, and have not altogether neglected that called moral, but their writings of the latter kind appear to contain nothing beyond naked maxims or dogmas enveloped in fable; and up to the present time at least, we have met with no works which deserve a comparison with those of the Grecian moralists.

In the same way that the Vedas are the real source of

[23] Jones's *Works*, vol. i. p. 165. Whoever will compare the respective accounts of Sir William and the *Ayin Acbari*, vol. ii. p. 428, etc., relative to the precepts of Jaimini, will easily see how uncertain must be the judgment which we could venture to pronounce on the philosophical systems of India.

[24] [See Colebrooke's essays on this subject in the *Transactions of the Royal Asiatic Society*, vol. i. pp. 92, 439, 549, where the reader will find ample proof that the philosophers of India allowed themselves as great, if not greater latitude of thought and expression than their brethren of the West; and that their speculations are by no means always in the most orthodox conformity with the Vedas. Transl.]

Hindu philosophy, so are they considered with respect to the other sciences and arts contained in the four Upavedas; that is to say, medicine, music in the larger sense of the term, as comprehending both poetry and dancing, the art of war, and architecture; under which last the mechanical arts in general are included. These are held to be derived immediately from the Vedas.[25] None of the Upavedas have yet been published, and of the above-mentioned arts, music is the only one respecting which we are in possession of learned inquiries drawn from original sources. The essay of Sir William Jones on this subject,[26] which has been translated by Baron Dalberg, and enriched with valuable remarks and additions,[27] will serve to show how nearly the music of the Hindus was connected with their religion. With the same view we need only repeat an observation already made, namely, that one portion of the hymns contained in the Vedas is exclusively devoted to the purposes of singing.

The study of the Sanscrit grammar may also be considered as forming a particular branch of the philosophical system of the Hindus. As in the other departments of science, so in the case before us, the credit of having invented grammar is usually attributed to a single author, named Panini, whose sutras, at least in India, are regarded as the most ancient grammatical treatise extant; and which, in the absence however of any correct data for their opinion, the natives assign to those remote periods when inspired sages appeared on earth as the instructors of mankind in arts and sciences. Panini is said to have been the grandson of Devala, an inspired lawgiver; of his work on grammar we know nothing beyond the account given of it by Mr. Colebrooke.[28] According to this learned scholar, the perfect coherence of all the parts of Panini's work

[25] JONES's *Works*, vol. i. p. 358, On the Literature of the Hindus. The term Upavedas denotes inferior or supplementary Vedas, translated by Sir William *subscriptures*.

[26] SIR W. JONES, On the Musical Modes of the Hindus, *Asiatic Res.* vol. iii. p. 55, etc.

[27] *On the Music of the Hindus*, by BARON DALBERG, 1802; together with a Collection of Indian National Songs.

[28] COLEBROOKE in *Asiatic Res.* vol. vii. p. 202, sq. The grammatical sutras of Panini were published at Calcutta, in the year 1809, but without a translation I believe.

evidently proves it to have been the composition of one person; nevertheless, it seems to imply the pre-existence of other inquiries of the same description, and Panini himself frequently quotes other grammarians who preceded him; and yet the general report in favour of its great antiquity appears to be fully confirmed by an examination of the work itself, for not only has it been commented on by a long series of grammarians belonging to very distant epochs,[29] so that we might in some measure consider it as the general text-book of all the Hindu grammatical compositions extant; but it is still more remarkable for the conciseness and obscurity of its precepts, which must have rendered the addition of commentaries a work of indispensable necessity.[30] It is probable, indeed, that a more accurate acquaintance with the relation in which Panini's rules stand to the language of the Vedas and the later classic poets, may enable us to determine their age with greater certainty.

The study of grammar would naturally be followed by the compilation of dictionaries. The most celebrated of which is the Amara Cosha, by Amara Sinha, who flourished at the court of Vicramaditya.[31] A manuscript copy of this work is preserved in the Royal Library of Paris;[32] and since the whole has been published and translated,[33] we are better able to form some correct opinion of its merits. The Amara Cosha is a vocabulary written in verse, and explaining in seventeen sections, the names of gods, men, the stars, elements, sciences, mountains, rivers, etc.; and is in its turn the subject of numerous commentaries explanatory of the derivation of words, by reducing them to their several primitives.[34]

[29] The most celebrated of these, Patanjali himself, belongs to the fabulous ages. In his *Maha Bhashya*, or great commentary, each of Panini's three thousand nine hundred and ninety-six rules is examined and explained at large.

[30] Colebrooke, l. c. p. 205.

[31] Ibid. l. c. p. 214.

[32] Langlès, *Catalogue des Manuscrits Sanscrits, etc.*, p. 22.

[33] *Amarasinha*, sectio prima, de Cœlo; Roma, 1798. This first part contains chiefly explanations of the names of Hindu gods; whole passages, and sometimes a number of verses, are cited. The entire work was subsequently printed in Bengal, under the title of Cosha, or Dictionary of the Sanscrit Language, with an English interpretation by Colebrooke; Serampoor, 1808.

[34] Colebrooke, l. c. According to Langlès, l. c. p. 25, the number of Sanscrit radicals does not exceed ten thousand. [In general the number of radicals in the ordinary lists is about one thousand seven hundred; as repeated in different classes they exceed two thousand. In Wilson's Dictionary the number is somewhat more than one thousand nine hundred. Transl.]

It has been already remarked in the commencement of this inquiry, what little reason we have for expecting to find any thing like critical history among the Hindus; and yet the subject requires a little more accurate investigation. The meaning we intended to convey in making the above remark, was the fact that Hindu, or in other words Sanscrit literature in general, presents us with no historical composition in the sense in which we commonly understand that expression, considered either as legitimate history or a simple enumeration of events.

With respect to the first of these assertions, it is incontestably true that no historical work has yet been discovered in India; even the pundits themselves have not been able to quote a single exception:[35] would they have omitted to do so had the case been otherwise? or could they possibly have concealed them from the ardent research of British scholars? would not national vanity or a thirst of gain induce them to exhibit these literary treasures were they in existence? Should any doubt however remain on the subject, it will soon be removed when we come to treat of the Hindu epic poetry. It is indeed hardly possible that critical history should ever exist among a people who had no sort of taste for that kind of literature, and consequently held it in little or no estimation. It is not with the soberness of historic truth, but with the meretricious ornaments of poetical fiction, that the Hindus are chiefly concerned; and hence it is that a narrative, to please them, must be directed less to inform the understanding than to captivate and amuse the fancy. To what extent, indeed, the great Indian epic poems may be founded on real matter of fact will appear in the sequel; and even admitting that they are, yet the facts themselves have been so metamorphosed by the poets as to present scarcely any documents available for the purposes of history. It will, therefore, be no exaggeration

[35] In the numerous collection of Sanscrit MSS. belonging to the Royal Library at Paris, there is not one properly historical work. This is expressly asserted by LANGLÈS, *Catalogue des MSS. Sanscrits*, p. 13.

[Mr. Wilson's translation of the Raja Taringini, or History of Cashmir, has clearly demonstrated that regular historical composition was an art not unknown in Hindusthan, and affords satisfactory ground for concluding that these productions were once less rare than at present, and that further exertions may bring more relics to light. See Col. Tod's preface to his *Annals of Rajasthan*, and *Asiatic Res.* vol. XV. TRANSL.]

to assert, that the Hindus never had the least idea of what we term an historic style. Many of the inscriptions, already alluded to,[36] will furnish striking evidence of the truth of our assertion: for in them even the most simple facts, such as a grant of land, for instance, cannot be recorded without putting into requisition the whole apparatus of poetry; and the achievements of princes there mentioned, are set off in such a style of pomp and amplification, as among us would scarcely be allowed even in a poet. Can we, therefore, reasonably expect any thing like critical history from a people with whom prevailed such a taste as this?

Assuming, then, that the Hindus possessed no regular historian, yet surely, like other Oriental nations, they might at least have had their writers of annals. In default of a Polybius, or a Gibbon, the banks of the Ganges might have cherished an Abulfeda, or a Mirchond? We shall certainly not deny the possibility of such an occurrence, though we have as yet heard of no proof in support of the conjecture; and were the case otherwise, can we imagine the Hindus less eager to recommend their annalists to the notice of a foreigner than the Arabians or Persians; we must consequently take it for granted that the pundits are acquainted with no such historian; and if even these learned natives are unable to inform us, where else shall we seek or expect to find any exception? In the mean time, however, we must reserve the further elucidation of this point to the commencement of the following section, where it properly belongs; the more as it can only be determined in any satisfactory manner when we shall have previously discussed the subject of Hindu epic poetry: it will then appear in what sense we must consider the history of this people as nothing more than a poetical history.

The geography of the Hindus bears the same poetical character as their history. They possessed several works in this department of science, some of them composed in Sanscrit, and others in the popular dialects, of which Wilford has given a circumstantial account in the eighth volume of the Asiatic Researches.[37] According to him, many of the

[36] See above, p. 100, the inscriptions cited from the *Asiatic Res.*

[37] *Asiatic Res.* vol. viii. p. 267. An Essay on the Sacred Isles in the West: of which however only the first part, viz. Of the Geographical Systems of the

Puranas, or mythological poems, contain particular sections on geography, which are termed Bhuchanda, (section of the earth,) or Bhuvana Cosa, i. e. the treasure of terrestrial mansions. These are the sources from whence the Hindu geographical knowledge found in books which treat of this subject, is derived.[38] Such treatises are however very rare, as the Brahmans are averse to their being generally circulated. "The people," say they, "have the Puranas, what do they want more?" Even Wilford himself was unable to procure two of the most important, both attributed to a royal hand, the one to Vicramaditya, the other to Munya.[39] The geography of the Hindus, considered in a scientific point of view, may be said to resemble that of the Greeks, which was borrowed from the writings of Homer and Hesiod, or the cyclical poets; though it does not follow that all is a poetical fabrication. The Hindu poets were naturally acquainted with their own country, and much of what appears in their writings, relative to its geography, may be explained on historic principles. Thus we cannot mistake the Holy River of India, the Ganges, with its seven branches of equal sanctity; the countries bordering on its course, especially Magada or Bahar, the scene of Krishna's fabulous history; the Himalaya mountains in the north, the island of Lanca or Ceylon in the south, as well as particular towns, such as Ayodhya or Oude, Canoge, and some others. But the geographical names in Sanscrit are usually very different from the modern appellations, and even the English commentators have been obliged to confess their ignorance of most of them. This circumstance alone is therefore sufficient to involve the ancient geography of India itself in very great obscurity. But as to their ideas respecting countries beyond the limits of their own, which the Hindu geographers

Hindus, is inserted in this volume. WILFORD himself says, p. 269, "With regard to history the Hindus really have nothing but romances, from which some truths occasionally may be extracted, as well as from their geographical tracts." It is, therefore, the more surprising that he should have endeavoured to prove the sacred Indian isles in the West to be—Great Britain! Unfortunately the zeal and assiduity of this writer were guided by no just rules of critical discernment, else what might not his great abilities have accomplished!

[38] "It is true," says WILFORD, "that in addition to the poetic there is a modern system of geography, but this is certainly the worst of the two." l. c. p. 272.

[39] WILFORD, l. c. p. 268.

represent as seven islands or peninsulas [Dwipas], and with regard to their notions as to the form of the earth, the researches and drawings[40] hitherto published on this subject, are quite sufficient to prove them to be founded solely in the imagination of their poets.

The discussion relative to Hindu astronomy and its age, we must leave altogether for professional men to determine, and shall confine ourselves to a mere literary notice of the science. This depends chiefly on the true age to be assigned to the Surya Siddhanta, the principal work on Hindu astronomy, and which the pundits extol as the most ancient of its kind. Its high antiquity however has been disputed by Bentley, who endeavoured to prove that the work in question, which is attributed by those learned natives to Varaha, one of their ancient sages, or at least a contemporary of Vicramaditya, was composed by Varaha Mihira in the eleventh century.[41] This assertion met with an opponent even in England, against whom Bentley defended himself in the eighth volume of the Asiatic Researches, and took that occasion of attacking the age of a considerable portion of Sanscrit literature in general; an argument to which we shall have another occasion of referring. Connected with this subject is the opinion of a learned German scholar,[42] who supposes the Hindus to have derived their astronomical science from the Arabians; this assertion will also require a more particular examination as we proceed.

Our inquiries hitherto have been occupied chiefly with the scientific literature of the Hindus, in assumed contradistinction to their poetical; though it must be observed, that a separation between the two cannot possibly be made with such definitive accuracy as in the case of European literature. All Hindu works of science, not even excepting such as by their subject would seem inapplicable to the purpose, are nevertheless composed in verse. The voca-

[40] *Asiatic Res.* vol. viii. p. 376.

[41] Compare Bentley's essay, On the Antiquity of the Surya Siddhanta, inserted in the *Asiatic Res.* vol. vi. p. 546, and his reply to the criticisms of the Edinburgh Review, in *Asiatic Res.* vol. viii. p. 195, On the Hindu system of Astronomy.

[42] M. Inspector Schaubach, in his two essays, De Astronomici studii apud Indos, etc.; and Ueber die Chronologie der Inder, (On the Chronology of the Hindus,) in Zach's Monatl. corresp. 1831, for Feb. and March.

bulary of Amara Sinha may serve for an example. It is true the Sanscrit contains also a few compositions in prose, but it seems that even these, at least those of any classical reputation, are composed in language nearly approaching to metre, a kind of style which some English scholars have termed *modulated prose*.[43] These modulations are without doubt of a rhythmical, or perhaps of an assonantial character; a point which a more accurate acquaintance with the language itself can only enable us to determine. For the present we may content ourselves with defining the expression poetical literature, to include those compositions which by their very nature and contents, as well as outward form, belong in a legitimate sense to poetry.

The various branches of poetry, such as the narrative and the dramatic, the lyric as well as the didactic, and the apologue, have all flourished in Sanscrit literature, and produced the most excellent fruits. Upon comparing, however, the several kinds with each other, we shall not long hesitate in deciding to which of them the preference belongs. The Hindus themselves award the prize to their great classical epic poems, which they consider as so many branches of their sacred literature. They, as well as the Vedas, are assigned to the most remote periods, and like them are supposed to be of divine origin. To the influence of epic poetry, the civilization of the Hindus is principally owing, as the former was the parent of their mythological system, which in its turn was the chief source of the other kinds of poetry as well as of art. The subject is consequently of very great importance, and deserves our special consideration; but, as a preliminary step, we must here also first determine the limits of our acquaintance with the Hindu epic, and ascertain our capability of forming a just opinion of its merits. Although neither the one nor the other are yet so complete and extensive as we could wish, and indeed as we had reason to expect, still our present knowledge is quite sufficient for enabling us to define its character with some degree of positive certainty.

The literature of the Hindus is rich in epic poetry;[44] and

[43] JONES's *Works*, vol. i. p. 319, 327, as for instance in the Bhagavat, see above, p. 110.

[44] See COLEBROOKE's treatise, On Sanscrit and Pracrit Poetry, *Asiatic Res.*

L 2

their most ancient classic works, of this kind, like the poems of the Ionian bard, have produced a number of imitations. But as in the Greek the Iliad and the Odyssey far outshine all the rest, so do the Ramayana and the Mahabharata eclipse all similar productions in the Sanscrit.[45] Of these two classical works we are more perfectly acquainted with the Ramayana; the two first books of which have been translated into English prose by the learned missionaries of Serampore,[46] and however we might otherwise regret the absence of the charms of verse, we have from that very circumstance less reason to doubt the scrupulous exactness of the translators. And we are the better enabled to give a general notion of the contents of the entire poem, as the

vol. x., in which are given the titles and contents of several epic poems, together with some specimens.

[45] POLIER, in his *Mythologie des Indous*, vol. i. p. 115, incorrectly places the age of the Marcandaya Purana anterior to both these great epics. The subject of this poem is the victory of the goddess Bhavani, mother of three great Deyotas, or, as she is frequently called, Durga, (one of her many names, see MAYER's *Mythological Lexicon*, under *Durga*,) over the giant demon Moisasur [Mahishasura]. LANGLÈS, in his *Catalogue des MSS. Sanscrits*, p. 54, gives an abstract of the one hundred and twenty-four sections composing the Marcandaya Purana, from which it appears that the history of Durga is only an episode of the whole poem. The mistake of Polier however is excusable, on the ground that this episode is circulated in India as a separate and independent poem, under the title of *Chandica*. And yet it is not very easy to tell what induced him to believe it more ancient than the two great classical epics, particularly as it is never placed in the same class with them.

[46] The Ramayuna of Valmiki, in the original Sungskrit, with a Prose Translation and explanatory Notes, by William Carey and Joshua Marshman. Vol. i., containing the first book, Serampore, 1806, 4to, pp. 656. [Vol. ii., containing a part of the second book, Serampore, 1808, pp. 528.] Vol. iii., containing the latter part of the second book, Serampore, 1810, pp. 493. The whole poem consists of seven books, each containing a certain number of sections, the first sixty-four, the second eighty.

A new and critical edition of this poem has just appeared under the title of, Ramayana, id est, Carmen Epicum de Ramæ rebus gestis, poetæ antiquissimi Valmicis opus. Textum, Codd. MSS., collatis recensuit, interpretationem Latinam, et annotationes criticas adjecit Aug. Gul. a Schlegel. Voluminis primi pars prior; Bonnæ ad Rhenum, 1829. This volume contains the text of the first, and a considerable portion of the second book. [Inedited note of the author.]

[The difference between these two editions is such, that many hundred verses occurring in that of Serampore are not to be found in that of Bonn; to say nothing of various other discrepancies. But the versions followed by the learned editor of the latter, are the most ancient, and every way preferable to those of Bengal adopted by the Serampore missionaries. See a detailed account in Schlegel's elegant and erudite preface, p. 22, etc.; the whole of which will amply repay an attentive perusal; while the typographical merit and general appearance of the work itself reflects infinite credit on all parties concerned. TRANSL.]

proper beginning (for the translation commences only with the fifth section) is replaced with an original abstract of the whole, which is probably of later date than the poem itself, though not the less valuable on that account.

The subject of this poem is the victory of the divine hero Rama over Ravana, prince of the Rakshasas or evil genii. It is possible, indeed, to consider the Ramayana as an allegory, representing the triumph of the good principle over the bad; but the question whether an epic poem be allegorical or not, depends less on the subject itself than on the manner of treating it. Now this in the Ramayana is not of an allegorical, but of a purely epic character; at least according to the Hindu notion of an epic poem. The Rakshasas had gotten the upper hand of the benevolent deities, by whom however they could not be overcome, as the latter were bound by a promise of making their adversaries invulnerable. None therefore except a mortal, but a mortal of no ordinary mould, could subdue Ravana. In this emergency the gods address themselves to Vishnu, one of their superiors, praying him to become man. Their petition is granted, but in such a manner that Vishnu divides himself into four parts, and assumes the mortal shape of four brothers, of whom Rama is chief. The principal hero therefore of the poem, is a god-man; he overcomes Ravana and puts him to death, and after this exploit returns back to his celestial mansion accompanied with the subjects whom he had governed in this lower world. Such, in few words, is the chief subject of the Ramayana, while the development and method of handling this simple argument, is so remarkably rich and copious as to suffer little from a comparison in this respect with the most admired productions of the epic muse; an opinion which a perusal of the first book only, as represented in the translation, will abundantly serve to confirm. It begins with a description of the city Ayodhya, formerly the residence of the wise and pious monarch, Dasaratha, in the person of whose son Rama was about to appear. "This city was founded by Menu, the first sovereign who ruled over mankind. Its streets and avenues were admirably disposed, and the principal ones well watered. Its walls of various hues resembled the chequered surface of a chess-board. It was filled with merchants of all sorts, with male and female dancers, with elephants, horses, and chariots. It was decorated with precious stones, filled with riches, amply furnished with all manner of provisions, beautified with temples and palaces, whose lofty summits equalled the mountains, and adorned with baths and gardens thickly planted with mango trees. The air was embalmed with incense, with the perfume of flowers, and the sweet-smelling savour of sacrificial offerings. It was inhabited by the regenerate,[47] profoundly instructed in the Vedas, endowed with excellent qualities, full of sincerity, zeal, and compassion; like the great sages, and perfectly masters of their passions and desires. In Ayodhya there was no covetous person, no liar, no deceiver, no one of an evil or implacable disposition. None of its inhabitants lived less than a thousand years; none of them but left behind a numerous offspring; none gave the Brahmans less than a thousand rupees; none flinched from performing the duties attached to their respective situations; none of them went without earrings, garlands of flowers, necklaces, perfumes, or richly ornamented apparel." Dasaratha their sovereign, already aged nine thousand years, would have been the most fortunate of princes if he had possessed children. With the advice of his Brahmans, he determines to offer the Ashvameda, or solemn sacrifice of a horse. This, which is one of the greatest religious ceremonies of the Hindus, is of such vast importance, according to the prescriptions of the Sastras, that it requires a previous preparation of many years. Hence arises a fresh subject, under the form of an episode, and of all others one most adapted to display the capabilities of the poet. In order to the success of the intended sacrifice it was necessary that a daughter of the king, named Shanta, who had been adopted by another pious prince, should wed a young saint, who led a solitary life in the forests, and occupied himself in studying the Vedas. But it was no such easy matter to draw Rishya Sringa, for that was the name of our youthful hermit, from his retreat. The task was deputed to a number of young maidens, well versed in the arts of seduction, and who were commissioned to entice him in the disguise of sages. Now Rishya Sringa had

[47] The name regenerate, or twice born, is applied to the three superior castes; pre-eminently, however, to the Brahmans.

never yet seen the face of womankind: he hears their song, discovers them dancing through the odoriferous shrubs and creeping plants, conducts them to his cell, and after being intoxicated with the wine they had offered him, is inspired with the flame of mutual passion, is led away captive, and becomes the husband of the lotus-eyed Shanta. On this fascinating picture are displayed all the charms of Hindu poetry. Then follows a description of the great sacrifice, to which princes and Brahmans are invited from afar, and its complete success insures Dasaratha the blessing of male children. This event consequently paves the way for the incarnation of Vishnu, and the poet introduces us to the mansion of Brahma, whither repair the Devas and heavenly sages, who had assisted at the sacrifice, and implore his aid against the impious Ravana. Here Vishnu arrives also. "The illustrious lord of the universe, clad in vestments of yellow, ornamented with golden bracelets, and riding on the eagle Vainataya, like the sun on a cloud, and holding his discus and mace in hand." Yielding to the entreaties of the gods, he promises them an incarnation of eleven thousand years, and the destruction of Ravana, who could only thus be overcome. Vishnu accordingly becomes man, in the persons of the four sons who were born to Dasaratha of his three wives; Rama the eldest of Kausalya, Lakshman and Satrughna of Sumitra, and Bharata the fourth of the beautiful Kaikeyi.[48] Vishnu, however, notwithstanding his incarnation, (so goes the Indian fable,) still retains his divinity in heaven. But at his demand an innumerable host of monkeys are produced as the allies and assistants of Rama in the approaching war. The introduction of monkeys into an epic poem certainly appears rather a strange idea: but their meanness vanishes when we find these animals to be of divine nature. In fact their origin proves them to be children of the gods, produced as they were by the latter at the command of Brahma; supernatural beings endowed with monstrous power, especially their chiefs and princes, Bali, Hanuman, etc.,[49] strong as tigers and lions. We might safely call them satyrs, if the appellation were not likely to convey a wrong idea. The poet, however, by creating such

[48] *Ramayana*, i. 217. [49] Ibid. i. 223—231.

agents as these, has contrived to open a fertile source of incident for the sequel of his poem. The action of the piece now, passing over the infancy of Rama, transports us to the time when he and his brothers were old enough to marry. At this period a certain sage of royal extraction, named Visva Mitra, who by a life of penance had elevated himself to the rank of saint and Brahman, comes into the presence of King Dasaratha. He had made a solemn vow of offering a particular sacrifice, but the opposition of the Rakshasas had hitherto prevented him from doing it in a manner acceptable to the deity.

Now his troublesome assailants could only be subdued by the power of Rama, and therefore he came to implore Rajah Dasaratha that he would allow his son, the youthful hero, to become his assistant. The narrative of the reception of Visva Mitra forms a truly patriarchal scene. The aged monarch cannot resolve to part with his darling child the lotus-eyed Rama; for how should a youth of sixteen be able to cope in battle with those impious demons? but, alas! he was bound by his promise of granting whatever Visva Mitra desired, and the latter severely upbraids him with the infraction of his word. "At the wrath of the sage, the earth quaked, and fear seized even the gods."[50] At this juncture the priest Vasishtha, the monarch's counsellor, interposes his advice, and overrules Dasaratha. The king himself summons Rama and his brother Lakshman, kisses them, and hands them over to Visva Mitra. At their departure, a shower of odorous flowers signifies the approbation of heaven, and the celestial inhabitants themselves celebrate the event with songs of joy. The description of their travels furnishes a new and exuberant subject for the poet's fancy; a number of adventures take place, some of them very artfully connected with the principal story, the enumeration of which occupies almost half the book. In the course of the expedition Rama obtains from Visva Mitra a present of celestial weapons, as in the Iliad Achilles receives the same from Thetis. But the weapons of Rama are of a very different temper, they are every where ready at the beck of the hero, on his pronouncing a certain

[50] *Ramayana*, i. 251.

formula; they are even personified, and hold conversations with their master.[51] Rama now achieves his first exploit by killing the sorceress Taraka. Pursuing their journey the travellers reach the banks of the Ganges, an occasion which serves to introduce a detailed account of its fabulous origin, for Visva Mitra carefully imparts information upon every remarkable object calculated to instruct the mind of the youthful Rama. The Ganges with its seven tributary streams are represented as females, but the fable contains so much of what is revolting to our notions of propriety, that the translators have only ventured a summary allusion to the subject. The holy river descends from the mountains of Himalaya, purifies the world, and goes to replace the waters of the ocean. The Ramayana likewise informs us that the Ganges was of little less consequence to the natives of India than the Nile was to the Egyptians; and that, together with its various branches, it was reputed to be of divine origin; moreover, we find that the transformation of female saints into rivers is no stranger to the genius of Hindu poetry. The thread of our history now brings us near to the marriage of Rama. The travellers having passed the Ganges and journeyed towards the north-east, arrive at the palace of a king named Janaka, who had an enormous bow which no person had yet been able to bend; the monarch was at that moment occupied with the solemnities of a sacrifice; his reception of the new comers is quite as imposing, if not more so, than any recounted in the pages of Homer,; while the distinguishing part of the Hindu character, is the awful veneration with which even royalty itself condescends to address an illustrious Brahman sage. The king, with his hands respectfully joined together, says to the principal of the wise men, Visva Mitra, "O thou godlike, take place among the great sages." Thus invited Visva Mitra sits down; upon which the king, surrounded with his counsellors, and with joined hands,[52] drawing near to him speaks in these words, "O thou heavenly one, to-day am I blessed with the water of immortality! to-day will my sacrifice have the desired effect!"—After which the pious king, with

[51] *Ramayana*, i. 295, 299.

[52] Properly with the palms joined together, which is a sign of devout respect.

a smile of delight, and with hands folded as before, proceeds to inquire, "Who I pray (may eternal prosperity attend thee!) are those noble youths of majestic gait like the elephant, courageous as the tiger and the buffalo, and with large eyes resembling the lotus? who are those heroes radiant in the bloom of youth, of godlike aspect, as if descended from heaven, and armed with daggers?" Upon hearing these words of the mighty king, the sage replies, "They are the sons of Dasaratha, and are come to inquire about thy great bow." The sage having thus spoken, was silent.[53] Now the king had promised that he who could bend this bow should be rewarded with the hand of his daughter, the fair Sita, who had been solicited by all the neighbouring rajahs in vain.

Here follows a long episode[54] recounting the history of Visva Mitra's penances, by means of which the sage, already a king in his own person, though of the Kshatriya caste, was finally successful in being admitted among the Brahmans.

The king then orders the redoubtable bow to be brought; it required the united efforts of eight hundred men to draw the eight-wheeled machine in which it was deposited. With one hand Rama grasps the bow, bends it, and lo! it breaks in the middle, with an astounding noise, like the crash of a falling mountain. It was now determined that Sita should become the bride of the successful hero, while Urmila her sister should wed Lakshman. His father, the king Dasaratha, is invited to the nuptials of his son; and after a four days' journey from Ayodhya, he arrives at the city Mithila, accompanied with his sages, his counsellors, and his army. The marriage is then celebrated, and his two remaining sons also espouse each of them a wife of the family of Janaka, from among his brother's daughters. Rama and his brother with their consorts and the king Dasaratha return home to Ayodhya; the king determines to associate Rama with him in the government, while he sends off his other son, Bharata, to his maternal grandfather, the wise monarch Kekuya; in order to receive under his super-

[53] *Ramayana*, i. 444.

[54] A German translation of this episode is given at the end of Fred. Schlegel's Essay, Ueber die Sprache und Weisheit der Inder (On the Language and Wisdom of the Hindus).

intending care the necessary and suitable education of a prince.

From this concise abstract of the first book we may easily perceive what a variety of incident the poet is furnished with in order to fill up an extended narrative. The table of contents relating to the other books,[55] and which is prefixed to the commencement of the poem, informs us, that the intrigues of Kaikeyi, who was desirous that her own son Bharata should succeed to the throne, prevented the elevation of Rama, and that in consequence Dasaratha was persuaded to banish him for a period of fifteen years. Rama, followed by his wife Sita, and his brother Lakshman, leaves Ayodhya, and retires into a forest, where he lives in penance. But the king soon repents his misguided action, and is unable to bear the loss of his favourite Rama. The complaints of his mother, and the lamentations of the people, unite in distracting the aged monarch; he falls down in a swoon, and immediately expires.[56] His corpse is laid in a vessel filled with oil, and his disconsolate widow Kausalya, the mother of Rama, determines to burn herself with him. In the mean time the state is without a king, and the poet takes occasion to give an animated description of the consequences attendant upon such a loss. The assembled counsellors and Brahmans, with the chief priest Vasishtha at their head, determine on sending messengers to Bharata the son of Keikeyi, who was still at the court of his maternal grandfather, inviting him to mount the vacant throne. The messengers set out, and their journey is described; Bharata, dismissed by his grandfather with rich presents and a numerous retinue, accompanies them home. Then follows a description of the funeral obsequies of Dasaratha; the royal body is clothed in vestments of silk, and being placed on a bier is committed to the flames. Bharata, how-

[55] In the third section. The poem itself commences properly with the fifth.

[56] It is with the death of Dasaratha that the third volume commences.

[This episode was elegantly published in 1826, at Paris, by the celebrated Chézy, under the title of Yadjnadattabada, or The Death of Yadjnadatta, together with a French translation, copious grammatical analysis, notes, and a preface exhibiting a brief view of some of the more striking peculiarities of Sanscrit grammar. The text is beautifully engraved in the Bengali character, and the whole followed by a literal version in Latin by M. Burnouf. It was subsequently edited in the Devanagari character by M. Loiseleur Deslongchamps, in 1829. TRANSL.]

ever, declines accepting the crown, which according to Hindu law belongs of right to the elder brother. Upon this the council of sages and Brahmans resolve to despatch him into the forests in quest of Rama, with the view of proposing him as the successor. Bharata sets out with a splendid retinue, and his travels are described. He passes westward beyond the Ganges, on his way to the residence of a renowned sage, Bharadaraja, who lived in that neighbourhood, and to whom he pays a visit, leaving his attendants and army behind. Bharadaraja, however, who by a course of penitence and devotion had elevated himself to the dignity of a Rishi, insists upon his numerous suite also coming and partaking of the entertainment he should provide for them. A description of the banquet then follows, which in a certain degree is a feast of enchantment; for the power of the saint is so prodigious, that all nature seems to be at his command. Here again is another opportunity of displaying all the richness of the Hindu epic. The rivers and forests appear to bring tribute to this wonderful Bharadaraja: a magnificent palace is raised, furnished with tables, richly decked with provisions of every kind. The princes and sages take their place, and next to them the commander of the army. Celestial music enlivens the scene, while thousands of beautiful damsels and dancing girls are sent by Brahma himself. The whole army prolong the feast until the morning, when, at the command of the sage, the enchantment is dissolved, and every thing returns to its usual order, as if the whole had been no more than the illusion of a dream.[57] Bharata now pursues his journey and arrives at the forest, where he finds Rama, with his brother and Sita, in the guise of penitents. He offers him the sovereignty, but Rama steadily refuses to accept it, until he has completed his engagement of fifteen years' penance. He surrenders to Bharata the royal insignia, the golden slipper,[58] and the umbrella, promising to resume them after the expiration of the above period. Bharata, in consequence, returns to the orphaned city of Ayodhya; he does not, however, stay there, but takes up his resi-

[57] *Ramayana*, iii. 304.

[58] A peculiar kind of high shoe was also in use among the Persians, and considered a mark of royalty.

dence in Nadigrama, from whence he administers the empire in the name of his brother;[59] while Rama with his wife and brother continue their penance in the woods. In the mean time Ravana prince of the Rakshasas conceives a violent passion for the beauteous Sita; and by stratagem and force succeeds in carrying her off to his city of Lanka, situate in the island of that name. The complaints and heroic achievements of Rama fill up the remaining books; he enters into an alliance with Hanuman chief of the monkeys, who engages to go in quest of Sita. Hanuman proceeds to Lanka, obtains an interview with her, and after delivering a message from her lord, hastens back to rejoin him. The grand expedition against Lanka is now undertaken; a bridge is constructed across the sea; the allied armies pass over, and lay siege to the fortress of Lanka. In the description of this war, the poet's imagination seems to have taken its highest flight. The scene of battle is not confined to the surface of the earth, for the hostile armies are represented engaging in the air itself. Rama and Ravana encounter one another on their war chariots; a combat ensues, which makes the earth tremble for seven days, until the prince of the Rakshasas, Ravana, is overthrown. Rama and Hanuman now make their entrance into Lanka, find Sita, and as Rama had thought proper to question her fidelity, she proves her innocence by submitting to the ordeal of fire. Brahma and the other deities appear and give them their benediction. Dasaratha also arrives; and afterwards the whole party repair home to Ayodhya, where no further obstacle remained to the elevation of Rama. He does not, however, continue on earth, but after committing the reins of government to his brother Lakshman, returns with all his people to heaven, his real abode.

The above sketch comprises only the main incidents of the Ramayana, as it would be impossible to unravel the whole contexture of the poem, and its endless variety of fiction, with no better assistance than we can derive from a

[59] Here ends with the second book the translation of the Ramayana. The contents of the remaining five, perhaps the most beautiful of all, are only known to us through a brief summary prefixed at the commencement of the poem.

meagre table of contents. There are many points, therefore, which require a critical investigation.

We can, then, as little doubt the existence of a great epic poem entitled the Ramayana, as we can doubt that there is such a book as the Iliad. The Ramayana, however, is not the only poem known under that title; there are several others[60] which are probably imitations, or, at least, variations of the same principal subject. But the one now before us is distinguished from all the rest by its being the production of Valmiki; and it is the general opinion that his composition is the original upon which the others have been formed. Nevertheless, the question relative to the poet himself, and the history of his poem, is involved in much greater obscurity than the works of Homer. The epoch assigned to Valmiki is very indefinite; he belongs to the same time as Rama himself, and is one of the great Munis or sages, who lived in the society of the gods.[61] In the last book of his poem he introduces himself as speaking in character; he is therefore something more than Homer, in that he is the confidant and familiar acquaintance of the gods themselves. This being the case, how can we reasonably expect any thing like chronological accuracy with regard to his life and works? Yet the Ramayana itself is certainly very ancient, and must have been composed at a time when Hindu poetry, altogether independent, and uncontaminated with foreign alloy, flourished in all its native purity and splendour. But whether the poem in its present state was the immediate offspring of one poet's imagination, or whether it has gradually become what it now is by the incorporation of many successive compositions, cannot be so easily determined. The Ramayana, it is true, exhibits a certain degree of epic unity, though from the frequent intermediate narrations put in the mouth of sages and heroes, the Hindu poem is of a more episodical character than the Greek. But ere we can proceed to offer any general remarks on this subject, it will be necessary first to examine another great heroic poem of the Hindus, the Maha-bharata.

[60] See LANGLÈS, *Catalogue des Manuscrits Sanscrits*, p. 14, where several other poems with this title are enumerated.

[61] He is so described in the first section of the poem.

Our long-cherished expectations of being presented with an English translation of this celebrated work[62] from the pen of Dr. Wilkins, have unfortunately not yet been realized. Only one episode, of moderate extent, the Bhagavad-Gita, has hitherto been translated by him; but this, as it contains a dialogue between Krishna and his pupil Arjuna upon religious subjects, introduced into the body of the Mahabharat, belongs rather to didactic than epic poetry, and under that head we shall have another opportunity of referring to it.

The Mahabharat was translated into Persian by order of the emperor Akbar the Great. In this translation each book is preceded by a short table of contents, which the editor of the Ayin Acbari has rendered into English.[63] Rajah Behrut (Bharata) reigned in the city of Hastnapur, (Hastinapura,) the metropolis of India. From him was descended in the seventh degree Rajah Chutterberi, (Bichitrabirya,) who left behind him two sons. The eldest, Dertrashter, (Dhritarashtra,) who was blind, had a hundred and one sons, called the Coros, (Koravas,) of whom the eldest was named Durjohn (Duryodhana); Pandu, the younger brother of Dertrashter, had five sons, Yudister, Bimsin, Arjun, Nekul, and Seddu (Yuddhishthira, Bhima-Sena, Arjuna, Nakula, Sahadeva); these are called the Pandos (Pandavas). After the death of Pandu his blind brother Dertrashter became king: but his eldest son Durjohn possessed himself of sovereign power, seized hold of the government, and apprehensive lest it should devolve upon the Pandos, he endeavoured to destroy them by setting fire to their dwelling, which had been filled with pitch and other combustible materials. Durjohn believed the Pandos were burnt; however, they contrived to escape, and fleeing through the de-

[62] The title Mahabharata is usually translated "the great war." But according to some writers, Bharata, is either the name of a king from whom were descended the families of the Coros and Pandos, or else the name of a city. Ohsonville, *Bhagavadam*, p. 129; and Sir William Jones, *Works*, vol. vi. p. 443. I have adopted the former interpretation.

[Mr. Wilson in his Dictionary notices a whimsical derivation of this word from Bhara, weight, the poem having been put by the Rishis in a scale and weighed against the four Vedas, which it was found to outweigh, thence its usual prefix of Maha, or great; a special grammatical rule, however, derives it from Bharata, the prince so named, because the war narrated in it occurred amongst his descendants. Transl.]

[63] *Ayin Acbari*, ii. p. 100, sqq. I have added in a parenthesis the Sanscrit form of the proper names as far as they could be ascertained.

sert, took refuge in the city Cumpela. They soon became renowned for their valour and generosity, and Durjohn afterwards resolved to divide his kingdom with them. He gave them one half, including Delhi, and reserved for himself the other, with Hastnapur. But Yudister beginning to distinguish himself, the jealousy of Durjohn was excited; and after inviting the Pandos to a feast, he unfairly won from them in a game at draughts the whole of their possessions. As a last stake, they promised, in case they should lose, to confine themselves for the space of twelve years in solitude, and after that term withdraw into private life. Being again unfortunate, they duly kept their promise; but at their return Durjohn behaved with such cruelty towards them that they flew to arms; and thereupon ensued the great war between the Pandos and the Coros. After a long series of mutual hostilities, a general engagement took place on the lake Kurkhet, which lasted eighteen days; Durjohn was slain, and a complete victory at length secured the throne to the Pandos.[64]

[64] The Mahabharat is divided into eighteen cantos, or books, (Parvas,) which, according to the Index prefixed to the Persian translation, contain the following particulars.—Book I. History of the families of the Pandos and Coros. II. Yudister sends his brothers into all parts to make conquests. The Coros arrange a sacrificial feast in order to play at draughts. Preparations for the same. III. The Pandos, having lost at play, retire into the desert, where they continue twelve years. Enumeration of events which happened in the mean time. IV. The Pandos remove from the desert to the city of Behrut, and conceal themselves there. V. They are discovered, and the war breaks out. General engagement on the lake Kurkhet. VI. Combats of heroes. The first ten days of the battle several of Dertrashter's sons are slain. VII. Durjohn holds a council of war. Derna becomes commander-in-chief, but falls in battle five days afterwards. VIII. Events of the two following days. Kurren is appointed chief; one of the greatest heroes of his time. He puts Yudister to flight, but is killed by Arjun. IX. Schul succeeds to the command of the army. His exploits and death. Durjohn hides himself. He is discovered by Bakiken. His death. This is the eighteenth day of the battle. The Pandos are at length victorious. X. Account of the last events of the war. Eight only of the Pandos survive. XI. Lamentations of the women on both sides for the loss of their respective friends. The mother of Durjohn curses Krishna. XII. Acts of Yudister after the victory. He wishes to abdicate, but is dissuaded by Vyasa, Krishna, and Bikum. This book contains many sublime religious and moral precepts, and rules of good government. XIII. Yudister wishes to retire into solitude, but Vyasa dissuades him. XIV. Preparations for the feast of Ismid. XV. Dertrashter and Kundehary, the mother of Durjohn, and Kuaty, the mother of the Pandos, go into retirement. XVI. Extinction of the race of the Yadus and other events. XVII. King Yudister and his brothers retire into solitude in the Himalaya mountains, and the former abdicates the throne. XVIII. Death of the Pandos. Yudister and his brothers mount

The index from which the above abstract is taken appears to give a general though very succinct view of the whole poem. From an additional notice we learn, that altogether it consists of 100,000 distichs, (slokas,) of which 24,000 are occupied in describing the war between the Pandos and the Coros, while the remaining, and of course by far the greatest portion, comprises episodes and digressions. The index is apparently confined to the mere history of the war and the events which followed it. This is, in fact, the principal subject of the poem, to which all the rest is subordinate; and it is not improbable that the Persian prose version of the Mahabharat may turn out to be merely an abridgement instead of a translation of the Hindu original. What indeed may surprise is the fact that the index makes no allusion to the influence of the gods; except once in the eleventh book, where Krishna is unexpectedly introduced upon the scene: may we not, therefore, reasonably consider this index to the Mahabharat to be an imperfect compilation?[65] What appears strongly to confirm this supposition, is a comparison of the extracts of the same poem given by Polier, in his Mythology of the Hindus. A great portion of this work is borrowed from the Mahabharat; but here arises a considerable difficulty, because the author having also mentioned the Bhagavat Purana as another source from whence he derived his information, it is almost impossible to determine accurately what belongs to the one or the other of these poems. The Bhagavat Purana contains chiefly the history of Krishna, which, however, is also interwoven with the thread of the Mahabharat, as we shall see presently, and as the former

up into heaven.—I am indebted for a translation of this Index to my learned friend Professor Mitscherlich of Berlin. It agrees almost exactly with the accounts given in the *Ayin Acbari*, ii. p. 100, and consequently serves to confirm their general correctness.

[65] Prefixed to the Mahabharat is a proem, relative to the inauguration of the poet Vyasa, by Brahma and Ganesha, and of which the second part contains also a general index to the poem. But in the English translation of this proem, inserted in the Annals of Oriental Literature, P. I. II. III., this part is altogether left out. *The chapter of contents is here omitted, being of a nature not to be translated.* II. p. 282.—The scarcely intelligible Latin translation of the proem in Frank's Chrestomathia, P. I. p. 122—147, gives only the first half of the English version, and consequently nothing of the index. Had Mr. Frank made choice of this instead of the other, he would have done us some service. In default of the index, therefore, we must be content with the other sources of information alluded to in the text.

poem itself bears witness.[66] Although the war of the Pandos and Coros is properly the subject, yet Krishna, or rather an incarnation of Vishnu under that name, is no less the principal hero of the Mahabharat: he is the defender and assistant of his relations the Pandos; and it is under his guidance, and through his power, that they are victorious. And consequently the legitimate object of the poem would seem to refer rather to the appearance of Vishnu upon the earth in the character of Krishna, and to the victory which by his means the good princes obtained over the bad. It is easy to see how the latter subject, properly speaking, has given the Mahabharat its poetic form, an observation which will appear still more evident from the following extract of the poem itself.[67]

The dominion of the bad spirits had become so excessive, that the earth could no longer endure their violence. Assuming, therefore, the form of a cow, she presents herself before Indra, the lord of the firmament, to complain of her wrongs: he directs her to Siva, who in his turn sends her to Vishnu. Vishnu repairs with her to the temple of Brahma the invisible, on the borders of the sea of milk, and is there commanded to become man, or to appear as an incarnation under the name of Krishna, in the city Matra, (Mathura,) situate on the banks of the Jumna, and in the house of Bosdajo and Deyoki. This Bosdajo was of the family of Yadu, son of Jayat, who had formerly reigned over the land (of India), and from whom were also descended the two branches of the Coros and the Pandos, who were now disputing the succession to the throne. This paves the way for a description of the genealogical descent of the family, which occupies the first book of the poem; and as it embraces the whole circle of Hindu mythology, serves to furnish the poet with a rich variety of subject-matter. With this is intimately connected the birth of Krishna, which, as one may easily suppose, could not take place unattended with miracle, in order to escape the persecutions of Kansa, to whom it had been prophesied that the eighth son of that marriage (and this was Krishna) would

[66] *Bhagavadam*, par OBSONVILLE, p. 303. Bhagavat is one of the surnames of Krishna.

[67] POLIER, *Mythologie des Indous*, vol. i. p. 395, etc.

take away his life. To prevent the accomplishment of this prediction, the whole empire of Daints, or evil genii, was put in motion, but all to no purpose. Even in infancy Krishna performed the most surprising actions; and the history of his youth, his education, and sojourn among the Gopis, or milkmaids, and his adventures with them, opens a wide field of display for the poet's imagination. When grown up, Krishna returns to Matra and slays Kansa, who had put his relations into confinement. The family of Yadu then governed in Hastnapur on the Jumna; and of the line of Pandu there were five princes, all born under circumstances of wonder, and all of them extraordinary beings. Of these, Yudister was the most just, Bhim the strongest, Arjun the most expert archer, Shekdajo the wisest, and Nakul the most handsome. They were not, however, in possession of the throne, for it had been usurped by the tyrant Durjohn of the house of the Coros, who having fraudulently invited the Pandos to play with him, had managed to cheat them out of their kingdom; since which he had never ceased to oppress and persecute them by all the means in his power. Krishna, apprized of the situation of his relatives by a confidential friend whom he had sent to Hastnapur, engages to assist them. In the mean time, Matra was attacked by the Rajah Jerasind, (Ugrasena,) the father-in-law of Kansa, who had solemnly sworn to avenge his death. But he was overcome by Rama the brother of Krishna, and would have been slain, had not the latter vouchsafed him his life. Jerasind, however, took up arms a second time, and with more formidable preparations than before. Then Krishna, to insure the inhabitants of Matra from all danger, summoned up an island from the middle of the ocean, on which by his order the architect of heaven, Biscurma, (Visvakarma,) constructed the wonderful city Dwarka, "whose walls and pavements glittered with gold, silver, and precious stones; its ramparts were formed of solid gold, and the houses of pure crystal. Vessels of gold adorned the portals of every mansion. The bazaars were decked with splendid stalls, the gardens were shaded with trees of Paradise, and refreshed with the waters of immortality. A multitude of temples raised their towering summits, and the smoke of incense from the altars perfumed the

M 2

air." To this wonderful city Krishna transports the inhabitants of Matra, where they remain in perfect security. Here also he places his first wife, Rukmini, who like her lord is of more than human origin, being an incarnation of his celestial consort Lakshmi. After this Krishna proceeds to Hastnapur to stand as mediator between the Pandos and Durjohn. The tyrant, however, has recourse to artifice, and prepares a banquet, to which he invites the Pandos, intending to burn them with the house where they are all assembled. But they escaped this violent death, (though Durjohn believed them to be destroyed, as he had confounded them with other strangers,) and withdrew into the solitude of a deep forest, where no one was acquainted with the place of their concealment except Krishna. The heroic exploits achieved by the Pandos, though unknown, during their residence in the forest; the marvellous city Dwarka and its destinies, the machinations and attempts of Durjohn and the Pandos respectively against each other, the assistance afforded to the latter by Krishna and his brother, the final war, and the great battles fought during its continuance, which terminated in the overthrow of Durjohn; all these particulars furnish an inexhaustible source of descriptive embellishment to the poet. He then concludes with an account of the absorption of the wonderful city Dwarka into the ocean from whence it arose, the Pandos recover their dominion in Hastnapur, and Krishna ascends up into his heavenly and original mansion of Vaikuntha.

Whatever judgment we may be disposed to pronounce on the merits of the poem before us, imperfect as that must necessarily be, when we are not even possessed of a simple prose translation, and of course can form no idea of its majestic style and metrical character, yet it will scarcely be possible to deny the Mahabharat to be one of the richest compositions in epic poetry that was ever produced.

Although, however, the summaries and indexes before mentioned are insufficient for enabling us to form a correct opinion of the whole poem, yet with regard to the subordinate parts, two episodes, taken from the Mahabharat, have not long ago been published in the original Sanscrit, and accompanied with an excellent translation, of which the Bhagavadgita, already alluded to, belongs to didactic, and the other (Nala) to epic poetry; our present business is therefore only with the latter, for which we are indebted to the labours of Bopp, the first scholar who fathomed the depths of Sanscrit literature in Germany.[68] We are now eagerly expecting the fulfilment of his promise of editing several other episodes from the great poem, in the same manner, which will enable us to pronounce a more determinate judgment on the merits of the whole. The episode of Nala is taken from the third book of the Mahabharat. When the Pandos, after having been cheated out of their kingdom by the unfair play of Durjohn, had retired into the forests, the sage Vrihasdana recounts to the eldest of the brothers, Yudhishthir, in order to console him, the history of Nala, who had met with a similar misfortune, but who nevertheless regained his kingdom in the end. Nala king of Nishadha, inflamed with the bare accounts of the beauty of Damayanti, the daughter of Bhima king of Vidharba, had fallen violently in love with her. A golden-winged swan[69] proposes to act as his ambassador. He accordingly despatches the bird with a message to Damayanti; and the princess, surrounded with her women, receives it with great complacency. In the mean while the king her father had invited the neighbouring princes and monarchs to Vidharba, in order that she might select a husband from among their number. Thither also Nala himself hastens to repair. The

[68] Nalus, Carmen Sanscritum e Mahabharata; edidit, Latine vertit, et adnotationibus illustravit Franciscus Bopp, Londini, 1819, pp. 216. The notes are chiefly critical. [Professor Bopp has since published four other episodes of the Mahabharat, under the title of "Diluvium cum tribus aliis Mahabharatæ episodiis præstantissimis, 1829." This publication contains the Deluge, so interesting to compare with the Mosaic account, the Mythic history of Savitri, the Rape of Draupadi, and Arjun's journey to Indra's Heaven, of which last, however, only the latter half is given. Inedited note of the author.]

[69] [The original word has usually been rendered by the very unpoetical term "goose!" but the Hansa of the Hindus bears little or no resemblance to that plebeian fowl. There are three distinctions: the Rajah-hansa, (or royal Hansa,) with a milk-white body and deep-red beak and legs; this is the Phœnicopteros or Flamingo: the Mallikaksha-hansa, (or Hansa with eyes like the Mallika-flower,) with brownish beak and legs; and the Dhartarashtra-hansa, (or Hansa of Dhritarashtra,) with black beak and legs: the latter is the European swan, the former a variety. It is somewhat remarkable, that the Egyptian Nile-Ibis (*Ibis religiosa* of Cuvier) is still called Abu Hansa (Father Hansa) by the Arabs, though it essentially differs from the embalmed specimens of the ancient Ibis, which correspond more with the Hindu bird. See *Asiatic Res.* vol. xiv. p. 29. CRAWFURD'S *Sketches of Hindusthan*, p. 150. SYMES' *Travels*, p. 363. TRANSL.]

report, however, of Damayanti's beauty had even reached the ears of the gods, for Indra too and some others enter the lists of competition. To mislead the princess they assume the form of Nala; but Damayanti contrives to recognise her lover, and, rejecting the celestial rivals, places the bridal garland on his shoulder. The gods approve her choice, load her with presents, and return back again to heaven. Damayanti, accordingly, becomes the wife of Nala, and bears him a son and a daughter. But unfortunately the gods on their return meet with two Rakshasas, Dwapara and Cali, who had also intended to present themselves among the suitors of Damayanti. They learn from Indra that they are too late, and Cali therefore determines to be revenged. He directs his route towards Nishad, where Nala and his spouse were enjoying the fruits of their happy union, and engages Pushkar the brother of Nala to invite him to a game at draughts, while he himself inspires the luckless prince with an uncontrollable desire for play. In vain Damayanti endeavours to withhold her husband; to no purpose does she send her two children out of the way to their relations. Nala has lost every thing, even to the clothes on his back: the latter are actually taken from him. But his faithful consort not only follows him in his distress and exile, but also shares her raiment with him. All this, however, could not satisfy the vengeance of Cali. He disorders the understanding of Nala, so as to make him desert his unfortunate Damayanti while sleeping in the forest! Who can describe her waking despair, and her wanderings in search of her bewildered lord! She meets with a caravan of merchants, but they can give her no assistance; for in the night they are attacked by a herd of wild elephants, and the whole caravan is torn in pieces. Damayanti alone manages to escape destruction, and makes her way to a city, where she is recognised by the mother of King Chadir, her relation, and is sent home to her parents at Vidharba. In the mean time Nala, pursuing his route through the forest, arrives at the residence of Carcothaca king of the serpents, who, giving him another form, sends him to Ayodhya in the character of a charioteer, in order to be instructed by Ratoparna in the art of playing at draughts. In requital Nala gives his instructor lessons in his own assumed art; and in process of time is enabled by this accident to win back the whole of what he had lost, and to recover possession of his wife, his children, and his throne.

Remarkable as this episode appears for inventive merit, it is not at all inferior in point of style; and some passages, especially in the first part, would do credit even to Homer himself.

The war of the Pandos and Coros seems to have furnished as abundant subject-matter to Hindu poets, particularly the epic, as the Trojan war did to the Greek. Several other epic poems, of which we know scarcely any thing at present beyond their names, have all been drawn from the same storehouse, such as the one entitled Magha, which is founded on the death of Sisupala, slain by Krishna in the same war; and that called Kiratarjuniya, which celebrates the victory of Arjuna over Duryodhama, by the aid of celestial weapons.[70] I have considered it necessary to enter into some detail with regard to these poems, in order to give greater effect to the ensuing remarks on the subject of Hindu epic poetry in general, and its influence on the civilization of the people. In comparing their epopee occasionally with that of the Greeks and the moderns, it is by no means my intention to draw any parallel between the two, but merely to throw greater light on the original character of the former.

The action of the Hindu epos is placed in an age far antecedent to all historical computation. The Mahabharat is supposed to be less ancient than the Ramayana;[71] and indeed it describes a later, that is, the eighth incarnation of Vishnu; but according to the pundits, the war of the Pandos and Coros, together with the poem, whose subject it forms, ought to be referred to the 105th year before the commencement of the Cali Yug,[72] (their present era,) an opinion which would therefore place them both in the fabulous times. In this sense the composition of the Ma-

[70] Colebrooke, in *Asiatic Res.*, vol. x. p. 405, etc. [The Magha Cavya consists of twenty cantos, and was published in the original Sanscrit, first by Professor Wilson at Calcutta in 1812, and subsequently by two learned natives, accompanied with a commentary, in the year 1815. Transl.]

[71] According to a passage in Polier, vol. i. p. 579, it would appear that the Mahabharat actually contains allusions to the Ramayana.

[72] *Ayin Acbari*, vol. ii. p. 99.

habharat has been usually attributed to Vyasa, who belongs to the same period.[73] What proportion, however, of the episodes, and other subordinate pieces, are really from his pen, can only be determined with some degree of probability, when we possess the entire poem itself. As to its great age, it will be impossible to entertain the least doubt on the subject, after having remarked that the ancient rock temples are ornamented with sculptured representations mostly borrowed from that source. The Mahabharat and the Ramayana determine the character of the Hindu epos, and to a certain degree also that of the whole range of national poetry. What constitutes their peculiarity, is the fact that they do not confine themselves exclusively to subjects purely human. The personages whom they introduce upon the scene are either absolutely supernatural beings, or, when they appear in human shape, are men of no ordinary kind. The Hindu system of religion has many ways of approximating gods to men, and of elevating men to the rank of gods. The illustrious sages, the Rishis and the Munis, who have purified themselves by continual study of the Vedas, by meditations in solitude, and by a long course of penance, are on a level with the Devas, and not unfrequently even superior to them. They are placed in the same heaven which is the abode of Indra, lord of the firmament, Siva, and Vishnu, to whose court and attendants they belong; they can even arrive at the high rank of Mukti, and enjoy the most perfect happiness in an intimate union with the deity himself. Another still more remarkable characteristic of the poetry of the Hindus is the incarnation of their divinities; which is, as it were, the very foundation of their epopee, and absolutely necessary for maintaining its essential form. These incarnations consist in making the superior and inferior Devas and Devanies assume for a definite period the form of man, be naturally born, and pass through all the vicissitudes of a terrestrial life, in order to attain a certain object, which was only attainable by these means. The ever playful fancy of the Hindus often treats this part of their mythology in a very complicated and artificial manner. The divinities, though in human shape,

[73] See above, p. 120—150.

continue nevertheless to preserve their heavenly relations; as Vishnu, during his appearance on earth under the form of Krishna, was still residing in his celestial abode of Vaikuntha. The same divinity also appears under various human forms at the same time, and while his first incarnation is going on, a second may have already commenced. These monstrous productions of Hindu imagination may no doubt offer their weak side to European criticism; but they are notwithstanding the grand lever of the national poetry, and indeed altogether indispensable in the epic; for it is only by such means that the superior beings of Hindu mythology can be made available for the purposes of the epopee. It depends upon the poet to give them what shape he pleases; and here we may remark, that the expression used above, viz. incarnation, as implying the assumption of a human form, is too limited in that sense for conveying the whole of what is meant by the term. The Hindu deities are not all confined to manifestations of themselves, exclusively human. They occasionally appear in the shape of animals. Many of the characters introduced by the poet, such as Hanuman leader of the monkeys, Yamvent king of the bears,[74] Garud prince of the eagles, and a hundred others, are all incarnations of this kind. It is easy to see how this must have altered the whole character of Hindu poetry, and that a neglect of the purely human form must have been the necessary consequence. Divine personages appear also in the Greek epos, and are represented as exercising an influence upon human destiny; but they appear there only in a subordinate capacity, or rather, to use a technical expression, as forming the machinery of the poem. In Hindu poetry, on the other hand, especially in the Ramayana, the case is exactly the reverse. Those superior beings are here the principal characters upon whose destinies the whole action of the epos turns; and even when simple mortals enter upon the scene, it is always in a subordinate relation to the former. Should any of them indeed be called upon to play a distinguished part, the poet almost in every case takes advantage of his discretionary power of approximating them to the rank of divine beings. We might here ven-

[74] Polier, vol. i. p. 579.

ture an observation which naturally suggests itself, that, considered in the above point of view, the Hindu epos has a greater resemblance to the religious poetry of the Germans and the English than to the Greek, with this difference, however, that the poet of India has a wider range afforded his imagination than the latter. Not confined to the single personification of the one eternal and invisible being, he can introduce at pleasure among the characters of his poem an innumerable crowd of Devas and Devanies, which again have not the monotonous uniformity attached to our notions of angelic personages, whether good or evil, arising from their want of sex, and the perfect moral excellence or depravity inseparable from their nature. Nevertheless, a certain degree of resemblance between the epic poetry of the Hindus and that of the English and the Germans, particularly the latter, is still incontestable ; and is so much the more curious, as the two kinds must have been formed and developed in complete independence of each other. May we not be allowed to conjecture that during a separation of some thousand years, admitting the former connexion of these nations, they have mutually preserved that sentiment of the divine and the heavenly which afterwards burst forth in their respective epic writers at the same time with the rise of their national poetry? And may we not suppose that Vyasa and Klopstock, Valmiki and Milton, though far removed from each other by the longest intervals of space and time, were nevertheless animated by the same spirit?

That neglect of the purely human character, which we have just noticed among the Hindu epic writers, would seem to explain certain other striking peculiarities of their epopee. The Hindu divinities, for instance, could never represent the perfect exemplar of corporeal beauty, as those of the Greeks did in all their principal modifications. The poet of India, it is true, allows some of them a general share in this privilege, but then he as little scruples to assign them attributes which are altogether incompatible with the true notion of purely human beauty. The blue colour of Vishnu, the many arms and heads with which other deities are represented, and a number of similar deformities, quite foreign to the mythology of Greece, all serve to confirm the truth of our observation. For the same reason it would appear further, that the Hindu epic poets themselves never knew how to draw the exact line of distinction between the simply wonderful and the outrageously extravagant. Where, indeed, could they draw it, as long as they had to deal with personages of such an extraordinary character, and furnished with such supernatural powers? The prodigious in every shape appears to be their peculiar object of search, even in cases where, according to our notions, it might very easily be dispensed with. In fine, the epic poetry of the Hindus, notwithstanding its rich luxuriance, is upon the whole less calculated to move the passions than ours, inasmuch as we are most strongly affected by purely human sympathies; though it is not on that account altogether without some scenes which are truly pathetic and affecting. But of all the various characteristic marks discoverable in Hindu epic poetry, the most sensible, and the most generally prevailing one, is the influence of a sacerdotal caste. Not only is the principal subject borrowed from religion, but the whole circle of the poem itself turns upon religious images and allusions. Whatever age we may attribute to the Ramayana and Mahabharat, yet it is pretty certain that the epic poetry of the Hindus could only have been developed at a period of time when the Brahman caste was already flourishing in all its splendour. Every thing therein seems calculated with the view of aggrandizing that caste, and this too not always in the most delicate manner possible. Were it allowable to speak of dates, in a case where chronology is quite out of the question, I should be inclined to refer the origin of this poetry to the time when, according to Hindu traditionary report, the sacerdotal caste had obtained the victory over the Kshatriyas, or warrior caste, and consequently, too, over the Rajahs, who belonged to the latter. The profound reverence with which the Brahmans are treated by kings themselves; the limits assigned to regal authority by religion; the scrupulous care to avoid offending a member of that holy order; are all capable of immediate explanation when referred to this source. But, above all, we must not omit noticing the terrible effect attributed to a Brahman's curse, which, sooner or later, was sure to overtake its object. This again was a powerful engine in the hand of the poet, and one which he did not fail to make use of; while at the same time it tended to increase and maintain the influence of the priests themselves. The religious character of this poetry gives it also an air of peculiar dignity, which, though it does not indeed absolutely exclude all notion of the comic, nevertheless admits it but sparingly and seldom.[75] The personages introduced observe towards each other, and especially towards the Brahmans, a kind of ceremonial, both in their behaviour and in their language, which has some resemblance to the dignified intercourse of Homer's heroes.

The introduction of supernatural beings would occasion serious embarrassment to the epic poet of India, as he felt himself under the necessity of assigning them limited powers both of mind and body; and it was therefore to obviate this inconvenience that he even made his incarnate deities amenable to the laws of fate.[76] Whenever it is destined that a certain event shall take place, at a certain time and under such and such circumstances, the gods themselves dare not attempt to counteract the fulfilment; which would, moreover, be to no purpose if they did. Another contradiction, arising from the assignment of limited knowledge to these superior beings, was very ingeniously removed by substituting an imaginary film, called Maya, or illusion, before their eyes, which prevents their seeing into the future. When this is withdrawn, the incarnate god immediately discovers the most hidden relations of things, and all futurity lies open before him.

In fine, with all these national peculiarities, the epic poetry of the Hindus, nevertheless, bears evident marks of that fabulous story-telling character so generally prevalent in all Oriental compositions. Most of the episodes, although artificially connected with the main thread of the narrative, may yet, however, be detached, and considered as so many independent tales by themselves, as the Ramayana sufficiently proves; and so no doubt would the Mahabharat, were we able to procure a translation of it. This very circumstance rendered the Hindu epic poetry so popular; for it lived not merely written on palm leaves, but spoken in

[75] See a proof of this in POLIER, vol. ii. p. 42, 43.
[76] *Ramayana*, iii. 165; POLIER, vol. i. p. 605; vol. ii. p. 243.

the mouths of all men. The productions of Valmiki and Vyasa, like those of the Mæonian bard, were originally intended for the public recitation of separate pieces, as indeed is the case at the present day.[77] And in exact proportion to the degree of respect and liberality which they every where strictly enjoin towards the Brahmans, so would it be the interest of the latter to make them as completely national as they could. Ought we, then, to be surprised at the powerful influence which the great epic poems of the Hindus have exercised upon the popular religion, upon arts and other branches of poetry—in one word, upon the whole civilization and intellectual development of the nation itself? Can we wonder that the Hindus should place the Ramayana and the Mahabharat immediately by the side of the Vedas?

Next to these great poems rank the Puranas, which also make a part of the Shastras, a general term under which the Brahmans include all their sacred writings.[78] Eighteen of these Puranas are enumerated, of which the last only is known to us, through an imperfect translation. Of the others, we possess little beyond the summary notices to be found in the catalogue published by Hamilton and Langlès of the Sanscrit manuscripts contained in the Royal Library at Paris. Sir William Jones has given a list of the eighteen Puranas; but upon comparing it with the account of M. Langlès, we can discover no kind of agreement between the two, even in the titles themselves.[79]

[77] According to Father PAULINO, (*Gram. Samscrd.* p. 70,) portions of the Ramayana were still sung in his time before the doors of the temples, to the assembled multitude.

[78] The signification of the word Shastras will be found in SIR W. JONES'S *Works*, vol. i. p. 361, "On the Literature of the Hindus," and is equivalent to *divine commandments.* But as it is not precisely agreed upon the number of those books which must be considered as of divine origin, the term Sastras, or Shastras, is consequently used in various limitations by different writers. According to Sir W. Jones, the Vedas, Vedangas, Upavedas, Dhermas, Dersanas, and the Puranas, together make up the six great Shastras. In the Ramayana it is frequently said of a person that "he was learned in the Vedas, Vedangas, and Shastras." See, for example, vol. i. p. 220.

[79] Names of the Puranas, according to SIR W. JONES, *Works*, vol. i. p. 360, are: 1. Brahma Purana. 2. Padma. 3. Brahmanda. 4. Agni. (These four he supposes to relate to the creation.) 5. Vishnu. 6. Garuda. 7. The transformations of Brahma. 8. Siva. 9. Lingam. 10. Nareda. 11. Scanda. 12. Marcandeya. 13. Bhavishya. (These nine treat of the attributes and power of the divinities.) 14. Matsya. 15. Varaha. 16. Kurma. 17. Varena. 18. Bhagavat Purana. Of these the catalogue of Langlès only gives Nos. 1, 2, 4, 5, 8, 9, 10, 11, 12, 14, (which is there designated as the first Pu-

The Puranas are mythological poems, in the more extended signification of the term, as comprehending not merely the fabulous histories of the gods, but also a variety of precepts,[80] which are the sources of the popular religion, of history, geography, and other sciences, as far, indeed, as we can expect to meet with science in a work on mythology. "Each Purana," observes Mr. Colebrooke,[81] "treats of five different subjects, viz. cosmogony, or the Hindu doctrine of the creation and renovation of the world; the genealogies of gods and heroes; chronology, according to the fabulous system of the people; and an heroic history, describing the exploits of demi-gods and heroes." Although this opinion is, perhaps, too generally expressed, yet it is certain that the principal subjects alluded to by him are contained in the Puranas, and it is not without some reason that he compares them to the cosmogonies and theogonies of the Greeks, and even attributes to them greater luxuriance and variety.

The Matsya Purana,[82] which is regarded as the first and most important of all, commences with a dialogue between Menu and Vishnu on the creation of the universe, of the gods and demons; it also contains a history of the kings, children of the sun and moon, descriptions of several feasts in honour of various divinities, certain chapters on the habitations of the gods, and different parts of the earth; a history of Parvati, the wife of Siva; the war between the Devas and Rakshasas, etc.

The Brahma Purana[83] comprises, in four sections, a copious Hindu theogony; but owing, perhaps, to some omission in the Parisian manuscript, it wants the genealogy of the kings, which, according to Hamilton, forms an essential portion of every Purana.

The Agni Purana,[84] one of the largest in the collection, is

rana,) and No. 18: instead of the missing Nos. 3, 6, 7, 13, 15, 16, 17, we have the three following, Kalika Purana, Vayu, and Narasinha, the contents of which are not indicated. Sometimes, though the arrangement is by no means general, the two great epic poems already described are also reckoned among the Puranas.

[80] The Puranas, or Hindu Mythologies, by COLEBROOKE, *Asiatic Res.* vol. ix. p. 290. Although certainly used for purposes of instruction, the Puranas are by no means, properly speaking, didactic, as some writers have endeavoured to make them.

[81] *Asiatic Res.* vol. vii. p. 202, not.

[82] LANGLÈS, *Catalogue des Manuscrits Sanscrits*, p. 58.

[83] Ibid. p. 36.

[84] Ibid. p. 44.

divided into three hundred and fifty-eight chapters, and may be considered as an abridgement of all the science, legislation, and medicine of the Hindus. Some other Puranas, on the other hand, such as those of Siva[85] and the Lingam,[86] are almost exclusively dedicated to the history of certain gods; or, as the Marcandeya Purana,[87] to the lives of renowned saints, devotees, and hermits.

Of the Kalika Purana we have nothing more than a translation of one section, relative to animal sacrifices, among which we find even those of human beings enumerated.[88]

The Bhagavat Purana,[89] the last of all, is at present, however, the only one of which we possess an entire, though very imperfect translation.[90] Its principal subject is the fabulous history of Krishna, who among his many surnames bears the one of Bhagavat, though it also contains a variety of information on other topics. "I should like to know," said King Parikyita to the wise Suka, son of Vyasa, "in what manner the soul is united to the body? How Brahma came into existence? How he created the world? How he recognised Vishnu and his attributes? What time is, and what the respective ages of mankind and the world? How the soul is absorbed into the godhead? What the dimensions and magnitude of the universe? Of the sun and moon, of the stars and the earth? How many kings have ever reigned in the world? What is the difference between the several castes? What are the various forms assumed by Vishnu? What are the three principal powers? What is the Vedam? What is virtue, and good works? What is the object of all these things?"—I considered it useful to select the above passage, in order to give the reader some notion of the contents, and the variety of subjects treated of in the Puranas.[91]

[85] LANGLÈS, *Catalogue des Manuscrits Sanscrits*, p. 49.
[86] Ibid. p. 29. [87] Ibid. p. 58.
[88] *Asiatic Res.* vol. v. p. 371.
[89] *Bhagavadam, ou Doctrine Divine ouvrage Indien canonique (par* OBSONVILLE). Paris, 1788. The translation is not immediately from the original Sanscrit, but from a Tamul version. According to Hamilton, it is merely an abridgement, of which the beginning is tolerably correct, but the remainder swarms with mistakes of every kind. LANGLÈS, *Catalogue*, p. 2. [Recent discoveries have proved that this so-called translation merits no confidence whatever. FR. TRANSL.]
[90] *Bhagavadam*, p. 49.
[91] The twelfth and last chapter of the Bhagavat contains a summary trans-

The Puranas occupy an intermediate space between epic and didactic poetry. They resemble the first in containing a great number of mythological fables; but as they are altogether devoid of that unity of action which prevails in the Ramayana and Mahabharat, notwithstanding the vast collection of episodes inserted in the latter, they cannot possibly be ranked in the same class. Their principal object is to convey instruction, and in this point of view they closely approximate to didactic poetry, and the resemblance is increased by the form of dialogue, which is their predominant feature, as they usually represent one of the great sages imparting instruction by way of answer to the inquiries of his diligent and attentive disciples. It is this circumstance which renders the Puranas so well adapted for being read in the schools of the higher castes, and is the reason why they are considered as the best preparative for studying the Vedas.

It follows, then, that the Puranas are the principal sources of Hindu mythology, and, as far as the divinities therein celebrated are objects of popular worship, of the national religion also; for the latter, as we have already shown in another place, could not be derived from the Vedas. It is, like the national religion of the Greeks, simply of a poetical origin, and borrowed from the epic poems, taken in a larger sense as comprehending also those of a descriptive character. But an important question still remains for us to discuss, viz. whether the Puranas are original or only secondary sources: in other words, are we to reckon them among the ancient compositions of Sanscrit literature, or must we assign them a more modern origin?

Before we can with any propriety venture upon a critical examination of the Puranas, we ought first to possess them in the original. At present, however, all that we can advance on the subject must depend upon the accounts of others, and upon imperfect abstracts of the works themselves. The common assertion of the Brahmans would refer the Puranas to an age as remote as that which produced the Vedas and the Mahabharat, in assigning Vyasa as the author of all three. Now, though it is impossible in our present circumstances

lated by Hamilton, (see LANGLÈS, *Catalogue*, p. 10,) from which it appears that all the above questions are therein discussed.

to institute a critical inquiry into the date of each Purana considered separately, yet it appears pretty certain that, taken altogether, and in the state in which they now are, they cannot be so old as the report would make them.

The Puranas are evidently for the most part nothing but compilations, and could therefore only be produced at a time when Sanscrit literature was already in a rich and perfect state of development in all its various branches. The literature of any nation could obviously never begin with compilations, for these require a previous age of learning, usually too of considerable duration, to have elapsed; and, moreover, they presuppose a demand for instruction. Now it was precisely with a view of satisfying this demand that the Puranas were composed, as in fact they are still used for the same purpose at the present day. They are by no means the work of a poetic genius like the great epics of which we have spoken; but, like the poems of Tzetzes and other grammarians, the fruit of extraordinary diligence combined with extensive reading. Add to this, we are assured that the historical sections of the Puranas contain several accounts of pretended prophecies, which, however, were evidently made after the events had taken place.[92]

Although I am convinced that the Puranas in their present state cannot possibly be referred to the earliest periods of Sanscrit literature, yet I am nevertheless far from considering them altogether as an invention of modern times, that is, of the middle ages. When and how they received their present form is a question hitherto undetermined. Apparently they are not the work of one person, as native tradition would make us believe, for they very frequently contradict each other on the most essential points, sometimes ascribing greater honour to Vishnu, at others to Siva. It is also very probable that even each separate Purana was not composed all at once, but by slow degrees. The form of these books is itself extremely favourable to additions and interpolations, for no one of them consists of a regular and consecutive whole; but appears more like a collection of detached pieces of descriptive and didactic poetry.

I am therefore inclined to believe that the Puranas are

[92] *Asiatic Res.* vol. viii. p. 486.

modern compilations, drawn from the works of ancient poets,[93] to which the compilers may perhaps have made several arbitrary additions of their own. The principal sources from whence they borrowed their materials, are undoubtedly the old epic poems of the nation; for instance, the Bhagavat, which is supposed to be one of the latest,[94] is almost wholly taken from the Mahabharat; to these, indeed, we should add the philosophical systems, discussed in poems of a different kind. All this, and much more, would naturally precede the existence of compilations of the above character.

Considered in this point of view, it is evident we may very properly regard the form of the Puranas as a work of comparatively modern date; though at the same time we have equal reason in attributing a much higher antiquity to their contents. A modern critic, Mr. Bentley,[95] contends that none of the Puranas are more than six hundred and eighty-four years old, because none of those writings which mention the chronological system, known by the name of Brahma Calpa, are any older. Supposing this assertion to be correct, which, however, is disputed by others, it would then only be conclusive with regard to the chronological sections of the Puranas, which bear but a very small proportion to the rest of their contents.

"In Europe, too," observes a most profound scholar,[96] "literary forgeries have been committed. But a native of India, who should argue from a few instances that the whole literature of Europe which is held ancient, consists of modern forgeries, would be justly censured for his presumption. We must not then indiscriminately condemn the whole literature of India. Even Father Harduin, when he advanced a similar paradox respecting the works of ancient writers, excepted some compositions of Cicero, Virgil, Horace, and Pliny. It is, however, necessary in India, as every where else, to be guarded against literary impositions: some fabricated works, some interpolated passages will be detected by the sagacity of critics; but the greatest part of those books which are considered ancient by

[93] Compare WILFORD, in *Asiatic Res.* vol. v. p. 244.
[94] *Asiatic Res.* vol. viii. p. 487.
[95] Ibid. vol. viii. p. 241.
[96] COLEBROOKE, in *Asiatic Res.* vol. viii. p. 487.

the learned among the Hindus, will assuredly be found genuine. I mean to say, that they are the same compositions which have been revered by the Hindus for hundreds, if not thousands, of years."

I am altogether of the same opinion. To suppose, indeed, as Mr. Bentley seems inclined, the whole collection of Sanscrit literature to be no older than the middle ages, involves a paradox even more monstrous than the one set up by Father Harduin. Admitting the accounts left us by the Greeks to be correct, in reporting the civilization of India to have been regarded as ancient even in the time of Alexander, we must necessarily infer the corresponding antiquity of Hindu literature, as the prime origin of the former. It were certainly just as impossible for the Hindus to have become a cultivated nation without their Vedas and their epic poetry, as for the Greeks to have attained their advanced state of refinement without the writings of Homer and his successors; the impossibility, indeed, appears even more striking in the case of the latter people, when we reflect that they had no Holy Scriptures like the Vedas to assist their intellectual development.

The mythological systems contained in these poems are but imperfectly known to us at present, through the medium of extracts and summary abridgements, which must for this reason be necessarily partial and disfigured, as it was the main object both of Father Paulino and the English writers who have directed their attention to this subject, to discover points of resemblance in the mythology of India as compared with that of the Greeks and the Egyptians.[97] They found what they sought after, and their opinions getting into circulation, contributed in no small degree to embarrass and confound the science of Hindu antiquities in general. Polier, who has supplied the latest, and by far the most complete information on the subject, has taken care to avoid this fault.[98] The form of dialogue adopted by him for re-

[97] Sir W. Jones's treatise, On the Gods of Greece, Italy, and India, (vid. *Asiatic Res.* vol. i. p. 221, and his *Works*, vol. i. p. 229,) gave the first impulse, and was followed in the same track by Father Paulino, in his *Systema Brahmanicum*, who is otherwise almost always the opponent of English writers.

[98] Mythologie des Indous, travaillée par Mdme. la Chanoinesse de Polier, sur des MSS. authentiques rapports de l'Inde, par feu M. le Col. de Polier.

porting a conversation with his instructor, Ramchund, and which is so agreeable to European taste, may also be regarded as truly Indian; and the whole dialogue itself appears to derive a considerable accession of probability from the circumstance of Ramchund's belonging to the sect of the Sikhs, who having turned back again to monotheism, regard Hindu mythology like ourselves, as nothing more than a tissue of poetical fictions. It is impossible to dispute Ramchund's extensive acquaintance with the fables of his countrymen; but whether he has correctly reported them, can only be determined when we are able to consult the original sources. The Mahabharat and Bhagavat are generally mentioned as the principal authorities, but whence each particular fable is borrowed we have no certain information. In the work before us, the critic will perhaps find much to supply with regard to details, but considered altogether it has the undoubted merit of having contributed materially to enlarge the circle of our acquaintance with the fables comprised in the epic poems and the Puranas; and of enabling us, with greater precision than before was possible, to judge of the character, the beauties, and the defects of Hindu my-

T. i. ii. 1809. Polier was a native of Lausanne, and having entered into the service of the East India Company, devoted himself with the greatest ardour, and, according to the testimony of Sir W. Jones and others, (*Works*, vol. i. p. 355, *Asiatic Res.* vol. viii. p. 377,) with distinguished success, to the study of Hindu mythology, and the collection of any thing that was remarkable in the country. Being unacquainted, however, with the Sanscrit, he was obliged to have recourse to a learned native, (Ramchund,) who explained to him the mythological fables according to the epic poems and the Puranas; and Polier immediately wrote down as the pundit dictated. With these notes he returned home to Europe, during the revolutionary troubles; but here a terrible fate awaited him. He was unfortunately murdered in his own house, near Avignon, by a band of French brigands. By good chance, however, his papers fell into the hands of a relation, the friend and disciple of Gibbon, Madame Polier, only a few years since deceased at Rudolstadt, who, already prepared for the undertaking by early studies, (see her preface,) arranged the scattered documents and published them. No one who has the least affection for the study of Hindu antiquities, can fail to pronounce the name of this extraordinary lady with veneration and gratitude; and it is certainly not the least among the curiosities of literature, that the most copious and accurate account we possess of Hindu mythology, should have been compiled by a woman in an obscure village in the heart of the mountains of Thuringia. [Considering the unusual circumstances under which this work was produced, it would hardly perhaps be reasonable to expect much critical accuracy in the details; and yet the laudatory judgment of the author requires some qualification. A less favourable, but more correct opinion of its merits, will be found in an excellent article by KOSEGARTEN, inserted in the *Hermes*, vol. xxvi. TRANSL.]

thology. We must here content ourselves with only giving a general outline of the subject.

The series of Hindu divinities commences, as we have already seen, with the three superior Devas, Brahma, Vishnu, and Siva. There being no incarnation of Brahma, he is for that reason less adapted to the uses of poetry.[99] He possesses a temple called Dheira, on the shores of the Milky Sea; whither Vishnu, accompanied with the other Devas, repairs to consult the oracle.[100] The response is communicated to them in a voice, which is only audible after many days of preparatory devotion and prayer. Would not this serve to explain the singular fact, that Brahma, notwithstanding his superiority of rank, is only the object of internal worship; that is, of meditation, and not of external ceremonies. Admitting the popular religion of the Hindus, together with their divinities, to be of poetical origin, does it not follow of course that a deity who was unserviceable to the poet, whatever might be his superiority in other respects, could never become an object of popular worship, or have his own peculiar sect, like the two other great Devas? But I must leave the further discussion of this argument to the professed inquirer into the religious opinions of India.

The case is quite otherwise with respect to Vishnu and

[99] European writers have involved themselves in a labyrinth of inextricable confusion, by employing the names of Brahma, Brehm, Birmah, Brumah, sometimes as synonymous, at others as different appellations. "Brehm," says Polier, (vol. i. p. 358,) "means the invisible, the deity; Birmah, the creative power of Brehm." On the other hand, according to Sir W. Jones, Brahma, in the neuter gender, means the deity, and when masculine, the creative power (*Works*, vol i. p. 249, 250). The Upnekhat always mentions Brahma as the being who is the self-existent, though it confounds with this simple notion much that is subtle and obscure. See vol. i. p. 240, 256, 320. A more intimate acquaintance with Sanscrit works can only, perhaps, dissipate these obscurities; it is, however, quite evident that the Hindu poets never troubled themselves with such metaphysical distinctions, and that an abstract being like Brahma was considered very little adapted to their purpose. [These assertions of Professor Heeren have been contradicted, and with reason, by Schlegel; the names Brahmă and Brahmā may be compared with the Greek Θεός and Θεῖον, except that they are never taken one for the other. Brahma means the divinity, in the most sublime and abstract sense that it is possible for the mind to conceive. See many passages in the Bhagavadgita.—*Note of the French Translator.*] [The confusion above noticed, seems only to exist in the vitious pronunciation and orthography adopted by Col. Polier. His Brehm is the same as Sir W. Jones's Brahma, the final short vowel being cut off, as is common among the vulgar; and Birmah, or Brumah, is probably a corrupt way of pronouncing Brahmā. TRANSL.]

[100] POLIER, vol. i. p. 398.

Siva. These two deities divide between them the principal religious sects of India; and are, under various denominations, (not a little embarrassing to the study of Hindu theology,) the objects also of external worship. They are no less the principal characters in Hindu epic poetry, and that indeed in a twofold sense, being gods in heaven at the same time they appear as incarnations upon earth. Their celestial palaces have been described by the poets of India in the most brilliant and glowing colours, but in a manner sufficiently at variance with the propriety of European notions. The residence of Vishnu is called Baikunt, or Vaikuntha.[1] He is there enthroned as a handsome young man, radiant with beams of light; but withal of a blue complexion, and furnished with four arms. One hand holds a shell, in another is a lotus flower, an equally important symbol among the Hindus as among the Egyptians; a third arm wields a mace; and in the fourth appears the ring called Sudarsan, from which, as well as from the precious stone depending on his breast, issues a stream of light which illumines the whole palace. When awake, he is seated on a resplendent throne; and when asleep, he reposes on the serpent Seshanaga, whose thousand heads serve him for a pillow. This reptile is himself a Deva, and becomes incarnate along with his master when the latter appears on earth; as does also the king of birds, the eagle Garuda, who carries Vishnu when he leaves Vaikuntha. By his side appears his wife Lakshmi, the fairest of the Devanies, who likewise accompanied her lord in human shape, as his terrestrial consort. A multitude of inferior Devas surround him, and two sentinels guard the entry of his palace. The mansion of Siva, or Mahadeva, called Kailasa Parvat, is not so brilliant as that of Vishnu: it is situate on the lofty peaks of Himalaya. The god, comprising in his own person both the powers of creation and destruction, is represented with corresponding symbols—the lingam to denote the former, and the trident

[1] Sir W. Jones, *Works*, vol. i. p. 267. Polier, however, always spells this word Baikunt. [The letters *b* and *v* in Sanscrit are, from similarity of form, very liable to be confounded; and, moreover, their occasional interchange is perfectly optional; see Wilson's *Dictionary*, preface, p. 41. Add to this, some of the Hindu dialects having no *v* in their alphabet, substitute *b*, and *vice versâ*, which is perhaps the reason why the Vedas are sometimes miscalled Beds. Transl.]

when he appears as the avenger and destroyer. His complexion is of a red colour, he is girt with an elephant's hide, and is seated upon the skin of a tiger, while near him stands his consort Parvati. But the manner of representing this deity, as well as his names, are subject to various modifications, according to the different ideas formed of his character.[2] The mansions of these superior Devas, belonging as they do principally to the invisible world, have not furnished such exuberant matter for poetical display as that of Indra, prince of Swerga, the firmament or visible heaven; notwithstanding Indra himself occupies a much lower rank in the celestial hierarchy[3] than the former. Lord of the inferior Devas, he inhabits his palace of Vaijayanta, constructed for him by the architect of heaven, Visvakarma, and situate in the middle of the gardens of Nandana. Here ever playing fountains maintain a perpetual verdure, and here also grows the celestial fruit, called Amrita, which confers immortality, the produce of the wonderful tree Parajati, transplanted by Krishna to the marvellous town of Dwaraka, with which it sunk again into the ocean. This surprising tree is adorned with the most brilliant flowers, and whoever reposes under its shade obtains the complete fulfilment of all his wishes. All that the earth contains of what is precious and excellent, is here found in its highest state of original perfection; such as Camada, the cow of abundance; the sacred horse Sajam, an indispensable requisite at the solemn sacrifices; and the white elephant, Airavata. These and many other animals are all produced from the Sea of Milk, which is the source of all perfection. As lord of the firmament, Rajah Indra rules over the winds and the weather; to him the earth addresses her prayers when she has need of rain; and subject to him are the innumerable hosts of inferior Devas, amounting to upwards of three hundred and thirty-two millions. These are divided into classes, but their chiefs alone have access to the Rajah, and the privilege of being admitted to his court of Mulasthan is

[2] As each sect gave the pre-eminence to their own respective deities, we ought not to be surprised at these variations and contradictions, whether apparent or real.

[3] Compare POLIER, vol. ii. p. 229, sq., with JONES's *Works*, vol. i. p. 248, sq. In Polier Indra is always called Ainder. [The latter way of spelling follows the corrupt pronunciation of the vulgar. TRANSL.]

considered the highest degree of happiness to which a created being can aspire. It is there he is represented as a beautiful youth, with four arms, sitting upon a throne; and before him dance the Apsaras, celestial nymphs, breathing the most exquisite perfumes. Notwithstanding all this splendour, however, the majesty and power of Indra had been sorely paralyzed for a considerable space of time; the Daints,[4] or bad Devas, who inhabit Pátála, or the infernal regions, under the command of their king Ravana, had waged war with him, and had overcome him; and it was in order to free the world from their unjust domination, that Vishnu was obliged to appear on earth in the person of Rama, and perform the heroic achievements described in the Ramayana.

The religion of the Hindus, though it admits in this manner both good and evil demons, nevertheless at the same time gives evident proof of that mildness of character so peculiar to it. Penances and purifications are held sufficient to wipe out the crimes of all, not only of mortals, but also of immortal beings; for in answer to the mediatorial prayers of the Devas, even the Daints themselves, after a complete expiation, are to be liberated from hell, and reinstated in all their original happiness. But what in a still more eminent degree contributes to enlarge the circle of Hindu mythology, is the fact, that its poetical fictions of Devas and Devanies are transferred also to natural objects, both animate and inanimate. The sun and moon, both of which are considered by the Hindus as masculine, the earth, mountains, streams, etc., no less than the brute creation, such as apes, bears, elephants, birds, etc., are all occasionally introduced as Devas and Devanies, and thus become available for the uses of poetry. We have already seen Hanuman king of the monkeys playing a distinguished part in one of the great epic poems; in the same manner we observe moral precepts superior even to those of Æsop's fables put in the mouth of animals; as, for instance, in the last book of the Ramayana, where the royal eagle Garuda is represented in sage conversation with a crow.

These primary elements of Hindu mythology, which it

[4] So Polier always calls them. In the Ramayana they are termed Rakshasas.

would be unnecessary further to develop in this place, as the reader will find an ample detail in the before-mentioned work of Polier, are sufficient, however, to show its extreme fecundity. What an inexhaustible fund of subject-matter does it not supply for the exercise and display of poetic genius! And when we consider the vast number of poets, who have separately made it the theme of song, each in his own peculiar manner, what an endless variety may we not conceive to be the result! If we compare the mythology of the Hindus with that of the Greeks, it will have nothing to apprehend on the score of intrinsic copiousness. In point of æsthetic value, it is sometimes superior, at others inferior, to the Greek; while in luxuriance and splendour it has the decided advantage. Olympus, with all its family of gods and goddesses, must yield in pomp and majesty to the palaces of Vishnu and Indra. On the other hand, we must not expect to find among the Hindu gods that beau ideal of the human form which the mythology of Greece supplies: a want of taste in this particular is no less evident in the Puranas than in the epic poems. To what extent, then, the mythology of the Hindus is adapted to the uses of their epic poetry will be sufficiently clear. This is obviously under such circumstances only as mark the peculiarities of the Hindu epopee, and so far only as the latter elevates itself above the consideration of humanity; and, like the sublime compositions of Milton and Klopstock, extends its poetic flight far into the regions of unlimited space.

The different kinds of poetry do not appear to have been so exactly distinguished from one another among the Hindus as among the nations of the West. The general character of the Indian epic poem, the unsettled connexion of its parts, and the frequent episodes, would easily permit the introduction of didactic pieces. Their dramatic poetry, however, is so far intimately blended with the lyric species, that it is often very difficult to draw a marked line of distinction between the two.

The lyric poetry of the Hindus appears to have consisted originally of hymns to their divinities, which bear some resemblance to those commonly attributed to Orpheus, in that they contain for the most part laudatory epithets in honour of the gods. Scarce any other mythology furnishes such a vast abundance of these epithets, and as they are often employed as surnames, and even as proper names, they give rise to considerable difficulty in reading the Hindu poets; for the same deity is designated by so many appellations, that it is nearly impossible to know or remember them all. Hymns, however, of a purely epic nature could not long remain unknown to the Hindus, while their mythology supplied them with such abundant subject-matter for the purpose; and even many of the episodes introduced into their great epopees bear the character of epic hymns, resembling those of Homer. We are indebted to Sir W. Jones for versions of several of these hymns in praise of the gods; but they are rather imitations in rhyming verse than correct translations; it would therefore be too hazardous to attempt drawing any satisfactory conclusion from them.[5] Father Paulino, however, and the scholars of England, have in their respective writings and essays furnished some complete specimens in the original, accompanied with a literal translation, not merely with the view of ascertaining their contents, but also of showing the variety of forms under which the lyric poetry of the Hindus is found, with regard to rhyme and metre.[6] The poetry in question was formerly among this people as intimately allied to song and music, as among the ancient Greeks; and the case is the same at the present day: both arts were treated by them in a theoretical manner, and both accordingly made the same progress.[7] But the Hindu lyric surpassed that of the Greeks, in admitting both rhyme and blank verse; and although we might compare it in this respect with the German, yet it would seem that the Hindu ear has much less affection for rhyme than the latter.

Among such a poetical people as the Hindus, however, lyric poetry would not be confined to merely religious hymns; and more than one writer has already remarked, that song in general has been no less extensively cultivated by them.[8] But the popular religion, and the various festal

[5] *Works*, vol. i. p. 313, sq.

[6] See examples of these hymns taken from the Vedas, in SIR W. JONES's *Works*, vol. vi. p. 423, 427.

[7] See BARON DALBERG's Treatise, *Ueber die Musik der Inder* (On the Music of the Hindus); see also *Asiatic Res.* vol. i. p. 35.

[8] DALBERG, loc. cit. p. 90. The Baron has also published the melodies of several Hindu songs.

solemnities it prescribes, opened such a wide field for the display of sentiment, that their lyric poetry almost always preserved some actual connexion with, or reference to, religious ideas. In what other nation besides the Hindu could the erotic species, for example, have found a more abundant supply of argument in the religion of the country? And with respect to the graver kind of lyric poetry, the songs of war and victory, was it possible to give them any other than a religious character, among a people who lived, as it were, upon the deeds of high emprise and heroic achievement performed by their gods and heroes.

A great proportion, nevertheless, of the Hindu lyric poetry belongs to the elegiac species. One of the most beautiful of this description, called the Mega Duta, or Cloud Messenger of Calidasa, has not long since been published in the original, and accompanied with an English translation in verse.[9] The following is a brief abstract of the contents of this poem. A Yaksha, or Deva, who was in the service of the god Cuvera, at his residence in the city Alaca, among the mountains of Himalaya, had drawn upon himself the angry vengeance of his master, for suffering Indra's elephant, named Airavata, to enter and lay waste a garden of which he had been left in charge. As a punishment for his negligence, he was exiled for one whole year to the mountains of Ramagiri, (which form the commencement of the Ghaut range,) where, during all this interval, he lived separate from his dearly beloved wife. Eight months of his banishment had passed over, when the rainy season began, and he beheld the clouds advancing from the south towards the north in the direction of Himalaya and Alaca, where his fond and bereaved consort was mourning his tedious absence. He commissions one of these clouds to convey her intelligence of himself, and describes the road which it must take in order to arrive at the celestial Himath, his own dear country, where he pictures to his mind's eye the form of his much-loved spouse, plunged in grief, and anxiously looking forward to the day of his return. He

[9] The Mega Duta, or Cloud Messenger, a poem in the Sanscrit language, by Calidasa, translated into English verse, with notes and illustrations by Horace Hayman Wilson, Calcutta, 1813. 4to. pp. 120. The notes contain many valuable explanations.

paints her distress in moving terms, and charges the messenger with the following words of consolation. "The thirsty plant looks up to thee; and a gentle shower is thy only answer." Could he have expressed himself with greater truth or delicacy?

The first Hindu lyric poet is considered by the natives themselves to have been Jayadeva, who, according to Sir W. Jones,[10] upon hearsay evidence, is reported to have lived even before Calidasa. This vague chronological date, which would therefore place him anterior to the first century of our era, is at present almost all we know of his history. He was born, as he himself states, at Kenduli, which, according to many writers, is situated in Calinga; but as there exists another town of this name in Burdwan, the inhabitants of the latter place claim Jayadeva as their fellow countryman, and celebrate an annual feast in his honour, when they pass the whole night in joyous revel, singing his poems and representing his idyls.

Although we are in want of positive data for assigning the real period of the golden age of Hindu lyric poetry, yet we are enabled to form some opinion on the subject from a review of one of the principal compositions in this department, the Gita Govinda.[11] We are indebted to the skill and industry of Sir W. Jones,[12] for a translation of this masterpiece of Jayadeva, which is so much the more valuable from being rendered into literal prose, with the omission, however, of certain passages rather too highly coloured in the original. The poem itself is composed in rhymed stanzas, and the subject is of an epic character, being borrowed from the Mahabharat; the whole is a species of idyl, intermixed with lyric songs, and has been incorrectly termed a pastoral drama, though it possesses nothing of the dramatic form. The subject of the poem is taken from the history of Krishna, what time the god, disguised as a youthful herdsman, sojourned among the Gopis, or milkmaids, and gave himself up to the enjoyments of love. Radha, the most

[10] Jones, *Works*, vol. i. p. 462.

[11] Govinda is one of the many surnames of Krishna, which he bears as the god of herdsmen; Gita means song; the whole expression is therefore equivalent to "the song of the god of herdsmen." *Asiat. Res.* vol. i. p. 262.

[12] Jones's *Works*, vol. i. p. 463. Sir William Jones's version was translated by Baron Dalberg into German, with the addition of explanatory notes.

beautiful of them, conceived herself slighted and despised, by the caresses he bestowed on the others. She pours forth the bitterness of her grief, until, through the mediation of one of her companions, the stray god is at length brought back to her arms, and they enjoy together the secret pleasures of amorous dalliance. Although there is a unity of action preserved through the whole poem, it is, nevertheless, no drama, but rather a series of amatory songs connected with the principal story.

The Gitagovinda may serve as a complete specimen of the erotico-lyric poetry of the Hindus. It exhibits a picture of love, confined to the sole gratifications of sense, and betraying rather the grossness of animal desire than the pure and refined enjoyments of intellectual passion. We need not, therefore, be surprised at the wanton luxuriancy of the poet's imagination, which has even occasionally obliged the translators to draw a veil over certain passages.[13] How much of the beauty of a lyric poem must inevitably be lost in a prose translation it would be superfluous to remark; and yet it is almost impossible to read the Gitagovinda even in a translation, without being charmed.

What immediately strikes us in the lyric poetry of the Hindus, is the perfect absence of any foreign alloy; purity and originality of character are predominant throughout, and we feel ourselves suddenly transported into the world of India. But how unable are we to appreciate its beauties, for want of clear and precise ideas of that gorgeous climate! Most of the comparisons are borrowed from Indian vegetation; and yet the melodious names of trees and plants, although reduced in the notes to the Linnæan system, are to our apprehension but empty sounds, while we are unacquainted with the plants themselves, and, consequently, are incapable of estimating the correctness of the allusion.[14] When to this we add the charms of verse and rhyme, not to

[13] The limits which separate the decent from the indecent, and which in general vary according to nation and climate, are utterly disregarded by Hindu poets, for the very reason that works of poetry are not intended for female perusal.

[14] [Dr. Wallich, in his magnificent work on the plants of India, which is now in course of publication, has in part supplied this deficiency. Mr. Colebrooke, in his learned notes to the Amara Cosha, Dr. Roxburgh, and particularly Mr. Wilson, in his Dictionary, had previously given the synonymes of a great number of Indian plants. FR. TRANSL.]

be conveyed in a prose translation, there will remain scarcely any thing of the original. It is impossible, however, not to notice the extreme richness of the poet's fancy, the strength and vivacity of his sentiment, particularly observable in his delicate taste for the beauties of nature in general; and which not even the ardour of passion was able to extinguish. In India the painter of love is at the same time the painter of landscape also, but such a one as could only be formed under the softness and luxuriant vegetation of an Indian climate. In fine, the poem before us shows clearly in what sense the epic of the Hindus may be regarded as the parent of their lyric poetry. The fable to which it refers is handled not only in the Mahabharat, but also in the Bhagavat Purana, and perhaps in many other poems of a later date. From thence the lyric poet borrowed the materials which served to inspire the outpourings of his genius and sensibility.[15]

From the Gitagovinda we proceed by a natural transition to consider the dramatic poetry of the Hindus. The English were the first to discover the fertility of Indian literature in this species of composition. For, upon theatrical representations of the British stage being introduced at Calcutta, Sir W. Jones heard a learned Brahman named Radhacanta remark, that their *nataks*, which had hitherto been considered historic poems, were almost the same thing.[16] The curiosity of Sir William was excited by this observation; he immediately informed himself of the best of these compositions, and it is to this circumstance we owe his discovery and translation of the Sacontala.

Although this interesting play, of which we shall presently have occasion to speak, has enabled us to ascertain the nature of the Indian drama, we are still in comparative ignorance of its extent, and the several branches belonging to it. Mr. Wilson, in his Theatre of the Hindus, has furnished us with additional information on the subject. According to

[15] The amatory poet above noticed, was no less the poet of religion; and we are obliged to Sir W. Jones for a literal translation of one of his odes to Vishnu or Hari, which contains a panegyrical account of all that god's incarnations. Jones's *Works*, vol. i. p. 289. So inseparably connected among the Hindus appear to have been the sentiments of love and devotion. [The same remark will apply to the Persians also. Fr. Transl.]

[16] Jones's *Works*, vol. vi. p. 202.

this learned scholar, the Hindu drama is sometimes of an elevated, at others of an inferior kind. The natakas, which belong to the first description, have this peculiarity, that the principal characters are always gods or heroes and heroines, and ought rather to be termed heroic plays than tragedies, for the catastrophe is invariably fortunate. The action of the piece must not occupy less than five, or more than ten acts, which are severally distinguished by the exit of all the players. The language of the superior personages is Sanscrit, that of the lower orders Pracrit and other dialects. The second class of the Hindu drama, called Uparupacas, comprehends smaller pieces, extending mostly from one to four acts, and the characters are ordinary men. We must, however, add to these two kinds a third, which is that of the allegorical drama, exemplified in a play entitled Chandrodaya, translated by Dr. Taylor, where Reason, Passion, and Desire are personified.

Imperfect as our knowledge of the Hindu drama at present is, we cannot mistake the sources from which it was derived; these are no other than the popular religion and epic poetry, from which last the religion itself originated. The histories of gods and heroes, therefore, supplied it with materials, and in this it coincides with the Grecian drama, however great may be the difference between the two in other respects. Although the constitution of Indian governments would not easily admit the introduction of any thing like the old Grecian comedy,[17] yet it did not altogether exclude the comic species, which was partly indispensable as a popular amusement. The fabulous histories of gods and heroes, conformably to the great epic poems, were represented upon solemn feasts in the vicinity of the temples, and are still occasionally at the present day. One of the most fertile subjects for the dramatic poet was furnished in the history of Rama, and the celebrated war of Lanka or Ceylon,

[17] [This is inexact, as there are specimens of Hindu comedy still extant, no ways inferior to the ancient Greek; and it would be curious to examine which of the two kinds had the advantage in all manner of licence. FR. TRANSL.] [It will be sufficient to notice, in confirmation of M. Suckau's opinion, the Hásyarnava, or Sea of Laughter, a farce in three acts, by Jagadisvara. It is a bitter satire on kings and their servants, who are described as profligate scoundrels; and on priests, who are represented as hypocrites! See SIR W. JONES's *Works*, vol. vi. p. 451; LANGLÈS, *Cat. des Manuscrits Sanscrits*, p. 80; and SCHLEGEL's *Ind. Bibl.* ii. 2. p. 161. TRANS.]

from the Ramayana; which is still frequently represented on his feast-day, and the exhibition closes, according to an eye-witness,[18] with the ordeal of fire, in which Sita, the wife of Rama, proved her innocence after being carried off by Ravana.[19]

The nature of the Hindu drama itself would lead us to infer, that it is of greater antiquity than we are enabled to determine with correctness. Its invention, according to Sir W. Jones,[20] is attributed to Bharata, an inspired sage. But, supposing the drama to have been founded upon epic poetry, it must of course be less ancient than the latter; and the Hindus themselves ascribe its perfect development to the comparatively modern age of Vicramaditya; while they are far from allowing their dramatic writings the same degree of veneration as their epic poetry. The former are not reckoned in the number of sacred compositions, which the superior castes only are permitted to read, but are classed with the national poetry; and in fact their prevailing language bears the same character. They are, it is true, written in Sanscrit, but not exclusively; the principal persons, especially the higher beings, alone talk Sanscrit; the women Pracrit; and the lower orders their respective popular dialects. The language is elevated or lowered according to the exigency of the subject; when that is sublime, the interlocutors use only poetry; in familiar conversation, on the other hand, they return to common prose.

How inexhaustible were the sources from whence the dramatic writers of India borrowed their materials, may be easily conceived, from what we have already said of the mythology and epic poetry of the Hindus. On the other hand, the general taste for these poems, and their being put in requisition at the public solemnities, must have increased their number to an extraordinary degree. The pundits, indeed, pretend they are innumerable; and we could willingly believe the assurance of Sir W. Jones, when he affirms, that the Hindu theatre would fill as many volumes as that

[18] *Asiatic Res.* vol. i. p. 258. [See an epitome of the Ramayana, as dramatically represented by the common people on the festival of Rama. *Asiatic Journ.* vol. iv. p. 130, 185, N. S. TRANSL.]

[19] See above, p. 157.

[20] See for this, and what immediately follows, his preface to the Sacontala. *Works*, vol. vi. p. 204, etc.

of any nation of modern Europe. More than thirty compositions, next to those of Calidasa, were pointed out to him as the flower of this branch of Hindu literature; of which, however, up to the present time, we know scarcely any thing beyond the mere names.[21]

The most brilliant period of Hindu dramatic poetry is undoubtedly that of Calidasa, whom the natives are unanimous in regarding as the first of their dramatic writers, though two only of his pieces are now extant.[22] He is reckoned among the nine poets who adorned the court of that friend of the muses Rajah Vicramaditya, the sovereign of India; who gave name to the era so called, commencing with his death fifty-six years before Christ; and which, as we have

[21] Sir W. Jones cites the following: The Ill-natured Child; The Rape of Usha; The Taming of the Dervasas; The Rape of the Lock; Malati and Madava; with five or six others, the subjects of which turn upon the adventures of incarnate deities. Mr. Wilford (*Asiatic Res.* vol. x. p. 450, etc.) has given an extract from the play entitled Malati and Madava, written by the poet Bhurivasu, and which has for its subject the loves of a youthful pair, whom their parents had already destined for each other, but who were only united at length after many obstacles. As far as I am able to judge, this play seems much inferior to the Sacontala. The translation of another drama, called Prabodha Chandrodaya, (i. e. Rise of the Moon of Intellect,) by Dr. Taylor, London, 1812, is only known to me by quotations.

[22] Sacontala, and Vikrama and Urvasi. SIR WILLIAM JONES, *Works*, vol. vi. p. 205. The drama entitled Vikrama and Urvasi has been published by Wilson in his "Theatre of the Hindus." The following is a brief account of its subject. The king Pururava appears in his chariot on the mountain tops of Himalaya, where he delivers Urvasi, a celestial Apsara, or nymph, who had been carried off from the court of Indra: a mutual passion is the consequence; but the lovers are obliged to separate, on account of Urvasi's return to heaven. The king gives himself up to melancholy, and communicates his misfortune to his friend Manava, who plays the traitor, and by means of a flying leaf discloses the secret to the queen his wife. Urvasi, impelled by love, returns to visit the king, and invites him to retire with her into the bosom of a wood called Rarikeya. The entrance of this wood was forbidden to all women, upon pain of being turned into vine-stocks, a metamorphosis which accordingly befell the luckless Urvasi, after giving birth to a son. At length, however, being disenchanted by Indra, she is received into his celestial abode together with her spouse and son. The plot and unravelling of the piece are evidently similar to those of Sacontala. The character of Urvasi, of the king and his companion Manava, a grossly sensual Banian, who acts the droll in this play like Madavia does in the Sacontala, are perfect counterparts of those found in the latter poem. Nevertheless, the character of Pururava is delineated with less vigour than that of Dushmanta, to whom he is besides generally inferior. *Inedited note of the Author.*

[The text of this play, and several other specimens of the Hindu drama, have been published by the Committee of Public Instruction at Calcutta. Another comedy, in five acts, entitled Agnimitra and Malavika, purports to be written by Calidasa, but it seems uncertain whether the great poet of that name or another. TRANSL.]

seen, was still in use during the middle ages. According to this computation, the age of Calidasa would coincide with that of Lucretius, and follow not long after Terence. It must be candidly allowed that we have no stronger proof of the correctness of this date; but surely the bare circumstance of an era having prevailed among the whole nation for upwards of a thousand years, is undoubtedly a strong presumption in its favour; and that the objections alleged by Mr. Bentley against the age of Calidasa rest upon no solid grounds, has, I think, been sufficiently shown already.[23] As far, then, as our present knowledge extends, we may feel ourselves justified in regarding the first century before Christ as the most flourishing period of Sanscrit literature, particularly of the drama. Whoever, indeed, examines with attention the only specimen of the latter kind at present known in Europe, will find ample reason, I imagine, for considering the play in question to have been composed, not for the people but the court, and for a brilliant court too: in this sense we might not unaptly term the piece a royal drama. A king, together with a heroine, is the principal character; and every thing is calculated with a view to his aggrandizement. The action of the play is confined to the court, and the society of gods and holy anchorites, which last are on the same footing with princes. The preparations requisite for enacting this drama, in whatever manner we may suppose that to be done, are on such a large and expensive scale, as none but a royal stage could either accomplish or afford.

The Sacontala[24] is already too well known to the learned of Europe to require a particular exposition of its contents. It was this celebrated drama which first gave us a more correct idea of the treasures contained in Sanscrit literature; and we must in truth allow Calidasa to be one of those poets who have done honour not merely to their own nation, but to all civilized mankind. At the same time it will not

[23] See above, p. 116, 117. We ought, however, to remark, that the question only concerns the age of Calidasa, and other poets his contemporaries, and has nothing to do with the work entitled Surrya Siddhanta, upon which it will be the appropriate task of astronomers to decide.

[24] Sacontala, or The Fatal Ring. SIR W. JONES, *Works*, vol. vi. p. 209, etc. The ensuing observations are grounded solely on this translation, without reference to the criticisms of other writers.

be too much to assert, that the number of those readers who can perfectly comprehend him must ever be small. He only who has become naturalized to an Indian world, and has been able to identify himself with the habits of thinking and sentiments peculiar to the natives, can ever thoroughly understand the most beautiful passages of this author.[25]

As the Hindus themselves regard the Sacontala as the first of all their dramatic compositions, there will be no impropriety, therefore, in our attempting to examine their whole drama, by referring it to the same standard. Notwithstanding the charms of language and versification are necessarily lost, yet enough remains, in the plan and development of the plot, for enabling us to make a proper estimate of the whole play, and thereby to ascertain the general character of the Hindu drama itself. That distinguishing feature of Hindu poetry, its not being satisfied with mere humanity, but confounding the divine with the terrestrial, yet so as that the former shall predominate, is no less conspicuous in the drama than in the epic poem. Both the principal characters are of supernatural origin; Sacontala is the daughter of a Rajah, and a Devanie;[26] Dushmanta the king is of the race of the Purus, who derived their lineage from the moon, and is at the same time the friend and companion of Indra, upon whose chariot he appears riding in the clouds. The action of the piece commences

[25] To cite a few instances, I need only allude to Sacontala's farewell address to her plants and flowers, expressed in as affectionate terms as if they were her sisters: to the fearful malediction of the Brahman Durvasa and its consequences, which form the principal groundwork of the plot; to Dushmanta's grief, and horrible presentiment of the ruin of his house, if he should die childless, and consequently lose the benefit of a funeral sacrifice to be offered by his heirs for the repose of his soul; and to his relationship with Indra, etc.

[26] The birth and history of Sacontala are related in the Mahabharat, from whence Calidasa borrowed his subject; but which he further detailed and embellished, as the nature of dramatic interest might require. The above episode has been translated by Fred. Schlegel, in his Essay on the Language and Science of the Hindus, p. 308; where at the same time that he shows how the dramatists of India borrowed their materials from the epic poems, he also informs us what freedom they allowed themselves in their respective methods of handling them. According to the Mahabharat, Sacontala was the daughter of Rajah Vishvamitra, who by his penances had raised himself to the dignity of a Brahman; whom, notwithstanding, the Devanie Menuca had seduced to her embraces at the suggestion of Indra, who was alarmed at the uncommon mortifications of the sage. In the drama she is called Causica, p. 222. The great simplicity of the narrative contained in the epic poem, compared with that in the drama, is another proof of the high antiquity of the former, and of the different ages in which they were severally composed.

on earth and terminates in the celestial mansions of the gods; all which gives to the poem a certain degree of majesty and elevation.

This is not the place for unravelling the web of this astonishing literary performance, or we might expatiate upon the intimate connexion of its parts, and the exact measure and proportion of the whole. We might show how the progressive and harmonious march of the action, commencing like an idyl, with the picture of a delicate young nymph surrounded with her plants and flowers, continually rises in majestic interest till the last act, where Sacontala, being again united to her husband and son, the youthful vanquisher of lions, is presented to the gods her relations, and the piece closes, as it were, with a species of transfiguration. Calidasa has been termed the Hindu Shakspeare;[27] and in truth there is as much affinity of soul between these two dramatists, as we have already noticed between the respective epic poets of the two countries. The action of the Sacontala, however simple it may be, is of no less extent than the great works of the English poet. Both are equally unrestricted by the unities of time and place; unity of action, indeed, is the only one which Calidasa recognises. Neither does he disdain, when the subject requires it, to interweave with scenes of ordinary life those also of a more elevated character; but his representations are always true and animated, in every variety of circumstance, whether he introduces us to gods or princes, to constables or fishermen. He paints with equal delicacy and force the graceful and the pathetic, the terrible and the sublime. Even the comic is not foreign to his pencil, though he employs it but sparingly, and always with design.[28] And if he does not express the passions so forcibly as the English dramatist, we should recollect that the grand aim of Hindu philosophy is to repress them altogether.

It would appear, then, that Calidasa raised the Indian

[27] JONES's *Works*, vol. vi. p. 205.

[28] Madhavya is certainly in some measure the droll in Sacontala, though incorrectly characterized as a buffoon in the English translation. He is represented as a Brahman by birth, and, in consequence, as the equal in rank and playmate of the king from his youth up, p. 236. It is not his wit so much as his dulness, in contrast with the lofty character of Dushmanta, to whom he serves as a foil, which produces the comic of the play.

drama to a degree of excellence, of which, previous to the discovery of his Sacontala, we had not the slightest conception. But what a course of preliminary mental improvement must the nation have gone through, ere they could possess a writer like Calidasa! ere they could understand and appreciate his genius! It is only from one of his two principal works that we are at present enabled to form any opinion of the poet himself, or of the whole dramatic literature of his nation. How confined, therefore, is our sphere of vision, and how much more correctly might we judge of both, did we but possess those thirty other pieces, which were represented to Sir W. Jones as the most valuable of this author's compositions![29] We can now only judge of the Indian drama, as we might of the English, supposing Hamlet were the only play we had to guide our judgment. It is, indeed, easy to conceive what we have lost, but scarcely possible for us to estimate its real value.

The poetry of no other nation exhibits in such a striking manner the didactic character as that of the Hindus; for no other people were so thoroughly imbued with the persuasion, that to give and receive instruction was the sole and ultimate object of life. How could such a sentiment fail to exercise a reflected influence upon poetry? A large proportion of the Vedas, the Upanishads, must be regarded in the light of philosophico-didactic poems, indissolubly connected, however, with religion. The case is the same with most of the Puranas, especially the cosmogonies and theogonies which those writings contain. The nature of the Hindu epic poem, so favourable to the introduction of episodes, is equally well adapted for conveying moral and philosophical precepts. The last book of the Ramayana, and the Bhagavat Gita in the Mahabharat, may serve as examples of the fact.

The Bhagavat Gita, which is in the form of a dialogue between Krishna and his disciple Arjuna, is one of the prin-

[29] According to Sir W. Jones, (*Works*, vol. vi. p. 205,) Calidasa was not only a dramatic, but an epic writer also. Two heroic poems of his composition are still extant: The Children of the Sun, and The birth of Curama the God of War. Some amatory tales are likewise attributed to him, and a poem on Sanscrit metre. "According to some," adds Sir William, "he revised the works of Valmiki and Vyasa, and arranged them in their present order." This last observation will serve to throw a considerable degree of light upon the obscure history of Sanscrit literature, a subject to which I shall very soon have occasion to refer.

cipal sources of the religious philosophy of the Hindus.[30] Krishna is there represented as the supreme being, through and in whom every thing exists. The poem certainly abounds in sublime passages, which remind one of the Orphic hymn to Jupiter, quoted by Stobæus. How far, indeed, the poet can be absolved from the charge of pantheism, when he represents the deity sometimes as a simple and indivisible being,[31] at others, as composed, and the substance of all things,[32] is a question for philosophers to decide. According to him, the body, when once become unserviceable, is thrown aside like an old garment, and the immortal soul is enveloped in another.[33] The government of the passions and the mortification of sensual desires comprise the whole extent of his moral system. Whoever, says he, can attain perfection in this respect, will after death be absorbed into the Divine essence, without being born again.[34] He adds a great deal of what is excellent and true upon this subject, though he also pretends that abstract meditation or devotion, accompanied with invocation of the deity by the mystical word *Om*, will conduct a man to supreme happiness.[35] Here, again, we remark the strong propensity of the Hindus to mysticism.

Although the didactic poetry of the Hindus, conformably to the general character of their civilization, remained in intimate connexion with religion, the descriptive, on the other hand, appears to have emancipated itself. To the latter kind belongs a poem of Calidasa, entitled Ritusanhara,

[30] We are indebted to A. W. Schlegel for a complete and critical edition of the Bhagavat Gita, from the Paris MSS. "Bhagavad Gita, id est, *θεσπέσιον μέλος*, sive almi Krishnæ et Arjunæ colloquium de rebus divinis Bharateæ Episodium." Bonn, 1828, 4to. This is the first book that was printed in the Devanagari character in Germany; the chapters of the Bhagavad Gita inserted in FRANK's *Chrestomathia*, vol. ii., being lithographed. As to Mr. Wilkins's edition printed at Calcutta in 1803, and accompanied with an English translation, scarce any copies appear to have reached Europe. [Wilkins never published the text of the Bhagavad Gita, which only appeared for the first time at Calcutta, in 1815; his English translation came out in 1785. FR. TRANSL.]

[31] Essentia simplex et individua est summum numen, p. 155.

[32] Mea natura in octonas partes distribuitur, p. 153.

[33] Page 135. [34] Page 143.

[35] Page 156. [*Om* is the mystic name of the deity, prefacing all the prayers and most of the writings of the Hindus; compounded of *A* a name of Vishnu, *U* of Siva, and *M* of Brahma; it therefore implies the Indian triad, and expresses the three in one. TRANSL.]

or the Seasons, which has been printed at Calcutta in the original Sanscrit: but Sir W. Jones, in his Works, only presents us with a title and a very short notice. "It is impossible," says he, "to commence the study of Sanscrit with a more elegantly written composition. Every line of Calidasa is elaborated with the utmost care; and each stanza of the poem describes an Indian landscape, always beautiful, sometimes strongly coloured, but never untrue to nature." The name and reputation of Calidasa were sufficient to justify the largest hopes; but unfortunately we must content ourselves with this imperfect account of Sir William, for neither original nor translation appear yet to have reached Europe.

The poetry of the Hindus particularly affects the form of dialogue, which it also employs in didactic poetry, as we have before noticed in speaking of the Puranas. But its peculiar feature consists in putting these dialogues in the mouths of animals, not merely for the purpose of enabling them to speak in character, like those in the fables of Æsop, or Reynard the Fox, but also, as beings of a higher and enlightened or at least of a rational nature, in order to convey precepts of wisdom and prudence. This peculiarity is strictly conformable to the light in which the Hindus regard the brute creation. We have already had occasion to remark the superior character which animals assume in the mythology of this people; that they are not only companions of the deities, but are themselves also of divine nature, and appear upon earth in an incarnate form by the side of the divinities. But in the case before us, a much stronger influence is exercised by the general belief in the transmigration of souls. According to the Brahmans, all life is an emanation of the deity; and this, too, not only with regard to men, but also to brutes, and even the vegetable world. The soul is supposed to migrate successively through the bodies of men and inferior animals, which are so many forms of purification, until at length it is raised to its original condition, and is absorbed again into the divinity;[36] though it is also pretended that this may take place immediately, through intense meditation, and extraordinary penances.

[36] Polier, vol. ii. p. 418.

Under such a system of belief, the whole race of brute animals appear in a much more dignified point of view; we are no longer astonished at seeing them, particularly as incarnations of gods, invested with all the reason and intelligence of man.

A striking example will be found in the last book of the Ramayana, of which Sir W. Jones has furnished us with a translation, or rather an abridgement.[37] The eagle Garuda, the attendant of Vishnu, having sinned in thought against his divine master, comes in penitent guise to the crow Bhushanda, who dwelt on the lofty summits of Nila, or the blue mountains, "rich in virtues as in vices; well acquainted with all that has happened since the beginning of time; sometimes wrapt in profound meditation on the being of God, at others pouring forth invocations, and proclaiming to the birds of land and water the praises of Vishnu." This sagacious fowl becomes the instructor of Garuda, recounts to him the number of his transmigrations, and gives him lectures on the greatness and power of Vishnu and Rama, to which latter personage he had belonged from his birth. He informs him that he once animated the body of a Brahman, but that, owing to the maledictions of a certain Rishi or saint, he had afterwards passed into that of a crow.

Another work of this description, but of much greater extent, is the celebrated Hitopadesa;[38] which, under the name of "The Fables of Pilpay," has already been translated into most of the Oriental and Western languages, but so disfigured by alterations and additions as scarcely to retain any feature of its original character.[39] As long ago as the sixth century it was translated into Persian, by order of Chosru Nushirvan; and from this, at a subsequent period, into

[37] *Works*, vol. vi. p. 399.

[38] Translated by SIR W. JONES, *Works*, vol. vi. p. 3—177; and also by WILKINS, London, 1810. [Mr. Wilkins only reprinted the text, after the Serampoor edition, which appeared in 1804, under the superintendence of Colebrooke and Carey. The original Sanscrit has since been published conjointly by Schlegel and Lassen, at Bonn, 1830. TRANSL.]

[39] The word *Hitopadesa* means *salutary* or *friendly counsel.* Instead of *Pilpay* it should be *Bidpay*, which, according to Sir W. Jones, is corrupted from *Vaidyapaya*, the trusty physician. [That illustrious Arabic scholar, the Baron De Sacy, in his excellent edition of Calila and Dimnah, has completely exhausted the subject of the different versions into which the Hitopadesa has been translated. See his preliminary *Mémoire Historique.* TRANSL.]

Arabic and Turkish; and lastly, into French and other languages, until Sir W. Jones presented us with a new version immediately from the original Sanscrit; to which last we shall confine ourselves in the ensuing observations. The Hitopadesa is a book upon morals, propounded through the medium of fable, and composed for the instruction of princes. The Rajah Sudarsana, king of Pataliputra, having froward sons, confided them to the care of the sage, Vishnu Sarman; who, under the form of apologue, delivered to them precepts of morality and wisdom. The whole work is divided into four books; which treat respectively on the acquisition and loss of friends, on war, and peace; all of them subjects of the last importance for princes to study.

The fables contained in the Hitopadesa are certainly like those of Æsop, but with this difference, that the animals in the former collection are made to speak not only according to the several characters we usually attribute to them, but also generally as rational and intelligent beings. The apologue is, without doubt, one of the most ancient kinds of Oriental poetry; and yet the Hitopadesa in its present shape can scarcely be reckoned among the oldest specimens of Sanscrit literature. The scene of these fables is laid in the city Pataliputra, by no means the most ancient in India; and the national literature must have already attained an advanced stage of development when they were composed, and the author himself have been a man of considerable reading; for, instead of the moral commonly subjoined to our fables, he always quotes illustrative passages from the poets; without, however, mentioning their names. But the Hitopadesa may also be considered as a collection of fables arranged by Vishnu Sarman, with a particular object in view; they may consequently have been invented by different authors. And on this last supposition who could possibly venture to determine their respective ages?

Having thus examined in detail the several branches of Sanscrit literature, together with the productions of each as far as they are at present known to us, we may now proceed to some more general considerations, which will probably assist us in replying to the questions proposed in the outset of our inquiry.

The literature of the Sanscrit language incontestably belongs to a highly cultivated people, whom we may with great reason consider to have been the most informed of all the East. It is true we are only acquainted with a very small portion of this literature, and that mostly through translations; but still these, in conjunction with the accounts derived from the researches of learned and credible persons conducted in the country itself, are nevertheless sufficient for enabling us to judge of its value and extent. It is at the same time a scientific and a poetic literature; and yet how much soever the national genius may have exercised itself upon particular branches of science, poetry notwithstanding was the predominant study; and its forms have even been applied to many subjects, which, according to our notions, do not admit of such application.

Further, Sanscrit literature is not only very rich, but also in a certain sense extremely ancient. Every thing concurs to establish the fact that alphabetical writing was known in India from the earliest times; and that its use was not confined to inscriptions, but extended also to every purpose of common life. When we call the literature of the Hindus extremely ancient, we mean to say that a great number of their principal works, considered with regard to subject and essential component parts, are the productions of remote antiquity, though at the same time we are far from asserting that they have always existed in their present form.

Sanscrit literature, perhaps more than any other, stands in need of critical examination; and yet this deficiency has hitherto been but very imperfectly supplied. The first discovery of its hidden treasures gave rise to an excess of enthusiasm and credulity. At a later period men went into the opposite extreme; they began to question the authenticity of particular works, or only particular passages; and forthwith, like Bentley, endeavoured to throw suspicion upon the whole. The truth, however, lies here also, as indeed every where else, in a mean between the two extremes. We have already observed that the principal works of this literature consist of compilations, which therefore presupposes the existence of earlier compositions; and that the epic poems, though severally forming a connected whole, are nevertheless of a character extremely favourable to the introduction of episodes. Now, in order to determine with precision the exact age of Sanscrit literature, we must previously satisfy ourselves upon these two points: how old are the works in question, considered with respect to their principal contents? and in what manner, and at what time, did they receive their present form? Something has been done already towards furnishing an answer; and if we resume our preceding observations, we shall come, I believe, to the following conclusions.

Sanscrit literature has had its respective periods. This we are assured, not only by the voice of national tradition, and the nature of its several works, but also by the progressive stages of development which we meet with in the language itself. The Vedas could not have been written at the same time as the classical epic poems, nor these latter have been contemporary with the Sacontala and other pieces of that kind. For want of accurate chronological data, we cannot absolutely determine these periods; we can only make a general reference to them. The first, we shall call that of the Vedas; though a still longer interval of time might have elapsed before they assumed their present shape. The various hymns and prayers contained in these books, are by very different authors; and are evidently not all of the same age, for how can we imagine the abstract theories which are found in the Upanishads, to have been simultaneously developed? And, moreover, how long might they not have existed in a separate form prior to their being reduced to order, and incorporated by some judicious compiler? Important as it would be to determine this question, we must stop here for want of materials; but that the compilation of the Vedas, or at least the three first, must have taken place at a very early period, has, I think, been sufficiently proved in a former part of our inquiry; with regard to the Atharvan Veda, it seems likely to be a continual subject of discussion whether we are to assign it an equal origin with the others.

The second period we shall call the epic; comprehending the interval in which the great epic poems were written, particularly the Mahabharat and the Ramayana, and no doubt several others at present unknown. That these are of later composition than the Vedas, will be evident on comparing their style and language; on the other hand, it has been elsewhere satisfactorily ascertained that the two poems themselves are of very great antiquity; and must be considerably older than the commencement of our era. The fact, however, contributes just as little towards illustrating the critical history of these works, as a similar presumption in the case of Homer's poems. If the history of these latter, which we possess not only in translations, but also in the original, and have besides so many other helps for explaining them, has never yet been cleared up, notwithstanding all the perspicacity and erudition of the most learned scholars; what better success can we, or ought we, to expect, from the researches made into Sanscrit literature? Nevertheless, when I consider the unity of action prevailing throughout the Mahabharat and the Ramayana, as well as the Iliad and the Odyssey, I can hardly persuade myself that they are nothing more than a simple collection of historic songs. At the same time, I am perfectly willing to allow that the form of the Hindu epic poems is much more favourable to episodes than the Greek; add to this, the manner of writing, and the materials used for that purpose in India, both afford singular opportunities for their introduction. The Hindus wrote ordinarily upon palm leaves, which did not admit of being folded or bound up, like rolls of parchment or papyrus, and at most could only be lightly strung together, when this method was not forbidden, as they even now pretend is the case with regard to the Vedas.[40] Under these circumstances, therefore, how easily might interpolations creep into the original text; and on the other hand, how difficult, we would almost say, how impossible, to arrange and collect the whole into one volume! The inevitable consequence of all this, and particularly in proportion as these songs came into popular use, would be their dismemberment, and ceasing to be regarded as one uniform whole. Fortunately, however, they met with the same lucky chance as the poems of the Ionian bard; and, like the

[40] Polier, vol. i. Preface, p. 21. The Vedas were only given to Col. Polier upon condition that they should not be bound with leather, (for, horrible profanation to a Brahman, it might possibly be made of a cow's hide!) but only with silk. It is easy, therefore, to conceive the extreme difficulty of procuring, even in India, a complete copy of the Vedas. A critical history of the various materials used for writing by the Hindus, would throw considerable light on the history of their literature. See above, p. 107.

rhapsodies of Homer, the Mahabharat and the Ramayana also found their Lycurgus or Pisistratus. In the absence of direct historical testimony on this point, we are nevertheless furnished with some hints from popular tradition, which are too important to be passed over in silence.

It was during the reign of the celebrated Rajah Vicramaditya, and one hundred years before the commencement of the Christian era, that this compilation is reported to have been made by order of the prince himself. The first notice of this circumstance we find in Sir W. Jones, who thus briefly alludes to the report: "He (Calidasa) is believed by some to have revised the works of Valmiki and Vyasa, and to have corrected the perfect editions of them which are now current."[41] Col. Polier has given us a detailed account of this transaction, though it certainly appears rather fabulous.[42] According to him, Rajah Vicramaditya, the Mecænas of poets and men of letters, convened an assembly of Brahmans at Benares, and expressed to them his desire of hearing the ancient books of sacred histories read. But as these, being written on detached palm leaves, were found to be incomplete, either through length of time or the negligence of their guardians, the Rajah accordingly directed them to be gathered together, and commissioned one of the most able among the Brahmans to execute the task. As none of them, however, were willing to engage in such a difficult labour, Calidasa, the most famous of all the wise men and Brahmans of his time, alone ventured to undertake it; and made a complete collection of these works, which even the learned men and Brahmans his rivals, universally regarded as authentic.[43]

This account of Polier, it is true, has no better foundation than the common saying of the Brahmans, for no other sources are quoted in support of it scorrectness. And yet, as Sir William Jones has also noticed the report, it would seem to be the object of pretty general belief; and we can hardly suppose it altogether devoid of historic probability. But,

[41] *Works*, vol. vi. p. 205. [42] *Mythologie des Indous*, vol. i. p. 104.

[43] Polier, in another passage, (vol. i. p. 185,) recounts the fabulous embellishments made to this traditional report, (which, however, chiefly concern the works of Valmiki,) the persecution which Calidasa met with from his rivals, and his final triumph over them.

admitting the reality of the fact as there stated, we must first inquire, what books were so collected together? The account only mentions historic poems, which would therefore seem to exclude the Vedas. The expression *all*, made use of by Polier, cannot possibly be taken in a literal sense, when we consider the great number of these poems; and as Sir W. Jones expressly mentions the works of Valmiki and Vyasa, we may safely include the Ramayana and also the Mahabharat in the report; without presuming to determine whether others of that kind were among the number. It is, perhaps, a more important question for us to decide, in what consisted the undertaking of Calidasa? Was it merely a compilation, or was it rather a critical and accurate edition of the poems alluded to? Now it is otherwise such an extraordinary thing to meet with what we call criticism among the Orientals,[44] that one cannot easily incline to the latter supposition; and yet this seems to be the meaning attached to the native report, when it ascribes all the current editions of their holy books to the supervision of Calidasa. We shall, probably, not be far from the truth, if we understand the report to mean, that Calidasa, and his assistants, collected together and arranged the separate poems, but that they excluded whatever in the poet's judgment seemed to be an improper addition. It is easy to see how much still remains for future discussion and inquiry; but researches of this kind can only be appropriately carried on in India itself.

Whatever be the result of further examination on the above point, we must in every case regard the age of Vicramaditya, as constituting the third period of Sanscrit literature. That the reign of this prince was a splendid one, may be inferred with great probability from the mere circumstance of his having given name to an era, which commenced with his death, and continued for a long time to be in general use. The literary character of this reign was not, however, confined to the mere revision of ancient works; it was no

[44] [The edition of the Ramayana published by Schlegel proves that manuscripts were in the habit of being critically reviewed in India, like the works of the ancient Greek poets were at Alexandria: the same may be said of many important works in Persian and Arabic; and it is well known that the Chinese, upwards of a thousand years ago, established the text of their sacred books by a mode of procedure analogous to that of the Masorites. Fr. Transl.]

less remarkably evidenced in the production of original compositions, by the poets and learned men who adorned the monarch's court. The Sanscrit literature of the time, indeed, seems to have assumed generally a courtly form; and the language itself and the study of versification to have reached the highest point of refinement. The drama was favoured beyond all other kinds of poetry, and gave birth to the greatest masterpieces in the art, which, however, were throughout constructed on principles of court taste. Besides the productions of poetic genius there appeared also works of science, in connexion with the artificial wants of polished society; and encyclopedic dictionaries, like that of Amara Sinha.[45] In short, the age of Vicramaditya is certainly one that in a pre-eminent degree recommends itself to the attention of the historians of India.

The fourth and last period of Sanscrit literature we may consider to have been comprised in that interval of time which we usually call the middle ages. That many Hindu compositions belong to this period is evident from Bentley's researches; and we have already shown that the Puranas then received their present form and arrangement.

All that we have hitherto laid before the reader is, we candidly allow, but a feeble attempt to trace even the outlines of this comprehensive subject. Much, very much, still remains for future inquirers to fill up, and probably to alter, as soon as a brighter ray of light shall have been thrown upon this interesting branch of Oriental literature. It is, however, with such an outline only that we can here commence operations; and, indeed, from the imperfect nature of our materials, it were hardly reasonable to expect much more than an outline.

At the same time, though it is sufficiently obvious, from all that has gone before, that our knowledge of ancient India is still very defective, yet we shall nevertheless be better able to estimate at their real value, not only the sober opinions, but also the wild reveries that have been indulged in by modern scholars with reference to Hindu antiquities.

[45] See above, p. 142. [The Amara Cosha can hardly be called an encyclopedic dictionary, being little more than a bare collection of words, arranged according to the order of their several subjects, without any explanation whatever. FR. TRANSL.]

Quitting the straightforward path of history, and turning aside in pursuit of etymological conjecture, and the results of comparison between the religious systems of India and those of other nations, they have attempted to prove that the Western world must have derived a great part of its mythology, and its civilization in general, from India. Now, though we are very far from wishing to deny the fact of such influence having taken place, yet we have to regret the want of previous acquaintance with the principles on which those comparisons and etymological conclusions are founded. Scarcely had the English become in some measure familiar with the names and attributes of the Hindu deities, than they immediately began to compare them with those of Greece, and to confound them together. Krishna and the Gopis were forthwith changed into Apollo and the Muses; and, in short, the prototype of Olympus was discovered in the Hindu Pantheon. To what erroneous consequences all this must inevitably lead, could not escape the observation of those even who fancied they saw some probable resemblance between certain Greek and Hindu divinities; for in the course of such a long passage from one country to the other, what various changes and modifications might not have occurred? While, therefore, the principal sources of Hindu religion and mythology are so little accessible, and as long as we can only have recourse to the information supplied by foreigners, who have too often examined things through a coloured medium, how can we possibly establish our inquiries upon any solid foundation? And even supposing we could freely avail ourselves of the sources alluded to, yet our progress would be little better, for it is in the very nature of the subject to contain much that will always be conjectural, and the question proposed for solution becomes a kind of enigma, which every one is at liberty to explain in his own way. Some of our modern mythologists, indeed, have made the attempt, and with such a display of sagacity and erudition, that it would be superfluous to enlarge upon the subject in this place, even though a particular inquiry into religious systems were less foreign to the object of the present work, in which we have only considered them in a political point of view. Still greater liberties have been taken with the etymological department:

here also the English gave the first impulse; but to what unwarrantable lengths have some natives of Germany proceeded! These latter, with no more assistance than could be derived from two or three meagre vocabularies (it were a solecism to call them lexicons) of the Sanscrit and the Zend, forthwith set about investigating the connexion between those languages; and a similarity of sound was quite enough, in their opinion, to establish what they were pleased to call derivations, but which might more appropriately have been termed the distortions of a playful fancy. A more profound study of Sanscrit literature, and a better acquaintance with its real sources, have contributed to remove such disorderly erudition; it is still, however, useful to remark, that mere etymological conjecture, unsupported by historic proof, is but a species of lottery, where for one prize we may reckon upon very many blanks.[46] In our researches, therefore, into these distant regions, we shall do well to follow the light of history rather than a deceitful meteor, even though it be not as yet the light of broad day, but only the faint glimmer of the morning dawn.

[46] [The rapid progress lately made in the study of Sanscrit has served to show that the etymological conclusions, which had been drawn by expert philologists, were much more certain than were formerly supposed. It is, indeed, astonishing to observe with what tenacity the synthetical languages, as they are called, preserve the forms of grammar; and conscientious researches have satisfactorily proved, that all these forms may be traced to the Sanscrit, or possibly to some more ancient dialect from which it is derived. The publication of the Vedas can alone enable us to determine the latter question with any degree of certainty. The numerous mistakes at first committed in the etymological branch of the study, originated with persons who were but little, if at all, acquainted with Sanscrit. So late even as the year 1823, M. Frank was for deriving that extraordinary language from the modern Persian; and still more recently, Dugald Stewart and Professor Dunbar have preposterously attempted to deduce its origin from the Greek and the Latin. The same remark will also apply to the mythological comparisons noticed by our author. FR. TRANSL.] [See Schlegel's Reflexions sur l'Etude des Langues Asiatiques, addressed to the late Sir James Mackintosh, p. 99—107. TRANSL.]

INDIANS.

CHAPTER II.

Fragments relative to the History, Constitution, and Commerce of Ancient India.

THE EXTREME REGIONS OF THE HABITABLE WORLD HAVE IN SOME MEASURE RECEIVED THE FAIREST GIFTS OF NATURE; — NOW THE MOST DISTANT COUNTRY TOWARDS THE EAST IS INDIA. HEROD. THALIA, 106.

ALTHOUGH the title of the present chapter will not lead the reader to expect any thing more than historical fragments, yet it will be necessary in this place to investigate somewhat more closely a question already touched upon in the foregoing pages, viz. To what extent are the Hindus in possession of a general history? and how far can a denial of the fact be reconciled with their vaunted pretensions to a very remote chronology?

The absence of regular historians, in our sense of the term, is a loss which India sustains in common with the other nations of Central Asia; among whom, as far as we are aware, the art of writing history has in no case exceeded the simple compilation of annals. The Hindus, however, do not appear to have ever possessed even their annalists, like the Arabians, Persians, and others; whose business it was to hand down the memory of events, if not in historical connexion, at least in chronological order.

And yet the Hindus are not altogether without some documents relating to history; such as the genealogies of their kings, which traverse a number of generations, and contain a great many proper names. The genealogies themselves, as we shall presently have occasion to remark, are found in the epic poems and in the Puranas; and were most likely, previous to their being consigned in those writings, preserved by means of oral tradition, as is common among other Oriental nations. For, in proportion to the degree of consequence attached by them to lineage and descent, so would be their anxiety to preserve some memorial of both; and as the recollection necessary for this purpose was less burthened with a weight of other knowledge to acquire and retain, they succeeded much better than we should at first imagine to be possible. In India, however, as we learn from the Ramayana, an additional degree of interest was attached to this kind of tradition; for as a preliminary step to the marriage of a prince's daughter, it was necessary that her genealogical table should be prepared, in order to establish her descent from a royal stock.[1] In this manner, consequently, the possession of a genealogical register would be an indispensable requisite in the houses of the reigning families.

Sir W. Jones, in his Essay on the Chronology of the Hindus, has already made us acquainted with some of these royal genealogies; among which, those of the kings of Maghada, or Behar, particularly deserve our attention. The sources from which he borrowed these tables will be found in the work of a learned native, called Rhadacanta Sarman, who was then still living, and who had published in Sanscrit an exposition of the Puranas;[2] from which, according to his own avowal, he had collected the genealogies themselves. The first of these specimens evidently betray their mythological character, in representing the kings as descendants of the sun and moon; at all events they go far back into the fabulous ages, and Sir W. Jones himself remarked their deficiency in chronological arrangement. The genealogical series of the kings of Maghada is distinguished by somewhat of a more historical character; these are reported to have reigned in five separate dynasties, from the year 2100 to 452 B. C., from which we might infer, with some probability, that in those distant periods of time, when the throne of the Pharaohs was in all its splendour in Egypt, an equally considerable empire might have

[1] *Ramayana*, i. p. 580. At the court of Dasaratha this is represented to be the peculiar office of Janaka.

[2] Sir W. Jones's *Works*, vol. i. p. 288. This work is entitled Puranarthapracasa, i. e. an explanation of the meaning of the Puranas.

flourished on the banks of the Ganges. If we inquire, however, for the authenticity of this chronological statement, we must be content with admitting the bare report of the Hindus themselves, who commence the series with the reign of Pradyota, 2100 B. C., and close it with that of Chandravidya, who died three hundred and ninety-six years before the era of Vicramaditya, or four hundred and fifty-six before ours. Now, though it is evident these statements are borrowed from the Puranas, we must still decide which of those writings have furnished the account; and as they differ very much from one another in regard to age, we must further ascertain the period of time to which they belong. In an inquiry of this nature, the critic is obliged to grope his way in complete darkness; and the numerous improbabilities with which these genealogical tables abound, as Sir W. Jones has remarked, must render us doubly cautious how we proceed.[3] Wilford made a fresh attempt to classify the dynasties of the empire of Maghada according to the Puranas;[4] but his work is so full of inconsistencies and arbitrary assumptions, that the critical historian will scarcely derive any more benefit from consulting this, than he will from his other treatises.[5]

A much more important undertaking was accomplished a few years since by Mr. Hamilton, who has arranged the Hindu dynasties, and assigned the names of their respective kings, in the genealogical tables which accompany his remarks on this subject.[6] In fact, he has adopted the only method capable of throwing a greater degree of light over these complicated successions of princes. The introduction

[3] Sir W. Jones's *Works*, vol. i. p. 804.

[4] *Asiatic Res.* vol. ix. p. 82, "On the Kings of Maghada." He quotes as his authorities the Vishnu, Brahmanda, and Vayu Puranas, loc. cit. p. 87.

[5] [While Wilford's general erudition and high attainments in Sanscrit lore eminently fitted him for archæological pursuits, his love of theory made him the dupe of designing knaves; and his works, which are mines of knowledge to those who can justly appreciate them, are pregnant with danger to the uninitiated. Transl.]

[6] "Genealogies of the Hindus, extracted from their Sacred Writings, with an Introduction and Alphabetical Index, by Francis Hamilton, Edinburgh, 1819, 8vo.; together with Genealogical Tables of the Deities, Princes, Heroes, and remarkable personages of the Hindus, extracted from the Sacred Writings of that people." The tables are twenty-six in number. The alphabetical index to the gods, kings, cities, mountains, rivers, etc., as far as they are connected with mythology, is very useful.

to his work contains certain preliminary observations and discussions relative to the two principal branches of the royal Hindu genealogies, already noticed by Sir W. Jones; that is to say, the dynasties of the sun and the moon. Of these, the dynasty of the moon appears in some measure best adapted to the purposes of classification; it is divided into several branches, particularly those of the Coros and Pandos, the quarrel between whom forms the subject of the Mahabharat. To this belong the kings of Mathura, Maghada, Ayodhya, Hastinapura, and others. The dynasty itself is derived from King Atri, and that of the sun from King Marichi, two contemporary sovereigns. To the latter belong the kings of Mithila, and Kasi, or Benares, etc. The tables give merely the names of the kings, distributed according to their respective families, without any chronological adjustment whatever. The author, in the body of his work, endeavours to arrange the several dynasties by centuries, beginning with the twentieth before our era, and terminating with the ninth after Christ; particularly those of the kings of Maghada, Mithila, and Ayodhya; and attempts to show how far they were contemporary with each other. In default, however, of more precise data, he is obliged to calculate by generations, reckoning from four to five for each century. It is easy to conceive how uncertain and inconclusive this method of demonstration must necessarily be, and yet it is the only one at our present disposal.

The principal question for us to determine is, what are the sources from whence these genealogies are derived? And here fortunately the author has not left us in doubt. They are four in number, viz. the Bhagavat Purana, for the twelve first tables; the Bangha-Lata, (probably another Purana, but of which we have no further information,) for the four next ensuing; the Harivansa, an episode from the Mahabharat, for the nine following; and the Ramayana, for the last table. Although we could have wished the author to have given a more detailed account of his several authorities and the use he has made of them, and to have informed us also whether he has perused them throughout, and in the original; yet one principal result of the whole is no less clear and intelligible, namely, that we must consider the Hindu epic poems, properly so called, and the Puranas, as the real sources of the history and genealogies of the ancient kings of India; and it is by reference to those writings that the critical inquirer must estimate the value of the genealogies themselves. In fact, he will not hesitate to class them along with the genealogies of the kings and heroes of Greece; for the tables before us stand almost in the same relation with Hindu mythology, as those of Apollodorus do with respect to the Greek; we ought not, therefore, to expect in them much critical exactness, whether of history or chronology. Composed and preserved as they were by the poets, we may not inaptly term them poetical histories, though at the same time we are not for that reason obliged to suppose them altogether the fruit of poetical imaginations. Indeed it would be unreasonable to conclude that the genealogies in question were solely invented by the epic poets, in direct contradiction to the nature of the ancient epic poem, as well as to the composition of the genealogies themselves, which only mention the bare names, without any distinction of time;[7] and for whose insertion we should be at a loss to conceive any adequate motive, were they not founded in ancient tradition, and probably also in written genealogical registers. It is just as certain that there formerly existed kings of Maghada, Ayodhya, and Mithila, as that there were such persons as the kings of Troy, Thebes, and Athens; but with regard to their further history, we must be content to take it for fabulous.

In opposition to this opinion might perhaps be objected what we are told respecting the Annals of Cashmire, which Abulfazl informs us in the Ayin Acbari, extend as far back as four thousand years.[8] According to this author, when the emperor Acbar made his grand entry into Cashmire, the inhabitants presented him with a Sanscrit work, entitled, "Raja Taringinî," containing this history, and which the emperor subsequently ordered to be translated into Persian. Abulfazl quotes the names of the kings who appear in these Annals, whose successive reigns are said to have occupied a space of four thousand one hundred and nine years, eleven months, and nine days; these, being a

[7] This remark will apply as well to the genealogies contained in the Ramayana as to those in the Mahabharat. See above, p. 162.

[8] *Ayin Acbari*, vol. ii. p. 157.

hundred and ninety-one in number, he has distributed in nine tables or dynasties, indicating at the same time the duration of each king's reign, except those of the first dynasty. The work of Abulfazl was for a long time the only available source of information on this subject. Modern researches, however, have since acquainted us with the actual existence of these annals in Sanscrit, and in a much more detailed form than in the Persian translation.[9] But all that we know of the work up to the present time, only serves to confirm our previous opinion, that these annals were extracted from the epic poems and the Puranas, enriched nevertheless with chronological dates; and consequently it follows that the history of Cashmire, as well as that of other parts of India, is nothing more than a poetical history, in the above sense of the term, since from the very beginning it was immediately connected with the Hindu epic poems. After giving a brief notice of the foundation of a colony in Cashmire, and the series of kings down to the Coros and Pandos, the author commences his history and list of kings, with a contemporary of Yudhishthir, named Gonanda, who was slain by Balabhadra, the elder brother of Krishna, and a principal character in the Ramayana. According to Abulfazl's own confession, the whole is every where intermingled with fabulous narrations, from which he has only selected those which bore some resemblance to historic probability; and even then merely because he was in want of better materials to supply their place. Some of the facts, however, recounted by him, are not without interest in an historical point of view; such, for instance, as the expulsion of the Buddhists from Cashmire through the agency of the Brahmans, an event which is referred to a very remote antiquity. "Among the successors of Gonanda," observes Abulfazl, "the religion of Siva was predominant until a usurper, named Bodhisatwa, introduced that of Buddha. This reformer reigned a hundred years; his successor, Abymaniah,[10] overthrew the worship of Buddha, and re-established the ancient form." We may also add, as another interesting historical fact, the submission of Cashmire to Vicramaditya, king of Ujjayani, after the death of Rajah

[9] See Colebrooke's observations on the Jains, *Asiatic Res.* vol. ix. p. 294.
[10] Called Nerk in the *Ayin Acbari*, p. 159.

Heren.[11] In conclusion, we may remark of the tables in question, that notwithstanding the apparent accuracy with which the duration of each reign is attempted to be laid down, they are nevertheless in certain dynasties so long, and in others again so short, as to be opposed to all historic credibility.[12]

It is true, the opinions hitherto set forth have reference only to those sources of Hindu history which are peculiar to the Brahmans and their religious followers. Another question, therefore, still remains to be answered, viz. whether there do not also exist historic writings and annals among the professors of Buddhism? We are at present but imperfectly acquainted with the literary compositions of this sect; and yet it is from one of their writings, entitled, Rajavali, that the "History of Ceylon" has been taken;[13] a work which has considerably enriched the province of Hindu literature, since, to the best of our knowledge, it is the only composition of the Buddhists that has hitherto reached Europe. The book commences with an account of the formation of the earth; and its contents in general are evidently derived from other sources than the Puranas of the Brahmans, though they contribute much less to history than even these latter; for the matters therein recounted are not so much of a mythological, as a simply fabulous character. The kings mentioned in the first part of the book, are made to reign upwards of a thousand years, and have often as many sons; and although the reigns of the kings comprised in the latter part are of much shorter duration, yet they are distinguished by no memorable event, if we except sundry invasions of the Malabars on the opposite coast, which are represented to have taken place at various times, and with various success. In short, we have little doubt that these narrations were borrowed from poetical works, though we may not be able to substantiate our opinion by a particular reference to the works themselves.

[11] *Ayin Acbari*, loc. cit. [Maharana?]

[12] Compare, for instance, Table ii. (which represents twenty-one princes to have reigned, collectively, a thousand and twenty-one years, and none of them, individually, less than thirty) with Table vii., where we have only fifty-four years' duration for the reigns of no less than ten princes.

[13] Translation of the Singhalese History of Ceylon; communicated by Sir Alex. Johnston, in the "Annals of Oriental Literature," Feb. 1821, p. 385, etc.

The attention of English scholars having been first directed to the antiquities of India, could hardly fail in the sequel, to include the chronology also of that country as an appropriate object of investigation, the two being so intimately connected together, that, according to our notions, whatever concerned the history could not but have some reference to the chronology of India. Add to this the reasonable expectation that was entertained of throwing some light upon general history, by the result of their inquiries into the chronology of such an ancient people as the Hindus. The result, however, was by no means commensurate with the extent of their hopes. The very first English scholar who directed his attention to this subject was obliged to confess, that the chronology of the Hindus set out from a point so extravagantly absurd, as to involve the destruction of the whole system.[14] He was followed in the same course by Wilford, whose opinion is not a whit more favourable, when he declares, that the chronological system of the Hindus is quite as extravagant as their geography.[15] In the mean time, considering the close connexion subsisting between their chronology and astronomy, the question might still be said to have remained in abeyance, so long as professed astronomers had not examined this litigious point. Accordingly, Mr. Davis[16] was the first to undertake the task, and after him Bentley, with the application certainly of much more rigorous criticism. The inquiries of both these scholars were principally directed to an examination of a work already mentioned, the Surya Siddhanta, which the Hindus themselves consider as the foundation of their astronomical and chronological systems; and as one of their most ancient literary productions, but which Bentley has proved to be of comparatively modern origin.[17]

With regard to the advantage which has or can be derived to history from this discussion, it is rather of a negative than a positive kind. The only fact which seems to be

[14] Sir W. Jones's *Works*, vol. i. p. 295.

[15] *Asiatic Res.* vol. v. p. 241.

[16] Ibid. vol. ii. No. 15.

[17] See above, p. 146. [In India, as well as elsewhere, works of science were in the habit of being remodelled from time to time, in order to keep pace with the march of discovery; but the fabulous name of the original author was generally retained in the improved work. This remark will apply to all that Bentley has advanced on the subject. Fr. Transl.]

proved is, that the present chronological system of the Brahmans is not so old as they represent it to be; that no traces of it are to be found in those works whose great antiquity has already been shown to be indisputable; and that consequently it has been derived as little from the Vedas as from the great epic poems.[18] Even the accounts left us by the Greeks respecting their first acquaintance with India, all tend to support the same conclusion. It is true, the Hindus even then boasted of a succession of kings, which they carried back to upwards of six thousand years,[19] thereby affecting the same pretensions to high antiquity which they do at the present day. But then we hear nothing of those enormous periods of time embracing thousands of millions

[18] According to Bentley, the Brahmans at the present time have three chronological systems: 1. the Brahma Calpa, invented one thousand and three hundred years ago, by Brahma Gupta; 2. the Padma Calpa, invented some eight or nine hundred years since, by Dhara Padma; and the third contained in the Surya Siddhanta, invented seven or eight hundred years ago by Varaha Mihira, *Asiatic Res.* vol. viii. p. 199. In addition to these, Bentley quotes from another astronomical work, entitled Graha Munjari, two more ancient systems, which he has endeavoured to reconcile and make available for the purposes of history, p. 224, etc.; an attempt, however, which appears to be conducted on very arbitrary principles, as may be seen by inspecting the treatise itself. Their application to history is founded on a comparison of the Puranas with the determination of the four ages, according to the first of the two systems, which makes the *Satya Yug*, or the golden age, to have began 3164 years before Christ; the *Treta Yug*, or the silver age, 2204 B. C.; the *Dwapar Yug*, or the brazen age, 1484 B. C.; and the *Kali Yug*, or the iron age, 1004 B. C.; in direct contradiction to the other systems, which place the commencement of the latter age, 3100 years before Christ. JONES's *Works*, vol. i. p. 318. The first age contains nothing of historical importance, but a fabulous account of the Deluge; the second, or silver age, comprises the origin of the Indian empire, and the dynasties of the Sun and Moon. It is here, too, the Puranas place Bhrigu and his descendants, Indra, Puradaksha, and others, and also Visvamitra and his relation Parasurama. In the Dwapar, or iron age, the war of the Pandos and Coros fell out; and during the same period lived Vyasa, Causica, Rishyasringha, and other renowned saints. But we are first entitled to ask, on what foundation that system is built; are they historical? if so, where are the authorities? or are they astronomical? In the latter case, according to Bentley himself, the Hindus possessed no scientific astronomy before the time of Brahma Gupta, who lived in the sixth century after Christ, p. 235. And further, were the Puranas composed with reference to that system? The supposition of four ages is probably of very ancient date in India; but the time of their respective durations, being the peculiar business of chronologists to determine, is independent of all fiction. Besides, both those systems comprise cycles of millions of years; and agreeably to what has been noticed above, we shall for that reason alone be less disposed to attribute to them a very remote antiquity. Of the fourth, or proper historical age, no remarkable events are given, and of course, its application will be of no service to the purpose of history.

[19] ARRIAN, *Op.* p. 175. From Dionysus to Sandracottus the space of six thousand and forty-two years is said to have elapsed.

of years. It is further extremely probable that the Hindus possessed no continuous system of chronological computation before the era of Vicramaditya, and that they reckoned by generations as the Greeks did for a long course of time. We know of nothing which would prove the existence of any era prior to the one just mentioned;[20] we only know that the Hindus themselves did not furnish the Greeks with any other notion of their method of computing time than that by generations.[21] Now it is perfectly impossible to suppose the existence of any thing like regular historic chronology without some fixed era. And even if we consider the chronological cycles of the Hindus as astronomical or poetical, or as a mixture of both, yet still history will derive no further benefit from the consideration, than merely venturing to assign the date of certain fables in general terms; and we must content ourselves with endeavouring to distinguish the more ancient from what is less so, without seeking to fill up the interval with positive and well recognised dates.

The question relative to the origin of a people to whom, notwithstanding the imperfect state of their chronology, it is impossible to avoid attributing a very remote antiquity, can only be solved by mere conjecture. But supposing we were to investigate the origin of the Hindus, considered as forming a principal nation by themselves, we must first of all determine whether they are actually one undivided and aboriginal people or no? A more particular examination of them, indeed, would lead us to doubt the correctness of the latter position, and to infer with much greater probability that this union among them was of a political character,[22] and brought about by religion and legislation, than that it was founded on an identity of race. The division of the Hindus into castes, extends as far back as their history itself; but the difference between these several castes is so very great, that we are almost obliged to admit a cor-

[20] The era of Yudhishthir indeed is said to have preceded that of Vicramaditya by the space of 3044 years, and to have commenced about 3100 before Christ; but, according to Wilford, we are to understand this, not of an historic era, but solely of an astronomical cycle. *Asiatic Res.* vol. ix. p. 86.

[21] ARRIAN, loc. cit.

[22] In this sense I understand the common derivation of the four castes, in respective order, from the head, arms, body, and feet of Brahma.

responding difference of original extraction. I shall reserve to another opportunity, when I come to speak of the Egyptians, an attempt to show how the division of castes is almost always based upon an original diversity of race, and shall confine myself in this place merely to the proofs which arise from variations in exterior appearance, and particularly colour. According to Niebuhr,[23] the caste of Brahmans and Banians have a complexion so clear, as almost to pass for white; "because," adds the same traveller, "they have preserved themselves pure from all foreign admixture," while on the other hand the lower orders are of a dark colour, often approaching to black. "It is remarkable," says a British observer,[24] "that the same fair complexion and caste of features distinguish this class (the Brahmans) through all the different provinces, from eight to twenty degrees of N. lat., (and by all accounts still further,) among nations varying so much in both as the Tamuls, the Telingas, the Canarins, Mahrattas, and Orias, the five families which appear to compose the body of the original inhabitants of the peninsula, at present distinguished by different dialects as by different features." A more extended examination of the Hindu castes, will serve to bring forward many other points of resemblance peculiar to the three higher ones, viz. that of the Brahmans, the Kshatriyas, or warrior caste, which no longer maintains its original form, and the Vaisyas, or mechanics; all three directly opposed to the Sudras, or inferior caste, and its various ramifications; and thus tend to confirm the supposition of a different origin upon other grounds. If we choose, with Sir W. Jones,[25] to derive the Hindus, as well as the other principal nations of Asia, from Iran, we must confine ourselves in making such an assertion to the three superior castes; these, however, especially that of the Brahmans, which yet appears to be the only one of all that has remained in its

[23] NIEBUHR'S *Travels*, vol. i. p. 450.

[24] CAPT. COLIN MACKENZIE, *Asiatic Res.* vol. vi. p. 426.

[25] *Works*, vol. i. p. 129, etc. [Sir W. Jones was the first who broached this opinion, which however reposes on no historic grounds. In point of fact, the Zend is derived from the Sanscrit; and a passage in Menu (x. 44) makes the Persians (Pahlava) to have descended from the Hindus of the second or warrior caste. As to the colonies in the Himalaya, it is very probable that they are much less ancient than the civilization of Aryaverta, or India properly so called. FR. TRANSL.]

original state, are so pre-eminently distinguished from the inferior caste, that they may be considered as properly constituting the nation. And although we cannot determine their original country upon correct historical principles, yet every thing induces us to believe that they first came from the north. The traditionary reports of the natives of Cashmire, mention the Brahmans as the earliest immigrants into that country.[26] Some additional light has been thrown on this subject by the researches of certain English travellers who journeyed in quest of the sources of the Ganges; an expedition which conducted them into the heart of the Himalaya mountains.[27] As early as the year 1807 Lieutenants Webb and Raper had penetrated as far as Bhadrinath, (in N. lat. 30° 42′,) and Gangoutri, (in N. lat. 30° 59′);[28] subsequently Capt. Hodgson in 1817 succeeded in reaching a spot situated in 31° 51′ N. lat., where a principal branch of the Ganges takes its rise in a cavern surmounted by a rock covered with snow. Beyond this point the further progress of the traveller was arrested by lofty mountains of snow, and tremendous glaciers, forming probably the highest part of the Himalayan range, and from which towards the south flow the Ganges and Indus with their tributary streams; and in an easterly direction the Brahmaputra, or Sampo, the principal river of Thibet.[29] It is here, however, in the heart of this Alpine country, that we still find the abode of Brahmans, which we can scarcely consider as any other than their original seat, together with the temples of their gods, and the accompanying body of priests. At the confluence of two branches of the Ganges stands the holy city of Devaprayaga, (in N. lat.

[26] *Ayin Acbari.*

[27] See Colebrooke, "On the Sources of the Ganges," with the accounts of Lieutenant Raper, *Asiatic Res.* vol. xi., and the "Journal of a Survey to the heads of the rivers Ganges and Jumna," by Capt. I. A. Hodgson, vol. xiv. Moorcroft has proved that the Ganges does not rise in the lake Mansarowar, in Little Thibet, as was formerly supposed. See his Travels, *Asiatic Res.* vol. xii. p. 380, etc.

[28] In Major Rennell's earlier charts the situation of these places was laid down two or three degrees further north. See Colebrooke, loc. cit.

[29] [M. Klaproth maintains, in opposition to the accounts of English travellers, but in accordance with the Chinese authorities, that the Sampo, or, as he calls it, the Yarou-dzangbo-tchou, is distinct from the Brahmaputra, and is identical with the Irawaddy of the Birmese empire. See a review of both statements in the *Asiatic Journ.* vol. xxv., and Mémoire sur les sources du Brahmaputra et de l'Irawaddi, par M. J. Klaproth. Paris, 1828. Transl.]

30° 8',) inhabited by Brahmans. Further on we find the temple of Bhadrinath, which is very opulent, and said to have upwards of seven hundred flourishing villages in dependence on the high priest.[30] To the same dignitary belongs also the commercial town of Mana, which contains fifteen hundred inhabitants of Tartar extraction, and is situate on the high road to Cashmire and Little Thibet, but is however only habitable in summer, owing to the snow under which it lies covered during the remainder of the year. At Gangoutri also, where the river issues from the bosom of lofty mountains, the interior of which seems to form one vast sea of ice, stands another of these ancient temples. The predominant sect throughout this part of India is that of Siva, without however being the only one; and the temples there existing are still holy places of resort to thousands of pilgrims, who assemble for purposes of devotion, as well as to carry on international commerce.[31] It was in this manner, at distant periods of time unknown to history, and in countries inaccessible to hostile invasion, that sacerdotal empires were formed and maintained, which subsequently produced similar establishments all over India, and perhaps also in other parts of the globe. The most ancient Hindu poems represent the neighbourhood of the Ganges to have been the capital territory of India, the cradle of her heroes, and the point of departure for expeditions undertaken into southern countries, as far as Ceylon; and the above described series of holy temples, extending throughout this vast country, both above and below ground, together with the figures of their divinities, are as it were a living chronicle of their progressive extension from north to south; the very reverse of what we find to have occurred

[30] [Since the period of the Ghurkhali invasion, these places have been in a miserable state of decline, and the pontificate is usually put up for sale to the highest bidder. TRANSL.]

[31] [If in the plains at the foot of the Himalaya we meet with no traces of ancient temples, it ought to be recollected that, owing to the nature of the soil, brick was the only available material for the purposes of building, as was the case also in Babylonia; and edifices of this kind would of course offer less obstruction to the hands of Moslem violence. But that there were many temples here in former times, is sufficiently attested by the Journal of a Chinese traveller, in the early part of the fifth century, discovered by the late Abel-Remusat, and the publication of which, had it not been for the lamented and untimely death of that illustrious scholar, would have thrown some new light on researches of this nature. FR. TRANSL.]

in Egypt, where the social and religious advance was in an opposite direction, from south to north.

What we may regard as an incontestable fact in the history of the Hindu nation, is the pre-eminence, or rather absolute sovereignty, of the Brahmans over the other classes of society. This dominion, it is true, was not exercised immediately, and without the intervention of kingly power; in other words, we are not to infer that the Brahmans themselves enjoyed the royal authority; for the Rajahs belonged not to this powerful body, but were selected, as in Egypt, from among the warrior caste, or from some particular families; the priesthood, however, restrained the power of the sovereign by religious enactments, and we have already noticed in the Ramayana more than one instance of the awful veneration in which the Brahmans were held even by kings themselves. The question is, did the Brahmans owe this distinction solely to the influence of religion, or did they acquire it by force of arms? Without doubt, religion may have served to confirm this power, and yet the national report has preserved to us the recollection of a violent struggle, which ended in placing the Kshatriyas and the Rajahs under subjection to the Brahmans. This is described as the work of Parasu Rama, an incarnation of Vishnu, under the form of a Brahman. After having gained twenty victories over the warrior caste, he was on the point of exterminating them, when the Brahmans themselves interceded in their behalf, vouchsafed them an asylum and permission to eat at the same table.[32] The Mahabharat, as well as the Ramayana, both allude to this struggle. In the former poem the narration of that event forms an episode:[33] in the latter, on the contrary, it is spoken of in reference to the remarkable story of the quarrel between Visvamitra, (who was Rajah of the Kshatriyas, before his penances had

[32] POLIER, vol. i. p. 288.

[33] At the end of the fifth book, according to the translation of M. Mitscherlich, Durjohn speaks in an assembly as follows: "And I will tell you a story which is very similar to the one just mentioned. There was in Malwa a king named Herghes, whose army consisted altogether of Kshatriyas, and between him and the king of the Brahmans a war broke out. The Kshatriyas, though the most numerous party, were nevertheless worsted in every engagement. At last they came and asked the Brahmans,—"What is the reason that you are always victorious, though inferior in numbers to ourselves?" The Brahmans answered,—" (Here is a break in the MS.)

elevated him to the rank of a principal sage,) with the Brahman high priest Vasishtha, who was counselled to offer resistance when Visvamitra demanded of him and carried off by force the holy cow, the fruitful giver of all abundance.[34]

Although it would be impossible to determine the exact period when this quarrel took place, yet it is no less evident that it must have been long anterior to the composition of the holy books above mentioned. For they every where notice the Brahmans as already the predominant caste, and the Kshatriyas as standing in a subordinate relation to them. The successive incarnations of Vishnu would seem to confirm this opinion; for that in which he appears in the character of Parasu Rama is the sixth, and by consequence must have preceded the incarnation which is sung of in the Ramayana. Accordingly, the Brahmans place its occurrence as far back as the second age. It is true, our knowledge of this event is only derived to us through a poetic medium, and if we conceive ourselves entitled to assume it as an historical fact, it is merely because we are thereby enabled to explain the relations subsequently established between the two castes.

Next to the establishment of Brahmanical influence, the war between the Coros and Pandos is the most famous event in the history of India, and one which has been the most celebrated in tradition and poetry. In this respect it has been no less important for the Hindus than the Trojan war was to the Greeks, in its influence upon their poetry, literature, and arts; we may naturally therefore inquire, whether it is the pure offspring of poetical imagination, or is it founded upon any historical fact? We might certainly furnish a more determinate reply to the question, were we in complete possession of the poem which has immortalized this war; we might then be enabled to ascertain whether the Mahabharat is interwoven with a sufficient number of geographical and historical details, as to imply the actual occurrence of the events therein related. An inquiry of this sort, however, would involve a more general discussion, narrowly concerning the ancient history of India itself, viz.

[34] *Ramayana*, i. 470, etc. "The power of the Kshatriyas is not greater than that of the Brahmans: O Brahman! thy power is of divine origin, and far superior to that of a Kshatriya."

the question whether in the most early times there has flourished one or more empires in the neighbourhood of the Ganges? Whatever we may have it in our power to advance on this subject, it must still be remembered, agreeably to an observation already made, that we have here to speak of a history which has only been preserved to us through the medium of the poets.

Tradition represents India, like Egypt, to have originally formed but one empire. The first kings of the fabulous period, such as Menu and others, are generally termed kings of India; but the two contemporary dynasties of the Sun and Moon, the one reigning at Ayodhya, the other at Pratishthana, or Vitora, would suggest the idea of a separation having already taken place.[35] A similar plurality of sovereigns afterwards continued to be an ordinary occurrence in Hindu mythology, with the occasional difference, however, that one of these monarchs was considered as lord paramount over the rest, who stood towards him in the relation of feudatory princes; nevertheless, his superiority in such cases appears to have been merely transient, and extorted by violence.[36] For in the epic poems India is generally represented as comprising a number of petty principalities, each under the government of its respective chief, who is independent of the others, and equal to them at least in rank, if not in power.

In speaking of India, we understand more especially by that appellation the northern parts of the country, containing Hindustan Proper, above all the land of the Ganges, in contradistinction to the Deccan, which forms the southern peninsula. Under the term, land of the Ganges, we mean to include the whole tract adjacent to the banks of that river, from its rise in the mountains to the sources of its confluent streams, particularly the Jumna, Goggra, and Sona. Though the position of certain towns may still appear subject to doubt, it will hardly be possible to mistake the geography of the whole, as the fables contained in the Ramayana, relative to the Ganges and its tributary rivers, are sufficient for enabling us to determine the general localities, which are still more precisely ascertained by reference to the Laws of

[35] JONES's *Works*, vol. i. p. 296.
[36] POLIER, vol. i. p. 598, etc., in reference to the fable of Rajah Jerashind.

Menu.[37] According to the latter authority, it is true, we find the land of Bramavarta, formerly the abode of the gods, and situate between the holy rivers Sarasvati and Ahrishadvati (the Deva and Ganges); and the country of Brahmarshi, with the cities of Kurukshetra, or Indraprastha, (Delhi,) Matsya, Kanyakubja, (Canoge,) and Surasena, or Mathura, (in Behar,) the place where Krishna revealed himself to mankind, and the favourite habitation of Brahmans; for it is said, (by Menu,) "From a Brahman who was born at Brahmarshi, let all men on earth learn their several usages." Contiguous to this is the country of Madhyadesa, or the Middleland, together with Ariaverta, extending from the eastern to the western ocean, and inhabited by honourable men; since it was exclusively destined for the abode of the three superior castes, a privilege refused to the country of the Nilechas, or Barbarians. In the above countries are found all those famous cities, which are celebrated in the Hindu epic poems. In the Ramayana, the capital of India appears to have been Ayodhya, situate in the land of Kushula, and the royal abode of King Dasaratha.[38] It was built on the river Suriya, no doubt the same as the Goggra or Deva, which flowing from the north-east, empties itself into the Ganges, not far from Sirpur. The upper part of this river is still called Surjew in Major Rennell's chart. It would follow, therefore, that Ayodhya is rightly considered to be the modern Oude, though the limits of the ancient territory appear to have been less extensive than the present; for at a distance of no more than three or four days' journey[39] was the city Mithila, in the kingdom of Videha, (now the province of Tirhut,[40]) where king Janaka resided. Ayodhya is represented in the Ramayana as the capital of one of the oldest Hindu states; and the genealogical register of King Dasaratha is there carried back through forty-two generations, as far as Brahma, whose descendant in the seventh degree, named Ikshvaku, was the first king of Ayodhya, and from whom, in the thirty-sixth remove, Dasaratha traced his descent.[41] It would therefore

[37] *Ramayana*, i. 345, sq. Compare Laws of Menu, ii. 17—23, and vii. 193. [The rivers Nerbudda and Mahanadi form the boundaries of Aryaverta, towards the south. Fr. Transl.]

[38] *Ramayana*, 94, sq. [39] Ibid. i. 563. [40] Ibid. i. 565. [41] Ibid. i. 574, sq.

follow, according to the usual mode of calculation, that the kingdom of Ayodhya had already existed nearly a thousand years previous to the birth of Rama, in the person of that monarch's son. On the other hand, the genealogical table of Janaka, the king of Mithila, only comprises twenty-two generations. Now, whatever be the measure of dependence we can reasonably place in these documents, this at least is certain, that Ayodhya is celebrated in Hindu tradition, which was repeated and confirmed by the epic poets as one of the most ancient states of India; and we do not, perhaps, assume too much, when, in accordance with the testimony just noticed, we venture to place its origin from 1500 to 2000 years before the Christian era. In a very remarkable passage of the Ramayana mention is made of certain foreign Rajahs, who were invited by Dasaratha to be present at his solemn sacrifice;[42] these were the sovereign of Kasi, or Benares, the Rajahs of Maghada, or Behar, of Sindu and Surashtra, (Sind and Surat,) of Unga and Suvira, (of which, one is conjectured to mean Ava, the other some district situate on the Persian frontier,) and, in fine, the princes of the South, or the Deccan. They are represented as the friends, and some of them also as the relations of Dasaratha, by no means, however, as his vassals. It is therefore evident, that the author of the most ancient Hindu epic poem, considered India to be divided into a number of separate and independent principalities.

The same manner of representation, as far as we can at present judge, prevails also in the Mahabharat. The kingdom of the Pandos is there described as the principal one, though by no means including the whole of India, according to the modern definition; as it merely comprised a considerable portion of territory along the Ganges, from the northern mountains as far as Bengal. During the separation between the two families, a kingdom was formed in the South under Yuddhishthir, chief of the Pandos, who established his residence at Delhi, or Indraprastha;[43] and another in the North, under Duryodhana, chief of the Coros, of which

[42] *Ramayana*, i. 159.

[43] The name of Delhi is of modern origin; but the foundation of the city itself (attributed to Rajah Bhagavat) is as old as the fabulous ages, (POLIER, vol. ii. p. 263,) at which time it was already celebrated for its splendour; vol. i. p. 606.

the capital was Hastinapura, and continued to be so upon the union of the two kingdoms, after the victory procured to the Pandos by the assistance of Krishna. In this manner the empire of the latter family became the principal, though it was by no means the only one in India.[44] The Mahabharat also mentions other Rajahs, such, for instance, as those of Canoge[45] and Mandota,[46] etc., of whom we know but little, from our not possessing a complete translation of the whole poem. The historical portion, however, of the Mahabharat, appears to be confined to the neighbourhood of the Ganges. The Deccan is of old the country of fable, and the abode of a numerous community of apes, under their several kings and generals; in the same quarter dwell the commander of the bears and the prince of the Rakshasas, lord of the marvellous island of Lanka. The mountainous regions seem to have always been the peculiar province of fable, and the Ghâts of Southern India, no less so than the snow-clad mountains of the north.

According to the Mahabharat, Canoge above mentioned is said to have risen in importance after the decline of Ayodhya. The latter had continued to be the seat of empire for upwards of fifteen centuries, when one of its kings, of the family of the Surayas, or children of the Sun, founded the city of Canoge, and he taking up his residence there, it became the royal capital. This event took place about the time when the simple worship of Brahma degenerated into pantheism, and gave way to the introduction of other gods and heroes, who had made themselves renowned by their conduct in peace or war. Temples and statues were erected to their honour, and the vanity of the princes, together with

[44] The empire of the Pandions, mentioned by Ptolemy and other writers in the time of the Romans, recalls to our mind that of the Pandos. The fabulous portion of whose history would certainly appear to have been known to the Greeks, and probably gave rise to the tradition relative to Pandea, who is said to have been a daughter of the Indian Hercules, and mother of the race of kings who governed India. ARRIAN, *Op.* p. 174. The very name of Pandion may perhaps be derived from that of the Pandos; but we must take care not to confound the later empire of the Pandions, (situate at the southern extremity of Malabar,) with the more ancient one of the Pandos. The term Pandion was probably a titular appellation common to the successors of the Pandos; as that of Porus belonged to the whole family of Puru, and was borne by many successive princes of that house, as is proved by MANNERT, *Geographie*, vol. v. p. 120, 126, 211.

[45] POLIER, vol. i. p. 519.

[46] Ibid. p. 546.

the superstition of the people, contributed to adorn Canoge with magnificent buildings.[47] The ruins which still exist of this city sufficiently attest its former splendour, and prove it to have been the capital of a great empire. And it would appear to have maintained its importance for a very considerable space of time; for as late even as the sixth century it was reported to contain not less than thirty thousand shops for the mere selling of betel-nut; and it only fell at last, in 1018, under the destructive invasions of the Ghaznevide sultans.[48]

Among the states situate in the land of the Ganges, next to Ayodhya, the kingdom of Maghada appears to have been one of the most ancient. According to the testimony of all writers, it comprised the modern Behar,[49] particularly the southern part; but considered in a larger sense, as a monarchy whose kings were in some degree lords paramount of all the rest of India, it will include the whole tract of country near the Ganges.[50] The Ramayana describes it as watered by the river Sumagodi, which flows towards the east.[51] Its capital, Hastinapura,[52] the ordinary residence of the kings, is particularly celebrated in Hindu mythological history. The kingdom of Maghada is mentioned in the poem just alluded to, as contemporary with Ayodhya;[53] and the Puranas so frequently speak of it, that we might, without much difficulty, collect and arrange the genealogical series of its kings from that source alone.[54] Maghada, therefore, may

[47] This account is repeated from MAURICE, (*History of Hindustan*, vol. i. p. 36,) who affirms it to be gathered from the Mahabharat. He makes Canoge to have been founded only 1000 years before Christ; it is, however, already mentioned in the Ramayana, if the editors of that poem are correct in supposing Kanyakubja to mean Canoge, and a different story of its origin is therein related. *Ramayana*, i. 230. It is possible, indeed, that the removal of the court thither, from Ayodhya, may have been considered as a second foundation, for the splendour of Canoge only commenced with that epoch; in which case, both the Ramayana and the Mahabharat may be right.

[48] RENNELL, *Memoir*, p. 54, second edition. According to this writer, Canoge was built more than a thousand years before the Christian era.

[49] *Asiatic Res.* vol. i. p. 304; vol. v. p. 263.

[50] WILFORD, in the *Asiatic Res.* vol. ix. p. 82.

[51] *Ramayana*, i. 325. Probably the Sona.

[52] POLIER, vol. i. p. 539.

[53] *Ramayana*, i. 159.

[54] ANQUETIL DU PERRON, in his *Recherches*, and TIEFENTHALER, *Beschreibung von Hindostan*, vol. ii. p. 232, etc., give another table of the ancient Hindu kings, together with the duration of their respective reigns, but without determining the places where they reigned. This register is borrowed from a modern Persian work, entitled, "Tadhkiratu-palatin," which its au-

claim the first place in Hindu poetic history; and whatever objections the critic may choose to allege against particular details in the account of it, he is not at all authorized to question the existence of such a kingdom in very remote times, while he allows the general antiquity of the Hindus as a polished nation. According to the evidence reported by Sir William Jones from the Puranas,[55] eighty-one kings are said to have reigned in Maghada, whose names he also mentions. The first twenty reigns are unaccompanied with any chronological determination: but the ensuing are divided by him into five separate dynasties, of which the first commenced with King Pradiota, about 2100 A. C., and terminated with King Namda about 1500 A. C., embracing a period of sixteen reigns: the second only comprises ten, and ends with the year 1365 before Christ: the third dynasty, that of Sunga, contains also the same number of kings, and terminates 1253 A. C.: the fourth, that of Canna, only consists of four names, and lasted till the year 908 A. C.: the fifth, that of Andrah, forms a series of twenty-one kings, and continued down to the year 456 before the Christian era, and 400 before that of Vicramaditya; since which time, say the pundits, there is no further account of any independent kingdom existing in Maghada.[56] Consequently, at this epoch India appears to have been placed in precisely the same situation as ancient Egypt, which was at first divided into several small states, but after the expulsion of the

thor, in his turn, compiled from Sanscrit books. "This treatise," observes WILFORD, (*Asiatic Res.* vol. ix. p. 132,) "is a most perfect specimen of the manner of writing history in India; for with the exception of one original list, almost every thing else is the production of the fertile genius of the compiler, who lived above a hundred years ago. In all these lists the compilers and revisers seem to have had no other object in view, but to adjust a certain number of remarkable epochs. This being once effected, the intermediate spaces are filled up with the names of kings not to be found any where else, and most probably fanciful. Otherwise, they leave out the names of those kings of whom nothing is recorded, and attribute the years of their reigns to some among them better known and of greater fame. They often do not scruple to transpose some of those kings, and even whole dynasties, either in consequence of some pre-conceived opinion, or owing to their mistaking a famous king for another of the same name," etc. After such an avowal, who would require further proof? The remarks, however, just quoted, are only to be understood as applicable to modern compilers of chronological genealogies; not to the epic poems and ancient Puranas, which usually affix no dates to their genealogical tables.

[55] JONES's *Works*, vol. i. p. 304; *Asiatic Res.* vol. ii. No. vi.

[56] JONES's *Works*, vol. i. p. 308.

Hyksos, or shepherd kings, was consolidated into one great empire under the sovereigns of Memphis. But if we are unable to trace the vicissitudes of the particular states in Egypt, much less can we attempt to investigate those of India; for with the exception of a few bare lists of names, we are deprived of almost every other source of information necessary for the purpose. Nevertheless, we are in possession of absolute proof from history, derived from the accounts of the companions and successors of Alexander, that at the epoch above noticed, there had already existed, for a long space of time, very flourishing empires in the country bordering on the Ganges. In these accounts, it is not merely Western Hindustan that presents to our view a number of small states, as we have already shown in our researches into Persian India; but we also remark at this period the grand empire of the Prasii, and their capital Palibothra, situate on the banks of the Ganges. Here, at length, then, we step from the regions of poetical tradition into the legitimate province of history; at the same time, however, and especially when we consider the long period of tranquillity which must necessarily have preceded the establishment of empire on the Ganges, we may be enabled to form some opinion also of the ages just then elapsed, by referring to the events of the epoch in question. Now if, at such an early period, we meet with a highly civilized nation, and endowed with a degree of refinement which could not but have required a long course of preparatory discipline, have we not sufficient grounds for recognising in the native tradition of the Hindus, if not critical exactness, yet, at least, some foundation in truth?

According to what the Hindus themselves informed the Greeks, it would seem that India, from the time of the expedition of Bacchus down to the invasion of Alexander, had never suffered any hostile aggression from without, nor been engaged in any foreign war.[57] As this piece of information

[57] Whatever the first Greeks, who established themselves in India, recount of Hindu mythology, must always be received with extreme caution. It certainly appears, as I have before observed, that some of the fables contained in the great epic poems had come to their knowledge; and, indeed, how could it well be otherwise? But unacquainted with the language of the country, they saw and heard every thing through a prejudiced medium, and were biassed in all their judgments by a strong spirit of nationality. Among

comes from Megasthenes, who heard it at Palibothra, we must understand it more especially of the countries in the neighbourhood of the Ganges, and not of the frontier provinces of India, which had been previously subjected by the Persians. To whatever distance this epoch be removed, it is no less evident, that during a long interval of time previous to the expedition of Alexander, the Hindus, unshackled by foreign dominion, and left to their own resources, had free and undisturbed liberty to develop the national character: this is obviously no unimportant circumstance, when we have to speak of the progress they made in early civilization and literature.

The exact determination of the locality of Palibothra is not unattended with difficulties, arising principally from our ignorance respecting the river Erannoboas, on whose banks it was situated. But according to the researches of Major Rennell[58] and Mannert[59] it would appear almost beyond a doubt, that the river in question can be no other than the Sona; and that in consequence Palibothra, which was built at its point of junction with the Ganges, must be sought

the number of those mythological stories which had undoubtedly reached their ears, we may probably reckon the expeditions of Bacchus and Hercules into India, so naturally explained by the incarnations of Rama and Krishna, and their heroic actions described in the Ramayana and Mahabharat. We can hardly doubt that Bacchus and Hercules are both of them Hindu deities, since they are not only represented as objects of general worship, but the particular countries and places are also specified, where both the one and the other had temples erected to their service. See ARRIAN, *Op.* p. 174; and STRABO, vol. xv. p. 489; according to whom, the inhabitants of the mountains principally adored Hercules, and those of the plain Bacchus. This fact would lead us to infer the existence of two sects, and at the same time bring to our minds the respective followers of Siva and Vishnu. Proof may be adduced in support of both one and the other interpretation, though sound criticism will not venture into the particular details; and besides, the principal conclusion that the Hindu Bacchus and Hercules derive their origin from a conception of the Hindu epic poems, remains the same in both cases. Compare MAURICE, *History of Hindustan*, vol. ii. p. 119, 153. According to WILFORD, *Asiatic Res.* vol. ix. p. 93, the subject of the Dionysiacs of Nonnus was borrowed from the Mahabharat; this, however, must be understood only of the expedition of Bacchus into India. But even where the scene is laid in that country, it is not very easy to discover in this poem any thing of the true Indian character. It must, therefore, have passed through several intermediate stages, before it reached the Greeks.

[58] RENNELL, *Memoir*, p. 50, sq. second edition. He had at first supposed Palibothra to be Canoge, but was subsequently convinced of his mistake by a personal examination on the spot itself. He shows that the Sona has changed its former course, having previously entered the Ganges nearly twenty-five miles from its present embouchure.

[59] MANNERT, *Geogr.*, vol. v. p. 100.

after, in or near the modern town of Patna, where even the ancient appellation still survives in the name of a certain district called Patalputhra; another opinion however, which identifies the Erannoboas with the river Cusa, would place that city farther east, and not far from Boglipur.[60] The empire of the Prasii, although described to the Macedonian conqueror as the most powerful of all, could nevertheless hardly comprise more than a part of the country of the Ganges. Towards the west it extended beyond the junction of the Jumna with that river, where at no great distance from the modern Allahabad, was situated the ancient Matura, called Methora by Arrian,[61] in the classic land, so famous for being the scene of Krishna's appearance among mortals, and the place where he spent his early youth. On the south-east, it was bounded by the country of the Gangarides, situate towards the lower Ganges, and forming Bengal Proper, which was already governed by its own Rajah, not improbably the vassal of some more powerful neighbour.[62] If the ancient empire of Maghada terminated, as the native reports affirm, in the year four hundred and fifty-six before Christ,[63] we might be allowed to conjecture the kingdom of the Prasii to have been founded on its ruins, possibly after a certain lapse of time. For like the former it also comprised Behar, and some of the neighbouring provinces. But as Alexander himself, though arrived at the banks of the Hyphasis, was nevertheless very far from having reached even the boundaries of this empire, and of which therefore he could only have uncertain information, it would follow of course that its limits were not much extended towards the west.

After the retreat of Alexander, there arose a conqueror in India, who was known to the Greeks by the name of Sandracottus. He was a native of low extraction, and yet formerly in his youth had seen Alexander.[64] This chief became the author and leader of a revolt, in which the Hindus

[60] WILFORD, *Asiatic Res.* vol. v. p. 272.

[61] ARRIAN, p. 174. In the land of Suraseni: we must not confound this ancient Matura or Madura, with the present Madurah, on the coast of Coromandel, a mistake which Langlès has committed. The names of Suraseni and Matura occur also in MENU, ii. p. 19.

[62] PLINY, vol. vi. p. 22.

[63] JONES's *Works*, vol. i. p. 308.

[64] PLUTARCH, *Op.* vol. i. p. 700.

shook off the yoke of allegiance to the Macedonian stranger, and put to death the governors he had established.[65] Placed at the head of his countrymen in the western provinces, as the restorer of liberty, he became a conqueror in his turn, and overthrew the reigning dynasty at Palibothra, at that time represented by a weak and odious prince. Although the victorious arms of Sandracottus extended over a portion of the modern Punjab, yet the principal seat of his empire was confined to the country of the Ganges, as specified in his treaty with Seleucus Nicator, to whose ambassadors he gave audience at his court of Palibothra, or at Canoge.[66] The scholars of England believed that they had at length discovered a fixed point in ancient Hindu history, when they found the Sandracottus of the Greeks actually occurring in the native genealogies. He was considered to be the same as the Chandra Gupta of the Hindus,[67] and the resemblance between the two names appears even more striking in the earliest editions of Athenæus, which, instead of Sandracottus, have Sandracoptus.[68] But even admitting an identity of name, will that prove a corresponding identity of person? On the contrary, this resemblance of name appears to be almost the only feature the two have in common. They are both indeed represented as Hindu princes, but with this sole exception all further comparison must cease. Chandra Gupta was by no means, like his namesake Sandracoptus, a man of low birth, but the son of King Nanda, upon whose death he took possession of the throne:[69] and

[65] JUSTIN, vol. xv. p. 4.

[66] MAURICE, *Hist. of Hind.*, vol. i. p. 38. It seems that Palibothra and Canoge were both one and the other considered as the capital towns of the Prasian empire; in the same way that Agra and Delhi were under the Great Moguls. According to Maurice, Sandracottus is said to have rebuilt Canoge.

[67] SIR W. JONES, on Asiatic History, in the *Asiatic Res.* vol. iv., and FRANCIS HAMILTON, *Genealogies*, Introduction, p. 14. According to the latter, Chandra Gupta was the second king of the house of Marija, ten of whom are reported to have reigned at Maghada during a space of one hundred and thirty-five years.

[68] ATHENÆUS, edit. Schweighäuser, vol. i. cap. 37.

[69] Compare the account of Chandra Gupta, given by WILFORD in the *Asiatic Res.* vol. v. p. 264, sq. In the list of kings arranged by SIR W. JONES, (*Works*, vol. i. p. 306,) the reign of Nanda is placed one thousand six hundred and two, and Chandra Gupta one thousand five hundred and two years before Christ; the latter therefore must have lived one thousand two hundred years before Sandracottus. Will any one pretend that there was another Chandra Gupta? in which case how comes it that his predecessor is likewise called Nanda? Is it still necessary to put the reader on his guard

far from being an enemy to the Yavanas, (under which term are implied the Greeks or Macedonians,) he is their friend and ally. If we pursue the history of Chandra Gupta further, we shall find it to be merely poetical, and borrowed partly from the epic and partly from the dramatic poets;[70] who, according to their particular exigencies, have so differently handled the same history, that we are sometimes led to doubt whether their Chandra Gupta be always one and the same person, and not rather a common title and appellation, applied to many individuals.[71]

After Sandracottus the history of his empire again falls into obscurity, in which it is involved for a space of two hundred years, when Vicramaditya, to whose splendid reign we have already had several occasions of alluding, appears on the scene, as king of precisely the same countries. Still, however, we possess no extract of what is recounted in the Puranas of this celebrated prince; a few partial and scattered accounts being all that we are able to collect of his history.[72] Vicramaditya is called the sovereign of all India;[73] without doubt, as having reduced a number of the petty Rajahs to his authority. The principal seat of his empire was in the land of the Ganges, on both sides of that river; and his residence seems to have been established alternately at Palibothra and at Canoge. He was also lord of Benares, whither he convened the already mentioned assembly of Brahmans. He rebuilt Ayodhya, so celebrated in the ancient history of the Hindus, but then in complete

against these abortive endeavours to apply fixed chronological dates to what is nothing more than a poetic history.

[70] These are cited by WILFORD, *Asiatic Res.* vol. v. p. 262; where also will be found a history of Chandra Gupta according to these authorities.

[71] WILFORD, loc. cit. The word Chandra Gupta means "protected by the moon." [WILSON, in the preface to his edition of the *Mudra Rakshasa*, which appeared at Calcutta in 1827, identifies Sandracottus with Chandra Gupta; in fact, the resemblance is too striking to have been the effect of mere accident. FR. TRANSL.]

[72] We certainly have a prolix treatise by WILFORD, *Asiatic Res.* vol. ix. p. 117, etc., "Vicramaditya and Salivahana, their respective eras," in which however the subject is rather obscured than illustrated. "The Hindus," observes this writer, "know but of one Vicramaditya, but the learned acknowledge four; and when at my request they produced written authorities, I was greatly surprised to find no less than eight or nine." When we recollect in what manner the lists of Hindu kings were made up, how can we doubt that these numerous Vicramadityas also owe their origin solely to the hypotheses of native chronologers?

[73] POLIER, vol. i. p. 104.

ruin.[74] His power extended northward as far as Cashmire, the governors of which submitted to him of their own accord; and he appointed a Rajah to administer the affairs of that country.[75] At one time the extent of his dominions embraced also the northern parts of the Deccan, as far as Tagara; but the Rajahs of that quarter having revolted from his authority, they gave him battle and he was slain.[76] These facts are sufficient to show in what sense Vicramaditya was called the sovereign of India, and how his court might easily have been one of the most brilliant of the age, and a central point of attraction to poets and learned men.

While the foregoing inquiries have made it evident enough that the country about the Ganges must have been for a long series of ages, not less probably than two thousand years before Christ, the seat of great empires and splendid cities; so, on the other hand, the various destinies which have befallen the western side of the peninsula, still remain involved in the deepest obscurity. It appears, as we have already remarked, even in the epic poems, as the country of fable. And yet it is precisely in this part of India, that we find those prodigious monuments of antiquity, both under and above ground, imperishable proofs of the spread of that caste, which, in the above-noticed sense of the expression, appears to have been the predominant one in the land of the Ganges; and, with the two other superior castes, was only allowed, agreeably to the laws of Menu, to reside in that part of the country. While the true origin of those remarkable structures, wrapped as they are in the gloom of centuries, will only permit us to advance conjecture, what can be a more natural and obvious supposition, than to refer their erection to the period of the victory gained by the Brahmans over the warrior caste; when the former, grounding the influence thus acquired on the support of religion, endeavoured to maintain it in the southern provinces also by the foundation of establishments similar to those already existing in the neighbourhood of the Ganges? And wherein could such establishments otherwise consist than in religious sanctuaries; which, as their nature and method of arrangement clearly show, were intended to serve for the

[74] Polier, vol. i. p. 185. [75] *Ayin Acbari*, vol. ii. p. 161.
[76] Wilford, in the *Asiatic Res.*, vol. i. p. 374.

residence of the divinities, as well as their attendant priests? The particular reason why these buildings were constructed under ground in preference to above, is sufficiently explained by referring to climate and locality; the latter presenting every convenience for such an undertaking; more especially, too, when we take into account the probable and easy adaptation of naturally formed grottoes to the purpose in hand; while the heat of the climate would furnish peculiar attractions to a residence in subterranean edifices. The supposition already made will also assign an adequate motive for the earliest establishments of this kind; like those of Elephanta and Salsette, being formed on some small island in the immediate vicinity of the coast, where they might be less exposed to attack from the barbarous aborigines of the continent. In the same manner, we can explain the gradual enlargement of these sanctuaries, and the progressive care bestowed on their decoration, while we consider them as central points of religious dominion; which it was the object to establish and confirm by all possible means; such as oracles, pilgrimages, and solemn feasts. And how satisfactorily can we account for the peculiarities above mentioned, when we refer to the spirit of rivalry which subsisted between a number of such establishments, each striving to outvie the other; while reputation, the love of gain, and above all, mutual jealousy, acted as a spur to sectarian opposition; and when probably the worshippers of Buddha endeavoured to supplant the followers of Vishnu or Siva; an attempt, however, which ended in the total expulsion of the former from the peninsula. In this manner the art must necessarily have been perfected by degrees; until at length a period of general tranquillity, succeeding the distraction of party spirit, permitted the secure erection of these sanctuaries in the heart of the mainland, such as Ellora, for instance, the most wonderful and magnificent of all. The gradual progress subsequently made in the formation of rock-temples above ground, and other buildings, together with the perfection to which the Hindus brought this kind of architecture, has already been shown in our description of the monuments themselves; and would seem to furnish a more convincing proof both of the long interval of time which must have preceded all these successive improvements, and also, by consequence, of the high antiquity of the nation, than we can derive from lists of kings collected from the poets, and laboriously arranged in chronological order; although certainly the general agreement of poetical fiction with these monuments, is an additional proof in favour of their antiquity. The monuments themselves, too, have their own language; it is concise and monosyllabic, but of unquestionable veracity to those who are acquainted with them, and with the people who erected those lasting memorials. The nature of sacerdotal states can only be seen in its true light, when we come to examine the corresponding phenomena which ancient Egypt presents to our view. The religion of the Hindus, in a greater degree than that of the Egyptians, was adapted, and indeed purposely calculated, to bind the people in strict connexion with their sanctuaries, while it prescribed the dutiful observance of pilgrimage thither, and made to depend thereon the hope both of present and future happiness. Even in modern times, notwithstanding the weight of foreign oppression under which they have languished for so many centuries, thousands of pilgrims still find opportunity and means to visit the temples and holy places; and to support, and even enrich them, by the number of their presents. What, then, may we conceive to have been the case in more fortunate times, when neither Moslem bigotry nor European avarice had yet quenched their zeal, or straitened their resources![77] In recurring to such an epoch, the imagination pleases itself with portraying the varied enjoyments of social and commercial intercourse, which these periodical assemblies of foreigners from all parts of India would naturally bring in their train; we see, as it were, before our eyes those vast grottoes and halls, peopled with living multitudes, that are now only the abode of frightful desolation, or ravenous wild beasts. But, to return to the Brahmans, how truly congenial to the spirit of that caste were establishments like those we have just mentioned, may be inferred from the Brahmanical colonies which Alexander found in the north

[77] [The whole amount of taxes collected from pilgrims to the four following places, viz. Juggernaut, Gya, Allahabad, and Tripetty, for a term of seventeen years, ending 1828, is reported to have been not less than a million of money, after deducting all necessary expenses. See *Asiatic Journal* for October, 1830, p. 103, sq. TRANSL.]

of India;[78] as well as those still existing in the recesses of the Himalaya mountains. In fact, does not the holy city Benares, at the present day, stand in precisely the same relation to the country of the Ganges, as, according to all appearance, Ellora and Deoghur did formerly to the Deccan?

It was only in the time of the Roman empire, during the first and second centuries of our era, and after the establishment of a regular navigation between Egypt and India, that the peninsula, under its present name of the Deccan,[79] began to emerge from obscurity. It is noticed, both by the author of the Periplus of the Erythrean Sea, and by Ptolemy; their accounts, however, cannot be applied to the elucidation of the earlier history of that part of India, except they make express mention of anterior epochs. In the time of the above writers, as well as fifteen centuries after, when discovered by the Portuguese, the Deccan appears to have been portioned out among a number of petty Rajahs, some of whom resided in the same cities as their successors of the present day. This was the case with Ozene,[80] the name of which is still preserved in Uzen or Ujein, (Ujjayani,) and which, as we have seen, the powerful Vicramaditya subjected to his arms for a certain time; it is now the residence of Scindia, one of the great Mahratta chieftans. A still more important place than the last is Tagara, without doubt the modern Deoghur, in the neighbourhood of the famous Ellora,[81] and, according to the author of the Periplus,[82] the grand capital of the district of Ariaca; which comprehended most of the present Subah of Aurungabad, and the southern part of the Concan; the northern parts of which, with the islands of Salsette, Bombay, and Elephanta, were subject to the Rajah of Larikeh. With the exception of a short interval of time, during which the residence of the kings was transferred from Tagara to Pattan, the former city continued upwards of two thousand years, down to the Mohammedan

[78] See Persians.

[79] ARRIAN, *Peripl. Mar. Erythr. in Geogr. Min.* vol. i. p. 29. According to the Ayin Acbari, vol. ii. p. 546, Ozene, Oude, Mahtra, and Maya, without reckoning Benares, are still holy places of the first order, and the resort of numerous pilgrims.

[80] ARRIAN, loc. cit. p. 72. He mentions it as formerly a royal city; for in his time the residence of the Rajahs had been transferred to Minnagara.

[81] Compare WILFORD's Essay on Tagara, *Asiatic Res.* vol. i. p. 369.

[82] ARRIAN, loc. cit. p. 29.

invasion in 1293, to be reckoned among the capital towns of India. We shall have occasion to show, in another place, that it remained also for an equal period of time the grand emporium of Mediterranean commerce.

Although it is extremely probable that the general condition of the peninsula and its line of coast, must have been for a long time previous the same as we find it represented in the Periplus, that is to say, divided into a number of small kingdoms, yet it would be hazardous to infer from the description there given, more particular conclusions respecting its constitution in earlier periods; for, considered in this point of view, many and divers changes might unavoidably have occurred; and more especially, as the active commercial intercourse kept up with India by the Romans after their conquest of Egypt, must necessarily have produced corresponding relations on the coast of the peninsula. It is a subject of regret, that the author of the above voyage had not visited the Coromandel, as well as the Malabar coast; we might then possibly have been favoured with some more important disclosures relative to the wonderful city of Mavalipuram, the ruins of which are at present almost the only proof we have of its former existence. But as, according to the remarks heretofore made, its antiquity must be very considerable,[83] we may at least infer, this part also of India to have once contained sacerdotal empires, like the other side of the peninsula, governed by Rajahs who possessed no inconsiderable share of territorial dominion.

Notwithstanding the early history of these ancient Hindu states (with regard to their destinies and extent) is still involved in obscurity, we are yet able to ascertain with somewhat more correctness, the nature of their political constitution. The Ramayana and the Laws of Menu are important sources of information, which we may advantageously consult in this part of our inquiry; and whatever be the degree of poetical merit awarded to the first of these works, we cannot but consider it as a valuable present to the general history of mankind. It transports us, as it were, into a new world, in every sense of the term; and, like the graphic representations of the Ionian bard, makes us immediately and personally acquainted with the various characters intro-

[83] See above, p. 81.

duced upon the scene. It exhibits before our eyes, not merely the external form of ancient Hindu polity, but what is of greater moment, the inward springs, and the very spirit of sacerdotal administration. That curious phenomenon, so abhorrent from the character of our times, the preponderance of the sacerdotal over the civil power, is there shown in all its nakedness; but not in those odious colours which we are accustomed to attach to the conception, and which we borrow from our experience or habits of association. The epopee, in the case before us, is closely united with the idyl; but it is with a religious idyl. Not kings alone, but the sons even of gods themselves, are there represented as looking up with profound veneration to those holy men, who, long celebrated for their penances, are almost equal to the Devas in point of rank; and thrice happy the princes whose court was honoured with their presence. The beau ideal of a prince is always there represented as the union of a monarch and a hero, with the character of a saint. Let us compare, for instance, the picture which the Ramayana gives us of Dasaratha, sovereign of Ayodhya: "Dasaratha, the descendant of Ikshvaku, perfectly versed in the precepts of the Vedas and the Vedangas; of consummate ability; beloved by his people; dexterous in the management of horses; indefatigable in sacrifices; pre-eminent in the holy ceremonies of religion; a royal sage, almost equal to a Rishi; renowned throughout the three worlds; the vanquisher of his enemies; the observer of justice; master of his desires; in magnificence like Shakra; protector of his subjects like Menu, the first of monarchs."[84] It is probably in delineating the portraits of their sovereigns, that the national character of any people is most conspicuously developed; and the Hindus, as we have seen, adopted by no means a contemptible exemplar for their own.

The code of Menu in connexion with the digest of law above mentioned, seem to present us with an exact notion of the forms of Hindu polity; and however divided we may always be in opinion with regard to the antiquity of that code in its present state, it nevertheless contains a collection of the oldest institutes and laws relative to public and private right; which may therefore owe their sanction to established usage, or to the fact of their having been drawn up and committed to writing. These legislative enactments are not confined in their application to particular states of India; because, being attributed to Menu, the first sovereign of that country, they recognise the whole as forming but one undivided kingdom. Whether, indeed, all of them were in actual force throughout every portion of India may admit of reasonable doubt; but that the groundwork of Hindu polity, and, by consequence, the fundamental laws, were the same in all states, is clearly evident from the Ramayana. Wherever the dominion of the Brahmans extended, the same order of things is found generally to have prevailed; we need not, therefore, hesitate to assume the code in question for the basis of our present inquiry.

The fundamental principle of all Hindu polity is the division of castes. In the laws of Menu this classification appears to have been completely organized already; and so it is also represented in the epic poems; we shall hardly, therefore, be liable to serious error in attempting the following description of them.

All Hindu writers are unanimous in assigning only four original castes,[85] viz. the Brahmans, Kshatriyas, Vaisyas,

[85] The Greeks alone differ from them, (Arrian, p. 176; Diod. i. p. 153; Strabo, lib. xv.,) in admitting *seven* castes instead of four: viz. 1. Sophists. 2. Agriculturists. 3. Herdsmen. 4. Handicraftsmen and artisans. 5. Warriors. 6. Inspectors. 7. Councillors. The whole of this statement is borrowed from one and the same source, that is to say, from the Indica of Megasthenes. A very slight acquaintance, however, with India will be sufficient to prove, that such could never have been the real division of Hindu castes; but there is less reason to be surprised that a Greek, who resided for a short time only at the court of Sandracottus in the quality of an ambassador, should not immediately have understood the subject, when we reflect, that no subsequent traveller has yet been able clearly to elucidate the matter, on account of the numerous intermediate castes, and their respective subdivisions. Megasthenes has sometimes divided one caste into two, as, for instance, the agriculturists and herdsmen; at others, he has mistaken (probably because he collected his information from the court) the simple classes of courtiers and public officers for distinct castes, and thus made out his sixth and seventh; and, in fine, he has omitted some, as the merchants and serving-men. His caste of sophists are, in fact, part and parcel of the Brahmans, as it was their business to superintend religious ceremonies; and this very name is expressly given to them in another passage, Arrian, *Op.* p. 134. Again, Megasthenes confounds the penitents or fakirs, who, as he reports, lived naked in the woods, enduring the extremes of cold and heat, (whence came the term gymnosophists,) with the Brahmans, to which caste they frequently, though by no means exclusively, belong. This mistake seems to have occasioned an-

and Sudras. Of these, the three first are distinguished from the fourth, or servile caste, not only by their manner of life, but also by their general appearance. The members of the former severally wear round their body a peculiar kind of girdle or cord, which is, however, different in different individuals;[86] and this being regarded as the emblem of a second birth, they are collectively termed by Menu the regenerate; an appellation which the epic poets nevertheless usually attach, by preference, to the Brahmans. The three superior castes have also the full enjoyment of their personal liberty, a privilege which is denied the Sudras. Further, they alone are permitted to derive instruction from the Vedas, in the respective degrees peculiar to each caste; so that we may not improperly term them, predominant castes, in contradistinction to that of the Sudras, who are absolutely debarred from all manner of acquaintance with those holy books.

The purity of the privileged castes would naturally depend upon their not confounding themselves with the others by marriage. On this point the laws are very precise; it is, however, a misapprehension to suppose, as the Greeks did, that marriages are only allowable between individuals of the same caste; for the laws of Menu permit the three higher castes to intermarry with each other, though only in the case of a second marriage; so that upon these terms, a man belonging to a superior caste may take a wife from an inferior one, without risking contamination;[87] a woman, on the other hand, is not allowed to profit by this concession. Nevertheless, the purity of caste was preserved by another fundamental law, which enacted, that those children only who were born to mothers of the same caste as the father, should properly belong to that caste. Whence it follows, that the son of a Brahman must also have a Brahman mother, in order to be reckoned a legitimate Brahman himself, and so of the rest.[88] The Sudras, on the contrary,

other, committed by Megasthenes, when he pretends that a Hindu of any caste may become a sophist.

[86] MENU, ii. 37, 42, 43, 44, 169. Compare the *Ayin Acbari*, ii. 509, where the modern custom is described.

[87] The principal passages are in MENU, iii. 12, 13; ix. 149.

[88] MENU, x. 6, sq. The principal passage; where are also found the various denominations of intermediate castes, arising from unequal marriages.

are not permitted to choose a wife, except of their own caste.[89]

While in this manner, notwithstanding the liberty of intermarriage, a strong barrier was raised between the principal castes, yet the natural consequence of these mis-alliances would be the formation of intermediate classes, the number of which, it is easy to conceive, would be very considerable; and, in fact, this circumstance renders the task of ascertaining the various shades of difference between them extremely difficult, and contributes to embroil an examination of the castes in general with perplexity and confusion. The law, however, has bestowed a great deal of care in attempting to determine these manifold subdivisions; each class has a particular name, and follows a definite trade or occupation.[90] Several of them, being the fruit of a connexion between Sudra fathers and the women of other castes, are impure, and considered the most despicable of mankind; they are not even allowed to dwell in towns,[91] etc. These appear to be synonymous with the modern Pariahs.

The caste of the Brahmans would seem to have spread itself all over India. It possesses the exclusive privilege of studying and explaining the Vedas.[92] This, indeed, is their principal destination; and as the Vedas are the source of all Hindu learning, whether religious or scientific, the priesthood is for the same reason in exclusive possession of knowledge. The Brahmans are, therefore, the only physicians in India; for sickness being considered as the punishment of transgression, it is remedied by the imposition of penance and certain religious ceremonies.[93] They are also judges; for who but themselves would have such a perfect acquaintance with the law?[94] They alone are the national priests, and offer sacrifice for themselves as well as for others. They make presents; but then they have an especial right to receive, and even to demand them in their turn;[95] while no

[89] MENU, ix. 157. The favour of marrying women of an inferior class, allowed to the three superior castes, is a concession of the Laws of Menu, which, as SIR W. JONES remarks, (Institutes of Menu, p. 362,) according to the Brahmans, was subsequently abolished.

[90] Compare the whole tenth chapter of MENU.

[91] MENU, x. 50—56. [92] Ibid. i. 88. [93] Ibid. viii. 1.

[94] Ibid. i. 88. [95] Ibid. x. 80—90.

one may refuse a liberal accordance to their petitions. A Brahman is also permitted to follow the occupations of the two castes next in order to his own; he may carry arms, and even embark in a mercantile profession, though not, indeed, with every kind of ware.[96] From this variety of occupation the several classes of Brahmans arise, among which, those who expound the Vedas take the first place. The latter are treated even by sovereigns with the most profound respect, and are represented as beings of a supernatural order, at whose bidding the powers of the invisible world are obedient. The landed possessions of a Brahman are free of all impost,[97] and himself exempt from the infliction of capital punishment; hence, to slay one of this privileged caste, even though he had deserved death by the commission of the most enormous crimes, would be a heinous and unpardonable offence. He can only be amerced in a pecuniary fine, or banished for a term of years at most.[98] Notwithstanding these high prerogatives, however, the Brahmans are bound to the performance of duties which, with the exception of celibacy, are as severe as the rule of the strictest order of European monks. Until they are thoroughly and intimately acquainted with the Vedas, they are obliged to pass a long course of previous study in the house of their Guru, or spiritual teacher, whom they are enjoined to regard in the light of a second parent. It is only then that they are allowed, or rather it becomes their duty, to marry and become heads of families.[99] Every day of their life appears to be subject to the performance of a severe ritual.[100] The many prayers, ablutions, and sacrifices they must go through, take up a great portion of their time; and the facility with which they may contract pollution, only to be cleansed by rigorous penances, require the most heedful circumspection. They are forbidden to eat in the company of any one of an inferior caste, and even with princes themselves; they must not kill any thing that has life, except for sacrifice, and consequently they may eat no flesh but that of victims. When arrived at a certain age, it is their duty, or at least their custom, to withdraw into retirement, in order to devote

[96] MENU, ix. 314—319.
[97] PAULINO, *Syst. Br.* p. 230, sq.
[98] MENU, viii. 380, 381.
[99] Ibid. iii. 1.
[100] Compare the whole twelfth chapter of MENU.

themselves to religious contemplation, by means of which they may attain to spiritual union with the deity. As to the interior organization of their caste, it is no where expressly mentioned that they recognise the authority of a sovereign pontiff, etc.: but when we read of the hundreds, and often thousands of Brahmans attached to a single temple, we are naturally led to infer the existence among them of some regular order and gradation of rank.[1]

The second caste, which is that of the Kshatriyas, or warriors, according to the express assertion of Menu, arose out of the first.[2] But although of the same origin, it has nevertheless undergone considerable modifications, partly arising, as we have before remarked, from the unfortunate issue of their struggle with the Brahmans, and partly from the common fate of all warrior castes, in a country which happens to be overrun by foreign invaders.[3] Under such circumstances this caste would not long maintain its primitive form; it would obviously be the first to suffer. So that notwithstanding the greater part of the present inhabitants of Northern India are in all probability descended from these warriors,[4] we can easily conceive the reason why they are no longer considered to belong to that caste. In this sense the Brahmans may justly affirm, that the old warrior caste no longer exists, and that it is altogether annihilated.[5] But another passage in Menu furnishes us with more decisive information on the subject; according to which, several tribes of the Kshatriyas, having neglected to observe the holy customs and to visit the Brahmans, became so degenerate that they were expelled the caste, and regarded as

[1] [The Buddhists alone introduced an ecclesiastical hierarchy; because, as they did not recognise the distinction of caste, such method of subordination was indispensably necessary; the reverse of what naturally obtained among the Brahmans. FR. TRANSL.]

[2] MENU, ix. 320.

[3] In the southern parts of the peninsula, the Nairs (a species of country nobility rather than a distinct tribe) are considered to belong to the warrior caste. Whether they are the dispersed remnants of the old Kshatriyas, is not yet sufficiently ascertained.

[4] See vol. i. sect. 3, sub fin. What is there said must be understood of the origin, and not of the ancient organization of the warrior caste. If we may believe modern report, the inhabitants of Multan, and its capital, (Malli,) from whom Alexander met with the most obstinate resistance, are the present Rajpoots. See ELPHINSTONE's *Account*, etc. p. 15.

[5] *Ramayana*, i. 584, not.

Dasyas, or robber-tribes.[6] Many of the neighbouring countries of Hindustan appear to be inhabited by these outcasts; and the sect of the Sikhs, for instance, who now occupy a considerable part of Northern India, can be looked upon by orthodox Hindus in no other light than as the offspring of those ancient exiles.

The old Kshatriya caste inhabited the northern parts of India; its business, according to Menu, was to defend the country, and of course to bear arms. The individuals of this class were not allowed, except in cases of urgent necessity, to follow the occupations of inferior castes; by no means, however, those of the Brahmans.[7] They might derive instruction from the Vedas, that is to say, read or hear them read, but they were not to impart this knowledge to others. It was also their duty to offer sacrifice, to give but

[6] Menu, x. 43. They are called Paundracas, Odras, Draviras, Cambojas, Yavanas, Sacas, Paradas, Pahlavas, Chinas, Kiratas, Deradas, and Chasas. Sir W. Jones, in his Treatise on the Chinese, (*Works*, vol. i. p. 99,) understands by Chinas, the Chinese, who, as the Brahmans report, are descended from the Hindus. The other names, which are apparently those of different nations, give rise to various conjectures. Are the Sacas the ancient Sacæ? are the Pahlavas Medes speaking Pehlvi? are the Cambojas the inhabitants of modern Camboja; and the Yavanas, as is commonly supposed, Greeks or Macedonians? But how are we to draw accurate conclusions from a bare recital of names? It is, however, certain, that several of these tribes designate foreign nations. "They are," continues Menu, "Dasyas, whether they speak the language of *Mlechas*, (that is, barbarians, or strangers,) or that of *Aryas*" (degenerated aborigines). There is a remarkable passage in the *Ramayana*, p. 326, 327, relative to this subject, in reference to the fable already mentioned of the quarrel between the Kshatriya Rajah Vishva Mitra with the Brahman Vasishtha. We here find Pahlavi kings, whom the editors interpret of the ancient Persians; Chacas, or Saces, whom they connect with the Yavanas; the Cambojas and Varvaras, (probably the Draviras of Menu,) and the Mlechas. They are fabulously reported to have sprung from portions of the sacred cow belonging to Vasishtha, and to whom they served as auxiliary troops. The explaining of the word Yavanas by Greeks, or Macedonians, is most generally adopted by English scholars; particularly as the name occurs in the history of Chandra Gupta, whom they identify with Sandracottus. *Asiatic Res.* vol. v. p. 264, 267. It is, however, difficult to say why the Hindus should call the Greeks or Macedonians Yavanas, even supposing the appellation to be derived from Yavan, or Ionians, because the latter was not their real name. [The word Javan, or Yavan, is found in Genesis, chap. x., and in Arabic, Persian, Coptic, and Armenian, is always employed to designate the Greeks. Moreover, in the early periods of Grecian history the name Iones is generally applied to the whole nation. See Homer, Plato de Leg. iii. p. 684, and Hesych. ad voc. Ἴωνες et Ἰαννα. According to Herodotus, vii. 62, the Medes were in former times universally called Arii: now, ārya, in Sanscrit, means 'noble,' 'venerable;' and India Proper is termed Aryāvarta, the Holy Land, or country of the Aryas. Transl.]

[7] Menu, x. 95.

not to receive alms, and to abstain from sensual indulgences.[8] These precepts, if we omit the latter, seem, it must be confessed, but little calculated to form a soldier; and they will perhaps furnish one principal reason why the Hindus have never been remarkable for warlike spirit, and have so frequently become the easy prey of foreign conquerors.[9] In general, however, the laws of Menu are extremely deficient in their notice of this caste. We are told nothing of its interior organization, of its divisions, its arms; nothing, in fact, of the essential character which belongs to it as a warrior caste. It might certainly have been the interest of the Brahmans to maintain the Kshatriyas in greater subordination to their authority than any other caste; but the people at large have suffered the inevitable and pernicious consequences of their ambition.

The third caste is that of the Vaisyas. It is a mistake to confine the individuals composing this class to merchants,[10] they being merely a subdivision, for it also includes husbandmen. Agriculture, breeding of cattle, commerce, and the lending of money upon interest, are their prescribed modes of occupation.[11] The Vaisyas, like the Kshatriyas, are also admitted to a knowledge of the Vedas, and to sacrifices. This caste would obviously be the most numerous of all.

The fourth, or Sudra caste, is separated from the preceding ones by a broad line of distinction. Its members being forbidden to wear the sacred thread, are, therefore, not counted among the regenerate; but, according to the Hindu expression, among those who have only been born once.[12] They are said to have sprung from the feet of

[8] MENU, i. 89.

[9] With regard to the present state of the Kshatriya caste, compare the *Ayin Acbari*, ii. 397, 398. "There are," says the author, "more than five hundred tribes bearing the name of Kshatriyas, but the real caste so called no longer exists."

[10] The modern name of Banians, as Hindu merchants are called by foreigners, properly means corn merchants; the Bannyeh being a subdivision of the Vaisya caste. *Ayin Acbari*, vol. ii. p. 399.

[11] MENU, i. 59. The breeding of cattle seems to have been the first destination of the Vaisyas, to which agriculture and commerce were subsequently added. Compare MENU, ix. 327, where it is said, "The Creator intrusted the management of cattle to the Vaisyas, as he did that of men to the Brahmans and the Kshatriyas."

[12] MENU, x. 4.

Brahma: although the lowest caste of all, they are not considered impure; but as they cannot marry out of their own class,[13] it is principally from an infraction of this law that the epithet impure is applied to the offspring of an illegitimate connexion with individuals of a superior caste. The Sudras are absolutely forbidden a knowledge of the Vedas; the mere reading of these books would entail upon them the punishment of death. They are born to be servants;[14] and are considered to do best when they wait upon a Brahman, then on a Kshatriya, and lastly on a Vaisya. If a Sudra meet with no opportunity of getting into service, he may, in such case, follow some useful occupation; he who serves a Brahman faithfully, has the consolatory hope of migrating, by some future metempsychosis, into a higher caste.[15] The respective relations of master and servant are not very explicitly defined in the laws; nor are we informed to what extent the latter is to be regarded in the light of a slave; they specify, however, the various ways in which a man may lose his liberty, either by being taken prisoner in war, or by birth, or by sale, or when condemned to slavery as a punishment.[16] Nevertheless, the Sudras are in general considered as placed in a state of slavery; because, even though a member of this caste should happen to be affranchised by his master, he does not, therefore, enjoy all the rights of a free-man, his natural condition being that of a slave.[17] This condition, however, admits of so many modifications that we can draw no positive conclusions from such indefinite premises; and although it appears certain that the Hindus had slaves at all times, the Greeks might nevertheless have sufficient reason for maintaining a contrary opinion;[18] because slavery in India was a very different thing from what it was in Greece.

The number of mixed castes, partly rejected and impure, was already so considerable, even in the time of Menu, that his laws do not mention the whole of them by name;[19] a circumstance which perfectly explains the relation of a

[13] MENU, ix. 157. [14] Ibid. ix. 334. [15] Ibid. ix. 335.
[16] Ibid. viii. 415. [17] Ibid. viii. 414. [18] ARRIAN, *Op.* p. 175.
[19] See the whole tenth chapter of Menu. The Sutas, Vaidehas, and Chandalas, are there mentioned as the lowest and most impure castes; the latter (the Chandalas) are the modern *Parias*. MENU, x. 26, sq.

modern traveller, who reckons in a general way, upwards of eighty-four.[20] Now, as the members of these castes were exclusively employed in certain occupations, particularly handicraft, their increase in number may be considered a proof of the advanced state of civilization at the early period when the laws of Menu were first compiled.

We can thus comprehend how the number of castes has gradually multiplied; but it does not, therefore, follow that all the inferior ones, many of them impure, should have been descended from the same stock as the higher castes. It seems evident, from what has been already advanced, that the three latter, which have so much that is common, both in outward appearance and in their religious and political privileges, constituted, properly speaking, the Hindu nation. Herodotus remarked long ago, that India was inhabited by a great many different nations;[21] and if we examine with attention that assemblage of various races, now generally termed Hindus by Europeans, we shall find sufficient reason to be convinced of the correctness of his remark. Religion is the sole bond of union which has joined all these nations together, and in a certain degree made them constitute but one people. With this exception, the variety of colour and features, the diversity of idiom and manner of life, all furnish so many proofs in attestation of a different origin.[22] And although it be impossible for us to draw a

[20] THEVENOT, *Voyages*, p. 84, last part.

[21] HEROD. iii. 98. He adds also, "Who do not use the same language;" an additional confirmation of the fact, that all the languages spoken in India were not equally derived from the Sanscrit; but that radical differences existed between them in this respect as well as in others. [It seems pretty clear that the ancients, in making use of the term "language," understood very often nothing more than idioms or dialects; which, although derived from one and the same original stock, were yet sufficiently distinct from each other to obstruct the purposes of verbal communication. And besides, Herodotus was only acquainted with that part of India which borders on the Sindhu, or Indus; whereas it is in the Deccan, and to the south of the peninsula, that we must search for languages radically different from the Sanscrit. FR. TRANSL.]

[22] It is not the reading of a dead letter description, but ocular testimony alone, which can convince any one of this difference. Could I lay before the reader a series of portraits of individuals belonging to different castes, taken on the spot, and for which I am indebted to the friendly communication of M. Blumenbach, he would probably dispense with my adducing further proof. The contrast exhibited between the Spanish Creoles and the Peruvians, in point of complexion and people, is by no means so striking as that between the Brahmans and the Parias. I have the rather made choice of this com-

marked line of distinction in the case, or to say positively how far the Sudra caste are of a different stock from the others; yet nevertheless there appears little doubt that generally the inferior castes, which are distinguished by a much darker colour,[23] were the primitive inhabitants of India; whom the predominant castes subsequently reduced under their authority, either by means of religion only, or by force of arms.[24]

The distinction of caste, though a fundamental principle of the constitution itself, at least in the three superior castes, based upon the organization of families. The desire of perpetuating the memorial of his house by heirs male, is, to a Hindu, one of the most lively importance; and the want of sons is considered a misfortune only to be remedied by adoption. The peculiar notions of the Hindus on this point,

parison, as the establishment of the Spaniards in the New World, effected not merely by the sword, but also by the cross, appears to be an exact counterpart of a similar establishment of dominion by the ruling caste over the aboriginal natives of India, did we but possess the history of the Brahmans as we do that of the Spaniards. At all events, the fable of Parasu Rama, the vanquisher of the Kshatriyas, seems to contain some allusions to that history. According to POLIER, (vol. i. p. 287,) this Parasu Rama reduced into subjection the Sanchalas, a wild and barbarous nation, who fed on human flesh. A traditionary report, current among the natives of Canara, makes a dynasty of seventy-seven kings to have reigned at Banavassi, 1450 years B. C.; who subjected the Parias, and plunged them into their present degraded state of slavery. LIEUT.-COL. MARK WILKS, *Sketches of Southern India*, p. 157.

[23] The *Ramayana*, i. p. 493, contains a remarkable passage, in which a Chandala, or Paria, is described as a man of dark colour. The sons of Vasishtha had uttered a terrible imprecation on the Rajah Trishanka, to the effect that he might be turned into a Chandala; "In the self-same night," proceeds the poem, "a complete metamorphosis took place in the king; on the morrow he appeared like a monstrous creature, in short, exactly like a Chandala. His nether garments were of a blue colour, and his upper in a soiled and filthy condition; his eyeballs gleamed like copper; while the complexion of his body resembled that of a hideous brown ape. His kingly robes were transformed into bear skin, and all his ornaments into iron." The same lot afterwards befell the sons of Vasishtha in turn; their imprecation upon the innocent Rajah having recoiled upon themselves. It would follow, therefore, that upwards of three thousand years ago, when the Ramayana was probably composed, the same diversity of colour was observable between the several castes as at present. How are we to explain this, except by supposing a difference of origin?

[24] [It is astonishing to observe the number of *Cerebral* letters there are in the Pracrit: M. Burnouf is of opinion that these letters were originally Tamul; and, from their not being found in the Zend, the Armenian, or any of the derivative languages, it is extremely probable that they were not incorporated into the Sanscrit till after its establishment in India. In this case, the migration of a foreign people into that country would become almost an historical fact. FR. TRANSL.]

are not so much the effect of political institutions as of religious precepts; as, for instance, those relating to funeral sacrifices; which are prescribed to be offered by children to the manes of their ancestors, in order to insure their entrance into Swerga, or paradise. Add to this the laws of succession; and especially the prerogatives attached to primogeniture, from which we may easily conceive the great importance of this question in the eye of the legislature.[25] We have already seen what frequent use the poets have made of this national peculiarity; and how, both in the epic poem and in the drama, the preservation of a male child is so often the main point on which the action of the piece turns.

To this place naturally belongs a question connected with the political organization of the Hindus; the solution of which, as I have already had occasion to remark,[26] is not unattended with difficulty; viz. to what extent is the social character of this people founded upon polygamy? That it was sanctioned in the higher castes by law, admits of no doubt whatever;[27] and we shall but deceive ourselves if we expect to find among the Hindus the same clear and rigorous conceptions of the marriage union, which in Europe are

[25] See Menu, ix. 104, sq. The great importance attached by the ancient Greeks and Romans to the maintaining family sacrifices, both on civil and religious grounds, is well known. The prize Dissertation of M. Bunsen, "De jure hereditario Atheniensium," Gottingæ, 1813, contains a profound and instructive investigation of this subject; and particularly deserves mention here, as the learned author has discovered a really surprising agreement between the laws of Athens and those of the Hindu Digest, v. 12; whence it follows that the sacrifices in question were offered in the same degrees of affinity; and also that the classification of families, and their descending branches, in a legal point of view, was the same among both people. [It is very singular, that notwithstanding the apparently ample means for deciding this point, no question is less determined than that of primogeniture among the Hindus. Some writers affect to deny its existence altogether; and assert that property descends to the whole family in common. Others again, and these great and honourable names, admit indeed this mode of equable partition, to obtain among individuals of the Sudra and Vaisya caste, but absolutely reject its application to the case of the higher classes; among whom it is maintained that primogenitureship is not only recognised, but reigns paramount. These contradictory opinions seem in great measure to arise from the conflicting nature of the authorities adduced on either side; those who deny the rule of primogeniture, grounding their arguments upon the abstract law of Menu and Jagannatha; while the supporters of the opposite side justify their view of the point at issue, by an appeal to the actually existing practice. See particularly, *Asiatic Journal*, N. S. vol. v. p. 46, 138; vol. vii. p. 297. Transl.]

[26] In the first volume.

[27] Menu, ix. 85.

founded on custom and the precepts of religion. The kings and great men had their harems in India, as well as elsewhere in the East; and the practice being authorized by the laws, was further confirmed and exemplified in the epic,[28] as well as dramatic poetry.[29] The difference between a wife and a concubine is not so clearly laid down by the Hindus as by other nations of the East; though it seems the law has endeavoured to specify the distinction.[30] And yet nevertheless the world of India, both as it exists in the fanciful descriptions of poetry, as well as in the sober realities of actual life, presents us with a sufficient number of characteristic traits to show that monogamy is the predominant custom. In mythology, for instance, each god is assigned his own proper wife, although some fables, particularly those relating to Krishna, attribute to certain deities the possession of well-filled harems.[31] While in innumerable passages of the poets marriage is represented in such a manner as only to be understood of the union of one man with one woman, and accompanied too with all the constancy and tenderness which the matrimonial tie is susceptible of: we need only appeal for an illustration to the married loves of Nala and his faithful Damayanti;[32] and to the tenderness with which the poet of the Mega Duta bemoans his absent spouse.[33] Corresponding to this, is the voice of Hindu legislation: "A man and his wife," says Menu,[34] "constitute but one person; a perfect man consists of himself, his wife, and his son." In another passage, the mutual fidelity of a married pair is regarded as the first of duties.[35] The law of succession, so favourable to the interests of the eldest son, appears to be founded on monogamy; while an additional proof of the existence of this custom may be discovered in the tender attachment of a wife to her husband, and which forbids her to marry a second time;[36] although nothing is said of the supposed duty of a wife's burning

[28] As in the *Ramayana*, i. p. 216, the three wives of Dasaratha.

[29] As Dushmanta's seraglio of a hundred wives, in the Sacontala. SIR W. JONES's *Works*, vol. vi. p. 251.

[30] MENU, vii. 77. In his precepts to kings on the choice of a wife.

[31] POLIER, vol. i. p. 627. [In a note on this passage, the French translator very justly questions the antiquity of the fables above alluded to, as an exception in support of polygamy. TRANSL.]

[32] See above, p. 165. [33] See above, p. 188. [34] MENU, ix. 45.

[35] Ibid. ix. 105. [36] Ibid. v. 161.

along with the corpse of her husband, either in the laws of Menu, or in the epic poetry of the Hindus.[37] From all these circumstances we may reasonably conclude that polygamy among the princes and great men, was the consequence of luxury and fashion; but that in general wherever it existed among the higher classes, it was principally founded on the necessity of preserving families; and, moreover, on the religious precept, which allowed a man to marry one or more additional wives,[38] on account of the sterility of his first. The members of the fourth caste, the Sudras, were only permitted to have one wife, taken exclusively from their own class.[39] These regulations will not therefore necessarily infer the seclusion of the women, though certainly the husband appears to be the legally constituted lord and master; and the principle is expressly laid down, that the dependence of the woman on the man is of perpetual obligation.[40]

As the partition of families, and the assignment of respective rights to each, formed the earliest bond of society, so was this additionally consolidated by the division and laws of caste. And, it is easy to conceive how the internal regulations of families and castes might become the fundamental tie of Hindu constitution in general. Add to this the common worship of certain divinities, originating in the family sacrifices, in such sort that the gods of a particular family, as the latter increased in process of time, became the gods of a distinct tribe descended from it; and the first

[37] The *Ramayana*, iii. 30, it is true, represents Kausalya to have formed the design of burning herself on the funeral pile of her husband, Dasaratha, but it never took place; a circumstance which would lead us to infer that this custom was considered among the ancient Hindus as a voluntary act, and not as an indispensable duty. See the enactments of modern legislators relative to this point, in the *Digests of Hindu Laws*, vol. ii. p. 451, etc.

[38] Menu, ix. 81. A barren wife may be replaced by another at the expiration of eight years. [Menu, viii. 362, mentions the existence, even in his time, of "wretches who lived by the intrigues of their wives; and conducted them to their paramours, or connived at the visits of the latter." In the *Ramayana*, ii. 297, mention is made of a husband who actually let out his wife for hire! The custom of Sati, i. e. a wife's burning herself with the dead body of her husband, only became general in consequence of the oppressive enactments of modern lawyers; which rendered the life of a widow more insupportable than death itself. Fr. Transl.]

[39] Menu, ix. 157.

[40] Menu, v. 148. Compare the detailed regulations on this head, in the *Digests of Hindu Laws*, vol. ii. p. 377, etc.

origin of sacerdotal states like those of India, is susceptible of immediate explanation. It would seem, however, that these states did not receive their full and perfect development, except by the colonization of detached branches from a similarly organized state, among foreign and barbarous tribes; in which case, the forms of religious worship introduced by the new comers, being first grounded in the establishment of sanctuaries, and subsequently maintained by oracles and solemn feasts, became the means of gaining over such tribes, and of founding thereon a powerful government, more substantial and secure than could possibly have been effected by mere force alone. The application of these remarks to the case of India has been already shown; and will admit of still further illustration in our inquiries into ancient Egypt. Such, then, was the origin of sacerdotal states, or theocracies, as we might term them, with which the progress of civilization in the earlier ages of the world was most intimately connected. As far as India is concerned, the oldest remaining specimens of her literature, the Ramayana, and in a certain degree also the Laws of Menu, furnish us with a correct representation of the fact; and it is not the least part of their value, that they place us, as it were, in immediate contact with the ancient world of India, as it appeared on the banks of the Ganges; just as the accounts of Moses and Homer serve to transport us back into the early periods of Western Asia and Greece. It is hardly necessary to observe, however, that India would not always remain in the same state as we find it represented in the ancient documents just noticed; but it is in them alone that we must seek, conformably with our present object, for any traces of the original condition of the people.

In the laws of Menu, as well as in the Hindu epic poetry, a monarchical form of government is that most generally introduced, hereditary it is true, and regulated according to the strict rule of primogeniture,[41] but nevertheless counterbalanced and limited in its powers by a sacerdotal aristocracy. Between the Brahmans and the Rajahs there was always a broad line of distinction kept up, as the latter did

[41] *Ramayana*, vol. iii. p. 146, 225, 388. The subject of the poem turns in great measure on the refusal of Bharata, the younger son of Dasaratha, to encroach upon the hereditary right of his eldest brother Rama.

not belong to the same caste as the former; and although this arrangement was probably, at first, the effect of necessity, as the king was of course a warrior, yet it appears no less probable that the sacerdotal caste considered it as a means of preserving their own power intact; because, were it otherwise, how could they have been able to confine within due bounds the influence of a Brahman Rajah? We do not indeed pretend to say that it was absolutely impossible for a Rajah to be elected into the Brahman caste, but as Hindu fable mentions only one instance of such election, in the case of Vishvamitra, already so often alluded to, as having acquired that distinction by the most unheard of penances, we may justly therefore infer the general dislike of the Brahmans to make exceptions of this kind.

The laws of the sacerdotal caste effectually limited the independence of the king, in prescribing to him his daily occupations and mode of life. He was to reside in a fortress, situate in a retired part of the country. He was to espouse a wife from his own caste. Early at break of day he rose from his couch, and paid a visit to the Brahmans, who possessed the three Vedas, after which, with the assistance of the priest of the household, he offered the proper sacrifices and prayers; then he devoted himself to the affairs of state, and deliberated upon them with his ministers in council. At mid-day he retired to his apartments, in order to take refreshment, composed only of lawful meats, and previously tasted by his servitors. The consequences of poison were further obviated by the use of medicaments and amulets. After dinner he amused himself a short time with the beauties of his harem; then he engaged in public business as before, and reviewed his army, steeds, and elephants. Immediately after sunset he resumed his devotional exercises, listened to the reports of his ambassadors, and again withdrew to the privacy of his harem, where he partook of a slight repast, enlivened by the sound of music, until the hour of retirement for the night.[42] Such, according to the laws, was the daily life of a Hindu Rajah; though of course many exceptions to this regular compliance with prescribed duty would necessarily occur, the conduct of

[42] Menu, vii. 75—79, 145, 146, 215—226.

each prince in that particular varying with his personal character.[43]

When the Rajah found himself incompetent to discharge the functions of his office with becoming propriety or convenience, he was free to select a representative, or first minister, who was to be a learned man, completely master of his passions, and of high birth.[44] The Rajah was also enjoined to admit from seven to eight persons to his councils, deeply read in the Vedas, and whose fathers had previously filled the same responsible offices; in concert with these he was to deliberate on the affairs of the nation. He should also make choice of some learned Brahman, to be the depositary of his secrets. And for the administration of foreign affairs he was to appoint a high officer well versed in the Sastras, of superior abilities, and of honourable descent; under whose directions were the emissaries of ambassadors, who communicated to him the designs of foreign princes.[45] Thus, in exact conformity with the laws of Menu, the Ramayana describes the court of the pious monarch Dasaratha, sovereign of Ayodhya.[46] "The courtiers of the son of Ikshvaku were richly endowed with good qualities, intelligent, and faithfully devoted to the interests of their royal master. Eight virtuous ministers directed the affairs of government. The two priests made choice of by him were the illustrious Vasishtha and Vamadeva. To them were added other inferior councillors to the number of six. With these holy sages were associated the ancient priests of the king, discreet, submissive, profoundly skilled in the law, and masters of their desires. With the assistance and counsel of such advisers Rajah Dasaratha governed his kingdom.

[43] To prove this, it is only necessary to compare King Dushmanta in the Sacontala with Dasaratha in the Ramayana. Both of them reverenced the Brahmans, but how much more independent is the former than the latter! [The reason of Dushmanta's greater share of independence, is rather to be attributed to the different time in which he lived, and which has produced similar effects on the character of European monarchs. FR. TRANSL.]

[44] MENU, vii. 141.

[45] Ibid. vii. 54—64.

[46] See *Ramayana*, i. 107, etc., and the events which took place upon the death of Dasaratha, iii. 92, etc., when, during the absence of the next heir to the crown, the high priest Vasishtha put himself at the head of affairs. The picture of an Indian court, filled with poets, panegyrists, parasites, eunuchs, and attendant officers, together with the severe etiquette of the court itself, is here represented in the most vivid colours, and with the most minute circumstantial detail.

Surveying the whole earth (India) by means of his emissaries, as the sun by its rays, the descendant of Ikshvaku found no person who was hostilely disposed towards him." The Sacontala presents us with a similar picture of the court of Dushmanta.

The government and administration of the interior, is wholly regulated in the laws of Menu, by means of cities or townships. The king is enjoined[47] to set a head-man over each separate town and its environs, one over ten, one over twenty, one over a hundred, and one over a thousand towns. The report of any disorders that may occur is communicated by the head-man of detached towns to the chief of ten, and by him to the others in regular succession. The intendant of a single town derives his income from the contributions of the inhabitants, which are paid in eatables, drink, and wood, conformably to the laws. The revenue of a chief of ten towns, is equivalent to the produce of two acres of land, that of a chief of twenty to five.[48] The chief of a hundred towns receives for his support the revenues of a small township, while the chief of a thousand has those of a large one. A superior officer is charged with the superintendence of all the local authorities; he is to appoint a particular commandant for each town, who by personal inspection, or by means of emissaries, shall inform himself of their conduct, in order that the king may defend his subjects against those magistrates who, instead of being the protectors, are the oppressors of the people; and that upon conviction he may punish such evil-minded servants, with confiscation of their property and banishment from the kingdom.

These enactments of Menu will enable us to investigate somewhat more thoroughly the primitive constitution of India. The whole seems to have originated in the partial organization of isolated communities; which, with their respective head-men, might be considered as so many petty states; and this fundamental institution still continued to subsist, even when several of these townships, or communi-

[47] Menu, vii. 115—120.

[48] That is, according to the commentary, so much land as a man can turn up with two or five ploughs respectively, each of them drawn by a yoke of six oxen. This passage, by the way, will also prove the high antiquity of the plough in India.

ties, were united under the dominion of one Rajah, and thus formed a larger state or kingdom. In the northern parts of India, particularly near the Ganges, where the irruptions of foreign conquerors succeeded each other like the waves of the ocean, all traces of the primitive form must have long since been obliterated; but in the southernmost division of the peninsula, in Mysore, and Malabar, etc., which were least of all exposed to foreign invasion, they are still in existence at the present day. A modern traveller who visited the places in question, has furnished us with some very interesting, as well as authentic, information on this subject.[49] "Each Hindu township,"[50] says this writer, "is, and indeed always was, a particular community or petty republic by itself; and furnishes us with a vivid representation of the early state of things, when men first joined themselves together in societies for the purpose of relieving their mutual wants. Every community of the above kind, in addition to the landed proprietors, contains twelve different members; the judge and magistrate (Potail); the registrar; the watchman of the place and the fields; the distributor of water for the purposes of inundation; the astrologer, for determining lucky and unlucky days and hours; the cartwright; the potter; the washerman of the few garments for which there is occasion, and which are generally manufactured in the family itself, or purchased at the nearest market; the barber; and lastly, the goldsmith, or maker of ornaments for the women and young maids, who is in many villages replaced by the poet (rhapsodist) and schoolmaster.[51] These twelve functionaries are paid either in land, or in a certain quantity of grain, furnished by the agriculturists of the community. The whole of India is nothing more than one vast congeries of such republics. The inhabitants, even in war, are dependent on their respective Potails, who are at the same time magistrates, collectors, and principal farmers.[52]

[49] *Historical Sketches of the South of India*, by LIEUT.-COL. MARK WILKS, London, 1810, vol. i. p. 117, sq.

[50] Ibid. p. 119. So the author corrected the term *village*, which he had previously employed. [See particularly on this subject, Mr. Colebrooke's excellent Memoir on Courts of Justice in India, in the *Transactions of the Royal Asiatic Society*, London, vol. ii. 166—196. TRANSL.]

[51] Most of these officers are already noticed by MENU; as, for instance, the goldsmith, ix. 292; the joiner, x. 100; the washerman, viii. 396, etc.

[52] Their modern names of Zemindars and Ryots, superior and inferior farm-

They trouble themselves very little about the fall and dismemberment of empires; and provided the township with its limits, which are exactly marked out by a boundary line, remain intact, it is a matter of perfect indifference to them who becomes sovereign of the country; and therefore their internal administration always continues the same."

Sir Stamford Raffles, in his account of the small island of Bali, situate to the eastward of Java, has furnished us with a remarkable instance of these petty states yet existing under their original constitution. "Here," says he, "together with the Brahman religion, is still preserved the ancient form of Hindu municipal polity, and its accompanying Potails, called by the natives Parbakes, in subordination to a Rajah of unlimited power."[53]

Will not the above serve to throw some light on the political situation of Northern India at the time of Alexander's invasion, and illustrate the remarks we have already made on the republics then found to exist in that part of the country?[54] Most of these petty communities, it is true, were then under subjection to the Rajahs; but some of them still maintained their original freedom, which, as we have just now seen, has been preserved even to a much later period. Such instances as these, however, were at that time, and continued to be afterwards, exceptions from the general rule; for although the laws of Menu made no change in the interior organization of isolated communities, they were nevertheless framed, as we have before observed, on a monarchical principle; which is the reason why they are so particular and express in defining the rights and occupations of the sovereign. As greater empires were formed, the number and gradation of persons employed about the court would naturally increase in proportion. A remarkable instance of this is exhibited in the ancient inscription found at Monghir, in Bengal; in which a royal grant is notified to near thirty of such public functionaries.[55] Among

ers, do not occur either in MENU, or in the *Ramayana*. [Certainly not; because the first is a Persian, and the second an Arabic term. TRANSL.]

[53] SIR STAMFORD RAFFLES' *Description of Java*, vol. ii. App. p. ccxxxvi. The expression "unlimited power," must certainly not be taken here in the strictest acceptation of the term.

[54] See the first volume. With respect to the boundaries, see MENU, viii. 245, sq.

[55] *Asiatic Res.* vol. i. p. 126, and the note, p. 130.

these we find the prime minister; the chief investigator of all things; the chief officer of punishments; the chief keeper of the gates; the generalissimo of the army; the chief obviator of difficulties; the chief instructor of children; the provost marshal of the thief-catchers; the supervisor of cultivation, and others; among whom we must not omit to reckon the king's charioteer, or gentleman of the horse.[56] The state calendars of our European courts hardly mention one of these titles, and yet we can easily imagine that all the officers just named had others again under their immediate orders.

The supreme judicial authority is vested in the king; and he may even exercise it himself, conjointly, however, with certain Brahmans, by whose advice he may guide his own judgment;[57] or he may nominate one of them, who is skilled in the laws, to the dignity of grand judge; adding three other Brahmans, equally instructed in the Vedas, to be his assessors; the whole then constitute the highest court of justice, emblematical of the four-headed Brahma, and are competent to decide in all causes, criminal as well as civil. Offences are punishable either by death, and corporal chastisement, (from both which, however, all of the Brahman caste are exempt,) or by fine; those committed against a Brahman are prosecuted with the most rigour, and the fines increase in a duplicate ratio according to the rank of the caste to which the offender belongs.[58]

The king is the commander-in-chief of the army. He is allowed to make war not only in defence of his own territory, but also for the purposes of conquest.[59] The enactments of Hindu law in this respect, are by no means conformable to our philosophic notions; they are rather maxims of precaution and prudence relative to the occasions when, and the manner in which, a war is to be carried on. Many of the ancient Rajahs are described as conquerors, whose victorious arms were extended over the whole of India, from the western to the eastern seas, and from the mountains of

[56] See Bopp's *Nalus*, p. 45—149. The king's equerry is one of the highest rank among the courtiers; and enjoys an especial share of confidence.
[57] As Dushmanta, in the fifth act of the Sacontala.
[58] Menu, viii. 338.
[59] Ibid. vii. 101, sq.

the north to the southern extremity of the peninsula;[60] but none of them are reported to have undertaken great expeditions beyond these limits, or to have invaded distant countries, like the Egyptian or Babylonian conquerors. As in its mythological system, India almost always continued to be a world by itself; so also the geography of the nation becomes fabulous, as soon as ever it steps beyond the natural boundaries of the country.

One of the most important, but at the same time one of the most difficult questions for us to determine, is, to what extent was the sovereign considered as the proprietor of the soil; and consequently whether the cultivators held their lands in fee-simple, or were merely tenants upon lease from the crown? The latter kind of tenure having been found to prevail, though under very mild forms, during the period of Mogul dominion, as far as this extended, it is therefore generally supposed to have been the case in earlier times also, when India was still an independent country.[61] The transition from absolute propriety in the soil, to mere leasehold tenure, would naturally take place when the contributions of the landed proprietors became so burdensome that their right, without being formally abolished, must necessarily lose its real value; but whether this might have occurred in the earlier ages of Hindu history, we cannot possibly venture to determine. The only question for us to decide in this place is, how far the laws of Menu and other ancient documents, recognise the principle as applied to the case of the sovereign? The remarks we have already had occasion to make, relative to the petty Hindu communities as they were originally constituted, are an evident proof that absolute propriety in the soil was not inherent in the crown; and the laws of Menu, so far from recognising the principle in question, contain an express assertion to the contrary. "The sages who are acquainted with the

[60] As, for instance, in the ancient inscriptions found at Monghir, and elsewhere.

[61] [This institution, (of tenure by lease,) of which we meet with no traces either in ancient Hindu or in Mohammedan law, would seem to have been introduced, like the system of villenage or feudal tenure in the middle ages, by usurpation during great political convulsions. Consult on this head, a passage hitherto little noticed in the "Proleg. ad Chron. de gestis consulum Andegav. ap. Achery, Spicileg.," iii. 272, fol. ed. FR. TRANSL.]

times of old," says he, "declare that cultivated land is the property of him who first cut away the wood, or who cleared and tilled it; just as an antelope belongs to the first hunter by whom it is mortally wounded."[62] Could the right of freehold have been laid down with greater clearness and precision, than in the passage just quoted? Moreover the same laws enumerate with great care the formalities to be observed respecting the alienation or sale of landed property;[63] to what useful or even necessary purpose, we would ask, unless propriety in the soil were a fully recognised principle?[64] In fine, wherever mention is made of the Vaisya caste, which comprises not only merchants but also agriculturists and herdsmen, the latter are never represented as leasehold tenants. Nevertheless, it is evident that princes, as well as the temples and sanctuaries, were in possession of considerable domains, from the frequent occurrence of royal and other grants of landed property, of which we have already given several examples in the former part of this inquiry.

But although, according to the most ancient institutions of the country, the kings of India were by no means abso-

[62] MENU, ix. 44. [63] *Indian Digest*, vol. iii. p. 432.

[64] [With reference to this knotty and much debated question, as well as to that concerning the law of primogeniture, the existence of which is absolutely denied by some writers and as vehemently asserted by others, see especially, COL. TOD's able defence of his view of the feudal system of Rajasthan, in the *Asiatic Journal*, N. S. vol. v. p. 40, sq. This ingenious writer thus distinguishes between the sovereign right to share in the fruits of the soil, and in the soil itself: "The proprietor of the soil, i. e. he who redeemed it from sterility, is the ryot cultivator, by whom a rent or land-tax (in kind) was paid to the prince. It is this rent, this tax, this tribute of the land, with which the prince enfeoffs; it is this alone which he alienates, or can alienate, because it is this alone over which he possesses dominion. Such is the state of landed property in Rajpootana; every where there are 'two properties in one thing,' viz. the ryot cultivator's property in the land, and the prince's property in the usufruct thereof. It is this usufruct with which the prince enfeoffs, which descends by 'fixed rules' to the eldest sons lineally of such proprietor." It will easily be seen that this view of the question involves no contrariety to the dictum of Menu. But see also, *Asiatic Journal*, N. S. vol. i. p. 81, and vol. iv. p. 282. It is extremely probable that a variety of systems have always prevailed in different provinces at the same time; some more, some less, favourable to the people; some admitting of private landed property, some rejecting it; that in the same province different systems have predominated at different times; and that the system of all land being the property of the sovereign has sometimes succeeded that of private landed property, and sometimes given way to it. See the excellent Minute of the late SIR THOMAS MUNRO, "On the Condition of Southern India," *Asiatic Journal*, N. S. vol. ii. p. 316, sq. TRANSL.]

lute proprietors of the soil, yet they were permitted by law to raise contributions therefrom, which in all probability formed the chief part of their revenue. In specifying the limits of sovereign right on this head, the regulations of Menu are particularly express.[65] In ordinary times it was restricted to an eighth of the whole produce; in cases of great emergency the king might exact as much as a fourth. On the other hand, the imposts laid upon movable property never exceeded a twentieth part of the profits. In other respects, these impositions pressed wholly on the industrious classes; the Brahmans, and no doubt their lands also, being exempt.[66] Individuals of the menial classes, handicraftsmen, and labourers, must endeavour to make themselves useful; but, adds the commentator, they never pay taxes.[67]

Another source of the royal income consisted in imposts laid upon merchandise, and the customs. In the direction of commercial affairs, indeed, the king was permitted to exercise an extraordinary degree of influence. He might absolutely forbid the exportation of merchandise, or reserve the whole monopoly to himself. He issued ordinances relative to the buying and selling of goods; he regulated the price of the market, and received as his customary dues five per cent. on the profits of sale. With respect to land and river toll, several other enactments are laid down; among which it is provided, that any person who is guilty of defrauding the customs shall pay a fine of eight times the value of the smuggled article.[68]

In examining the spirit of these ancient constitutions and laws, we discover evident traces of a germ of republicanism; which, however, could never come to the full growth of political freedom. This germ was produced by the organ-

[65] MENU, x. 120. The subjoined commentary says, "In good times, a twelfth; in bad, an eighth or a sixth, which is the average; and only in times of necessity, a fourth part of the produce." Some other regulations more exact will be found in chapter vii. p. 130, 131, relative to the contributions in fruit, flesh, honey, butter, etc., on which a sixth of the clear produce is levied. In the *Ramayana* also, (iii. 170,) the king is allowed a sixth part of the whole revenue of the land. [A tenth is the traditional share paid in Hindustan before the sixth was instituted. It is the portion paid in the territory of Koorg to this day; and the Dutch found and continued it in Ceylon. TRANSL.]

[66] This exemption is, however, qualified with the condition of their understanding the Vedas. MENU, vii. 133.

[67] MENU, x. 120.

[68] Ibid. viii. 400—406.

ization of separate communities, while its further development was obstructed by the institution of caste. The authority of the prince was limited, not by the nation itself as constituting the body politic, but solely by the influence of a sacerdotal caste; and the character of despotism, though considerably modified by the priesthood, was nevertheless exhibited in its true form by the executive power, being vested in the king as a mark of sovereign right. "Punishment," says Menu,[69] "governs the whole race of mankind, and keeps them in order." And, as a further indication of the same character, Hindu legislation, otherwise so mild in its nature, becomes savage when it has to determine certain punishments; especially for offences committed against the Brahmans.[70] Moreover, in addition to the spirit of caste, is it not possible that polygamy also, by changing the form of domestic society, may have operated unfavourably to the development of free constitutions? Whatever be the real state of the case, it certainly appears that nothing of the kind, at least in the European acceptation of the term, ever came to maturity on the banks of the Ganges.

The foregoing observations naturally lead us to a discussion of the ancient commerce of India. What we have to advance on this subject, will not so much refer to the commercial intercourse of the Hindus with foreign nations, (which has been already partly examined, in our inquiries into the Phœnicians and Babylonians, and will receive further illustration, when we come to speak of Egypt,) as to the interior commerce of the people, arising from their own particular industry; though we shall necessarily have occasion to touch also upon their foreign commerce as we proceed.

As a preliminary step, it will be requisite to describe the sources of information which have been consulted in this part of our inquiry, as well as the use here made of them. The most valuable of these, both for its purity and extent, is undoubtedly the circumnavigation of the Red or Indian Sea, performed in all probability during the first, or at latest during the second century of our era.[71] The work itself,

[69] MENU, vii. 18. [70] See, for instance, MENU, viii. 270, 271.
[71] Periplus Maris Erythræi in HUDSON, *Geogr. Min.* vol. i. The excellent commentary of Dean Vincent, of which a new and very correct edition sub-

which is usually attributed to Arrian, commemorates the voyage of a certain merchant, from Egypt to the western coast of the peninsula on this side the Ganges, and contains some valuable and authentic information, with respect to the commercial traffic as well as the navigation of these parts. In the present inquiry, which is principally devoted to the commerce of India as it existed prior to the times of the Macedonians and the Romans, we cannot in reason apply all that is reported of the latter period, to the elucidation of its commercial relations at an earlier epoch: though it is at the same time quite certain that much of what Arrian reports of the commerce in question may with proper care be adapted to such purpose. Whenever, therefore, we have had occasion to speak of the early commerce of the Hindus, little use has been made of the accounts furnished by this writer. The case however is altered, when the national industry, and consequent impulse given to internal traffic, becomes the subject of discussion: it is then evident, that many of the data communicated by Arrian have reference to anterior epochs, and we are enabled to appreciate the value of his information by comparing it with that derived from ancient Hindu sources, which are now at our disposal. Having thus premised, we shall not incur the imputation of confounding different periods of time, if we adopt these principles as the basis of our present inquiry.

The Hindus in their most ancient works of poetry are represented as a commercial people. And it is one evidence of the prosperity and well-being of a country, that its merchants can travel from one place to another with perfect security to themselves and their merchandise.[72] But further, the regulations of society appear to have awarded a high rank to persons who were employed in the business of commerce. In the Ramayana we are informed, that at the triumphal entry of Rama into his capital, "all the men of distinction, together with the merchants and chief men of

sequently appeared, containing also the voyage of Nearchus, under the title of, "The Commerce and Navigation of the Ancients in the Indian Ocean," in two volumes, London, 1807, 4to, has spared me the trouble of entering at large into geographical and various other discussions, which would be so much the more out of place as I have no intention of commenting on the work itself.

[72] *Ramayana*, iii. 97.

the people," went out to meet him; and the procession is closed by the warriors, tradesmen, and artisans.[73]

The internal commerce of India could not have been inconsiderable, as it was in a certain degree prescribed by nature herself. For the sandy shores of the peninsula, not producing in sufficient quantity the first necessaries of life, and particularly rice, the importation of these articles from the country bordering on the Ganges became absolutely indispensable. In return for which the latter received chiefly spices; and among other valuables, precious stones, and the fine pearls only to be procured in the ocean which surrounds the former. Although cotton, one of the most important materials used for clothing, is common all over India, and manufactured with the same activity on the coasts of the peninsula as in the land of the Ganges, yet the fabric of the two countries differs so much in texture, that a commercial interchange of both kinds would naturally be introduced. The mode of life peculiar to the higher classes, especially in courts and cities, as represented to us by the poets, imply the existence of a multitude both of natural and artificial wants,[74] only to be satisfied by a corresponding system of active internal commerce. The constant experience we have of Asia, which shows that royal cities are always the principal depôts of inland traffic, will serve to establish the same fact also with regard to India; let us only compare the picture which the Ramayana draws of the capital town of Ayodhya.[75] "It was filled with merchants, and artificers of all kinds; gold, precious stones, and jewels were there found in abundance; every one wore costly garments, bracelets, and necklaces." And in another passage, in allusion to the mourning which took place on the death of the king, the poet says, "The tables for the

[73] *Ramayana*, iii. 245.

[74] *Ramayana*, iii. 98, in the description of the mourning for King Dasaratha, which put a stop to the fashionable amusements and occupations of the luxurious Ayodhyans. At other times the town always resounded with the noise and bustle of men and women, like the shout of contending armies. The great men were ever going to and fro upon chariots, elephants, and prancing steeds. The gardens of pleasure were always crowded with eager inquirers after their friends and lovers." In all descriptions of this kind, we constantly meet with strong proofs of a highly refined state of social life among the ancient Hindus.

[75] *Ramayana*, i. 94.

sacrificial offerings are empty, the shops where they sold garlands are closed; and the bankers and merchants do not show themselves as usual."[76] Such descriptions as these, even though we make every allowance for poetic colouring, will nevertheless show what was the Hindu idea of a rich and flourishing city; and we may be sure it would represent nothing but what was perfectly well known.

The great quantity of the precious metals, particularly gold, possessed by India, may well excite our attention and surprise. Though it had neither gold nor silver mines,[77] it has always been celebrated even in the earliest times for its riches. The Ramayana frequently mentions gold as in abundant circulation throughout the country. And the nuptial present made to Sita, we are told, consisted of a whole measure of gold pieces, and a vast quantity of the same precious metal in ingots. Golden chariots, golden trappings for elephants and horses, and golden bells, are also noticed as articles of luxury and magnificence;[78] and it has been already shown, in the course of our inquiries into the ancient Persians, that the Hindus were the only people subject to that empire who paid their tribute in gold and not in silver.[79] The quantity of this metal then current in India will therefore enable us to infer, with reason, the existence of a considerable foreign commerce and trade with the gold countries. Where these latter are to be sought for, will be shown in the sequel, when we come to ascertain the connexion subsisting between India and Thibet, as well as the country situate beyond the Ganges; at present we shall content ourselves with remarking, that it is evident from the Periplus, that commercial transactions with India during the time of the Romans, and for some time afterwards, were principally carried on in ready money, which is more than once mentioned as an article of importation.[80]

[76] *Ramayana*, iii. 128.

[77] PLINY, (vi. 20,) indeed, quotes the existence of gold and silver mines in the mountains of Capitalia, which are represented by him as the highest of the Ghât range; but we have no other proof of the fact. The Periplus also (p. 36) speaks, from hearsay, of certain gold mines situate on the Lower Ganges; where, however, there is nothing of the kind to be found now.

[78] *Ramayana*, i. 605, 606. See also the introduction to the Mahabharat in FRANK's *Chrestomath*. vol. i. p. 147.

[79] See the Persians, in vol. i.

[80] As, for example, in p. 28 of the *Periplus*. Δηνάριον χρυσοῦν καὶ ἀργυροῦν,

And who does not recollect the complaints of the elder Pliny, of the vast sums annually absorbed by the commerce with India?[81] How, indeed, could the case have been otherwise, when a country, which produced in superabundance every possible article, whether required for the necessaries of life or the refinements of luxury, would of course export a great deal, while it imported little or nothing in return; so that the commercial balance would always be in its favour. Hence it followed, that from the moment she possessed a foreign commerce, India would enrich herself with the precious metals by a necessary consequence from the very nature of things, and not by any fortuitous concourse of circumstances.

This naturally brings us to the question, whether the Hindus possessed a regular coinage, and how far back the use of it extends? There is no doubt that the precious metals, gold and silver, particularly gold, were in very ancient times the established medium of exchange in India; but this, however, will not prove it to have been coined. If we can repose any confidence in the published translations of native works, the use of coined money would appear to have prevailed in very remote times; for it is expressly mentioned in the fable of Krishna: but it is uncertain whether the passage is taken from the Mahabharat, or the Bhagavat, or from one of the other Puranas.[82] In the Ramayana a distinction is made between gold pieces and gold unwrought;[83] but it does not follow that the pieces bore any impression. In the Laws of Menu, the respective weights of paras and racticas of copper, silver, and gold, are very exactly determined, without, however, any allusion to their being stamped. The list of kings given by Tiefenthaler also makes mention of various changes introduced into the coinage by different monarchs; but we know not on what authority the account rests,[84] and we have already noticed the

which was, moreover, actually exchanged against the native money, *ἐντόπιον νόμισμα*. The Hindu gold coinage was termed *καλτεις*, (p. 76,) the *Kaltris* of the present day.

[81] PLIN. *Hist. Nat.* xii. 18.

[82] POLIER, vol. i. p. 456. "Une grande quantité d'argent monnoyé."

[83] *Ramayana*, i. 606. "He also gave a full ajuta (of pieces) of gold; and a like quantity of unwrought gold." Mention is also made of presents of from ten to twenty crores. Ibid. iii. p. 114.

[84] According to this list, King Savein, the thirty-fifth monarch of the first

very little credit to be attached to the list in question.[85] The Periplus expressly mentions pieces of Hindu gold coin, under the name of Kaltris, which were exchanged with profit against the Grecian and Roman money.[86] But whatever may have been the value and character of the ancient Hindu coinage, it is quite certain that its use is of very remote antiquity. This is sufficiently attested by the permission to lend money upon interest, and by the exact definitions laid down in the Laws of Menu with respect to the rate of interest. And, again, in the Sacontala we find the discovery of a lost ring rewarded with a sum of money;[87] and in the Hitopadesa, among other persons, we frequently meet with money-changers.[88]

Precious stones and pearls, both of them indigenous productions, may be comprised among the most ancient objects of Hindu luxury, and, therefore, of commerce; and they are even expressly recommended by Menu, together with coral and woven stuffs, as the most important articles on which the Vaisyas were carefully to inform themselves as to price,[89] etc. It would be superfluous to adduce proofs on this head from native works;[90] for even the oldest specimens of Hindu sculpture, found in the rock temples, sufficiently attest it. According to the Periplus, precious stones of every kind were brought from the interior to the port of Nelkynda;[91] among these, diamonds and rubies are particularly noticed;[92] and as the former is a native of India,[93] we may reasonably conclude that some of the mines where

of the nine races, that of the Pandos, had already issued a gold and silver coinage, containing an effigy of the sun. Rajah Sernaut, of the second race, was the first who added his name; Rajah Bempal, of the seventh race, coined pieces with his name, and the representation of some divinity; and Rajah Gobenchand, of the eighth race, first gave the rupee, which was hitherto square, its present circular form. But we may justly ask, how the author came to know all this? Now it has been already shown that these lists deserve no sort of confidence: the question, therefore, still remains where it did. Is there even any Hindu coinage older than our era? We certainly know of none. There are, indeed, plenty of coins impressed with some emblematical device, but none of them have either date or inscription of any kind.

[85] See above, p. 229.

[86] *Periplus*, p. 26, 36.

[87] JONES's *Works*, vol. vi. p. 280.

[88] Ibid. p. 27, 44, 47.

[89] MENU, ix. 329.

[90] Whoever wishes to see them may read the Gitagovinda, which frequently mentions the ornaments still in use among Hindu women at the present day. See also *Ramayana*, iii. 157.

[91] Λιθία διαφανῆ παντοία ἐκ τῶν ἔσω τόπων.

[92] Ἀδαμας and ὑάκινθος.

[93] Compare VINCENT, vol. ii. App. p. 6.

they are found must have been worked at a very remote period. In another passage we find mention made of the onyx-stone, which was brought from Ozene, and consequently from the Ghât mountains, to Barygaza.[94]

Although pearls were as anciently used for ornament as precious stones, and are, moreover, indigenous to the country, yet it is surprising we find no sort of allusion to the pearl fisheries, in any works of the ancient Hindus that have come down to us; whereas, the islands and sand-banks between Ceylon and the main-land, where these fisheries exist, and where Rama built his famous bridge when he made war upon Ravana, are precisely those spots which are most celebrated in Hindu mythology. But this circumstance is undoubtedly owing to our very limited acquaintance with the ancient literature of India; because the fable reported by Arrian, of Hercules' having searched the whole Indian Ocean, and found the pearl with which he adorned his daughter Pandæa, is of Hindu origin.[95] That the fisheries in question must have existed before the time of Alexander, is evident from their being mentioned by his companions.[96] The author of the Periplus informs us, not only that pearls were found near Manaar, a small island situate between Ceylon and the continent; but that they were also bored there.[97] It is, therefore, pretty certain that these fisheries existed from time immemorial;[98] for the pearl is of no use till it is bored; while the operation itself requires no inconsiderable degree of skill. In the time of the writer just quoted, the principal market for pearls was the town of Nelkynda, or Neliceram.[99]

The use and manufacture of ornamental works in ivory is equally ancient throughout India. Pendants for the ear, and necklaces, both of that material, form the ordinary decorations of the divinities of Elephanta, as was observed to

[94] *Periplus*, p. 28.

[95] ARRIAN, *Op*. p. 174. Καὶ ταῦτα μετεξέτεροι Ἰνδῶν Ἡρακλέους λέγουσι. Supposing Hercules to have been of Phœnician extraction, we might also understand this tradition to allude to the Phœnicians having pearl fisheries in the Indian seas, as they had in the Persian Gulf.

[96] ARRIAN, *Op*. p. 194.

[97] *Geogr. Min.* vol. i. p. 34. In this work Manaar is called the island of Epiodorus, probably from the name of some Greek who discovered it.

[98] *Periplus*, p. 32.

[99] Situate to the northward of Calicut, in 12° N. lat.

be the case even in Alexander's time.[100] Above all, the art of working in ivory must have attained a high degree of perfection, from the circumstance, that the ornamental chains above noticed seem to have been carved out of a single piece.

According to the unanimous report both of history and tradition, weaving is reckoned among the most important manufactures of ancient India; a country which nature has abundantly furnished with all kinds of raw material for the purpose, and especially cotton. We are not informed, however, who was the inventor of the simple loom used by the Hindus, which from its first origin does not appear to have undergone any alteration. The variety of cloth fabrics mentioned even by the author of the Periplus, as articles of commerce, is so great, that we can hardly suppose the number to have increased afterwards. We there read of the finest Bengal muslins; of coarse, middle, and fine cloths, either plain or striped; of coarse and fine calicos; of coloured shawls and sashes; of coarse and fine purple goods, as well as pieces of gold embroidery; of spun silk and furs from Serica.[1] As it is certain this variety of cloth manufactures was then found to exist in India, so is it extremely probable that such was the case long prior to the time of the Periplus; for the industry which produced them was not the fruit of external commerce, but of the national wants themselves. With respect to earlier times, indeed, we cannot expect to find such an accurate enumeration of manufactured articles, as the Periplus is the oldest work we have on the subject; but that they were generally the same, there is every reason to believe; for the Greeks who visited India four hundred years before, in the train of Alexander and his immediate successors, observed the same state of things prevailing. The cotton garments of the Hindus were the first to draw their attention, from the extraordinary whiteness of the cloth; and they are described as being made and worn in the same manner as at the present day.[2] The accounts we find of this cloth in the prophet Ezekiel would lead us to similar conclusions.[3] That the "coloured cloths and rich apparel" brought to Tyre and Babylon from distant

[100] ARRIAN, *Op.* p. 179.
[1] *Periplus*, p. 13, 16, 22, 28, 32, 36.
[2] ARRIAN, *Op.* p. 179.
[3] Ezek. xxvii. 23, 24.

countries were partly of Indian manufacture will scarcely be doubted, after what has been already said of the extent of the Phœnician and Babylonian commerce.[4] But still older and more important testimony will be found on this subject in India itself. The coloured garments usually worn by the inhabitants of Ayodhya have been before noticed, in the description of that city quoted from the Ramayana.[5] The principal passage, however, to which we would now refer, is the one descriptive of the nuptial present made to Sita by her father the king of Videha.[6] It consisted of woollen stuffs, furs, precious stones, fine silk, vestments of divers colours, princely ornaments, and sumptuous carriages of every kind. Now, what can we understand by the term woollen stuffs, but those Cashmir shawls, which still form part of the female attire in Eastern countries, and even in modern Europe? Only the finest cloths of this material would be a suitable present to a king's daughter, and especially, too, upon such an occasion. The passage, therefore, just quoted, supplies an additional proof in favour of the high antiquity of these celebrated fabrics. Mention is also made of coarse woollen cloths, or tilts to cover waggons.[7] Articles of furriery, so much sought after in warm countries, as in China, for instance, more by way of ornament than for defence against the cold, would of course only come from northern climes. With respect to silk stuffs, they are probably what we should least of all expect to meet with in India at that early period. The above, however, is not the only passage in the Ramayana where they are mentioned. Vestments of silk are usually worn on festal occasions, and even in the interior of the royal harems. Such, also, we find to have been the case upon the reception of Rajah Dasaratha's four beautiful daughters at the court of Ayodhya.[8] "Kausalya, Sumitra, the fair Keikeyi, and the rest of the king's wives, eager to embrace their beauteous daughters, received the happy Sita, the far-famed Urmila, and the two daughters of Kusa Dhwaja. All these ladies, sumptuously clad in silk, and entertaining each other

[4] See the first volume.
[5] See p. 150 of this volume.
[6] *Ramayana*, i. 605.
[7] Ibid. i. 201.
[8] *Ramayana*, i. 627. Compare iii. 204, 282.

with agreeable conversation, hastened to the temples of the gods to offer incense." From the circumstance of these garments of silk being worn on state occasions in the harems of princes, we might immediately conclude the stuffs to have been of foreign manufacture; but to this subject we shall have another opportunity of reverting in the sequel.

Besides the materials hitherto noticed, Herodotus and Ctesias both mention the bark of trees being used in India, from very remote times, for the purpose of manufacturing cloth.[9] In the Sacontala, we find garments of this description worn by pious hermits and penitents;[10] and Sacontala had a mantle of the same kind, expressly distinguished from the magnificent apparel which was presented to her by the Devanies, when she became the wife of Dushmanta.[11] The king also, during the time of his penance, laid aside his robes of muslin and silk, and put on garments of a similar coarse texture.[12] The manner in which this cloth was manufactured, is no where particularly described; but there is a remarkable passage in the Sacontala, which says, that it was dried in the sun.[13] It must, therefore, have been different from that made by the South-sea islanders of the same material, as the latter will not bear moisture. Or, might it not have been first wetted during the process of manufacture, and then exposed to the sun?

Among articles of food, rice, according to the Ramayana, occupies the first place. Of this, various kinds are there distinguished; and in the flourishing city of Ayodhya, the most esteemed, as well as the most usually eaten, was that called *shali*, which ripened in the cold season.[14] One of the most curious passages in the above poem, relative to this subject, is the list of provisions and drink, with which Rajah Vasishtha regaled the well-fed army of Vishva-Mitra:[15] "Every man had what he desired, sugar-cane, honey, laja,[16] mireja,[17] wine, and the most generous liquors; an immense

[9] HEROD. iii. 98. ἐσθὴς φλοίνη. CTES. *Indic.* 22. ἱμάτια ξύλινα.
[10] JONES's *Works*, vol. vi. p. 225, 226. [11] Ibid. p. 257.
[12] Ibid. p. 283. [13] Ibid. p. 289. [14] *Ramayana*, i. 104.
[15] *Ramayana*, i. 463. Compare the description of an entertainment given by Bhurdmaja, iii. 296.
[16] A dish consisting of rice. [Fried grain, in WILSON's *Dict.*]
[17] A fermented drink of molasses and water.

variety of dishes piled mountains high, and containing dainties for sucking, licking, chewing, and drinking,[18] together with rice-curries, sweetmeats, pastry, and large vessels filled with excellent curds and whey; all adapted to the six kinds of taste, and served out in every direction, in thousands of vessels sweetened with the inspissated juice of the sugar-cane." What may excite our surprise in this copious enumeration of provisions is the fact, that although the question concerns an entertainment given to soldiers, we nevertheless find no allusion to more substantial food than mere sweetmeats. The sugar-cane is not only mentioned in the Ramayana, but also in the Laws of Menu[19] and in the Periplus as an article of exportation.[20] The juice of it is sometimes drank in a raw state, at others it is thickened and preserved in vessels for future use; but we meet with no traces of its being refined. Of strong and intoxicating liquors, ancient India was acquainted with more than one sort; the use of them, however, was by no means general. The Ramayana distinguishes the Surs, who indulged themselves in these liquors, from the Asurs, who abstained from them;[21] two sects which even at that time must have been of pretty ancient standing, as they are noticed in the old fable about the descendants of Aditi (who are the Surs) and Diti (who are the Asurs).

Under the head of strong liquors, wine is more than once mentioned in the Ramayana. If we suppose this to mean wine made from grapes, it must, in that case, have been imported; because, to the best of our knowledge, they do not press the grape in India itself.[22] It is very doubtful, however, whether this sort of wine is to be understood in the passages alluded to; and even admitting it to have been introduced into the country as early as the time of the Ramayana, it would scarcely be the usual drink of common soldiers, any more than it is at the present day. It appears, indeed, much more probable that palm-wine is intended by the expression; as this could be easily made in any part of

[18] Let the reader fancy himself in India, where they *suck* the juice of the sugar-cane and other succulent fruits, *lick* ice, and *chew* the betel-nut.

[19] MENU, viii. 341. [20] *Periplus*, p. 9. [21] *Ramayana*, i. 416, not.

[22] In the *Periplus*, wine is several times mentioned as an article of importation; for instance, in p. 22—28, where it is said to have been brought from Italy and Syria.

T 2

India, and was, moreover, in the time of the Periplus, imported from Arabia, which is the reason of its being called Arabian wine.[23] The strong liquors, however, in most general use throughout India, appear to have been those obtained by distillation. The Ramayana mentions a beverage of this sort procured from fruits and the sugar-cane;[24] and in Menu we find three principal kinds distinguished,[25] according as the liquors in question were distilled from molasses, bruised rice, or the Madhuca-flower.[26] Of the last we know nothing beyond the mere name; the two former are most likely equivalent to the arrack and rum of modern times. The Brahmans are forbidden the use of all three.

India is the mother country of spices; and we have already shown, in the course of our inquiries into Phœnician commerce, that, from the most ancient times, she supplied the whole western world with that article. Although in the few native works at our present disposal there is no particular mention made of spices, yet we cannot possibly doubt of their consumption in the country itself. This silence, however, is merely the effect of accidental causes; for neither Menu or the Ramayana had any special occasion of alluding to the subject. But it is quite certain that pepper was very early known to the western world as an article of commerce; for Theophrastus even distinguishes several varieties of it.[27] Together with the spice itself, the name also of pepper seems to have migrated, probably through Persia, into the countries of the West.[28] There is little doubt that it came originally from the southern parts of Malabar, from Cochin and the neighbourhood; which was noticed for its growth of pepper by Cosmas in the sixth century, and indeed is so at the present day.

With respect to articles of perfumery, we are enabled to speak more decisively. These are of various kinds, partly foreign, as frankincense, and partly indigenous, as the san-

[23] *Periplus*, p. 21. [24] *Ramayana*, iii. 289. [25] MENU, xi. 95.

[26] Bassia Latifolia. [Called also Mahwah by the natives. See an interesting description of this very curious and useful tree in the *Asiatic Res.* vol. i. p. 300, sq., together with an account of the native method of distilling the flowers, p. 309. TRANSL.]

[27] THEOPHRAST. *Hist. Plant.* ix. 22.

[28] The Sanscrit name is *pippali*, whence the Greek πέπερι, Latin *piper*, pepper, etc. DR. HUNTER's Remarks on the species of Pepper, etc., in the *Asiatic Res.* vol. ix. p. 384.

dal-wood, which is frequently mentioned in the Ramayana and the Gitagovinda,[29] and was in common use throughout India as well as China. Perfumes in general, and particularly frankincense, were from the most ancient times not confined solely to the purposes of sacrifice; they were also indispensable requisites in Hindu private life, and above all on festal occasions; an example of which will be found in the Ramayana, where the poet describes the solemn entry of Bharata into his grandfather's capital:[30] "The inhabitants, after having watered the streets, had sprinkled them with sand, and garnished them with flower-pots, ranged in order, and containing fragrant plants in full blossom. The city was adorned with garlands, and exhaled the odours of frankincense and sweet-smelling perfumes." The quantity of frankincense consumed in India deserves to be particularly remarked, as it is not an indigenous production, but imported from Arabia.[31] Many other kinds of perfume are mentioned in the Periplus as being of native growth; we can scarcely, therefore, doubt their having been used in very remote antiquity.

This is not the place for enumerating in detail all the objects of commerce mentioned in the earliest accounts of India; such, for instance, as female slaves, destined for the replenishing of harems;[32] different sorts of colours, as lac[33] and indigo;[34] together with base and precious metals; not

[29] *Ramayana*, iii. 125, and elsewhere; *Gitagovinda*, p. 58, 65, 84. According to which, it grew chiefly on the mountains of Malaya. An odoriferous unguent was also prepared from this tree, by reducing the wood to powder and mixing it with oil. BECKMANN (*Waarenkunde*, vol. ii. No. i. p. 112, sq.) has furnished us with a learned inquiry into the nature and properties of this wood. The passages above quoted must be understood, in all probability, of the best species of sandal-wood, viz. the yellow, which grows in Malabar, and not of the red sort.

[30] *Ramayana*, i. 636.

[31] [MR. COLEBROOKE has satisfactorily shown, that the resinous gum called Olibanum (the frankincense of the ancients) is an indigenous production of India as well as of Arabia. See his "Account of Olibanum," in the *Asiatic Res.* vol. ix. p. 377, sq. According to NIEBUHR, however, (vol. i. p. 202,) it is not even a native of Arabia, but originally brought thither from Abyssinia; in which opinion he is supported by Bruce. See MICHAELIS, Question xxix. TRANSL.]

[32] *Ramayana*, i. 606. Rajah Janaka is there represented as adding to his other presents a thousand female slaves, adorned with collars of gold.

[33] CTESIAS, *Indic.* cap. 21.

[34] Indian black, (called μέλας Ἰνδικὸν in the *Periplus*, p. 22,) as well as cinnabar, (p. 18,) are also mentioned. At the present day indigo, called by the

forgetting the celebrated Indian steel,[35] and many other valuable productions. But enough has been already said for the purpose of showing the extent of ancient Hindu commerce, considered with reference to its principal objects.

The nature of the country, however, rendered the internal commerce of India different from that of the rest of Asia, in respect of transportation; for it was not necessary, nor indeed was it always possible, to employ caravans, as in the extensive tracts of Inner Asia. That this mode of conveyance was nevertheless occasionally resorted to, we learn from the beautiful episode of Nala, where Damayanti in her flight is represented to have joined a caravan of merchants.[36] But the beasts of burden made use of, in this instance, are tame elephants, which were therefore attacked in the night and dispersed by their wild brethren of the forest; and besides, the caravan in question appears to have belonged to some royal personage, rather than to a company of private merchants.[37] The greatest part of India, that is to say, the whole of the peninsula, being traversed with rocky mountains, would scarcely, if at all, admit of the employment of camels;[38] and the moderate distances between one town and another, and the general spread of civilization, would enable merchants to travel alone with perfect security, while river-navigation and the coasting trade afforded unusual facilities for transporting merchandise. The Ganges and its tributary streams were the grand commercial routes of Northern India; and mention is also made of navigation on the rivers of the peninsula in the south.[39] It is not improbable, indeed, that artificial routes between the Ganges and the Indus, as we find to have been the case in after-times,[40] existed even at an earlier period. The great high roads across the country are not only frequently mentioned in the Ramayana;[41] but we also read of a particular

natives *nil*, (i. e. dark blue,) still forms a principal branch of the commerce between India and Bokhara.

[35] CTESIAS, *Indic.* cap. 4.

[36] *Nalus*, ed. BOPP, p. 88, etc. See p. 166 of this volume.

[37] It is called the caravan of King Chandir. *Nalus*, xii. 132.

[38] The *Periplus* (p. 29) expressly remarks, that merchandise was transported from the commercial towns of the interior to the sea-coast on carriages (ἁμάξαις).

[39] *Periplus*, p. 31. The river-tolls are specified in MENU, viii. 406.

[40] *Strabo*, p. 1010.

[41] As, for example, *Ramayana*, iii. 228.

class of men who were commissioned to keep them in repair.[42] According to Arrian, the commercial intercourse between the eastern and western coasts was carried on in country-built vessels; and when we consider the high antiquity of the pearl-fisheries in the straits of Ceylon, together with the necessary requisites thereto, we can hardly doubt that such was also the case many hundred years before his time. It would appear, then, that conveyance of merchandise by means of a caravan, as in other countries of the East, continued always foreign to the practice of India, unless the multitudes of pilgrims and penitents, that were continually resorting to places of sanctity, may be said to have compensated for the want of it. The almost innumerable crowds that yearly flock to Benares, Juggernaut, and elsewhere, amounting to many hundred thousands of souls, would obviously give rise to a species of commerce united with devotion;[43] and markets and fairs would be a natural, and indeed an indispensable requisite to satisfy the

[42] The principal passage is in book iii. 226, where the poet describes the preparations made for Bharata's journey. "The people were collected together who superintended different parts of the roads; able carpenters, diggers, engineers, hired day labourers with carts, hewers of wood," etc. It is not, indeed, positively mentioned that these were regular artificial roads; for there is nothing of the sort even at the present day to be found in India; but they were at least beaten or levelled ways. However, in p. 231, we read that "Bridges are built, rocks broken through, canals and wells dug, and the roads planted with flowers and trees: thus adorned, they resemble the causeways of heaven." There is no allusion to milestones, though otherwise well known in the East.

[43] It will be sufficient by way of illustration, to quote Capt. Hardwicke's account of the pilgrimage and fair held at Hurdwar on the Ganges, in 30° N. lat. See *Asiatic Res.* vol. vi. p. 312. "This fair," says the Captain, "is an annual assemblage of Hindus, to bathe, for a certain number of days, in the waters of the Ganges, at this consecrated spot. The multitude collected here on this occasion, might, I think, with moderation, be computed at two and a half millions of souls. Although the performance of a religious duty is their primary object, yet many avail themselves of the opportunity to transact business, and carry on an extensive annual commerce. In this concourse of nations, it is a matter of no small amusement to a curious observer to trace the dress, features, manners, etc., which characterize the people of the different countries of Cabul, Cashmir, Lahore, Butan, Sirinagur, Cummow, and the plains of Hindustan. From some of these very distant countries, whole families, men, women, and children, undertake the journey; some travelling on foot, some on horseback, and many, particularly women and children, in long heavy carts, railed, and covered with sloping matted roofs, to defend them against the sun and wet weather; and during the continuance of the fair these serve also as habitations." And yet Hurdwar is by no means in the first rank of holy places! Markets and fairs are expressly mentioned in the *Ramayana*, iii. 432.

wants of such throngs of people. And consequently, too, the establishments already noticed under the appellation of choultries, the erection of which was considered a religious duty, and whose forms not unfrequently displayed all the magnificence of native architecture, might be said to have a similar destination with the caravanserais of other Eastern countries, without, however, the resemblance between the two being exactly perfect.

Although commercial traffic was not carried on in India, as elsewhere, by means of caravans, yet there was necessarily an occasion for the establishment of certain intermediate depôts and places of mercantile resort. These were partly in the interior of the country, and partly also on the coast; and the names of three of them are given by the author of the Periplus: Ozene to the north of the peninsula, and Tagara and Pluthana in the interior. The first of these, Ozene, or, under its modern appellation, Oujein, is the present capital of Scindiah, one of the most powerful of the Mahratta chieftains, but it is also represented by Arrian as an ancient city, and "formerly" a royal residence.[44] At first, Ozene was the market for internal traffic, and supplied the neighbouring country with necessaries; at a subsequent period, however, it also became the emporium of foreign commerce for inland productions, such as the onyx-stone, muslins, coarse and fine calicos, which it transmitted to the haven of Barygaza for exportation; and probably it was also a depôt for the produce of more distant northern countries, of which we shall have occasion to speak hereafter. Ozene was at all times reckoned in the number of holy towns, and indeed of the first rank, the surrounding territory, for

[44] *Periplus*, p. 27, 28. The modern Oujein is one mile distant from the ancient town, which was overwhelmed by an earthquake, as report says, in the time of Vicramaditya. At the depth of from fifteen to eighteen feet, entire walls of extraordinary sized bricks, pillars, various utensils, and ancient coins have been discovered; and, what is more singular, a large quantity of wheat. Adjoining these ruins is a subterranean palace, said to have been the abode of Rajah Bhirtiry, the brother of Vicramaditya. It contains a court, galleries, and apartments, curiously carved with figures of men in high relief. It is, however, impossible to explore the whole, a great portion of the ruins being choked up with rubbish. See HUNTER's narrative, in the *Asiatic Res.* vol. vi. p. 36. Oujein is, therefore, certainly one of the most ancient towns in India, and it is also a place of great sanctity; both which circumstances would concur in proving it to have been originally an establishment altogether resembling those of Ellora and Elephanta, etc.

the space of two coss in circumference, being held to be sacred.[45] It is, therefore, of course, the resort of pilgrims; and every year, at a particular season, an immense number of people flock together from all parts into the town, a circumstance which immediately explains the reason why Ozene, as the residence of kings and a place of such peculiar sanctity, should become the principal depôt of interior commerce.

In the interior of the Deccan, two places, Tagara and Pluthana, are expressly mentioned as the most important commercial staples in the whole province.[46] The first of these is the ancient Deogur, or Devagiri, "the hill of the gods," celebrated for its pagodas, and also for the close proximity of the still more celebrated Ellora;[47] and consequently we have here, too, another proof of the intimate connexion subsisting between the establishment of inland commerce and religion; for Tagara, being considered one of the most famous sanctuaries in the country, would of course owe all its importance as a place of mercantile resort, to the great number of pilgrims who for more than a thousand years had been wont to assemble there. The author of the Periplus reckons Tagara among the largest cities of India, even in his time; a circumstance which would naturally lead us to infer a long period of antecedent splendour. From hence coarse and fine cotton goods, different kinds of muslin, and other indigenous productions, were conveyed over difficult roads to the port of Barygaza, to be shipped for foreign countries.

The situation of Pluthana is not so well ascertained. According to the present text of the Periplus, it should be sought for at a distance of twenty days' journey to the southward of Barygaza; and Tagara is said to have been ten days' journey to the east of Pluthana. At first we might suppose it to be the same with the modern Patual, which in fact is about a hundred and fifty miles distant to the westward of Tagara, and consequently the journey between the two places would require a space of ten days to accomplish with heavy laden carriages over difficult and mountainous routes; but then the distance from Patual to

[45] *Ayin Acbari*, ii. 546. [46] *Periplus*, p. 29.
[47] See p. 72 of this volume.

Oujein,[48] instead of being only twenty, is at least thirty days' journey. The passage, however, in the Periplus is manifestly corrupt; and we must therefore be content with mere conjecture. Nevertheless, under all the circumstances, it is quite clear that Pluthana was situate among the Ghâts, for it was the general market for onyx-stones, which were transported from this town over very bad roads to Barygaza.[49]

The most active internal commerce, however, was that carried on in the northern parts of India, along the course of the Ganges. Here was the royal highway, extending from Taxila on the Indus, through Lahore, to Palibothra on the Ganges; and which, measured by *schœns*, was upwards of ten thousand stadia in length.[50] The first writer, we believe, who makes any mention of this road is Megasthenes; but whether it existed before the time of Alexander is very doubtful, as Arrian does not expressly notice it; and the admeasurement by *schœns* is not of Indian but Persian origin. On the other hand, the facility with which Alexander was able to advance, as well as the frequent use of chariots among the ancient Hindus, would clearly show that there was no want of levelled roads in this part of India. Even the Ramayana describes in a circumstantial manner, the road leading from Ayodhya over the Ganges, by Hastinapur and the Jumna through Lahore, to the city of Ginibe-raja in the interior of the Punjab; and by which Rama, after the death of his father, was conducted to Ayodhya.

The observations hitherto made, will at least serve to throw some light on the internal commerce of India; and the latter probably will receive additional illustration by combining therewith the results of our inquiry into the commerce of the same country, as it existed in times anterior to the reign of the Ptolemies. In conducting this in-

[48] [The author probably means Barygaza, though both towns appear to be equidistant from Patual. TRANSL.]

[49] *Periplus*, loc. cit. [WILFORD, with every appearance of probability, supposes Pluthana to be the modern Pultanah, situate on the southern bank of the Godavery; about two hundred and seventeen British miles to the southward of Baroach. See *Asiatic Researches*, vol. i. p. 369, sq. TRANSL.]

[50] STRABO, p. 1010. CASAUBON has demonstrated the true reading to have been 10,000 stadia, instead of 20,000. It is the same road spoken of by PLINY, *Hist. Nat.* vol. vi. p. 21, and which WILFORD (*Asiatic Res.* vol. ix. p. 48, etc.) and other writers have endeavoured to explain; but they do not inform us whether its antiquity reaches as far back as the times of which we are treating.

quiry, we shall confine ourselves to the same limited principles of criticism already prescribed for examining the other; that is, we shall only make use of the information contained in later writers, such, for instance, as the Periplus of Arrian, in so far forth as it either directly refers to more ancient times, or is capable of throwing some light on them, in connexion with the accounts furnished by earlier writers. In the mean time, however, we would request the reader always to bear in mind a remark, the propriety of which must by this time be sufficiently evident, and will be further corroborated in the sequel: viz. that the internal commerce of the East has undergone little other change than what would arise from partial deviations in the route; while on the contrary, the direction of Western commerce has been subject to considerable modifications.

The nature of the country and its productions, together with the peculiar genius of the people themselves, both contributed to render Hindu commerce of a passive rather than an active character. For as the productions of India were always in high request with the Western world, the Hindus would clearly have no occasion to transport them to foreign countries themselves; they would of course expect the inhabitants of the latter to come and fetch what they wanted. And again, the Hindu national character has no pretensions to that hardy spirit of adventure, which is capable of achieving the most extraordinary undertakings. While their fables abound with prodigious enterprise, the people themselves are content to lead a quiet and peaceful life, with just so much activity as is requisite to guide the plough or direct the shuttle; without running the risk of hazardous and unnecessary adventure. Their India—their Jambu-dwipa, comprised in their estimation the limits of the known world. Separated from the rest of Asia by a chain of impassable mountains on the north; while on all other sides the ocean formed a barrier, which, if their laws are silent on the subject, yet at least their habits or their customs would not permit them to transgress; we can find no certain proof that the Hindus were ever mariners.

These remarks, however, must only be understood as applicable to the great body of the nation, without at all implying that some particular individuals were not enterprising enough to pass the seas, and establish themselves in foreign countries, in order to profit by commercial speculation. Merchants of this kind are expressly mentioned in the Ramayana, who "traffic beyond sea and bring presents to the king."[51] In fact, no law had ever forbidden this species of commerce; on the contrary, the Institutes of Menu contain several regulations which tacitly allow it, in giving the force of law to all commercial contracts relative to dangers incurred by sea or land.[52] Moreover, the religion of the Hindus does not recognise the Egyptian principle of the sea being impure. The latter is assigned its own peculiar sovereign; and according to mythological report, the sea, that is, the Bay of Bengal, owed its origin to the influx of the holy stream, the Ganges.[53] It is well known that the Hindu merchants, called Banians, are in the habit of traversing the ocean, and settling in foreign countries. And a modern writer observes,[54] that, "The commerce of Arabia Felix is entirely in the hands of the Banians of Guzerat; who, from father to son, have established themselves in the country, and are protected by the government, in consideration of a certain impost levied upon their estimated property." We can easily conceive this to have been the case also in much earlier times. In the Hitopadesa[55] it is said, "A ship is a necessary requisite for enabling man to traverse the ocean;" and in another passage we read of a "certain merchant, who, after having been twelve years on his voyage, at last

[51] *Ramayana*, iii. 237.

[52] [See Menu, iii. 158; viii. 157. Sir W. Jones has supposed that from bottomry being mentioned in the laws of Menu, the Hindus must have been navigators in the age of that work. Now, that ships belonging to Hindus went to sea, and that a proportionate interest for the hazard of the sea was to be paid on money borrowed, must be perfectly true; but it remains to be proved that the seamen were Hindus. And Sir W.'s endeavour to prove that they used the sea in former ages, proves that it is contrary to their principles and practice in later times. It is only within these few years that the English have been able to carry their sepoys to sea; and in doing this, there seems to have been employed money, discipline, and a variety of fictions, to salve their conscience. Fishermen there are, but they can cook and eat their food on shore; and even fishermen are an abomination in Malabar. Merchants, however, may grow rich at home while other nations are their carriers; and the Armenians, who are no navigators themselves, freight ships in every port of India. Transl.]

[53] *Ramayana*, i. 400.

[54] From the accounts of M. Cloupet, in the *Allgem. Geogr. Ephem.* for November, 1810, p. 235.

[55] Sir W. Jones's *Works*, vol. vi. p. 94.

returned home with a cargo of precious stones."[56] But what makes the case still more evident, is the story told in the Sacontala of the merchant Danavriddhi, whose immense wealth devolved to the king on the former's perishing at sea, and leaving no heirs behind him.[57] If, in addition to these authorities, the reader wishes for more decisive historical proof, he will find it in the Periplus; which, besides merchants of Arabia and Greece, mentions also the Banians of India, who, for commercial purposes, had established themselves on the north side of the island of Socotra.[58]

The foregoing remarks will, it is hoped, serve to explain in some degree the manner in which the Hindus took a part in external commerce. We have seen that although it was not their general practice to travel in caravans, or to man vessels for the purposes of commerce, yet it by no means follows that private individuals had not extensive mercantile transactions with foreign countries, and even occasionally undertook long voyages themselves. We shall now then proceed to inquire into this foreign commerce of the Hindus, according to its several directions, towards the north, east, and west; and examine each quarter in succession.

The only country in the north with which India had commercial relations was China.[59] Notwithstanding all the obstacles which nature herself has interposed, such as apparently inaccessible mountains, and pathless deserts, it is impossible to doubt the existence, even from very remote times, of a commercial intercourse between the two countries; particularly as we meet with articles of Chinese merchandise in India. Silk stuffs, and garments of the same material, are mentioned in the Ramayana as ordinarily worn in the harems of great men.[60] Whether, indeed, the rich nuptial vestments spoken of in the Sacontala,[61] might not likewise have been made of silk, we shall leave our readers to determine. The Periplus, however, expressly mentions silk stuffs, and also spun silk, as articles of

[56] SIR W. JONES's *Works*, p. 80. [57] Ibid. p. 292.
[58] *Periplus*, p. 17. There called the island of Dioscorides.
[59] VINCENT, vol. ii. p. 574, 575, has already shown that the name of China is of Hindu origin, and came to us from India. [The word Sinim occurs in the Bible, Isaiah, xlix. 12. Compare also a passage in *Mengsteu*, i. 121; and the "Nouveaux Mélanges" of M. ABEL, *Remusat*, ii. 334. FR. TRANSL.]
[60] See p. 273, of this volume.
[61] SIR W. JONES's *Works*, vol. vi. p. 257.]

foreign importation.[62] That silk is the indigenous production of China and the neighbouring country of Tangut, on its western frontier, both comprised by the ancients under the indefinite appellation of Serica, is a fact too well known to require proof;[63] we have, therefore, only to ascertain by what route, and in what manner, the commerce in question was carried on.

It is an undeniable fact, that a land traffic between India and China has existed heretofore, and probably is still in being at the present day. But the obscurity in which this part of our subject is involved, cannot altogether be cleared away, in consequence of the very small number of European travellers who have investigated the countries bordering on the route. With regard to the commerce itself, we shall begin by quoting some decisive testimony from the Periplus, which will set the matter beyond a doubt. The first place mentioned in that work, as being situate on the eastern side of the peninsula, is Masalia; which extended a considerable way along the coast, and was famous for the manufacture of cotton piece goods.[64] That this can be no other than the modern Masulipatan, is sufficiently proved by its situation, name, and produce.[65] The next commercial town mentioned by our author, is one situate on the mouths of the Ganges, and bearing the same name as the river, where betel, pearls, and the finest sorts of muslin were sold. Then follows an account of the island, or rather peninsula, of Chryse, which is mentioned as the furthest part of India towards the east; comprising, in fact, the modern Ava, Pegu, and Malacca. To the northward of this, and contiguous to the ocean, lay a country in the interior of which we find the large city Thina;[66] from whence raw and spun

[62] *Periplus*, p. 36.

[63] [It is not at all improbable that silk was also indigenous in India even at a remote epoch. See SCHLEGEL, *Berlin Kalender*, 1829, p. 9. FR. TRANSL.] [It is worthy of notice, that the Rudra-Yamala-Tantra, in an enumeration of Hindu castes, mentions the Pundracas and Pattasutracaras, or feeders of silk-worms, and silk-twisters; this authority, therefore, in conjunction with the frequent allusions to silk in the most ancient Sanscrit books, may be considered as decisive of the question, provided the antiquity of the Tantra be allowed; of which Mr. Colebrooke seems to have no doubt. See his Essay on Indian Classes, in *Asiatic Researches*, vol. v. p. 61, sq. Silk is known throughout the Archipelago by a Sanscrit name, *sutra*. TRANSL.]

[64] *Periplus*, p. 35.

[65] VINCENT, vol. ii. p. 523.

[66] *Periplus*, p. 36. Πόλις μεσόγειος μεγίστη, λεγομένη Θῖνα, ἀφ' ἧς τότε ἔριον,

silk and silk stuffs were conveyed by land through the country of the Bactrians to Barygaza; and also by the Ganges to Limyrica. From the last words of this passage it is evident that silk was imported into India by two different routes; one towards the west altogether by land, through Bactra, and the other towards the east by the Ganges. The city Thina, whether it be Pekin[67] or some other large town in Western China, was in either case the great emporium of silk merchandise in these parts. The next question, therefore, for us to decide is, by whom and by what routes was this traffic in silk carried on?

With regard to the persons engaged in the above commerce, there is a very remarkable testimony contained in a passage of Ctesias, already quoted on another occasion,[68] and which we have always considered as presenting the earliest traces to be found of any connexion between China and the Western world. "The Indians," says he, "who live near the Bactrians, make expeditions into the gold desert, in armed companies of a thousand or two thousand men. But, according to report, they do not return home for three or four years."[69] Now we have before shown that the desert here mentioned is the great one of Cobi, and the "Indians" are the northernmost inhabitants of the country, or those who bordered on the Paropamisus. But the expeditions through this desert, made in such numerous caravans, and for so long a space of time, for what region could they be intended, or whither, in fact, would they lead, except into China? The writer, it is true, having only heard of gold as the object in quest of which these expeditions were undertaken, makes no mention of silk, with which, probably, he was unacquainted. It were superfluous, however, to prove

καὶ τὸ ὀθόνιον τὸ Σηρικὸν εἰς τὴν Βαρύγαζαν διὰ Βακτρῶν πεζῇ φέρεται· καὶ εἰς τὴν Λιμυρικὴν πάλιν διὰ τοῦ Γάγγου ποταμοῦ. That the Thina of the Periplus must be looked for in the north, that is, in Serica or China, is quite evident from the express words of the passage just quoted. Ptolemy, however, and other writers, place a town of that name in Malacca, near the modern Tenasserim. Concerning this determination and the reasons for it, see MANNERT, vol. v. p. 234, 275.

[67] Some writers identify it with the "Senim Metropolis," of Ptolemy; others take it to be the present Se-Chuen.

[68] See the chapter on the Babylonians.

[69] Apud ÆLIAN. *Hist. An.* iv. 27. This passage is not to be found among the Fragments of Ctesias, because it stands only at the end of the chapter, but that it is really borrowed from that writer is evident from the context.

that silk might have been used as a medium of exchange for gold, and that the most valuable production of China would surely not have been suffered to remain a useless commodity in the hands of the merchant. The individuals in question, then, were North Indians, that is, inhabitants of Cabul and Badakshan, who travelled in numerous caravans for the productions of China, which they either exported themselves, or transmitted for that purpose to their neighbours the Bactrians, in whose country the first principal mart of the carrying trade for Media, as well as India Proper, was most probably situated. At all events, these merchants are represented as travelling through Bactra in order to reach India[70] and Barygaza; but whether their route was altogether by land, or partly down the Indus, can only be determined by conjecture. The accounts we have of Alexander's expedition evidently show, that an active navigation must have existed on that river and its confluent streams long before his arrival; otherwise he could not in so short a time have collected a sufficient number of vessels, for enabling him to embark the greatest part of his army, and so transport them down the Indus to its mouth, passing in his way by Pattala, a commercial port situate on the delta of the river.

That part of our question which relates to the particular routes by which this commerce was carried on, may be answered by applying the accounts of later times, as the nature of the subject will allow us to do, to the elucidation of an earlier period. These accounts are furnished by Ptolemy,[71] who calculates the distances between the Euphrates and Serica according to the determinations of Marinus. He mentions as a principal commercial station, a certain *lithinos pyrgos*, or stone tower, which was situate under the same parallel of latitude (42°) as Byzantium and the capital of the Seres, from which latter place it was seven months' journey distant. The approach to this tower was through a defile at the point of junction between the north and south chains of the Imaus, that is, where the great mountain range

[70] According to the latest Russian accounts, the principal rendezvous of the caravans which set out for India, Persia, and Asiatic Russia, as well as China, is the modern Bokhara. So that what the ancient Bactra was formerly, Bokhara is now.

[71] Ptol. i. cap. 11, 12.

of Taurus, on the western frontier of Little Bucharia, divides itself into two branches, skirting the vast plain of the desert of Cobi.

It is only within these few years that additional light has been thrown on this statement of Ptolemy; and the tower itself, so interesting a monument for the history of commerce, been actually proved to exist. We are indebted for this information to Wilford, who had it from a Russian of the name of Czernichev, who had been made prisoner on the frontiers of Siberia by the Kalmucks, and sold as a slave to the Usbeck Tatars. In the year 1780, his master, who was a merchant, went to trade from Bokhara to Cashgar, Yarkand, and Cashmir; and being pleased with his behaviour, gave him his liberty; upon which, in company with some Armenians, he came to Lucknow, where he was relieved by Sir Eyre Coote, whose generosity enabled him to revisit his native country. According to the Russian's narrative of his travels,[72] Wilford says, "The elevated plains of Meru are, perhaps, the highest spot, or at least the highest flat, in the old continent. Its height towards India and China is prodigious: it is not so considerable toward the north, and is still less toward the north-west, where the ascent between the stone-tower and the station of the merchants trading to China, is by no means very difficult. The stone-tower still exists under the name of Chihel-Sutun, or the Forty Columns,[73] and is famous all over these countries. The station of the merchants is still their place of rendezvous to this day, and is called Takhti-Suleiman, or the Throne of Solomon. The tower is at the extremity of a small branch, jutting out of a range of mountains to the left of the road, or to the north, and which projects toward the south, and ends abruptly in the middle of a plain.[74] Its

[72] *Asiatic Res.* vol. viii. p. 323.

[73] The ruins of Persepolis are also called by the Persians Chehl-Menâr, agreeably to their usual custom of expressing an indefinite number by the use of a definite, such as *forty*. Can this tower be the Temple of the Sun, mentioned by Ctesias in the eighth chapter of his Indica? See Persians, p. 94.

[74] In 41° N. lat., 69° 6″ E. long. [In the maps hitherto published, the geography of these countries is extremely defective. The new Atlas by Sidney Hall has a place called Takhti-Suleiman laid down in lat. 31° 20″, which is much too far south to be in the route of merchants travelling from Bokhara to China; to say nothing of its being represented on the left bank of the Indus, on a plain, and far away from any mountains. TRANSL.]

extremity, consisting of a solid rock, has been cut into a regular shape, with two rows, each of twenty columns. The front part is in a very ruinous condition, and the upper row of columns remains suspended from the top; the columns below answering to them, with their entablature, having been destroyed. It is a most wonderful work, and ascribed by the natives to supernatural agents, as usual." The latest Russian information which we have been able to procure, relative to Bokhara, serves to confirm the above account. Bokhara is now what Bactra formerly was, the grand mart of Indo-Chinese traffic. Upwards of three hundred Banians are established there, and the road leading from thence to India through Bactra, which is twelve days' journey distant, is still in common use. The route from Bokhara to China passes through Samarcand, Cocan, Takhti-Suleiman, or the Stone-tower, and the neighbouring town of Owsh, where the mountains begin.

This tower so called was therefore a building of considerable extent; probably a large caravanserai, with a sanctuary attached. According to the Russian accounts, it is still much frequented by pilgrims: it is here also we find the miraculous stone,[75] said to be of sovereign application in all diseases. At the entrance of the desert, some such monumental edifice as the above would naturally enough be required, and therefore easily become an important commercial station. By means of this building, it is easy to determine the particular route as well as the length of time employed by the Hindu merchants in their journey to China.[76] If we assume Cabul, or rather Bactra, as their place of departure, the expedition would take a north-easterly direction as far as the forty-first degree of north latitude. It would then have to ascend the mountains, and so arrive at the stone-tower through the defile of Hoshan or Owsh. From hence the route led by Cashgar, beyond the mountains, to

[75] Qu. The stone called Yusche probably?

[76] The route of Czernichev from Cogend to Cashgar is as follows. From Cogend to Cucan, two days' journey; to Marhelan, one day; to Gheraba and Chihel-Sutun, two days; to the pass of Hoshan, one day; to the lead mines, ten days; to Girrel and the entrance into the plains, two days; to Cashgar, one day. In a "Chart of the Country of the Kirgheez Tatars," (Weimar, 1804,) designed after a Russian MS., we meet with the following places: Cucan (Kotschan); Machalan (Murgalan); the defile of Hoshan (Adjan); and Cashgar; with the distances marked as above.

the borders of the great desert of Cobi, which it traversed probably through Khoten and Aksu (the Casia and Auxazia of Ptolemy): from these ancient towns the road lay through Koshotei to Se-Chou on the frontiers of China, and thence to Pekin, a place of great antiquity, if we are to understand it as the metropolis of Serica, which, indeed, the accounts of Ptolemy would hardly leave any room to doubt.[77] The whole distance amounts to upwards of two thousand five hundred miles; and though the journey to and fro, together with the necessary delays there, is said to have required a space of no less than three years to accomplish, we shall not be disposed to consider this calculation exaggerated.[78]

But the Periplus mentions another route, by which silk was imported into India: viz. down the Ganges to its mouth, and from thence to Limyrica.[79] This way, though it was the shortest, was yet the most difficult, as it must have passed through the lofty mountains of Thibet, in the heart of which the Ganges has its source. Nevertheless, whatever hinderances nature might have opposed to such a route, it is, however, certain that motives of religion and a thirst of gain have been able to overcome them, and have done so for a long time. In prescribing to its votaries the duty of pilgrimage to the sovereign pontiff, who resides in the interior of Thibet, the religion of Lama furnishes strong inducements to undertake the journey. We are in possession of an itinerary of the Dalai Lama himself, from his residence to Pekin, whither he had been invited by the emperor Kien-Long, and where he died of the small-pox.[80]

[77] The latitude given by Ptolemy is nearly correct.

[78] Among the moderns who have travelled this route, we may notice the missionary Goez. He proceeded to Pekin from Cabul, by way of Samarcand, Cashgar, and Yerkand, at which latter place the caravan from Cabul exchanged their merchandise with another coming from China. *Purchas Pilgrim*, vol. iii. p. 312.

[79] *Periplus*, loc. cit.

[80] This journey was undertaken in the year 1780; and an authentic account of it will be found in TURNER's *Embassy to Thibet*, p. 443, 457. The principal stations on the road were Ducbu, situate on a river of the same name, forty-six days' journey; Tuktharing, twenty-five; the town of Cumbu-Gumbaw, nineteen, where the Grand Lama was detained four months by a heavy fall of snow; the town of Tumdatelu, fifteen; Nissaur, nine; Karambu, thirty; Tolowar, twenty-nine; Singhding, fifteen; as far as which latter the emperor had come to meet him. The Lama only reached Pekin a year after leaving his residence in Thibet. It is worthy of remark, that the presents made him by the emperor, consisting of silks, pearls, and furs, are precisely similar to those so often occurring in the Ramayana.

U 2

This itinerary, however, containing only the names of towns, with which we are otherwise unacquainted, and supplying no accurate determinations of their geography, will not throw much light upon the subject. Nevertheless, every thing concurs to prove that some such commercial route must have already existed in the time of the Periplus: and though we are, indeed, unable to assign the particular stations, yet as in after-times merchandise was usually conveyed down the Ganges, it is quite certain that the route in question must have followed the course of that river, and consequently have proceeded from the south-west of China. The modern route passes by a town called Teshu-Lumbo, situate in 29°·4′ 20″ N. lat. and 89° 7′ E. long.; and as it reaches the Ganges in a direct line from hence, there is less reason to doubt the probability of its being also the ancient one. Teshu-Lumbo is a place in Thibet where the great commercial roads cross each other; and Mr. Turner, from his residence, was able to see at once the roads leading to China, to Nepal, Mongolia, and to Cashmir, through Ladak, the principal market for shawl-wool, and the point of junction for the road leading from Cashgar.[81]

At the mouth of the Ganges, merchandise was conveyed to a town of the same name; situate probably in the neighbourhood of Duliapur, to the south-east of Calcutta, and on the central branch of the river.[82] The Periplus does not inform us in what way the transport of goods was effected from hence to the last Hindu market, Limyrica; but as the whole coast of Coromandel was navigated, we can scarcely doubt that it took place by sea.

The passage above quoted from Ctesias evidently shows that the first described route by land is much older than the Periplus; but whether the second has an equal claim to remote origin, must be left undetermined. That articles of silk, however, were imported into India from China by one or other of the two routes, if not by both, as early as

[81] TURNER, p. 296.

[82] According to MANNERT, vol. v. p. 232. Its situation, however, cannot be defined with precision. It was not merely the emporium for Chinese commerce, but also for the productions of Bengal, particularly fine muslins. As the Ganges, with its tributary streams, formed the high road of inland commerce, we can hardly doubt that the commercial town situate at its mouth was a place of considerable importance.

the composition of the Ramayana, is too well established to admit of the least doubt.

Silk, however, was not the only article of commerce which India received from China. The Periplus mentions a second, under the name of "skins from Serica,"[83] an expression which may be understood in two different senses, either as denoting furs or prepared leather. Whichever mode of interpretation be adopted, the skins certainly came from the land of the Seres. In the first case, supposing furriery to be intended, the expression would prove, that one branch of the fur trade, of which we have already spoken in our inquiry into the Scythians, must have been transmitted through Serica into India; and the supposition is confirmed by a passage in the introduction to the Mahabharat.[84] In the second case, assuming these "skins" to have been dressed or prepared, it is not at all improbable that the preparation of Morocco, and the finer kinds of leather, was formerly as well known in Asia as at the present day, being still indispensable for the manufacture of slippers, usually worn by the great people of both sexes. But what may be considered as certain is, that this species of commerce existed long before the time of the Periplus, and was indeed of very remote antiquity. In the Ramayana we find skins of animals[85] mentioned among the nuptial presents made to a king's daughter, that is, to Sita, together with shawls, garments of silk, and precious stones. So that, whether we understand the term to imply fine leather or furs, the skins in question were obviously, in either case, of considerable value, and an article of foreign merchandise.

The Periplus describes a third branch of commerce, as remarkable as the mode of procuring it was attended with difficulty. We shall quote the passage entire: "It is not easy," says the writer,[86] "to arrive at Thina, and but few individuals have made the journey and returned back again. This country is situate under the Little Bear, and is said to touch upon the Black and Caspian Seas, at the point where the lake Mæotis empties itself into the latter. Every year

[83] δέρματα Σηρικά. *Periplus*, p. 22.

[84] These skins are translated by *pelles villosæ* in FRANK'S *Chrestomath. Sanscrit.* vol. i. p. 147.

[85] "Deer-skins." *Ramayana*, i. 605.

[86] *Periplus*, p. 36, 37.

there come to the borders of Thina a set of ill-formed, broad-faced, and flat-nosed people, who are called Sesatæ,[87] and resemble savages; they bring with them their wives and children, and carry great burdens in mats, which look like vine-branches. They stop short at a certain place between their own territory and that of Thina, where, seated on their mats, they celebrate a kind of festival, which lasts for some days; and afterwards they return home into their own country. The natives of Thina then arrive upon the ground, collect the mats left by the strangers, take out the haulm which forms the *betre* so called,[88] and, joining the leaves together, make the whole up into balls, through which they pass the fibres of the haulm. Of this there are three several kinds, the large, middle, and small, prepared in the above manner, and conveyed by the persons whose occupation it is to prepare it, into India. The country situate beyond Thina is unexplored, either in consequence of cold and severe frosts, which render travelling thither very difficult, or because the immortals have so willed it." From this description we come to the following natural conclusions, viz.

First. The peculiar kind of merchandise here alluded to, though not expressly mentioned by name, can evidently be no other than the betel, that is to say, the areca-nut, enveloped in the leaves of betel, which, as is well known, the Orientals are in the general habit of chewing. The method of preparation described above, though not altogether correct, is yet, however, sufficiently so in its essential points. The betel is a species of pepper, the fruit grows on a vine, and the leaves are employed to wrap up the areca-nut.

Secondly. The people called Sesatæ belong to the Mongol family; and it is scarcely possible to describe them in more striking colours than in the passage before us. They are nomads, and travel for purposes of commerce to the borders of Serica; the festival they celebrate, as is usually the case, is at the same time also a fair. The goods they

[87] Besatæ by Ptolemy.

[88] *Πέτρος*. We cannot mistake the Hindu name surviving in the Greek appellation: the term elsewhere used in the Periplus to denote betel is *μαλάβαθρον*, (VINCENT, vol. ii. p. 735,) which is also applied to the prepared balls. The names of the three kinds are Malabathrum hadrosphærum, mesosphærum, and microsphærum. It is evident, therefore, that the passage alludes to the preparation of betel.

bring with them are disposed of to the Seres, by whom they are subsequently transmitted to the Indian markets.

And thirdly. This fair must have been held in some northern country; because Thina itself was situated so far north as to touch upon that region, which is represented to be inaccessible on account of the extreme rigour of the climate.

In this last point, however, lies all the difficulty; as the betel grows only in warm countries, in the two Indian peninsulas, in Malabar and Arracan,[89] and consequently could not have been brought into India from any distance north of the latter. The solution adopted by Vincent, who supposes it to have been imported from Arracan by the Tatars of Thibet, does not seem to bring us any nearer the truth.[90] The author of the Periplus evidently places the mart in question far north; and makes the Sesatæ inhabitants of Middle Asia, under the same parallel as the Black and Caspian Seas, and, in fact, as the lake Mæotis, which is the most northerly part of the former.

At the same time, however, it is impossible to deny that the author of the above work must have had very confused notions of these northern countries, which he had never visited himself, but drew all his information from hearsay. Can we, therefore, do him any wrong, or offend against the laws of true criticism, if we venture to assume that he has, in the passage before us, confounded two very different narrations, one relating to the northern traffic and its commercial mart, and the other to the traffic in betel, which he has incorrectly stated to belong to the former? We shall not take upon ourselves to decide this point; but that the

[89] And so, indeed, the author of the *Periplus* himself had before correctly stated in p. 32, when speaking of Nelkynda, that the Malabathrum was brought thither from the interior, that is, from Malabar.

[90] VINCENT, vol. ii. p. 527. By the Tatars, Vincent understands those of Lassa, or Thibet. But the inhabitants of the latter country have no sort of resemblance to the Mongol physiognomy. WILFORD, in the *Asiatic Res.* vol. ix. p. 60, gives another explanation, according to which, the Sesatæ, or Besatæ, were a nomad tribe on the frontiers of Bengal, supporting themselves by the occupation of basket-making. This opinion, however, will not serve to explain the difficulty in question, as the Sesatæ of Arrian are located in countries much further north than Bengal. It is much more likely that the author has here confounded two different narrations. Nor does it seem difficult to account for the fact, in supposing him to have mistaken Thina for Tzina, which latter appellation was used even by Cosmas to designate China.

Sesatæ of the Periplus were a nomad Mongol tribe, appears to be as little questionable as the fact of their residing, not in Southern Thibet, but in Middle Asia, which is obvious from the description itself. Supposing them to have been, as is probable enough from their origin and place of residence, a branch of the Issedones of Herodotus, whom we have already seen to be a nomad mercantile people,[91] this circumstance would serve to explain the commercial intercourse carried on through Central Asia, and establish the existence of a regular chain of mercantile nations, extending from China to India, as well as to the Black Sea. At all events, we are fully justified in applying these accounts of the Periplus, not merely to the time in which that work was composed, but also to the elucidation of an earlier period. The use of betel is very ancient in India; and, besides, the northern commerce just noticed stood in no kind of connexion with that of Alexandria, and consequently, therefore, could not originate from that source.

The second direction which the commerce of India took was towards the east, that is, to the Ultra-Gangetic peninsula, comprising the countries of Ava, Pegu, and Malacca. These are not, it is true, expressly so mentioned in ancient Hindu records; but the pundits are unanimous in understanding Anga, the powerful sovereign of which country is noticed in the Ramayana,[92] to mean Ava;[93] and Yamala is interpreted by Malacca.[94] The traffic with these countries would of course be carried on by sea only, though the transmission of goods across the Bay of Bengal could not be attended with much difficulty. That this navigation existed in the time of the Periplus, is evident from that work itself, as it actually mentions a place situate on the Coromandel coast, from which the passage was usually made to Chrysa.[95] This appellation is manifestly used by Ptolemy to denote Malacca;[96] but in the Periplus it seems to be applied indifferently to the whole region on that side the Ganges. How far the commercial intercourse with this country extended beyond the time of the Periplus, cannot be deter-

[91] See the chapter on the Scythians.

[92] *Ramayana*, i. 159.

[93] Ibid. i. 119, et ib. not.

[94] WILFORD, in the *Asiatic Res.* vol. viii. p. 302.

[95] *Periplus*, p. 34.

[96] See MANNERT, vol. v. p. 242, sq.

mined with certainty; as no particular kind of merchandise is there mentioned which would enable us to ascertain the question, if we except gold, from the abundance of which, the Greeks gave the peninsula its name of Chryse, whence we may very reasonably infer that metal to have been an article of foreign export. Nevertheless, the antiquity of this connexion may be inferred from other sources; because, in the first place, the Hindus themselves were in the habit of constructing vessels, in which they navigated the coast of Coromandel, and also made voyages to the Ganges, and the peninsula beyond it. These vessels bore different names according to their size.[97] Nothing, indeed, could furnish better proof that this commerce did not originate from an intercourse with the Greeks, but was the sole product of ancient native industry; a fact which receives additional confirmation from the existence of commercial towns and ports on the Coromandel coast, from time immemorial. Masulipatam, with its cloth manufactures, as well as the mercantile town situate above the mouth of the Ganges, have already been noticed as existing in the time of the Periplus; and if we allow these places to have been, even then, very ancient, of which there is scarcely any doubt, have we not also equal reason for believing their commerce and navigation to be so too? The coast of Coromandel, especially the southern part, is represented by Ptolemy to have been thickly studded with a series of commercial towns; a circumstance which may not improbably serve to throw some light on the ruins of the wonderful city, Mavalipuram, already described.[98] Even as early as that writer's time it was called "a place of commerce," (Emporium,)

[97] *Periplus*, loc. cit. The smallest kind, formed of a single piece of timber, (μονόξυλα,) and used for navigating along the coast, were called *sangara*; the larger sort, in which voyages were made to Malacca, bore the name of *colandiophonta*. This last appears to be a compound term. Are they both of Malay origin? If so, it would prove the navigation in question to have been carried on by the Malays, a fact of which there appears to be little doubt. They are not to be found in Marsden's Dictionary of the Malay, though we might reasonably expect the insertion of naval terms; but there are several words very much like them, which tend to support the above conjecture.

[Colandiophonta has been derived from the Hindustani, *coilan-di-pota*, coilan boats or ships; *pota*, in Sanscrit, signifies a boat or ship, and *di*, or *da*, in the western parts of India, is either an adjective form, or the mark of the genitive case. *Asiatic Res.* vol. v. p. 283. Transl.]

[98] See above, p. 79.

that is, if we assume his Maliarpha to be the same as Mavalipuram, a supposition which its geographical site and the magnificence and extent of its buildings abundantly tend to confirm. In what sense Mavalipuram might become a town of very great commercial importance, is clearly shown by its peculiar situation; and admitting it to have been at a remote epoch the central point of intermediate commerce between the two Indian peninsulas, similar to what Malacca became in subsequent ages, we have then a sufficient reason to account for its splendour.

The same observation will also apply to the neighbouring isle of Ceylon. It was through the followers of Alexander that the fame of Taprobana, as the first of Indian islands, and its pearl-fisheries, became known in Europe, and increased with the progress of time. In the accounts of Ptolemy, we find its shores well furnished with commercial ports;[99] and if we cannot venture to refer the precise information which this author gives, not only of the coast, but also of the interior of Ceylon, to a Phœnician source, yet the stupendous monuments, still found there, are amply sufficient to show, that at some distant time, as we know also to have been the case, according to Cosmas, even in the sixth century,[100] this island was the centre of Hindu com-

[99] Ptol. vii. cap. 12.

[100] Cosmas *Indicopleustes* apud Montfaucon, *Bibl. Patr.* vol. ii. p. 336. The whole passage is too important, in reference to Ceylon, and the ancient commerce of India, to be omitted here. "Taprobana, called by the Hindus Selandiv, (Sinhala-Dwipa,) is a large island in the Indian Ocean, where the hyacinth-stone (ruby) is found; it is opposite to the pepper country (Malabar); and in the vicinity are numerous other small islands (the Maldives). It is governed by two kings, one of whom rules in the country of the hyacinth-stones, (the mountain tracts of the interior,) and the other on the coast, with its harbours and commercial towns. From all India, Persia, and Ethiopia, between which countries it is situate in the middle, an infinite number of vessels arrive at, as well as go from, Ceylon. From the interior of the continent, as, for instance, from China, (τζινιτζα,) and other commercial countries, it receives silk, aloes, cloves, and other productions, which it exports to Malabar, (Μαλα,) where the pepper grows, and to Calliene, from whence is brought steel and cloth; for this latter is also a great commercial port. It likewise makes consignments to Sinde on the borders of India, whence comes musk and castoreum; and also to Persia, Yemen, and Adule. From all these countries it receives articles of produce, which again it transmits into the interior, together with its own productions. Selandiv is consequently a great emporium; and being situate in the middle of India, it receives merchandise from, as well as sends it to, all parts of the world." It is therefore evident, from this passage, that Ceylon was, in the year 500 of our era, the principal mart of the carrying trade of India; and that it was so three hun-

merce; for which purpose, indeed, its natural situation and commodious havens afforded singular opportunities.

The western coast of the peninsula on this side the Ganges, contained in the time of the Periplus a chain of ports, of which Barygaza in the north, and Muziris, together with Nelkynda, in the south, were the most considerable. The first is Beroach, not many years since reduced by the British arms, and which in modern times has lost much of its ancient splendour, owing to the neighbourhood of Surat; Muziris in Limyrica, will be found in the present Mangalore; and Nelkynda survives in Neliceram.[1] Pattala, which was a place of considerable importance even in Alexander's time, would appear to be more ancient than the former; according to the illustrations furnished by Pottinger, this town is not to be identified with Tatta, as was once supposed, but with the modern Hydrabad,[2] situate on the Delta of the Indus, in lat. 25. If, as it is said, the word Pattala, in Sanscrit, means "a commercial town," this circumstance would prove the extreme antiquity of the navigation carried on by the Indus; and Agatharchides,[3] who wrote upwards of three hundred years before the time of the Periplus, had previously noticed the active commercial intercourse kept up between Pattala and Yemen. Of the other towns, we shall only mention Calliene, the modern

dred years earlier, in the time of Ptolemy, is also certain, from that author's own account. And so it was also in the time of the emperor Claudius, according to PLINY, *Hist. Nat.* vi. 24. From this writer, who quotes the testimony of ancient historians, (*prisci memorant,*) namely, those of Alexander's age, "who first discovered Taprobana to be an island," we learn that Ceylon enjoyed this commercial reputation in the time of the Ptolemies, and even in that of Alexander. If we extend this period but a century and a half further back, which no one, surely, will consider unreasonable, we come at once to the interesting historical fact, that during a space of a thousand years, that is, from 500 before Christ to 500 after, the island of Ceylon, so conveniently situated for such a purpose, continued to be the great emporium of the Hindu carrying trade, from Adule on the coast of Africa, Yemen, Malabar, and the Ultra-Gangetic peninsula, even to China. On the other hand, in the mythology and in the oldest epic poems of India, Ceylon does not at all appear in this matter-of-fact shape, but only as the land of fable; a circumstance, however, which tends to establish its claim to remote antiquity. With regard to the ancient monuments still existing in Ceylon, particularly the ruins of Mandotta, and the gigantic reservoirs to be found there and at Trincomalee, see especially BERTOLACCI's *View of the agricultural, commercial, and financial Interest of Ceylon*, London, 1817. See Appendix XII.

[1] See the map in VINCENT's edition of the *Periplus*. These places are somewhat differently laid down in MANNERT.

[2] See on the Persians, vol. i.

[3] *Geogr. Min.* i. p. 66.

Gallian, situate over against Bombay and the islands of Salsette and Elephanta, as a proof that in the vicinity of these famous sanctuaries, commerce had once fixed her abode. Calliene is expressly mentioned as having been formerly a place of considerable importance, but that its decay was owing to a certain king, named Sandanes.[4]

From these and other similar towns, the commerce of India was directed towards the west. We have already observed that it would be precipitate to apply what the Periplus reports of their flourishing condition to an earlier period; because the commercial prosperity alluded to in that work, originated altogether in the direct intercourse of India with Egypt; which only commenced under the Romans, and was not even in existence during the Ptolemies. Independently of this, however, a very ancient connexion subsisted between India and Arabia, and mediately with Egypt also, by means of the commercial towns established on the Nile as well as on the Euphrates and Tigris. This point has been already in great measure ascertained, in the course of our inquiries into the Phœnicians and Babylonians; and will receive additional confirmation when we come to treat of the Egyptians and Ethiopians. Without, therefore, repeating what has been formerly said on another occasion, or anticipating the regular series of our remarks, we shall content ourselves with observing in this place, that if Arabia drew largely upon the productions of India, yet in its turn this latter country was no less indebted to those of the former. Frankincense forms an article of commerce peculiar to Arabia, though in part originally imported thither from Africa. Now we have already shown how general was the use of this perfume in India, and yet, according to the express testimony of the Periplus,[5] it all came from Arabia; from which country, indeed, India, in common with the rest of the world, must have derived her supplies of that article from the earliest times.

Besides this commercial intercourse between India and

[4] *Periplus*, p. 30.

[5] *Periplus*, p. 18. The principal mart of the frankincense trade on the coast of Arabia, was Mocha; to which place vessels came from Barygaza and Limyrica, and received in exchange for cotton goods, etc., the incense from the king's officers. From this it would appear that the trade in question, at Mocha, was a royal monopoly.

Arabia, the Periplus informs us of another scarcely less remarkable trade, carried on with the opposite coast of Africa; comprised by us under the general denomination of Zanguebar, that is, the Black, or Caffre coast. After having enumerated the commercial stations as far as the promontory of Rhapta, now called Delgado,[6] which was the most southerly point of his geographical knowledge, and after describing their mercantile relations with Egypt, the author continues,[7] "Moreover, indigenous productions, such as corn, rice, butter,[8] oil of sesamum, coarse and fine cotton goods, and cane honey, (which we call sugar,) are regularly exported from the interior of Ariaka, (Concan,) and from Barygaza to the opposite coast. Some particular vessels are purposely destined for this trade, others engage in it only as occasion or opportunity offer." It is obvious that the navigation just noticed, could have had no sort of connexion with the Græco-Indian commerce; but was perfectly independent, and for that reason, of much earlier origin than the other. From what follows, it is also evident that both the persons and vessels engaged in this trade were Arabian; for the whole coast, though parcelled out among several petty chiefs, was nevertheless dependent on Arabian princes.[9] But further, observes Arrian, "This navigation was regularly managed;" an expression which, as applied in reference to those seas, can mean nothing else than that it was regulated according to the monsoons. Here, then, we have an indisputable proof of the existence in very ancient times of a maritime commerce, carried on by the Arabians between India and the opposite coast of Africa; we see in what manner, and by whom, the productions of the former country were conveyed into the latter; though it is possible, indeed, that the importation of Indian produce into Africa,

[6] Situate in lat. 10° South. See VINCENT's map, vol. ii. p. 121.

[7] *Periplus*, p. 8.

[8] Ghee, or melted butter; an indispensable requisite in India, for religious as well as common purposes. It appears also to have been known to CTESIAS; for the "oil of milk," noticed by him in his *Indica*, cap. xxii., can be nothing else. We may remark, by the way, that several of the stories related by this writer, and which have usually been considered as incongruous absurdities, may be explained in a similar manner. His Cynocephali, for instance, or people with the head of a dog, appear to mean the Pariahs, or some other impure caste.

[9] *Periplus*, p. 10, 18.

by means of the intermediate traders of Arabia Felix, was much more considerable. "Here," says the Periplus, "was Muza, (the present Mocha,) wholly inhabited by Arab ship-owners and sailors, who traded at the opposite port of Barygaza, with the productions of their native country."[10]

It is surprising, that under this head the Periplus makes no mention of gold. Now, the eastern coast of Africa, towards the south, contained precisely those countries where this metal is found; and when we observe in later times, that the exchange of African gold for the spices and cloth of India was of regular occurrence, and considering moreover that similar commercial transactions took place on the Indian Ocean both before that time and afterwards, we are naturally led to inquire whether the exchange above mentioned did not exist also at a much earlier period. In the time of the Periplus, the establishments, or at least the dominion of the Arabs on the African coast, extended as far down as Rhapta;[11] and when Pliny wrote, the same adventurers had already naturalized themselves in Ceylon; and had even introduced their religious worship into that island.[12] Admitting then the fact of the Arabs having navigated the Indian seas, can we possibly imagine them to have neglected an article of commerce, which, more than any thing else, was calculated to excite their love of gain? It is true, indeed, that we have no positive testimony in support of the direct commercial intercourse between India and the eastern shores of Africa; but then if we conceive the navigation to Ophir as extending not merely to Yemen, but also with great probability to Africa, we have immediate proof that the gold countries of the latter were well known even in the time of Solomon, and that the natives of Yemen enriched themselves by the discovery. In this manner, therefore, it might, if not by direct means, yet at least indirectly, find its way into India; a circumstance which will also serve to explain the great abundance of this precious metal in the latter country.

Whatever opinion we may choose to entertain on this point, for I merely adduce the above as a probable conjecture, yet the early navigation of the Indian seas, and the

[10] *Periplus*, p. 12. [11] Ibid. p. 10. [12] PLINY, vi. 24.

commercial intercourse of the surrounding nations, are facts not the less generally certain. They are indeed completely established by the consumption of Indian produce in the Western world; that is, in Egypt and Western Asia. Nor is it less true, that from time immemorial the Arabs, as a seafaring people, had monopolized the whole carrying trade of the Indian Ocean; and continued in undisturbed possession till the discoveries of the Portuguese.

The preceding observations, referring as they do to Africa, naturally bring us to a point which I have reserved for the termination of this part of our inquiry; as it prepares us, in some measure, for the transition from Asia to Africa; I mean the affinity existing between the Hindus and the Egyptians. By the term affinity, I would merely understand the resemblance discoverable between the two nations; as it is by no means my design to attempt deducing the origin of either from the other. When I shall have placed in juxtaposition, not only the various points of resemblance, but also the peculiar shades of difference which distinguish both people, I shall then leave it to the reader to determine whether such comparison leads to the conclusion that one is derived from the other. With regard, however, to my application of the term people, it is necessary to observe beforehand, that I merely allude to the higher classes, or castes, of each nation; as, on account of the greater degree of interest attached to their superior civilization, they may not unreasonably be said to comprehend the whole people respectively.

Upon comparing, then, the Egyptians and Hindus together, many and very remarkable points of resemblance will certainly strike the observer. First of all, we notice a physical similarity in colour, and in the conformation of the head; the brighter complexion of the higher Indian castes has been already mentioned, and the ancient paintings still found in Egypt attest the same peculiarity with regard to the upper classes of the latter country; a fact which will be incontestably demonstrated in the volume on the Egyptians. As to the form of the head, I have now before me the skulls of a mummy and a native of Bengal, from the collection of M. Blumenbach; and it is impossible to conceive any thing more striking than the resemblance between the two, both as respects the general form, and the structure of the firm portions. Indeed, the learned possessor himself considers them to be the most alike of any in his numerous collection.

But the resemblances we discover between these two people, upon comparing their civil and religious polity, their arts, customs, and manner of life, are no less striking, while they are much more varied than the other.

The constitution of the ancient Hindu and Egyptian states evidently bears the same character. Both were sacerdotal; legislation, and every other species of science, was in the exclusive possession of a caste or tribe of priests, who also confined the power of the sovereign; elected, in both cases, not from their own body, but from the warrior castes. The same form is observable in the courts of these limited monarchs; their authority and occupations, as well as familiar connexions, are perfectly similar.

The rise and progress of these states in political civilization appear to have followed the same course. Originally, Egypt also contained several petty communities; which, however, owing to their limited extent, might be consolidated into one great kingdom, more easily and more permanently than was possible in India, where nature, by the interposition of lofty mountains, pathless deserts, and broad and rapid streams, has thrown almost insuperable obstacles in the way of such a union.

In both countries, the constitution was based on a division of caste; which, as far as the higher orders were concerned, was perfectly similar; and the only difference with regard to the lower classes, necessarily arose from circumstances of a purely local character. In Egypt, as well as India, the impure castes are distinguished from the pure. The sacerdotal orders of both countries exhibit various points of resemblance. Their possessions and their rights are the same; their manner of life is connected with a similar ritual; and the costume of the one differs not from the cotton garments of the other. Both are married, and yet in neither country is there any female priesthood. Each order possesses its holy books, the perusal of which is confined to its respective members alone. The influence of both is established by the same means; that is, by their being the sole depositaries of knowledge; for they are not only priests, but also astrologers, physicians, judges, etc.

The warrior castes of both countries present an equally striking resemblance to each other; the Egyptian, however, was the more powerful of the two; though even this in the end was obliged to emigrate. Their costume, and manner of equipment, appear to have been alike.[13] They had their war-chariots, but no cavalry, precisely as the Hindus, only the Egyptians did not employ elephants in battle.

In all states of this kind, the inferior classes naturally form themselves according to local circumstances. In Egypt as well as India the right of propriety in the soil originally obtained; and we learn from the Bible that the patriarch Joseph, during his abode in the former country, took occasion of a famine to transfer the landed property from the original owners to the king.

Whether the gods of Egypt were derived from those of India, is a question which I must leave for the professed inquirers into mythological history to determine. In such an undertaking, however, it is scarcely possible to advance much beyond simple conjecture, more or less probable; that in certain divinities, common to both people, we may recognise the same general idea prevailing is certainly very true; but it does not at all follow therefore, that either were borrowed from the other. The worship of the Lingam was as natural to Egypt as it was to India; but might not the natives of each country have invented and introduced it independently of the other?

The most surprising resemblances, however, are those we meet with in their external worship. This among both people is attached to particular sanctuaries and particular localities. Bloody and unbloody sacrifices are prescribed by the religion of both, as indeed they have been also among other nations. The same authority required the observance of pilgrimage; whence the numerous assemblies

[13] Compare the representation of two Kshatriyahs, from an Indian drawing in DALBERG's treatise *Ueber die Musik der Inder*, tab. ii., with the numerous designs of Egyptian warriors in the *Description d'Egypte*. It is remarkable that the head-dress of these two Kshatriyahs, is the same as that of the Indian warriors represented in vol. ii. plate 10, of the *Description d'Egypte*. See vol. ii. p. 820.

of people that crowded together upon festal occasions; with these were connected penances, and even personal sacrifices. Not only bathing in the holy river, but drowning also is supposed to confer peculiar sanctity.[14] The religious processions are likewise similar in certain points of view. Images of the gods too are not only carried about the person, but also conveyed from one temple to another on enormous stages, erected upon four-wheeled cars.[15] The worship of animals is found in both countries, but not so generally nor so fully developed in India as in Egypt. As much reverence indeed is paid to the Bull Nandi of the former, as to the Apis of the latter; and the cow is an equally sacred animal, which it would have been as great a profanation to sacrifice on the banks of the Nile,[16] as it still is on those of the Ganges. But we hear nothing of the worship of any other species of animal in India;[17] and indeed, it is sufficiently evident from what has gone before, that the Hindu idea of the brute creation was totally different from the Egyptian.

With respect to the state of the soul after death, the notions of both people were pretty much the same, their priesthood inculcated the doctrine of a metempsychosis; the popular creed contained the same representation of Hades. And even the judgment of the dead, so celebrated in Egypt, is reproduced in India with every feature of exact and astonishing resemblance.[18]

The progress of art among these two people generally followed the same path. The study of architecture was the predominant taste, to which sculpture and painting, in Egypt as well as India, served only as accompaniments.

[14] HEROD. ii. 90. [15] Ibid. ii. 63; see also above, p. 96.

[16] HEROD. ii. 18.

[17] [The Hindus have also a religious veneration for monkeys, probably out of respect to Hanuman, so celebrated in the Ramayana: the late Bishop Heber in his Journal alludes to a case of two young officers, who shot at one near Bindrabund, being driven into the Jumna, by a mob of Brahmans and devotees, where they perished. And MENU, ii. 132, 136, enumerates a list of animals, the slaughter of which by an individual of the Sudra caste would entail the punishment of death. TRANSL.]

[18] POLIER, ii. p. 426. Jamray (Yama) the Hindu judge of the dead, like the Egyptian, has also two assessors, one of whom enumerates the good, and the other the bad actions of mankind. The resemblance in fact is so strong that the designs lately published of the Egyptian doomsday might be almost explained by referring to the Hindu representations alone.

The architecture of the Egyptians, however, is not precisely the same as that of the Hindus, though it is impossible to mistake a similarity of general character prevailing in both. That of India evidently took its rise in grotto constructions, and the same feature prevails in that of Egypt. The internal arrangement of the great temples, their component parts, the flat-roofed halls supported by a forest of pillars, the pyramidal form of the large entrances or porticos, found in both countries, involuntarily remind the observer of one another.[19] The same taste and the same mode of procedure obtains likewise in the ornaments of both. Colossal statues of gods and animals, reliefs on the walls covered with stucco and painted in various colours,[20] the grand entrances of the sanctuaries adorned on festal occasions with flags[21]—all this is still seen in India as formerly in Egypt. We nevertheless meet with certain variations; the general character only of the art was the same in both countries, as its ulterior development in the one as well as in the other necessarily varied according to local circumstances. The ornaments of the capital of a pillar, for example, are in both cases copied from native plants. Add to this another more important distinction: in India, where they burn their dead, the grottoes are inhabited by the living; in Egypt, on the contrary, where they did every thing to preserve them, they were the receptacles of the dead. What influence this distinctive peculiarity would naturally exercise upon the architecture of the Egyptians, will be shown hereafter, when we come to treat more particularly of that people. In sculpture and painting the two nations appear to have reached very nearly the same degree of perfection; and both undertook the execution of complicated subjects in relief: in this department, however, the Egyptians perhaps succeeded better than the Hindus. In painting, neither people understood the art of blending colours, or paid any attention to the rules of perspective.

Both nations had their literature; but that of the Egyptians was by no means so rich, in poetry at least, as that of

[19] See above, p. 93, sq., and compare the general accounts of Egypt.
[20] *Asiatic Res.* vol. vi. p. 389.
[21] *Ramayana*, iii. 209, 212, in connexion with the vignette title of vol. ii. book ii.

the Hindus. The epic poem, so intimately connected with the civilization of India, appears to have been completely unknown in Egypt. How, indeed, could the poesy of that gorgeous world have flourished in the narrow valley of the Nile, hemmed in on both sides by a wilderness of sand? The clime of Egypt seems to have been equally unfavourable to the other higher species of song. And even though we allow her to have possessed what we may term her sacred books, in the writings commonly attributed to Hermes, yet these latter do not appear, in an equal degree with the Vedas, to have been the sources of the sacerdotal religion. The knowledge of history, apart however from accurate chronological determinations, was confined in both countries to the family registers of the kings, and the popular traditions of their individual exploits; but the Egyptian, nevertheless, depended more upon public monuments than that of the Hindus.

But the most remarkable dissimilarity between the two nations is exhibited in their different modes of writing. The Egyptians had their hieroglyphics, of which there appears to be no sort of trace among the Hindus. As far as we know, the latter were only acquainted with literal writing, which in fact was not unknown to the former people; but then, owing to the circumscribed extent of their literature, it evidently would not be so comprehensive as that of the Hindus. But how unfavourably must the hieroglyphic writing of the Egyptians have operated, not only upon their general literature, but also upon the free development of its particular branches, scientific (astronomy, for instance) as well as religious and ceremonial! Had indeed that intimate connexion subsisted between the religious opinions of the Egyptians and those of the Hindus, which some modern writers are inclined to suppose, could the Vedas have been unknown in Egypt, or the hieroglyphics in India?

In their customs and manner of life, the two nations as closely resembled each other as the different nature of their respective countries would allow. Agriculture was the principal occupation of both; and exercised principally on the same objects, wheat and rice. To this, both people added another branch of industry, which their other indigenous productions, and above all cotton, seemed naturally to call for. The art of weaving, which in both countries was more the business of men than of women, goes back to as remote a period of antiquity in Egypt as in India. The simple Egyptian loom coincides with the Hindu; as does also the ancient plough, if we may judge from a representation of it copied from the monuments of Thebais. The domestic society of either nation was organized on the same principle. Polygamy was allowed, without however being generally practised; and therefore also the many legislative enactments bearing upon this subject, would of course be nearly similar among both people.[22]

The foregoing comparative sketch of these nations will furnish the reader with abundant matter for reflection; and must itself necessarily precede our discussions upon Africa. It is by no means my present intention to confine the circle of our view, and terminate this inquiry by asserting the derivation of the Egyptians from the Hindus. That is not at all my own opinion. But as we have already proved the antiquity of a commercial intercourse between the natives of the southern world, there is nothing improbable in such an opinion; on the contrary, it is perfectly agreeable to Hindu manners that colonies from India, i. e. Banian families, should have passed over into Africa, and carried with them their native industry, and perhaps also their religious worship.[23] The objection drawn from the fact that the Hindus were not a seafaring people, proves nothing to the contrary; for the Egyptians were even less so, and yet it is notorious that they planted colonies in Crete and Greece. And as the latter probably employed Phœnician vessels for that purpose, so might the Hindus have had recourse in a similar way to the Arabians. Whatever weight may be

[22] [Whoever wishes to see this question examined more in detail, should consult the excellent work of P. BOHLEN; especially dedicated to a comparison of ancient India with Egypt. TRANSL.]

[23] [The colonization of the eastern coast of Java, a fact so well established by Sir Stamford Raffles, is sufficient to prove that they were Brahmans, and not Banian merchants, who effected these settlements. And had any portion of the ancient literature of Egypt been preserved to our time, it is more than probable the author's supposition would be found correct. FR. TRANSL.] [See SCHLEGEL's *Ind. Bibl.* tom. i. p. 400—425. A writer in the *Asiatic Journal* (vol. iv. p. 325) gives a curious list of the names of places in the interior of Africa, mentioned in Park's Second Journey; which are shown to be all Sanscrit, and most of them actually current in India at the present day. TRANSL.]

attached to Indian tradition, and the express testimony of Eusebius,[24] confirming the report of migrations from the banks of the Indus into Egypt, there is certainly nothing improbable in the event itself; as a desire of gain would have formed a sufficient inducement. Moreover, how could such a thickly peopled, and, in some parts, over-peopled country as India, have disposed of her superabundant population, except by planting colonies; even though intestine broils (witness the expulsion of the Buddhists) had not obliged her to have recourse to such an expedient?[25]

Supposing, however, the Hindu origin of the Egyptians to admit of historical proof, which it does not at present, and most probably never will, yet the fact would allege nothing against the civilization of Egypt being exclusively of native growth. In such case, the germ only would have been introduced, and in an Egyptian soil, and under an Egyptian sky, must have developed itself somewhat differently from what it did in India. And let not the reader forget that the question before us concerns an interval, not of one, but of many hundred years. Such a germ as we speak of was transplanted from Egypt into Greece; but how very different were its fruits in the latter country from those which had ripened on the banks of the Nile!

Here, then, with a mind still free and unprejudiced, we take our leave of Asia, in order to examine the political and commercial phenomena which Africa presents to our notice. And should we succeed in rendering the subject as familiar to the apprehension of our readers, as we have endeavoured to make it with regard to Asia, the dark cloud which now hangs over that interesting portion of the globe will be dispersed, and a new and instructive prospect unfold itself to our view.

[24] See MARSHAM, *Chronicon*, p. 335. [The most decisive evidence of the fact, may be found in Philostratus and Nonnus. FR. TRANSL.]

[25] It is hardly possible to maintain the opposite side of the question, viz. that the Hindus were derived from the Egyptians; for it has been already ascertained that the country bordering on the Ganges was the cradle of Hindu civilization. Now, the Egyptians could not have established themselves in that neighbourhood; their probable settlement would rather have taken place on the coast of Malabar.

APPENDIX.

APPENDIX I.

FARGARD I.

I. *The two first Fargards of the Vendidat, from the Zendavesta.*[1]

ORMUZD, speaking to Sapetman Zoroaster, said as follows: "I have created, O Sapetman Zoroaster, a place of delights and abundance, such as no other being besides myself could have formed. It is called Eeriene Veedjô, and is more beautiful than the whole wide world. Nothing, indeed, can be compared to it for pleasantness.

"I have acted first, but Peetiarê,[2] whose soul is immortal, has exercised his own power after me.

"The first abode of happiness and abundance which I created without any mixture of impurity, was Eeriene Veedjô. Upon this came Ahriman, pregnant with death, and prepared in the river which waters Eeriene Veedjô, the great serpent of winter, the offspring of Div.

"Here there were then ten months of winter and two of summer; whereas formerly the warm weather lasted seven months, and the cold only five. The winter spreads cold all over the water, land, and trees; and is very severe in the middle of Eeriene Veedjô. This scourge, however, is highly beneficial to mankind; for scarcely has winter begun to appear, than all good things shoot forth in abundance.

"The second place of happiness which I, Ormuzd, created

[1] *Zendavesta*, by KLEUKER, tom. ii. p. 299.
[2] The source of evil, Ahriman.

for an habitation was Soghdi,[3] abounding in men and herds. But the pernicious Peetiarê Ahriman produced swarms of flies, which destroyed the herds.

"The third place of abundance which I fashioned for an abode, was the great and holy Môore;[4] then came Ahriman and introduced evil speeches.

"The fourth place of delights created by me was the pure Bakhdi,[5] decorated with lofty standards; thereupon came Peetiarê Ahriman, bringing death, and produced an army of ants.

"The fifth place of abundance which I, Ormuzd, created was Nesa,[6] between Môore and Bakhdi; then came the deadly Ahriman, and brought forth there reprehensible doubt.

"The sixth place of plenty created by me was Haroin,[7] celebrated for the number of its inhabitants. Upon this, Ahriman the destructive produced there the highest degree of misery.

"The seventh country and town of abundance which I created, was Veékéreânte[8] with numerous villages. Here the deadly Ahriman instituted the worship of Peris, (Fairies,) which inflamed the anger of Gueshap.

"The eighth country and place of felicity created by me, was Ornan,[9] fertile in pastures. Thereupon came Ahriman breathing death, and poisoned men's hearts.

"Khneântê,[10] the abode of wolves, was the ninth place of abundance created by me; but the destructive Ahriman there perpetrated an act which rendered the passage of the bridge Tschinevad impossible, which is a sin against nature.

"The tenth place of felicity which I, Ormuzd, created, was

[3] Without doubt, the modern Al Sogd, or Sogdiana. Whether this country is still infested with gadflies must be determined by future travellers.

[4] Môore, in Chorasan, the Margiana of the Greeks.

[5] Certainly Balkh or Bactria. How formidable an invasion of ants may be, is well known from their ravages in Guinea and the West Indies.

[6] Nesa, a city in Chorasan, the position assigned to it in the text will not allow us to confound it with Nysa on the Indian frontier.

[7] Probably Herat or Asia, properly so called.

[8] In Pehlvi Kawûl, which bears a striking resemblance to Kabul.

[9] Perhaps Lahore, though we have not sufficient evidence of its identity.

[10] This place is uncertain; some writers suppose it means Kandahar. The bridge of Tschinevad leads from the mountain Albordi to the vault of heaven, the habitation of the blessed.

the pure Heerekheeti.[11] Hereupon the deadly Peetiarê Ahriman instigated men to a crime, which obstructs the passage of the bridge; namely, the burial of dead bodies in the earth.

"The eleventh country and town of abundance created by me, Ormuzd, was Heetomeante,[12] the intelligent and happy; but the pernicious Peetiarê Ahriman introduced there magic, the bad art which produces all manner of illusions and procures all things. Specious as it may seem, it is nevertheless the offspring of the evil principle, the father of all calamity. Far is it from the great one, from him who doeth good!

"The twelfth place of felicity created by me, Ormuzd, was Raghan,[13] the abode of three germs, rich in understanding and free from passion. But the deadly Peetiarê Ahriman sowed there the seeds of fatal doubt and presumptuous insolence.

"The thirteenth country and town of abundance created by me was Tschekhre,[14] the powerful and holy. Here, however, the destructive Peetiarê Ahriman instigated to an action which prevents the passage of the bridge, namely, the practice of burning the dead.

"The fourteenth place of happiness created by me, who am Ormuzd, was Verene,[15] with four corners, forming a square, and the birth-place of Feridoun the vanquisher of Zohak. But the deadly Peetiarê Ahriman introduced there, and into all its dependencies, the monthly purgations of women.

"The fifteenth place of felicity, which I, Ormuzd, created, was Hapte Heando,[16] which rules over the seven Indies. India surpasses all the rest of the world in power and extent. But the destructive Peetiarê Ahriman, the enemy of nature, inflamed (precipitated?) the monthly terms of the women.

[11] In this word we may recognise Arokage (Arachotus) on the borders of India.

[12] Probably Hendmend in Shehestan.

[13] Supposed to be the town of Rey or Rages.

[14] This should be Chark in Chorasan.

[15] Apparently the district of Pars; if any doubt remains as to the identity of name, it is removed by the circumstance of its being mentioned as the country of Feridoun, a great hero among the Persians.

[16] There can hardly be any doubt, that Heando is the Zend form for Hind. The end of this, as well as the preceding verse, seems to allude to the premature puberty of women in hot climates.

"The sixteenth country and town of happiness and abundance which I created, was the mighty Rengheiao;[17] the abode of numerous cavaliers who acknowledged no superior. But the deadly Peetiarê Ahriman brought hither, and into all its dependent villages, the raw cold of winter, the pernicious gift of Div.

"These countries and towns were all pure and embellished with fruitful valleys—there was not the least uncleanness among them.

"Abundance and Bihisht are the reward of him who is upright and pure.[18] He alone is holy and pure who doeth holy and pure actions."

FARGARD II.

Zoroaster asked Ormuzd as follows: "O Ormuzd, surrounded with majesty, thou equitable judge of the universe, who dost exist by thine own power, and who art purity itself; what man has first interrogated thee before myself, O thou who art Ormuzd? To whom hast thou communicated thy law?" Ormuzd replied, "The pure Jemshid, the chief of men and herds, was the first man who inquired of me as thou doest now, O Zoroaster! To him I imparted a knowledge of the law.

"'I am Ormuzd,' was my reply to him; 'be obedient to my law, O pure Jemshid, thou son of Vivengham; meditate upon it and convey it to thy people.' 'But,' answered Jemshid, 'I am not just enough to execute thy law, to meditate upon it, or to convey its blessings to mankind.' Upon this I replied, O Zoroaster, I who am Ormuzd, 'Cannot Jemshid execute my law; can he not meditate upon and communicate it to mankind? still less then will he be able to make happy the world, my property; to bless it with fertility and abundance, to be its nourisher, its chief, and its sovereign.' In answer to this, O Zoroaster, the pure Jemshid replied, 'Yes, I will make the world thy peculiar possession, both happy, fruitful, and blessed; I will provide

[17] The locality of this place is uncertain: according to some, it is to be found in Assyria.

[18] The ordinary formula of benediction.

for its necessities, will nourish and govern it like a father, so that under my sovereign care there shall be no frosty or scorching wind, no corruption, no death; and the dews shall disappear as soon as I repeat the words of thy law.'

"The holy zeal of Jemshid was great before me, and therefore he reigned. Whatever his sublime tongue commanded, was done immediately. I gave to him and his people nourishment, intelligence, and a long life; his hand received from me a poniard, the blade and hilt of which were gold. Upon this, King Jemshid traversed three hundred parts [19] of the earth, inhabited by domestic animals as well as savage, by men, dogs, and birds, and filled with ruddy and brilliant fires. Before him there were neither tame nor savage animals, nor men, nor red-flaming fires; the pure Jemshid, the son of Vivengham, produced all.

"Jemshid arrived in the country of light (the south) and found it beautiful. He clave the ground with the blade of his golden poniard, and said, 'Sapandomad,[20] bless us!' He proceeded still further, and pronounced the holy word, accompanied with prayers for wild and tame animals and for men. Accordingly the expedition of Jemshid through these countries became the source of happiness and prosperity to this third part of the world. The domestic animals and wild beasts as well as men ran together in great crowds.

"In the same manner did Jemshid traverse the two other parts of the world.

"Jemshid now built Ver, the vast extent of which was comprehended in a square enclosure. Hither he brought the germ of wild and tame animals, of men, dogs, birds, and the ruddy bright flame of fire. The water burst forth in torrents, and surrounded the grand palace of Ver. Here were fowls of all kinds; and the ever-fruitful golden fields produced every thing that was good to eat. Here too the youth were shamefaced, modest, respectful, strong, and well nourished.

"Into Ver Jemshid brought the seed of men and women. The land was charming and excellent, and as pure as Bihisht. Hither, too, Jemshid conveyed the germ of all kinds

[19] That is, the third part.

[20] The Ized (genie) of the earth.

of animals, of all trees, and all nourishment. The little hills of this country exhaled agreeable perfumes.

"Among all the inhabitants of Verefchue,[21] there was no man who commanded with severity; no beggar; no impostor who would seduce people to the worship of Diu; no concealed enemy; no cruel tyrant, the oppressor of mankind; no ravenous tooth.

"Jemshid caused nine streets to be built in the large towns, six in those of moderate size, and three in the small ones. Jemshid constructed at Ver a palace on an eminence, which was surrounded with a wall, and its interior was divided into several apartments and well lighted.

"Jemshid endeavoured with all his might to render Ver complete, according to the commandment which I, Ormuzd, gave to him."

Abundance and Bihisht, etc. etc.

[21] That is, Ver, rich in every blessing.

Alphabetum Zendicum Persepolitanum.

É.			M.		
S.	س		O.		
E.			K?	ق	
V.	و		Dj?	ج	
R.	ر		Tsch.	چ	
D.	د		A.		
N.	ن		Sch.	ش	
B/p.	پ ب		Zolaats:	ز ژ	
G.	گ		Ü.		
Ö.			Kh.	خ	
Gh.	غ		Ng.	نک	
incerta.			H.	ه	
E/a.	ا		I.	ي	
Th?			F /ph.	ف	
T.	ت		(compl.) rex.		

[illegible]

APPENDIX II.

On the cuneiform character, and particularly the inscriptions at Persepolis, by G. F. Grotefend.

You request me, Sir, to furnish you with a brief sketch of the result of my inquiries into the cuneiform character, and particularly the inscriptions at Persepolis, for the purpose of subjoining to the new edition of the first part of your Researches into the Politics and Commerce of the Nations of Antiquity. To a request so flattering, I shall endeavour to furnish the best answer I am able, and so much the more willingly, as I have been for some time waiting for a favourable opportunity of publicly testifying my acknowledgments to your kindness and friendship. Although in the present sketch we have only to do with the inscriptions of Persepolis, and specially with the kind I have deciphered, I shall nevertheless take advantage of your permission, to extend my remarks to the other kinds of cuneiform inscriptions, as far as may be compatible with the limits of the present essay; it having been discovered that the general conclusions drawn in my first Treatise, were only applicable to the inscriptions at Persepolis. I shall therefore, first of all, endeavour to determine with exactness the particular as well as general character of all the known species of cuneiform writing, and then submit the results obtained from an examination of all the species, before I proceed to a detailed notice of the Zend inscriptions which I have succeeded in deciphering.

In my first Treatise, the cuneiform inscriptions are divided according to the countries where they are found, into three classes; viz. the Babylonian, the Persian, and the

Ægyptico-Persian. But as both the Persian and the Babylonian species have been discovered in Egypt, it is obvious the above division is inadmissible, in a case where the cuneiform character is to be examined with reference to its distinctive peculiarities. Neither can we admit of a classification of these inscriptions, according to the nail or arrow-headed form of the letters, because the very same characters, which, on the Babylonian bricks, resemble nails, or daggers, are observed to take the form of an arrow or hammer, or even simple lines, when graven on a finer sort of stone. Under these circumstances I shall endeavour to define the several species in some other manner, first pointing out the distinctive character of cuneiform writing in general, and then classifying the different kinds according to the different construction of their letters.

In the first place, I exclude all kinds of writing, more or less alike, which were used in the west and north of Europe, and confine to the term cuneiform those inscriptions only which have been discovered in the different provinces of the ancient Persian empire.[1] These inscriptions are distinguished from all other modes of writing adopted in the East, by the absence of every thing like roundness: some specimens, it is true, present the appearance of circular characters; but upon comparing them with others, it is evident, that this form is rather a fault of the copier than the true shape of the original. In my opinion, the cuneiform letters appear to have been exclusively destined for the purpose of engraving on stone, or other durable materials employed in public monuments; on urns, gems, seals, talismans, or amulets, etc.; and were never intended for the ordinary purposes of writing, as in the latter case they were, like the hieroglyphics of Egypt, probably replaced by another kind of character more adapted to the wants of the people.[2]—The

[1] With respect to the extent of country over which cuneiform writing prevailed, see the *Hall. Allg. Litt. Zeitung.*, for April 1820, No. 106.

[2] A particular kind of very hard baked bricks, found in the ruins of ancient Babylon, of which I gave the first account, in the *Fundgruben des Orients*, vol. vi. No. 2, p. 161, and on which Münter fancied he discovered some astronomical observations, have been compared with other specimens, and found to contain documents. On certain of them the name of Darius, or some other Persian king, is engraved, in the third species of Persepolitan character, which is the same as the Babylonian; most of them are sealed on the sides, with a device, under which is found the name of the witness; or

Exempla comparationis trium cuneiformium quae Persepoli exstant scribendi generum.

1. Inscriptiones ap. Niebuhr. Tom. II. Tab. XXIV. G. F. E.

I. Niebuhr G.	II. Niebuhr F.	III. Niebuhr E.	Versio.
[illegible]	[illegible]	[illegible]	Xerxes
[illegible]	[illegible]	[illegible]	rex
[illegible]	[illegible]	[illegible]	fortis.
[illegible]	[illegible]	[illegible]	rex
[illegible]	[illegible]	[illegible]	regum.
[illegible]	[illegible]	[illegible]	Darii.
[illegible]	[illegible]	[illegible]	regis.
[illegible]	[illegible]	[illegible]	filius.
[illegible]	[illegible]	[illegible]	orbis rector.
2. Inscriptio vasis ap. Caylus. Tom. V. Tab. XXX.			
[illegible]	[illegible]	[illegible]	Xerxes
[illegible]	[illegible]	[illegible]	rex
[illegible]	[illegible]	[illegible]	fortis.
3. Inscriptio Cyri Pasargadis ap. Morier. Tab. XXX. N. 3			
[illegible]	[illegible]	[illegible]	Dominus.
[illegible]	[illegible]	[illegible]	Cyrus.
[illegible]	[illegible]	[illegible]	rex.
[illegible]	[illegible]	[illegible]	orbis rector.

E primo scribendi genere. E secundo scribendi genere. E tertio scribendi genere.

elementary strokes of all cuneiform writing are composed of wedges, so called, and angles, which M. Murr has also denominated swallow-tails. Those writers who consider angular forms simply as the union of two wedges placed obliquely, and who therefore assume the wedge as the only stroke peculiar to this species of writing, are certainly mistaken, because, in consequence of such union the character receives quite a different form. Besides, these small angles, in many of the inscriptions, except those of Persepolis, appear to make up but one perfect triangle, the principal angle of which inclines to the left, so that, particularly when connected by a transverse wedge, they bear the appearance of a single wedge turned towards the left. In addition to the wedge-like and angular forms, we find on bricks, gems, and cylinders, and in both the large inscriptions discovered in Babylon and Persia, certain marks of conjunction, which however cannot be considered as integral portions of the cuneiform character, because in precisely similar cases, where they would be no less essential, they are altogether wanting, and in fact do not occur in any of the Persepolitan inscriptions. On the other hand, when, upon comparing similar passages in different inscriptions, we find these marks of conjunction employed instead of small wedges, this interchange of the two characters must be attributed to a mistake of the copier.[3] The elements of the cuneiform character

instead of a seal, they bear the impress of a cylinder. Two of them are furnished with an illegible inscription, the characters of which partly resemble Chaldee; though they do not appear to differ from the Pehlvi engraved on ancient monuments, still unexplained. This writing, engraven by some more recent possessor of the documents, (one of which is subscribed with the name of Darius, and the second with that of another king, in the cuneiform character of Babylon, the original being partly erased, in reference to which the new inscription is upside down,) has been confounded by M. Kopp, in his *Bilder und schriften der Vorzeit*, (hieroglyphics and writing of antiquity,) vol. ii. p. 154, with a Phœnician inscription also of later date, and faintly inscribed in three lines on a Babylonian brick, in such a way, however, that, to use the expression of M. Bellino, it is very easy to leave the characters out altogether, though not, as M. Kopp supposes, to decipher them. In these characters, which are graven on a brick, simply baked in the sun, I think I can discover the words "Ben dulkalnin," (son of the rays of the sun,) though M. Kopp is of a different opinion.

[3] It is necessary to repeat here an observation which has not been sufficiently attended to. It is, that the most exact copier has not always, or indeed even could copy an inscription with such minute accuracy as to represent all the peculiarities of the original. Nay, more, it is very possible for mistakes to have crept into the original itself, as well as the copy; and an enlightened critic is therefore free to correct the draught of an inscription when

from the ruins of Persepolis are exhibited in the most perfect manner, and in their full size, by M. Murr, in the *Journal zur Kunstgeschichte,* vol. iv. tab. i. fig. E. 1, 2, 3. In order to characterize them with definitive accuracy, I shall make the following observations.

1. The wedge-shaped characters, whether primary or accessory, great or small, in every specimen of inscription, assume chiefly four directions, but always so that their principal inclination is from top to bottom, or, in other words, from left to right. They are either perpendicular or horizontal, or inclining obliquely upwards or downwards: but their points are neither turned directly upwards, nor transversely to the left. Should they appear occasionally to assume the latter direction, it is either owing to the fault of the copyist, or else the particular character is composed of an angle. The initial sign upon all the bricks, which represents an assemblage of all the directions of the cuneiform character crossing each other, is copied in Murr's Journal (vol. iv. tab. i. fig. C.) under the form of a star with eight rays. Pietro della Valle, who discovered the same sign on some bricks in the desert, compares it, in like manner, to an eight-rayed star; but in no one species of cuneiform writing are all these eight directions found to exist at the same time.

2. The angular-shaped character, whether great or small, affects only one direction, so that the opening is constantly turned to the right. When it happens to be otherwise, it is in consequence of the copier having confounded the angular with the wedge form, as for instance, in the inscription of the royal mantle quoted by Le Bruyn; or from his having reversed the character, as is the case with the name of Gushtasp in Niebuhr, fig. C, which M. de Murr has cited as the only instance in Niebuhr's inscriptions where the angular letters are placed one over the other, like a roof. The Babylonian angular character, the opening of which is turned towards the left, is composed for the most part either of lines of conjunction crossing each other, as is observable upon a comparison of certain bricks, or of the union of two

he can do so on valid grounds. In fact, had I depended solely on Niebuhr's copy, my attempts to decipher these inscriptions would have succeeded just as little as those of my predecessors who were more scrupulous.

oblique wedge-shaped letters. Accordingly, we find on some bricks a character which appears to consist of two half moons turned to the left, and placed one over the other, but which, in point of fact, according to its real design, is composed of four oblique wedges, so placed as to form a zigzag.

This very character, which on the cylinders ordinarily stands at the commencement of the second line, has, in various copies, the appearance of a Latin B unrounded, thus |⋦, or without the stroke of conjunction which precedes it, that of a Latin W placed sideways, as ⋦, besides many other distorted and connected forms, which seriously augment the difficulties of deciphering them.

These preliminary notices are enough to show, beyond the possibility of mistake, in what direction we are to read a cuneiform inscription. That is to say, we must place ourselves in such a manner, that the points of the vertical wedge letters may look downwards, and those of the oblique ones, as well as the openings of the angular letters, may be turned to the right. This being observed, we shall find that no cuneiform writing has a perpendicular, but always a horizontal direction, and that the accompanying figures occurring on gems and cylinders, afford no sort of criterion as to the real direction of the writing. The fragment of a stone covered with cuneiform letters, which was found near Suez, and copied by Gen. Dugua for Denon, (*Voyage*, pl. 124,) and which represents the head of a Persian, with a hawk's wing above it, in token of apotheosis, will furnish a striking example of the very little connexion subsisting between these figures and the direction of the writing by their side, as well as the slight dependence to be placed on some copies. The inscription on the above stone, is only distinguishable from the cuneiform writing in the Zend language at Persepolis, by the absence of any division between the words; and, with the exception of two or three inconsiderable mistakes in the copy, and an unfinished U standing by itself, represents pretty clearly the words *Dârheûsch Khschêhiôh eghrê* (that is, Darius the valiant king); in the beginning, however, three letters and a half, and at the end, three are wanting, and the royal title is expressed in the ordinary manner by a monogram. We cannot reasonably doubt the correctness of this interpretation, as Count Caylus has already published an account of an Egyptian urn furnished with a similar inscription relative to Xerxes, and the hawk's wing alludes to the apotheosis of Darius, an honour which, according to Diodorus in his first book, was never rendered in Egypt to any other living monarch but Darius. Supposing our explanation to be correct, we may remark, that the characters of this inscription are traced in such an inverted manner, that it is almost impossible to read them, except by elevating the stone itself above one's head.[4]

The different species of cuneiform writing are determined by the degree of simplicity apparent in the formation of characters, by means of the two elementary strokes before noticed. The letters on the monuments at Persepolis are the least complicated of any; and of the three kinds of writing there found, the first place is assigned on the urn discovered by Count Caylus to the most simple, and the second to the more so of the two others. According to this arrangement, therefore, the various kinds of cuneiform character may be classified in the following manner.

1. First of all, rank the cuneiform characters of the Persepolitan inscriptions, which in their turn may be subdivided into three classes, each of them exactly indicated on the ruins of Persepolis, as well as on the urn of Count Caylus. The first, deciphered by me in the Zend, that is, in all probability, the Median language, is found above one of the windows of Darius's palace. The second, which is to the right of these windows, would seem to belong to the Parsi, the language of the true Persians. The third, which is situated to the left, or to the right of the spectator, likewise exhibits all the characteristics of some other Persian dialect; the absence of any prefixes shows that it cannot belong to the Semitic family. The second species, which occupies an intermediate rank between the two others, is distinguished from the first, which I consider to be the ancient Assyrian

[4] It has subsequently been ascertained that the inscription and figures upon this stone were copied from different parts of a monument erected under the Persian king Darius, on the canal which joined the Nile with the Red Sea; and that the absence of any division between the words was entirely the fault of the transcriber. A perfect copy of this inscription would furnish the best proof of the correctness of my interpretation. Compare my treatise in the *Fundgruben des Orients*, vol. vi. No. 3, p. 252, sq.

writing mentioned in one of the letters attributed to Themistocles, by the circumstance of its containing less of the angular than the oblique wedge letter; while it differs from the third kind by the absence of any oblique, or crossing wedge letters.

2. Next to the above, we must class the writing on a stone described by M. Millin, (Monumens Antiques, pl. viii. ix. No. 1,) the characters of which partly resemble the Persepolitan of the third kind, and partly those of the Babylonian bricks, gems, and cylinders, without however being perfectly similar. We may also remark in this writing some of the strokes of union which characterize the Babylonian cuneiform letters.

3. The third and last rank will be assigned to the characters of the large inscription found in the ruins of ancient Babylon, together with those on the bricks, gems, and cylinders, recently published at London by the East India Company. These are the most complicated of any, and present not only the same characters, but also the same words, and occasionally even the same contents. This kind of writing is distinguished by the multiplication of the strokes of union, and by the sign resembling a star with eight rays, which occurs at the commencement of all writing on bricks, as may be seen in the large inscription of London. As this peculiar sign is only met with in the cuneiform writing of this class, I have for that reason included under it the bricks and gems of the desert extending from Basora to Aleppo, which are mentioned by Pietro della Valle, as well as the jaspers, made known to us through the medium of the East India Company.

Of each of these specimens of cuneiform writing, I shall venture to submit the following elementary principles, as the general result of my examination.

1. The cuneiform inscriptions are all written in a horizontal direction, from left to right, by no means however vertically, or alternately from right to left, and from left to right.

It is almost two hundred years since Pietro della Valle (Voyage, Paris, 1745, tom. v. p. 320, sq.) and Figueroa, the ambassador from the court of Philip III. of Spain, came to a similar conclusion from examining the wedge-shaped and angular inscriptions of Persepolis; viz. that the cuneiform writing proceeded from left to right; and this general principle has been confirmed by so many particular examinations of each species, that I have not room to notice them all. When Chardin, however, (Travels, p. 168,) accompanies the remark of Figueroa with the observation, that cuneiform writing is also read from top to bottom, like the Chinese, (alluding particularly to the inscriptions over the windows of Darius's palace,) he no more contradicts our opinion, than if he said that it was also read in a circular manner, as is actually the case with an inscription which completely surrounds the head of a cameo in Tassie's collection, (*Raspe Catal. No.* 655,) because in the latter instance the characters are arranged like the legends on our money, so that the direction from left to right is still preserved, as in the horizontal situation. The analogy between the three species of the Persepolitan writing proves incontestably that they are to be read from left to right; and the same holds good also with regard to the Babylonian bricks. It is evident also, that Niebuhr must have drawn the same conclusion, from his having remarked, (vol. ii. p. 143,) that in the inscriptions graven on the door-posts of the building I. (Nieb. tab. xxiv. E. F. G.) two characters occurring on one of the doors to the right, at the end of the third line, were repeated on the other door to the left, at the commencement of the fourth line.

When M. Hager, at the end of his last treatise, *Illustrazione d'uno Zodiaco Orientale*, maintains that the cuneiform writing of Babylon descends like the Chinese in perpendicular columns, of which the farthest to the right is the first; his opinion certainly corresponds with the series of signs I have adopted, though he reverses the inscriptions themselves, being misled by the lines drawn as a mark of separation, and by the position of these inscriptions on the cylinder alongside of the figures. That all the Babylonian inscriptions are to be read in the manner I have before prescribed, that is to say, in the initial sign of all the bricks, the vertical wedge-letters turn their points downwards, while the oblique ones, on the contrary, turn theirs to the right, is proved by the great London inscription, which is written from left to right, as demonstrably as M. Millin has already shown in the case of the stone found near Tak-Kesra. The same may be said of the gems and cylinders charged with similar writing; though being intended for impression, and for the purpose of attesting documents, they generally present the characters reversed. M. Lichtenstein was therefore too precipitate, when he inferred from the Oriental origin of the cuneiform writing, that it must in consequence be read from right to left. He was supported in this conclusion by a specious argument of M. Wahl, (*Algemeine Geschichte der Morgenländischen Sprachen, General History of Oriental Languages*, p. 618,) (who however really maintained a different opinion,) and forthwith he set about deciphering the cuneiform character, upon principles altogether arbitrary, with the assistance of some known alphabet, without having previously compared the different inscriptions together. In confounding the term Oriental with Aramean, it never occurred to him that the writing of an Oriental people might very well have a direction quite contrary to the Aramean; and that there might be inscriptions engraven on stones from left to right, while the ordinarary mode of writing followed an opposite direction.

2. All cuneiform writing is composed of letters, and not merely of syllabic signs.

The principle which I have just laid down has scarcely been combated, except by a single writer; and yet in reference to the more complicated species of cuneiform writing, almost all my predecessors have taken an opposite view of the question. It will therefore be worth my while to establish its correctness by a particular review, under certain limitations, of each kind of cuneiform writing.

It is perfectly certain that none of these writings are composed of signs or compendious characters, for, generally, several enter into the composition of one word; and there are words compounded of as many as eleven characters in the first species of Persepolitan writing, of nine in the second, and of seven in the rest. Besides, under the supposition that any of the complicated specimens of cuneiform writing were hieroglyphic, I cannot conceive why the same characters should be so often repeated, or why several of them should even immediately succeed each other two or three times running. In the first case, supposing the mode of writing to be by signs, it is obvious, the circles of ideas must be extremely confined; while the other supposition is inadmissible, except we limit the number of these signs to a few such words as "king," "lord," "prince," "sacred," etc., not expressed in as many characters. It is very true, that the reduplication of a sign might signify the dual number, as its triple repetition might stand for the plural, because in Du Perron's Vocabulary of the Zend and Pehlvi, the dual is usually marked by the number two, as the plural is by three. But then the repetition of these signs would be more frequent than it is; we should meet with several signs following each other in immediate succession; and, what is of much more consequence, the triple repetition, as a mark of the plural, would be more common than the simple reduplication; the reverse of which, however, is evident from examining the inscriptions. I am convinced, therefore, that none of the cuneiform writings are composed of signs or whole words. It would be less easy to prove that they do not consist of simple syllabic writing in the strict acceptation of the term; but that, on the contrary, the whole of the signs employed, though with considerable variations, might be arranged under one alphabet. It is essential to remark, that the more complicated the characters are, the fewer of them enter into the composition of a word; a circumstance which would lead us to infer, that even though all cuneiform writing was alphabetic, yet the manner of composing syllables and words of letters was necessarily subject to considerable variation. I shall therefore endeavour to enumerate all the possible varieties of compounding alphabetical signs before I proceed to examine each species of cuneiform writing in detail.

Literal writing then may either employ consonants alone, and designate the vowels by intercalated signs, placed above or below the consonants, as is the case in several Eastern alphabets; or, agreeably to Western usage, it may elevate the marks for repeating consonants, as well as those for vowels, to the rank of independent letters; or, in short, it may employ particular signs for denoting a short or long vowel, an acute or a grave, as, for example, in the ancient Persian. Accordingly the letters of a particular syllable might be written in an isolated form, or they might be joined together, and in fact, like several alphabets of Southern Asia, certain accessory marks might be added to the consonants, according to the different vowels subjoined to them, so that the writing would appear at first to be syllabic, while in reality, from its alphabetical construction, and the analogy of its signs, it would truly be a writing composed of separate characters. If we consider this last species of writing as formed of letters, I will boldly venture to assert, that every kind of cuneiform writing is in like manner composed of characters; but if the propriety of that appellation be disputed, I must certainly allow the most complicated species of cuneiform writing to be syllabic, though it may also possess certain signs to represent the vowels; thus in the Persepolitan inscriptions we meet with monograms to denote whole words. The perfectly opposite nature of the Persian and Aramean tongues will not allow us to suppose, in the case of the Persian or Babylonian remains, the existence of any syllabic writing, like that of Japan.

It is now time, however, for me to speak of each kind of cuneiform writing in particular, for it becomes necessary in this place more especially to mark the distinction between them.

The first of the Persepolitan kinds of writing is now generally allowed to be alphabetical, since M. M. Tychsen and Münter were so fortunate as to discover the sign, denoting the separation of words, and which intercludes from two to eleven characters on both sides, though the sum of all the primitive characters never exceeds forty. M. Tychsen has observed, that in several inscriptions, the series of signs so frequently occurring is replaced by a monogram; and very probably he might have succeeded in deciphering the whole writing before myself, had he taken this monogram for the title, and not for the name of the king. A more successful attempt has now proved that this species of writing has not only particular signs to represent the vowels as well as the consonants, but that, like the ancient Zend inscription discovered by Anquetil Du Perron, it also distinguishes the long vowels from the short and acute. M. Tychsen appears to consider the second and third kinds as specimens of this mode of writing; while M. Münter regards the second as syllabic and the third as hieroglyphic. For myself, I am no more at liberty than my predecessors entirely to reject this opinion, as long as the inscriptions in question have not yet been completely deciphered; nevertheless, from the comparison I have made of analogous inscriptions, I feel myself justified in asserting, that neither of these two kinds is a writing of signs; since both in one and the other, though less frequently in the third, we may remark the occurrence of inflections composed of several signs. With respect to the second kind, owing to the great number of multiplied signs which it exhibits for detached words, I must allow its employment of particular signs for the long and short vowels, as well as signs of consonants, including the vowel, provided I am not mistaken in my opinion, that certain words of the first kind are cited literally in the second. On the other hand, as to the third species of writing, which has occasion for very few signs in the composition of words, though the number it employs is nevertheless much greater than that of our alphabets, I must absolutely deny it the use of vowel signs altogether; and therefore I concede the employment of consonants, including a vowel, in cases where one consonant alone would be insufficient. As far as regards the other specimens of cuneiform writing, I have not been able to compare them with any that has already been deciphered, such as the Persepolitan; but after having compared them with several analogous inscriptions, such as those on bricks, and collated numerous passages from the large inscriptions, I can confidently venture to assert, that they do not contain a compendious writing of signs, because it is easy to discover in them instances of four or five characters following in succession, and, as it were, connected together. I have already observed in another place,[5] that I consider syllabic and literal writing, to a certain extent, as identical terms, as long as we can apply them indifferently to a species of writing which, like the Hebrew, excludes the vowels from the rank of consonants, and unites, by means of connecting strokes, such of the consonants as are immediately dependent on each other. Whoever wishes to know my reasons for holding this opinion, will find them detailed at length in the literary periodical already alluded to; I shall only add, that

[5] *Intelligenzblatt der Jenaischen Allgemeinen Litteraturzeitung*, 1824, No. 101.

considered under this point of view, I allow the great inscription, published by Millin, to possess the same character as the Babylonian cuneiform writing. It would be unreasonable to expect more decisive proofs, till such time as we possess a complete interpretation of one of the most complicated specimens of this kind of writing; for the present, it will be enough to have shown, that none of the cuneiform inscriptions are stenographic, or composed of signs representing whole words, and that consequently their explanation is by no means impracticable.

Let us now, then, proceed to an examination of my own method of deciphering the first species of Persepolitan writing; after which I shall endeavour to furnish a brief sketch of the results obtained from my interpretation as far as they may interest the general historian. With regard to my mode of procedure and manner of deciphering, they are both so excellently laid down by the Baron Silvestre de Sacy, in a letter to M. Millin, (Magasin Encyclopédique Année VIII. tome v. p. 438,) that I need only refer the reader to that source. But as it might prove interesting to know how a person, without any profound acquaintance with Oriental languages, has been able to decipher a species of Asiatic writing of the most remote antiquity, of which the alphabet, the language, and the contents, were equally unknown, I may as well enter into a few details relative to the history of my interpretation.

Among the inscriptions of the first kind, there are two very accurately copied by Niebuhr, vol. ii. tab. xxiv. B. and G. They are accompanied with translations evidently made from the two other kinds of writing which are of the same size, and, according to all appearance, of the same contents; and therefore as the first kind is in general the most simple of all the cuneiform writings, my predecessors have applied themselves to decipher it in preference to the rest. From the same point also I took my own departure, particularly as the word recognised by Tychsen and Münter as the key of the whole alphabet occurs most frequently in the species in question; and supposing with Tychsen, that we must look for titles of kings in the inscriptions placed over their portraits, (Niebuhr, *Travels*, vol. ii. p. 112, 117,) I felt convinced that the word so often repeated, must signify "*King*." Having therefore arrived at the same principle as Tychsen and Münter, without perusing any work upon cuneiform writing, and without seeing any other copies than those of Le Bruyn and Niebuhr,[6] I translated the two inscriptions according to the analogy of those in Pehlvi deciphered by M. de Sacy in the following manner.

N. N. REX. MAGNUS (?) REX. REGUM. (REX.—UM.) FILIUS —. (REGIS). STIRPS. ACHAEMENIS (?) (-----)

I was thus naturally led to infer, that these two kings must be father and son, because the king in Niebuhr's pl. *G* was called the son of the king in pl. *B;* and because in both the translations of the other kinds of writing, there existed the same connexion between the two names. Upon this I examined Heeren's Researches, and the essay of M. Münter, in order to ascertain the particular age of the Persian kings, to which the bas-reliefs in the ruins of Persepolis belonged, and thereby to discover the names applicable to them, the only way in which I could possibly succeed in finding out the signification of certain letters, and ultimately by this means elucidate the whole of them. Being fully persuaded, from the examination of the contemporary Greek historians, whose writings are the most circumstantial of any we know, that I must in this case look for two kings of the dynasty of the Achæmenides, I in consequence ran over the list, and successively applied the names to the characters of the inscriptions. These names could obviously be neither Cyrus nor Cambyses, because the names occurring in the inscriptions do not begin with the same letter; Cyrus and Artaxerxes were equally inapplicable, because in reference to the characters, the first is too short and the second too long; there only remained, therefore, the names of Darius and Xerxes; and these latter agreed so exactly with the characters, that I could not hesitate in selecting them. Besides, in the inscription relative to the son, the royal title was also

[6] I cannot omit expressing my obligations to my fellow-helper and friend M. Fiorillo, at that time secretary to the library, and afterwards *magister legens* at Göttingen, who first persuaded me to attempt deciphering these inscriptions, and assisted me with his advice for the first eight to fifteen days, during which I was busied in establishing the general principles. To the same person I am also indebted for the liberal and friendly communication of whatever essentially concerned the literature of cuneiform writing.

attributed to the father, but not in the one relating to the latter; an observation which holds good with regard to the Persepolitan inscriptions generally. Having thus found out more than twelve letters, among which were precisely those composing the royal title, with the exception of only one, the next business was to give these names, hitherto merely known to us by Greek pronunciation, their true Persian form, in order, by ascertaining the correct value of each character, to decipher the king's title, and thereby also to determine the particular language in which the inscriptions were written. The Zendavesta of Anquetil Du Perron appeared to furnish the best information on the subject, especially as the frequent use of vowels had already inclined M. Münter towards the Zend. From this authority I learned that the Greek name of Hystaspes was pronounced, in Persian, Goshtasp, Gustasp, Kistasp, or Wistasp. Here, then, were the seven first letters of the word Hystaspes in the inscription of Darius, already pointed out; while a comparison of all the royal titles led me to conclude, that the three last formed the inflection of the genitive case singular. It is scarcely possible to admit the conjecture of M. Du Perron, that the name of Darius was pronounced, in Persian, *Eanteraffesh;* for in Reland's Dissertation, *De vet. ling. Pers.*, I observe the following quotation from Strabo;[7] τὸν Δαρειαύην (consequently in the nominative *Dariaves*, or, according to the Persian system, *Dariavesh*) Δαρεῖον ἐκάλεσαν; and it is not easy to conceive why the Greeks and the Hebrew writers should have transformed *Eanteraffesh* into *Dareios* or *Dariavesh*. I confined myself, therefore, to the word Darius, or Dariavesh, and only endeavoured to find out the Persian sounds in the name of Xerxes. Without stopping at the name of Artaxerxes in the Pehlvi or the modern Persian, I gave the preference to the Zend, taking as a model the word Araxes, on which Du Perron makes the following remark in the *Mémoires de l'Académie Royale des Inscriptions*, tom. xxxi. page 367. "Araxes is formed from Weorokeshe or Warakshe, simply by dropping the first letter; and *Kshe* is always represented in Greek by ξ." In consequence, I had no hesitation in transforming the name of Xerxes into Ksharshe or Ksharsha, being guided by

[7] STRAB. xvi. sub fin.

the letters indicated in the words Hystaspes and Darius; the only difficulty was the occurrence of an additional sign between the first *sh* and the *e*, which last Münter rightly conjectured to be the first letter of the Zend alphabet, and which has also the value of an open *a*. Having compared afresh all the inscriptions given by Niebuhr and Le Bruyn, in order to assure myself that the names were faithfully copied, I found that the fourth character in the word Hystaspes ought to be composed of three principal wedges of the same length; but that in the name of Xerxes, the third character ought to be written with only one, and the fifth, on the contrary, with three transverse wedges. This circumstance led me to remark, that the third character in the name of Xerxes was synonymous with the fourth and last of the royal title; and as the three first signs in his title had been ascertained by means of the name of Xerxes, and the last but one by that of Hystaspes, I endeavoured to decipher the whole, in order to find out the meaning of the unknown sign, which also occurs in the name of Darius, after the three first characters representing the syllable *Dar*. The vocabulary of the Zend language, by M. Du Perron, presented no word under the letters *Kshe*, signifying *King*, but a number of equivalent forms under *Kshhe*, which led me to understand the language of the inscription, and proved to a certainty that the first letter in the name of Xerxes was *Kh;* but I found no clue to the meaning of the unknown sign. In the mean while, however, as no form of the Zend accorded better with the characters of the inscription than that of *Khsheïo*, I assumed this unknown sign as the mark of aspiration, or a long *h*. I was the less scrupulous in admitting some such sign of aspiration, as I had before observed in the Zendavesta a number of words written sometimes with, at others without an *h;* and had also met with a remark (in the *Mémoires* already quoted, page 365) to the effect, that "a final *a* is aspirated as if it was followed by an *h*." This also would serve to explain satisfactorily the third character in the name of Xerxes, as well as the fourth in that of Darius; and the *h* would apply with equal propriety to the inflection of the genitive case singular *ahe*, and to the end of the word *ah* so often occurring, as *tsh* does to the inflection of the genitive plural *etshao*. I have recognised this aspiration in several words of the Persepolitan inscriptions; as for example in *Dahutshao*, which I at first supposed to stand for *Daharum*, but which a continued study of the Zend language has shown me to be synonymous with *populorum*. But since M. de Sacy has made several well-grounded objections[8] relative to the names of Xerxes and Darius, I began to conjecture, that this sign might also serve to determine the correct pronunciation of the names in which it occurs, and provide against their being enounced *Khsher-she* instead of *Khsh-ershe*, or *Da-reush* instead of *Dar-eush*.[9]

In this case, one might imagine the aspirate to be changed, after certain consonants, into *w* or *y*, so that the two names just mentioned would be pronounced *Khshwershe* and *Daryeush* or *Darycoesh;* a supposition which may serve to explain how the Hebrews, like the Egyptians, by placing an *a* before each word commencing with two silent consonants, in order to facilitate the pronunciation, as the French would employ an é for the same purpose, might easily change the name of Xerxes into אחשורש *Ahhashverosh*, and Darius into דריוש *Daryavesh.* In all probability the Persian name of Xerxes might contain the sound of *w*, omitted by the Greeks for want of a corresponding sign, as in the case of Ἀρόξης for *Worokeshe* or *Warakshe;* such at least might be gathered from the different ways of spelling this name, that is, if we admit the words Ἀσσουῆρος, Ὀξυάρης, Ὀξυάρτης, and Ἀξάρης (in Κυαξάρης) to be nothing more than

[8] I am not so scrupulous as M. de Sacy about the transposition of *h* in the word *Khshhershe*, instead of *Khshehrshe;* particularly as that learned scholar himself observes in his *Mémoire, M. de Sassanid.*, p. 175, (see also, p. 191,) "In the name of *Sapor*, the *heth* of the last syllable is placed after the *resch*, which makes *Schapourh*."—"On the reverse, the name of the king is well engraved, but the *vaw* of the syllable *pouhri* is placed after the *heth*, which makes *Schahphouri*."

[9] The names of Darius and Xerxes do not appear to be simple, but compound words, of which the first part is an abbreviation of *Dara* (Lord) and *Kshah* (King); which is the reason why Œlius Lampridius in Alex. Severus, calls Artaxerxes "*potentissimum regem tam re quam nomine.*" Herodotus, on the other hand, (vi. c. 98,) explains Artaxerxes by μέγας ἀρήϊος, and Ammianus Marcellinus by "*bellorum victor.*" Herodotus seems to have merely translated the latter parts of the names Darius and Xerxes by ἑρξείης and ἀρήϊος, imitating, after the Greek fashion, the sound of the Persian word, though in an inverted order: at all events ἑρξείης is a term fabricated by Herodotus himself, for ῥεξίας or πρηκτήρ, that is to say πολεμικὸς, according to the explanation of the *Etymologicum magnum*, in which Δαρεῖος is, after Hesychius, derived from the Greek δῆρις, i. e. φρόνιμος.

different modifications of Ξερξης, just as Ἀρτοξάρης, Ἀρταξάρης, and Ἀρταξάσσης, are of Ἀρτοξέρξης or Ἀρταξέρξης, (in Zend *Artakhshethr*, in Pehlvi *Artashir*, in Persian *Ardeshir*, in Arabic *Azdeshir*,) with the initial *Art* or *Ard* (strenuus, magnus, fortitudine pollens, Herod. vi. 98). Not being myself sufficiently versed in the Oriental languages to pronounce decisively on this point, I shall merely add that M. de Sacy himself has confessed his complete failure in every attempt to give the characters another signification. M. de Rozière, in his *Déscription de l'Egypte*, (Antiquités, Mémoires, tom. i. livraison iii. p. 265, 276,) objected to the introduction in the name of Darius of the letter *h*, so difficult for French organs to pronounce; and M. Saint-Martin also, in his last essay has changed it into *é*, a mode of procedure which has led him to other deviations from my method of deciphering; but he adduces so little reason for his alterations, that I cannot venture to adopt any of them. The hieroglyphics engraven on the urn of Count Caylus, entirely confirm my interpretation, as, according to M. Champollion, they exhibit the name of Xerxes in literal characters, *Khshharsha*. Again, the name of Hadrian, in which the sign asserted by M. Champollion to represent a Greek *h* precedes the letter *a*, proves that this sign is rather a Latin *h*, or the fifth character of the phonetic alphabet, which, instead of vowels, has only their *fulcra*, and therefore employed the *hé* to designate the Greek *e*. This remark alone is sufficient to overthrow the whole structure of M. Saint-Martin's plan of deciphering, as far as his determination of the sign in question is concerned, even though it were free from numerous misconceptions of another kind.

There is no occasion for me to detail the particular method which I followed, in gradually tracing out the signification of all the other characters, as it must be sufficiently evident, from what has already been said, that my mode of procedure, so far from being conducted on arbitrary principles, has been as circumspect as possible, and that my plan of deciphering least of all deserves the imputation of blind chance, which certain partisans of my antagonist have been pleased to throw upon it. I shall only observe, that if I flatter myself with having succeeded in deciphering the first specimen of

Persepolitan character, it can scarcely in fairness be required of me to furnish also a satisfactory explanation of the writing itself, though it is too much the general custom to confound the business of a decipherer with that of an interpreter. Being little acquainted with the Oriental languages, I have merely endeavoured to determine the value of each sign by a species of logical induction, founded on a comparison of all the cognate inscriptions, and the different combinations of their characters. The way being once laid open, it will be the appropriate task of the Orientalist alone to furnish a complete interpretation of the writing now first rendered legible; it were too much to call upon the decipherer himself to prove the validity of his system by engaging in such an attempt, particularly when there is no such thing as dictionary or grammar of the deciphered language in existence, but only a few detached fragments. This will serve as an answer to those who, inconsiderately enough, require what is beyond one's power to effect. In the mean while, however, the following corroboration of one of my conjectures may be advanced as a satisfactory proof of the little reason there is to doubt the reality of the Persepolitan Zend alphabet having been actually deciphered.

M. Münter informed me by letter, that M. Fuglsang, a clergyman, well versed in the Sanscrit, and who returned two years since from Tranquebar, had communicated to him, among other things, the remark, that some Englishmen were in the habit of writing and employing the word *bun*, as a Sanscrit term, signifying *descendants, race;* and that in consequence they made use of the expression, *surya buns*, and *chandra buns*, to denote, *descendants of the sun and moon*. Whoever is acquainted with the striking analogy existing between the Zend and the Sanscrit, will immediately recognise in the above fact no small confirmation of the truth of my rather daring hypothesis at first, when asserting that the word *bun* must signify *stirps*, though M. Du Perron had only given *root*, *foundation*, as its meaning. Further, M. de Sacy assures us that he met with the word *pun* (as he writes it, though M. Du Perron constantly has *bun*, *bon*, or *bonem*) in the above sense, on several monuments of the Sassanide dynasty. Nevertheless, I cannot help thinking that this word, as well as *pothré*, or *pothrém*, which Du

Perron (Zendavesta, i. 2, p. 179, No. 2,) translates by *son* and *germ*, might also signify *son;* and I refer it to the preceding genitive cases, because in the great inscription of Le Bruyn, (No. 131, lin. 14,) we read *bon darheaush khshehiohahe,* and the word *bome* (lin. 12, in Pehlvi, *boman;* "son") is expressed in the translation of the second species of cuneiform writing by the same character as *bon.* So that there is no occasion to supply the word *son* in the titles of Darius and Xerxes: and the word *akheotshoshoh*, which ordinarily follows that of *bun*, may perhaps be considered as an epithet of the latter.

I shall not detain the reader any longer with unseasonable conjectures relative to the interpretation of these inscriptions, as there is reason to expect, that M. Du Perron's observations on the Zend will at some future day be entirely cleared up. It is sufficient to have shown that the Zend is the language of the first class of inscriptions, and that my deciphering of the alphabet, a few signs only excepted, reposes on solid grounds. Although I cannot flatter myself with having done as much in this case as M. de Sacy has for the Sassanide inscriptions, yet I feel abundantly recompensed for my labour by the conviction, that the rational system I have adopted has at length set bounds to the prevailing mania for arbitrary hypotheses, and secured the public from an inundation of writings, which threatened to embroil rather than to elucidate the question. From my researches then I come to the following conclusions.

1. All the cuneiform inscriptions of Persepolis at present known, have reference to Darius Hystaspis, and his son Xerxes; consequently to these kings belong all the edifices on which they are inscribed, and the bas-reliefs of which attest the high degree of Persian civilization and taste at this early period. In order, therefore, to furnish the reader with an exact notion of what concerns the two monarchs respectively, I shall proceed to a particular enumeration of all the inscriptions alluded to; first of all remarking, that those found on the royal mantle, which Le Bruyn (No. 133) assures us that he put together again from several broken pieces, are in fact fragments of two inscriptions, relating to the two kings whose portraits are placed side by side, and which inscriptions are written in all the three kinds of

character, but have been confounded by Le Bruyn into one, and in such an inverted manner, that it is necessary to read them from bottom to top, so that in consequence the four first lines contain the inscription relative to Darius, and the fifth, sixth, and seventh, that concerning Xerxes. The former is almost entire, at least in the first kind of writing, and evidently represents these words:

DARHEUSH K - - - - H EGHRE GOSHTASPAHE BUN AKHEOTSHOSHOH. DARIUS REX FORTIS HYSTASPIS FILIUS (?)

The inscription which refers to Xerxes can only be restored by a comparison of all the three species of writing, as it exhibits for the most part only fragments of isolated words. Upon comparing it with the inscription of Darius, above deciphered, and with Niebuhr's perfect copies, E. F. G., we find the contents to be:

XERXES REX FORTIS DARII REGIS FILIUS (?)

Somewhat more circumstantial than these are the inscriptions over the figures of the kings, placed on the doors in the interior of the buildings;[10] those relative to Darius (Niebuhr, B. D. C.) are from the building marked G. (Nieb. tab. xxvi. in Heeren's ground-plan *s*); those of Xerxes, on the other hand, (Nieb. G. F. E.,) are from the building marked I. (in Heeren's plan, *t*.) This circumstance confirms the opinion of Niebuhr, (vol. ii. p. 142: compare vol. i. p. 150, of this work,) who, from the interior form and architecture of these buildings, was led to assign them a different origin; at the same time, however, it shows that Niebuhr mistook the more ancient building to be a later erection.[11] The inscriptions over the windows prove that the edifice marked G, was intended for Darius, to whom also they themselves refer: only at the south-west angle of the building there is an upright stone, about twenty feet in height, presenting on its upper face the long inscription, (Le Bruyn, No. 131,) relative to Xerxes, the contents of which are almost the same with the one marked A, in Niebuhr, engraven on the front of the principal terrace of

[10] See *Lettre de M. Silvestre de Sacy à M. Millin sur les inscriptions des monumens Persépolitains:* Extrait du Magasin Encyclopédique, année VIII. tome v. p. 438.

[11] Unless, indeed, as appears likely from the four words subjoined to the end of the inscriptions relating to Darius, we suppose this building to have been erected by Xerxes himself, in honour of his father.

the esplanade. According to Le Bruyn, this stone was erected at a later epoch. There are no other inscriptions relating to Darius, besides the one marked H. I. K. L. in Niebuhr, which is found nearly in the middle of the southern wall of the building, on a stone twenty-six feet long by six in height. The other cuneiform inscriptions are scattered about in all directions over the ruins of Persepolis; a proof that the whole of these ancient buildings were erected by the two kings above mentioned; that Darius began them, and that Xerxes made considerable additions, without, however, completely finishing them; for, in the portions constructed by the latter prince, we still meet with stones bearing no inscription. M. de Murr (Journal, vol. iv. p. 125, sq.) has enumerated thirty-five Persepolitan inscriptions, reckoning some of them over again as many times as they are repeated, though they are all the same, and omitting on the other hand a number of others, of which we have no copies. Of the twelve inscriptions enumerated by him as occurring on the pilasters of the grand entrance, we possess no copies that are legible; their height from the ground rendering it difficult to distinguish them. Gemelli Carreri, who visited Persepolis about the end of the seventeenth century, alone pretends to have transcribed two lines, (Voyage, tom. ii. fig. i. p. 246,) the first of which corresponds with the former half of the twenty-first line in Niebuhr's A., and the second contains the isolated characters of an inscription which appears to have been the same as Niebuhr's G. Tavernier (*Relations de divers voyages curieux*. Paris, 1663) had already given the same characters, and in the very same order. I consider the opinion of M. Tychsen rather too hazardous, when he affirms the grand palace, marked L., to have been erected by the Arsacides; though the ruins of Nakshi-Rustam appear to belong in part only to the era of the Sassanides, as together with some inscriptions in the cuneiform character, they contain others in that of the Pehlvi dialect.

2. The language of the first species of Persepolitan writing is the Zend; the ancient existence of this dialect, first discovered by M. Du Perron, being as little subject to be called in question as that of the Pehlvi or Parsi, we may therefore consider the Zendavesta as a genuine religious

code of the old Persians, by reference to which we are enabled to judge of their peculiar notions in matters of religion. Although the language of the deciphered inscriptions does not exactly correspond with that of the Zendavesta, if we may conclude from the forms and inflections published by Du Perron, (for the Zend must necessarily have undergone considerable modifications during the time when it flourished,) yet the conformity in point of language discoverable upon comparing the inscriptions with the manuscripts of the Zendavesta, proves equally beyond a doubt the ancient existence of the Zend, as the Sassanide inscriptions deciphered by M. de Sacy prove that the Pehlvi flourished some centuries later.[12] It is possible, indeed, that the Zend alphabet published by Du Perron might have been in use even under the old Persian monarchy, and might just as possibly have been written from right to left, while the cuneiform character was engraved in an opposite direction. For however beautiful and convenient the latter is for engraving on stones, it must have been equally tedious and troublesome for ordinary purposes. I am, therefore, decidedly of opinion that it was only employed for inscribing on public monuments, solemn deeds, seals, and amulets, as a kind of sacred and venerable writing, and do not think it improbable even, that its two elementary signs might originally have contained some mysterious meaning.

The direction of the characters would seem to be explained by the Oriental custom of sitting cross-legged to write, in which position the order from right to left is the most natural, as it is the most convenient; while, on the other hand, in monumental inscriptions the eye loves to follow a contrary direction.[13] Such was the case in ancient Egypt, where the

[12] In a recent publication, breathing the very spirit of dogmatism and conceit, the writer coolly asks, "To what country and epoch does this pretended language belong? Has any ancient dialect ever borne the name of Zend? or is it not rather a corruption of the Sanscrit *Chhandas*, one of the most usual appellations of the Vedas?" As to the Zendavesta, our literary dictator supposes it to be a comparatively recent forgery by Guebres or Parsees of Guzerat; an opinion indeed which others besides himself have entertained. See *Réflexions sur l'étude des Langues Asiatiques*, par A. W. DE SCHLEGEL, etc. Bonn. 1832, 8vo, pag. 69. TRANSL.

[13] This distinction seems rather fanciful; it is not very easy to see why the direction from right to left should be considered the most natural, or even the most convenient, or why any connexion should be supposed to exist between the eye and the material on which the characters are traced. Few,

hieroglyphics were occasionally written from left to right, as I observe by a comparison of certain inscriptions resembling each other, and disposed in a square; whereas the ordinary mode of writing evidently proceeded from right to left. Admitting the cuneiform writing, like the hieroglyphics of Egypt, to have been a sacred writing, only employed on public monuments and amulets, etc.; it must of course have declined in estimation with the fall of the Persian empire, and gradually have come into disuse. Perhaps however it might have been still known in the time of the Sassanide dynasty, as the inscriptions at Nakshi-Rustam are copied from those of Chihel-Minar. But that it was understood as late as the fourth century of the Hegira, which is the opinion of M. de Sacy in his explanation of the cufic inscriptions at Persepolis, is utterly groundless and improbable.

3. The inscriptions of Persepolis that have been deciphered, speak of Hystaspes, Darius, and Xerxes, as grandfather, father, and son; but they never attribute the title of king to the first, while the two others are represented as kings even on the monuments of Egypt; and it is in this latter quality that the sign manual of Darius appears on two Babylonian documents hitherto unpublished. Here then we meet with a full confirmation of the history of the Persian kings, as preserved to us by the Greeks: a history which is as little liable to be affected by the monstrous traditions of the modern Persians, as by the unconnected narratives of the sacred writers, and which, notwithstanding the corruptions it may have undergone, bears nevertheless so many marks of intrinsic credibility, that I cannot but consider its agreement with the inscriptions as one of the strongest proofs of the correctness of my interpretation. The very manner in which Darius is said to have come to the

perhaps, if any, who have seen the Arabic sentences so beautifully sculptured on the walls of Mohammedan mosques, complain of their eyes being annoyed by having to read them from right to left, or seem to have thought this circumstance any diminution to the beauty of the writing. Besides, there need be no question about posture in the case, for the Hebrews followed the same direction in writing as the Arabs, and yet there is nothing to show that they wrote sitting cross-legged. In the abstract, indeed, either direction appears equally natural; or if there is any difference, it should be in favour of the European system from left to right; because, were the Asiatic method the most natural, how came the European ever to be adopted? TRANSL.

throne, is altogether in the true spirit of the Persian religion; agreeably to which, the sun, as representing the visible apparition of the divinity, could only communicate an oracular response by the neighing of his sacred animal the horse, at the moment of his own appearance above the horizon. The history of a foreign people, written by contemporaries, naturally deserves more credit than that which the natives themselves have composed several centuries after the events recorded. An attempt, therefore, to illustrate the ancient history of Persia from modern Persian sources, would be just as futile as to study the ancient history of our own country in the chronicles of the middle ages. The expectations which were conceived by learned men of being able to form new conclusions respecting the ancient history of Persia by means of the cuneiform writings, have not yet indeed been realized; but that person would betray no small want of taste for true learning, who should regard all the attempts hitherto made in deciphering these inscriptions as abortive, the study itself as useless, and its consequences as unimportant! Because, when once the true method of interpreting the character has been pointed out, to what important results may not a scrupulous collation of the inscriptions already known, as well as the discovery of others of the same kind, lead us, and particularly the documents and inscriptions at Hamadan and Bissutun, together with those found on the canal of Suez, or in the desert between Aleppo and Bassora. Besides, in those ancient monuments, which have been supposed to contain profound mysteries, or interesting information on curious subjects or remarkable events, every step towards positive certainty, and even the very conviction that we shall be disappointed in our search, is a positive gain, which none but a frigid compiler can affect to deny, to whom every additional acquisition made in the knowledge of history is of much more consequence than the limitation of his materials for constructing hypotheses.

Postscript by Prof. Heeren.

M. Grotefend, in the preceding essay, has so expressly declared that his object was merely to decipher, and not to explain the inscriptions, that it would be superfluous to call the reader's attention to this point, were it not for the extreme partiality with which his labours have been reviewed by some of our critics. Whoever reflects on the scanty knowledge we have of the Zend, confined as that is to a meagre list of two or three hundred words, furnished by Anquetil Du Perron, will rather be surprised that so much should have been effected, than complain of so little. Up to the present time no person has succeeded in refuting M. Grotefend's method of explanation; for dogmatic assertions prove nothing to the contrary, even when emitted by Oriental scholars, who being unacquainted with the Persian, cannot possibly be considered judges of the question, the Zend having just as little connexion with the Semitic dialects, as the German has with the Turkish. In England, on the other hand, his method has been generally recognised as correct. It is no business of mine to undertake the defence of M. Grotefend; he has already done it himself to the satisfaction of every unprejudiced mind. Within these few years, however, a decided adversary to his system presented himself in the person of the late M. Saint-Martin, who read before the Asiatic Society of Paris a memoir relative to the ancient inscriptions of Persepolis, an extract from which is given in the *Journal Asiatique* for February, 1823. But if I may be allowed to judge from a perusal of this extract, M. Grotefend has every reason to congratulate himself in meeting with such an opponent, who, so far from confuting his interpretations, actually appears to confirm them in their essential points. What Saint-Martin finds fault with in Grotefend, is confined chiefly to his method of deciphering certain characters, (which the critic asserts to have been too arbitrary,) and to his explanation of a few words. In other respects, Saint-Martin himself adopts the whole system of M. Grotefend; allows him the credit of having first correctly read the names of the kings, which furnished a clue to the rest of the alphabet; and in his explanations, a few points of secondary importance excepted, comes to precisely the same conclusions as the German scholar. According to M. Saint-Martin, the inscription relating to Xerxes reads thus: "*Xerxes the powerful king, king of kings, son of king Darius, of an illustrious race.*" According to Grotefend, (see vol. i. p. 253,) "*Xerxes the valiant king, king of kings, son of Darius the king, successor of the sovereign of the world.*" The inscription on Darius, as translated by the first-mentioned scholar, is, "*Darius the powerful king, king of kings, king of the gods, son of Vyshtasp, of an illustrious and very excellent race.*" By Grotefend, "*Darius the valiant king, king of kings, king of the people, son of Hystaspes, successor of the sovereign of the world.*" Such being the general agreement of these two scholars in their respective modes of interpretation, we may, I think, safely leave them to settle their other differences together in an amicable manner, without any apprehension that the system adopted by M. Grotefend will eventually turn out to be false, or that any other scholar will venture to contest with him the merit of discovery. Being desirous of enabling the reader not merely to form an opinion of this branch of study, but even to prosecute it himself should he feel curious to do so, I have accordingly subjoined to the end of this volume a copper plate, tab. i., in which, with the assistance of M. Grotefend's treatises, I have laid down the whole apparatus necessary for reading the cuneiform inscriptions of the first species, written in the Zend language, and found on the ruins of Persepolis, which up to the present time have been deciphered by the above scholar only. In this table then we observe,

1. The deciphered Zend alphabet, not however in grammatical but in chronological order, so that the student may proceed from the most simple to the most complicated method of arranging the wedge-letters, and subsequently to the composition of the angular with the wedge-form. It is evident this order must throw some light on the origin and development of the alphabet itself.

2. Opposite to each character of the Zend is placed the corresponding one in Latin and Persian. But as the latter possesses no marks to denote the vowels, they are only represented in the Latin. The last sign is an abbreviation of the royal title *Khshêhiôh*, (Pers. *Shah.*) *Rex.* composed of the initial and final characters of the word.

3. By the side of the alphabet descends a column entitled *sphalmata*, which contains the mistakes of the transcriber.[14]

[14] The letters N and B stand for Niebuhr and Le Bruyn.

In the course of deciphering the alphabet itself, as well as upon comparing the several copies made by Niebuhr, Le Bruyn, Chardin, and others, M. Grotefend was led to notice the occurrence of numerous errors, rendered almost inevitable by the state of the inscriptions, and the peculiar circumstances under which they were copied. It was altogether necessary to point out these mistakes, otherwise the reader would have been stopped by the frequent recurrence of characters not to be found in the alphabet. They are therefore so arranged in the table, that by the side of each letter he will also observe the corresponding erroneous form.

4. Although the preceding directions might seem sufficient for enabling the reader to commence the study of deciphering, I have judged it convenient to add also a specimen of reading, in order to remove the serious difficulties he would still have to encounter; this specimen I have taken from M. de Sacy's *Lettre à M. Millin sur les inscriptions des Monumens Persepolitains;* and together with the alphabet, and the rest of the apparatus, has been copied with the most scrupulous fidelity, Professor Tychsen having had the goodness to undertake the trouble of revising the plate.

5. M. Grotefend had also enriched the third edition of this work with another plate, (tab. ii.,) containing the abovementioned specimen in all the three kinds of writing, together with the cuneiform inscription on the urn of Count Caylus, which is the same as the former, word for word. His object in making this addition was partly to explain what he had previously remarked of the character of cuneiform inscriptions in general, and of the three Persepolitan species in particular; and partly also to show that these three species of writing read from left to right, correspond verbally with each other; and that each of them is composed of letters, of which several go to make up a single word, with the exception of the royal title, which is represented by a monogram, either with or without inflection. From the same plate, also, we learn the peculiar method by which M. Grotefend, notwithstanding the absence of any division between the words of the second and third species of writing, succeeded, nevertheless, in effecting their separation; and before he had actually deciphered any part of them, put himself into a way of translating a considerable number of

detached words, with the assistance of the first species, and also of discovering the ὕστερον πρότερον, already referred to, as committed by Le Bruyn, (No. 133,) in confounding together the fragments of two different inscriptions.

It must, however, be confessed, that, notwithstanding the progress hitherto made in deciphering and explaining the cuneiform inscriptions, we have as yet scarcely passed the threshold of the science, for want of other aids than we now possess, towards understanding the ancient Persian dialects, and particularly the Zend; nevertheless the attempts made by learned scholars, up to the present day, are quite sufficient to interest the attention of every friend of antiquity in their favour. Independently of the new conclusions they promise to supply with respect to the ancient history of Persia, they serve also to make us better acquainted with one of the most important of all human inventions next to language, I mean the art of literal writing. And if they do not throw a full blaze of light on the art itself, and the place where it originated, they at least supply us with a feeble ray to guide our researches into these distant regions, which indeed is all that we have reason to expect.

The cuneiform writing is so simple in its character that it evidently bears all the marks of an original invention. It only consists of two signs, the wedge and the angle, and it is impossible to construct a literal writing with a fewer number of elements. This is the reason why a single letter is often composed of more wedges or angles than at first sight would be thought necessary; which is the more remarkable, because, from the total absence of curved lines, it would be impossible to connect the signs together without considerable difficulty. At the same time it is equally clear, from the very nature of this kind of writing, that it could not have proceeded from hieroglyphics, as the latter from their first origin necessarily retain a character of variety, which an alphabet derived from them (admitting such to have been the case) would scarcely fail to betray: and even if we regard the two elementary signs above mentioned as hieroglyphical, that is, for example, supposing them to represent the idea of two sexes, yet the writing itself still remains essentially distinct from that of hieroglyphics. That it is neither a syllabic writing has already been proved by M. Grotefend; and, in fact, it is not very easy to see how its elementary characters could be composed of syllables. What other supposition, therefore, can we entertain, than that the writing in question was originally formed of letters only, allowing even that it was developed slowly, and by degrees? It is, however, true, particularly with respect to the first species of cuneiform writing, that it appears in a remarkable manner to betray all the characteristics of an infant state of the art, in the quantity, or rather the superabundance of letters in certain words. Does not this peculiarity evince an anxious effort on the part of the inventor to leave no sound, however insignificant, or even aspiration, without its appropriate symbol? or, in other words, does not this writing bear all the marks of having been carefully written in conformity with the spoken language? In the second and third species, the fact just mentioned is much less frequently observable; a circumstance which might lead us to infer, though they contain more complicated specimens of particular character , that they are less ancient than the former.

As to the question, in what country this writing was invented, we may answer without hesitation, that it is of Asiatic origin. It differs to such a degree from the Egyptian writing, not merely that of hieroglyphics, but also the literal, as existing on the Rosetta stone, that they scarcely deserve a moment's comparison. The discoveries made at Persepolis and at Babylon, prove further, that its use extended over a considerable portion of Upper Asia, and that being divided into several alphabets, (of which the three kinds found on the ruins of Persepolis are again distinguished from those engraven on the Babylonian bricks,) it was adopted by several different nations, the original elementary signs being variously modified in constructing the new alphabet. It appears certain, that the invention of cuneiform writing was long anterior to the Persian monarchy, from the circumstance of its being engraven at this early epoch, under three forms, on the buildings of Persepolis; but to determine the precise spot where it was first brought into use, is not so easy. As there can be no doubt, however, that the first Persepolitan species, which is also the most simple, was employed for writing the Zend language, we might with great probability assume its original country to have been Media, where the Zend, and with it the doctrines of Zoroaster, once flourished. But when, on the other hand, we find in the ruins of Babylon bricks and tablets, themselves of very remote antiquity, covered all over with cuneiform inscriptions, we feel equally disposed to attribute to them an Aramæan origin. The latter hypothesis derives great confirmation from the fact, that in all probability the writing which the Greeks and Persians termed Assyrian, was no other than the cuneiform. I am particularly led to this conclusion by a passage in Herodotus, (iv. 87,) where he speaks of the two columns on which Darius, after crossing the Bosphorus in his Scythian expedition, caused the names of the different nations composing his army to be engraven, on one in Greek, and on the other in Assyrian characters; the latter of which columns the historian himself saw in the temple of Bacchus at Byzantium. Now the cuneiform character being in general use among the Persians for inscribing on public monuments, is it likely that Darius would have employed any other in the case just alluded to? There is no sort of occasion to suppose that the Babylonian or Assyrian writing was of Aramæan origin, under the idea that it was brought to Babylon by the Chaldæans, at the epoch of their power, because it has been already shown, in another part of this volume, that the Chaldæans were a branch of the great Persico-Median tribe.

APPENDIX III.

On Pasargadæ and the Tomb of Cyrus; by G. F. Grotefend.

THE Essay contained in the preceding Appendix had already been printed off, when, during an accidental stay at Göttingen, I received from M. d'Olenin, director of the Imperial Library at St. Petersburg, through the medium of Prof. Rommel, a cuneiform inscription in all the three forms of the Persepolitan character, which had been copied from a pillar in the neighbourhood of a village called Murghâb, distant about fifty-two miles from Persepolis, by Sir Gore Ousely, the British envoy at the court of Persia. Upon comparing it with the Persepolitan inscriptions already deciphered by me, I found that it consisted of four words in the three known species of writing, the first of which formed the beginning of Niebuhr's I. and K. Judging by analogy from the inscriptions of Persepolis, the second word should represent a certain name, which in the third and fourth is followed by the titles of "king" and "sovereign" respectively. In the first specimen of writing, this name consists of six characters, which, according to my alphabetical table, and presuming Sir Gore Ousely's copy to be correct, furnish us with the word "*Zushudsh*." But the uppermost wedge representing the letter *d* is made so long, that we might suppose it to have been drawn over three perpendicular wedges instead of two, which would in that case give us *á* or *é*, the first letter of the Zend alphabet.[1] It is true I have in my table explained the first and third signs by *z* and *sch* respectively, because I conceived them

[1] A later copy of the inscription made by Sir Robert Ker Porter, shows that the above character does not exist in the original.

to be synonymous with certain other characters of similar import; but a more scrupulous examination has convinced me that they are different, as it is only in particular words that they occur without variation; the first sign in the forms "*ezutshush*," "*ezutsheo*," and the other in those of "*pshutsheo*," "*pshueotshetshao*." I have no hesitation therefore in considering the first to represent a *k*, and the second the double consonant *sr*; the whole inscription then may be interpreted in the following manner:

Edo. Kusruesh. Khshehioh. Akheotshoshoh.

Dominus. Cyrus. Rex. Orbis terrarum rector.

What leads me to infer that the inscription contains the name of Cyrus, is the circumstance of its being expressed in the two other specimens of writing by no other than three signs, which could hardly stand for a name of greater length than the one in question.[2] The reason why this name in both the other kinds of writing presents no sign common to those of Hystaspes, Darius, or Xerxes, is because the original appellatives of the kings of Persia sounded differently in different languages; a circumstance which, in addition to the titles of "king" and "sovereign" being designated by a monogram, has prevented my deciphering the other specimens.

The occurrence of the name of Cyrus in the above inscription necessarily excited my curiosity to know whether the ruins of Murghâb had ever been the residence of that monarch. Upon this, M. Blumenbach, with that kindness which always distinguishes him, was so good as to lend me a copy of Morier's Travels, in the French translation of 1813, in which I was not a little surprised to find the very inscription itself, and the ruins of Murghâb described in such a manner as to make me unite with Morier, in believing them to be the identical remains of Pasargada. And as the further I examined the subject only served to confirm me in my opinion, though Pasargadæ had hitherto been sought for in quite an opposite direction from Persepolis, I willingly complied with the request of Prof. Heeren, to explain my reasons for this conjecture in a separate treatise.[3]

[2] M. Saint-Martin reads *Huschusch*, which he considers to be synonymous with *Ochus*. How far this supposition is admissible will be shown in the sequel.

[3] A particular defence of my hypothesis, in opposition to the attacks of M.

The name of Pasargada occurs only in Ptolemy and Solimus (cap. 55). All the other writers, with the exception of Q. Curtius, who in one place (v. vi. 10) has "Persagadum" (i. e. Persagadarum) "urbs," and in another (x. 1, 22) "Persagadæ," uniformly call it by the name of "Pasargadæ," or "Passargadæ;" which latter appellation deserves the preference, as we generally find it attributed to the Persian tribe surnamed from this place. The method of spelling it Pasagarda adopted in modern maps, is founded solely on the untenable supposition, that its site was on the present Fasa, near a river of the same name. It is far more probable that the term Pessargadeh, signifying "the abode of princes," has been corrupted into that of Persepolis by a very common transposition of the letter *r*, because Stephanus of Byzantium explains Passargadæ by "Persian camp," just as Kyreshata (Koreshgadeh) has been converted into Cyropolis. We must confess, however, notwithstanding the similarity of name, that Pasargadæ, where the tomb of Cyrus was, is altogether distinct from the Persepolis, (i. e. Persarum urbs, called by Arrian simply Πέρσαι, the *Pârs* of the cuneiform inscriptions,) which was burnt by Alexander. At the same time, we are not to look for it at such a distance from Persepolis as the ruins of Fasa, or in so perverted a direction as to suppose the modern Shiraz, merely on account of the resemblance between Cyr and Chyâs, as written by the French, to have been the ancient capital of Cyrus.

The Greeks first became acquainted with Persepolis and Pasargadæ in consequence of Alexander's expedition. According to the unanimous accounts of all writers, the Macedonian conqueror in his progress towards the east, arrived first at Persepolis, and afterwards at Pasargadæ, so that the possession of the former immediately led to the capture of the latter. Upon this is founded the statement of Pliny, (Hist. Nat. vi. 26, compare Solinus, cap. 55,) and also of Strabo, that Pasargadæ was situated at the eastern extremity of Persis. A still more decisive passage is that of Strabo, (xv. p. 1060, or 729,) where he says, that in the country of Pasargadæ, the river Cyrus, a name altered from the original one of Agradates by Cyrus himself, flowed through

M. Hœck and Hammer, is inserted in the *Hallische Allgem. Litt. Zeitung*, No. 140, for June, 1820.

Hollow Persis, so called. The latter appellation evidently denotes the valley extending from Persepolis to Murghâb, along the banks of the Ruh-koneh-siwond, which is also termed by Oriental writers the Abkhuren or Kervan. We must not however look for Pasargadæ in a direction due east from Persepolis, because the eastern part of the plain in which the latter is situated abuts upon the marble mountain of Rachmed, where, according to Diodorus, (xvii. 70,) the tombs of the Persian kings were to be found; while a similar chain of marble rocks form the boundary of the plain towards the north. But in the neighbourhood of the ruins of Istakhar, and along the banks of the above river Kervan, which flows between Nakshi-Rustain and Chihel-Minar into the Bend-Emir or Araxes, we find a valley, (represented in Morier's chart, further to the east; in that of Kinneir, on the contrary,[4] more to the east,) which runs in a north-easterly direction, parallel to the road from Shiraz to Ispahan. The same road conducts us over two mountain-chains to the ruins from which the inscription before alluded to was copied; after passing these mountains, which, on account of the snow, is only practicable in summer, we arrive by another route at the "valley of Heroes," the favourite hunting-place of the ancient kings of Persia, and where Bahram-Gur, who is said to have derived his surname from the wild asses of this country, (*Gur* or *Khor*,) had seven palaces all of different colours. As early as the year 1471, these ruins had been visited by Josaphat Barbaro, the Venetian envoy; Morier, however, is the only traveller who has examined them with attention. Kinneir, who has made us acquainted with several routes leading through this valley, observes, in his Geographical Memoir, that "he saw nothing remarkable along the above road, except a singular edifice in the neighbourhood of Murghâb, called Takhti-Suleiman, which was in a superior style of architecture, and, to judge from an inscription[5] on one of the pillars of a portico, seemed to be contemporary with the buildings of Persepolis. This pillar, which is round, is about forty feet high and eight in circumference. A hill in the vicinity bears evident traces of having been once fortified; and about a mile fur-

[4] In his *Geographical Memoir of the Persian Empire*, London, 1813, 4to.

[5] This is the one copied by Sir Gore Ousely.

ther to the west, is an ancient structure, said to have been erected to the memory of a certain sultan Suleiman." From the circumstantial description and drawings furnished by Morier, we learn that the very edifice in question is the tomb of Cyrus, and that the surrounding ruins are no other than those of ancient Pasargadæ.

The writers from whom the Greeks, and subsequently the Romans, derived their first knowledge of this country, were Onesicritus, Nearchus, and Aristobulus, the contemporaries of Alexander the Great. Of these, Onesicritus appears to have mixed up a good deal of what is fabulous in his accounts; the second has led both Ptolemy and Pliny into the error of confounding the rivers of the coast, which empty themselves into the Persian Gulf, with those of the interior, to which latter, according to Kinneir's Geography, (p. 59,) the Cyrus of Pasargadæ and the Araxes of Persepolis belong.

The only writers likely to be of service in determining the locality of Pasargadæ, are those who have borrowed their accounts from Aristobulus, the principal of whom are Arrian and Strabo. According to the last-mentioned author, (compare also Diodorus i. p. 43; Ælian. Hist. Anim. i. 59,) Pasargadæ was built by Cyrus to commemorate the victory which secured to the Persians their dominion over the Medes; and Morier informs us, that the mountainous defile leading from this country into Media, considered in a military point of view, presents very favourable advantages for obstructing the march of an enemy. For that reason Cyrus made Parsagardæ the principal seat of empire, of his treasures, and, as Plutarch writes, the place of coronation for the Persian kings, where the newly-elected monarch, in order to his solemn inauguration at the hands of the Magi, was obliged, in addition to many other ceremonies, to put on, in the *temple* of the *goddess of war*, the robe formerly worn by Cyrus before he came to the throne. Here also did that monarch erect his own tomb, which, by its peculiar form of architecture, was distinguished as much from the tombs of his successors, as it was from all others. The burying-places of the Persian kings and the satraps were in general lofty edifices, into which the coffins were wound up by means of machinery, and afterwards placed in shrines; the tomb of Darius Hystaspis, however, according to Ctesias, (Pers. cap. 15,) was hewn out of a rocky mountain; that of Cyrus, on the contrary, is reported by Arrian, (vi. 29,) and Strabo, (p. 730, or 1041,) on the authority of Aristobulus, to have been built of square stones in the midst of a delightful paradise. Making every proper allowance for the great alterations which must necessarily have taken place in this ancient monument since it was pillaged in the time of Alexander, it is worth while to examine the following circumstantial description of it furnished us by Arrian. "It was in the royal paradise at Pasargadæ," says this writer, "that the tomb of Cyrus was erected, on a foundation of square blocks of stone, above which was raised a building also of stone, with a roof, and having a doorway so extremely narrow, that it was difficult for a small-sized man, and altogether impossible for a large one, to enter. Within the building stood a golden sarcophagus, which contained the body of Cyrus; near this was a kind of throne, the feet of which were carved in gold; and underneath the sarcophagus were carpets of Babylonian manufacture, while over it were spread rich vestments and coloured stuffs in the Median and Babylonian taste, together with collars, scimitars, earrings of gold, and precious stones. In the neighbourhood was built a small habitation for the Magi, to whom was committed, in hereditary succession, the guardianship of the tomb. According to Aristobulus, the tomb of Cyrus is reported to have borne the following inscription, written in the Persian character and language. "O man, I am Cyrus, (the son of Cambyses,) who laboured to give empire to the Persians, and who reigned over Asia. Therefore, envy me not the possession of a monument." Onesicritus and Aristus of Salamis, give this inscription in a more concise form, as in the following hexameter:—Ἔνθαδ' ἐγὼ κεῖμαι Κῦρος βασιλεὺς βασιλήων. Although it is not likely that the Greek verse, as pretended by some, should have been engraven in Persian characters alongside of the other inscription, yet it certainly corresponds better with the spirit of the Persepolitan inscriptions, than that mentioned by Athenæus, (Diepnos. x. 9. p. 434,) Ἠδυνάμην καὶ οἶνον πίνειν πολὺν καὶ τοῦτον φέρειν καλῶς. The latter betrays the same fictitious character, as that of Sardanapalus in Cilicia, or as the inscription represented to have been engraved on the tomb of Darius. Φιλος ἦν τοῖς φίλοις· ἱππεὺς καὶ τοξότης ἄριστος ἐγενόμην· κυνηγῶν ἐκράτουν· πάντα ποιεῖν ἠδυνάμην.

The town of Pasargadæ was destroyed by Alexander, (Arrian, iii. 18,) but the tomb of Cyrus still remains uninjured, though no longer exhibiting the sumptuous ornament described by Aristobulus, or the same appearance it did when restored by Alexander after the pillage of its treasures. The building is situate at no great distance from the mosque, as it is called, of Solomon's mother, (*Mesjidi-Madari-Suleiman*,) and on account of the peculiarity of its structure is named the "devil's court;" it still subsists entire, just as described by Arrian, and a representation of it may be seen in Morier's Travels, pl. 18. It consists of a stone apartment raised upon a foundation of large blocks of marble in several layers, which are so disposed, that each upper one, in succession, comprehends a less extent of surface, and consequently the whole foundation or base of the structure has a pyramidal form. The general outline is that of a parallelogram, the lowest course of masonry being upwards of 43 feet long, and 37 in breadth. The apartment above measures 20 feet, by 10 feet 5 inches, and the roof terminates in a sharp angle just like our houses. The whole is constructed of one kind of marble, and the blocks are held together by cramps of iron. One of the blocks composing the base is 14 feet 8 inches long, 5 feet high, and 8 feet 6 inches broad. In the interior of this marble edifice, by peeping through a chink in the door, (for the key is in the hands of a woman, who permits nobody but those of her own sex to enter,) we observe a small chamber blackened with smoke; the door itself is so narrow, that to effect an entrance would be attended with no small difficulty. The guardians of the key declare that nothing is to be found in the inside except a large stone, which probably supported the sarcophagus of Cyrus.

Although there is not the slightest resemblance between this ancient monument and the tombs of the Mohammedan saints, the common people nevertheless imagine it to be the burial-place of the mother of Solomon, a name with which they connect all sorts of miraculous legends. In the vicinity is shown a spring of water, a draught of which is said to cure the bite of a mad dog, and prevent all dangerous consequences arising therefrom. All around the edifice is strewn a vast quantity of blocks of marble, and fourteen shafts of pillars, which appear to have once formed a colonnade; at present, however, they are half buried under a mound of earth, which encloses the whole of these ruins. The paradise in which the tomb of Cyrus was formerly situated, is now a cemetery, filled with grave-stones of modern date. The building itself is covered on all sides with inscriptions, written by persons who have been led to undertake a journey thither, from motives of superstitious veneration; among which Josaphat Barbaro read the words *Madari Suleiman*, in the Arabic character. Morier, however, no where discovered any traces of ancient Persian writing, inscribed on the walls; though at no great distance, near the abovementioned mosque of Solomon's mother, he found three pilasters so inscribed, and which appeared to be the ruins of some hall or other, adorned in the inside with columns. From one of these pillars was copied an inscription, which resembles that taken by Sir Gore Ousely, though it is not so well executed.[6] At a distance of a hundred and sixty feet, we meet with similar ruins, and similar inscriptions, while the whole plain is covered with fragments of marble, which Morier considered to be the ruins of some large city. There can scarcely indeed be any doubt that it was Pasargadæ; for every particular, even the most minute, recorded of this capital of Cyrus, is perfectly applicable to the situation before us. To the left of the above-mentioned pilasters are the ruins of a fire-temple, which, in its dimensions, style of architecture, and ornament, altogether resembles Nakshi-Rustam; and about a thousand feet more to the east, is a hill on which are the remains of a fort, constructed of marble blocks, as large as those found in the buildings of the plain. This marble is white, and polished in the most exquisite manner. The village of Murghâb, situated about ten miles from the fort, contains several fine springs, which water the whole plain, and derives its appellation (of Murghâb, i. e. Birdwater) from the very singular property

[6] See pl. II. at this end of the volume.

ascribed to the water of one of these springs, which is said to attract certain red and black coloured birds, which, like starlings, follow the course of the stream in large flocks, screaming incessantly all the time, and are very useful to the inhabitants, in exterminating the immense swarms of locusts which infest the country. What is more extraordinary, if bottles be filled with this water and exposed, uncorked, in the open air, the birds are equally attracted to them by some unknown charm; and it is incredible with what quickness and voracity they despatch all the locusts they find on their passage. Villamont also, (Livre ii. p. 39, 40,) alludes to properties something similar belonging to the water and birds of the island of Cyprus; and says, that the Persians and Turks dignify these birds with the appellation of Mohammedans. According to other authorities, they are called Abmelekh, or locust-eaters, and the water, Abi-murghân. Chardin (Voyage en Perse, édition de Langlès, tom. iii. p. 390) makes this water spring from a source in Bactriana; but Father Angelus à St. Joseph, (Ange de la Brosse,) a Carmelite friar, who travelled in the East as a missionary, and wrote a book, entitled "Gazophylacium Linguæ Persarum," (Fol. Amstelod. 1684,) places the source of the Birdwater in the district of Lâdjân, (the Laodicea of Pliny,) between Shirâz and Ispahân; while Villamont, whose Travels Chardin himself is in the habit of quoting, says, it is in the neighbourhood of the Persian town of Cuerch, by which it seems likely he meant Khoneh-Kérgab, situate about nine miles from Murghâb.

We must beware of confounding two different edifices, both named from Solomon's mother, a mistake which Chardin, nevertheless, has committed. Almost all the travellers who have visited Shirâz, mention a building so called, and which Chardin, (Voyage en Perse, tom. viii. p. 432,) has described and illustrated with the most complete drawings; this building, however, is in the plain of Shubsâr, scarcely more than five miles from Shirâz. Kæmpfer indeed, (Amæn. Exot. Fasc. II. Relat. vi. p. 357,) speaks of a place called Abi-murghân, from the springs it contained; but then the marble ruins of a building which he calls the temple of Solomon's mother, (p. 354,) are in fact the three porticos to be found at Shubasâr, built of the same kind of marble, and furnished with the same figures and ornaments so generally prevailing at Chihel-Minâr. Besides, there are several ancient structures in Persia, bearing a similar appellation; thus, among others, we meet with a Takhti-Suleiman on the high road from Cocan to Cashgar, about nine hours' distance beyond Murghelan; so also the river Margus of the ancients, which flows through the province of Margiana, and rises in the mountains near Gur, bears the name of Murghâb. It is not improbable that Chardin confounded this river with the Birdwater, in the neighbourhood of Pasargadæ, just as, in the passage already alluded to, he has confounded Josaphat Barbaro's tomb of Solomon's mother, (according to Bizari, Rerum Persicarum Historia, Frankf. 1601, p. 325,) with his own three porticos of the same name at Shubasâr.

APPENDIX IV.

On the Indian Words occurring in Ctesias; by Professor Tychsen.

It was long ago asserted by Reland, that the remains of the Indian language, preserved by Ctesias in his *Indica*, might to a certain extent be interpreted with the help of the Persian, and accordingly that scholar himself first made the attempt.[1] His explanations, however, seeming neither complete nor altogether satisfactory, I have myself undertaken to comment on the Indian glosses of Ctesias without any reference to the explanations of Reland; and will now therefore proceed to submit the result of my study to the learned reader.[2] In order to facilitate the comparison of our respective essays, I shall also subjoin the interpretation proposed by Reland. The particular words we have severally endeavoured to explain, are the following, arranged according to the order of the paragraphs, in the *Excerpta* of Ctesias:

1. Ctesias (§. 2) speaks of a stone, called *pantarba*, (περὶ παντάρβας τῆς σφραγῖδος,) which had the property of attracting precious stones when thrown into the water; he has not, however, supplied any explanation of the word itself, and therefore it is not very easy from his description of the stone to determine what Persian word it corresponds with. *Pandâr*, (پندار) means *firm, stable.* If the letter ء is the sign of the Greek genitive, we might explain the last member of the word in question by پاي *pây*, i. e. *running water;* the

[1] Reland, *Diss. Miscellan.* Pars I. Diss. vi.

[2] An extract from this Essay will be found in the *Gott. Gel. Anzeig.* for 1796, p. 1997, sq.

whole would then signify, *firm in running water;* or perhaps the word may be interpreted by بند در پاي *Bend der páy,* i. e. Band or attraction in the water. These comparisons, however, are too artificial to lay much stress upon; and Reland has omitted to notice this word altogether.

2. The name of the parrot, βίττακος, (Ctesias, §. 3,) is compared by Reland, (*De Ophir*, p. 184,) with the Persian تدك, *tedek,* which is the modern appellation of the bird. From this might come τέδακος, τίδακος, σίτακος, and finally, ψίττακος; it is just possible that Ctesias may have written it with ب instead of ت as βίττακος.—All this, however, it must be allowed, is mere conjecture; though I have nothing better to substitute in its place.

3. The name of *martichora,* (Ctesias, §. 7,) applied to a fabulous animal, having the body of a lion, the face of a man, with the tail of a scorpion, may be very satisfactorily explained from the Persian. According to Ctesias, μαρτίχορα means in Greek, ἀνθρωποφάγος, the man-eater; this is neither more nor less than the Persian مرد خور from مرد *mard,* man, and خوردن *khorden,* to eat. *Khor,* the eater, is an abbreviated form of the participle *khordeh,* which is still in use. The Persians usually style an intrepid warrior *mardam-khor,* the eater of men, which is the same expression at bottom. *Mardam,* however, at present is the general form, *mard* being for the most part employed in a more elevated sense to denote a hero or warrior.

In the above comparison we have considered the final α to be merely the Greek termination: if on the other hand it be viewed as a component part of the Persian word, we have only to substitute the participial form, مردخورا *mardikhorá,* (abbreviated from مردخوران *mardikhorán,*) as Reland has already done, (p. 223,) and we obtain precisely the same signification.

4. The Greek term for *griffin,* γρὺψ, (Ctesias, §. 12,) seems to be of Persian origin; at all events it may easily be derived from that language. For example, كرفتن *giriften,* means to gripe or seize: upon cutting off the termination we have كرف *girif.* which in sound as well as meaning corresponds well enough with the word γρὺψ. The modern appellation for griffin in Persian, is *Si-murgh,* (i. e. thirty

birds,) or *Si-reng*, (i. e. thirty colours,) equivalent to "great," or "variegated." The two last names are obviously nothing more than epithets.

5. The bird δίκαιρος is reported to be synonymous with δίκαιος, *just* (Ctesias, §. 17). I can compare this word with no other than the Persian دي *di*, good, the good principle, and كار *kar*, doing, a participle of the verb كردن *kerden*; the whole then means benefactor, and might possibly allude to the supposed custom of this bird's taking care to bury its own excrement, which is said to possess very deadly properties. Reland supposes the word to be altogether of Indian derivation, and he may be perfectly right in his conjecture; but the Persian ديلمك *dilmek*, which he compares with δίκαιρος, (p. 221,) is too far-fetched, and moreover signifies a venomous spider.

6. The tree called πάρηβον, (Ctesias, §. 18,) in Apollonius πάρυβος, the wood of which is said to have the quality of attracting any substance, may be compared with the Persian بار, *bár*, weight, burden, and آور *âver*, bearing, drawing, the participle of اوردن, *âverden*. *Bár-âver* would then signify *drawing a weight*. This comparison however is too defective; we are not told the meaning of πάρηβος, and the sound is very different from that of the Persian term. Reland has forgotten to notice this word.

7. In India, says Ctesias, (§. 19,) there is a river called ὕπαρχος, which means φέρων πάντα τὰ ἀγαθὰ, i. e. "*producing all good things*." To explain this word I adduce the Persian آور *âver*, bringing, carrying, from the verb آوردن *âverden*; and خوش *khosh*, good; consequently *âver-khosh*, bringing good, which corresponds exactly with the signification pointed out by Ctesias. The word should properly have been written ἄβαρχος or ὕβαρχος in order to represent the Persian; but it is well known that the Greeks, who were seldom able to appreciate foreign sounds with correctness, generally expressed them according to Greek etymology, or a fancied resemblance to certain words in their own language; as, for instance, in the case of Ἱεροσόλυμα for Jerusalem, Ἱεραμαξ for Jarmuch. We might also compare برخوش, *berkhosh*, good, so that the initial letter ὕπαρχος would be merely euphonic, but then, the participle φέρων

would not be expressed. Reland (p. 46) compares it with اوبرخ *av-perkh*, from *áv*, water, and *perch*, utility, convenience; the whole expression thus amounting to *aqua utilissima*.

8. In the same passage with the above, Ctesias also speaks of an Indian tree called σιπταχόρα, from which *electrum*, probably some odoriferous gum, distilled, and which likewise produced a kind of fruit something like a grape. *Siptachora* is represented to signify γλυκὺ, ἡδὺ, sweet, agreeable. We may compare this with the Persian شيفته خور, *shifteh-khor*, that is, "agreeable to eat," which applies very well to the signification alluded to. *Shifteh* from *shiften*, "to be in love," properly means "amorous," but is also attributed to any object that inspires affection, and thus comes to signify "agreeable." In the same manner the Persians call an apricot شيفته رنگ *Shifteh reng*, literally "agreeable colour." The other part of the word خورد or خور *khôrd* or *khor* means "eating," "food." Reland (p. 229) follows the reading in Höschel's edition of Photius, viz. σιπαχορα, and derives the word from صفا *safa*, "pleasing," "delightful," and خوردن *khôrden*, to eat. *Safa* however comes from the Arabic, a language we dare not have recourse to for explaining the Persian words of the age of Ctesias. But the correctness of the former reading, even with the τ, is confirmed by a passage in Pliny, (Hist. Nat. 37. 2,) where the word occurs, though in a disfigured shape; he says "arbores eas Aphytacoras vocari." It is otherwise not a little surprising, that Reland preferred the reading of σιπαχόρα, because forsooth it came nearer to his proposed Persian etymology, as if the convenience of the commentator ought to decide when such and such a reading is to be adopted as the correct one!

9. The mountains in the neighbourhood of the Indus, according to Ctesias, (§. 20,) were inhabited by a wild race of beings, with dog's heads, of a black colour, and speaking an unintelligible language; these the Indians termed καλύστριοι, that is, κυνοκέφαλοι, or the dog-headed. Admitting the Greek translation of the name to be not altogether literal, and that the Indian sound has not been correctly expressed, I would nevertheless venture to compare

it with the Persian كلك *kelek*, or *keluk*, a wolf, and سر *ser*, the head; that is to say, كلكسر *kelukser*, wolf-headed; which in Greek would properly be καλυκσιριος, and in the plural, καλυκσιριοι. But pronounced rapidly, the word might sound to a Greek ear like καλυκσρ, from whence came καλυστριοι.

Another word more exactly answering to the sound of the Greek, would be كالوسترين *kalusterin*, the superlative degree of *kalus*, stupid, foolish, which would convert these "dog-headed" people into "blockheads." But although this latter epithet agrees well enough with the description of the Cynocephali, it is nevertheless too little consonant with the translation of the term as furnished by Ctesias, to admit of our regarding it as the more probable etymology.

Reland (p. 213) compares the Persian كله شكاري *kalla shikâri*, caput caninum, dog-headed. He supposes that Ctesias at first wrote καλίσκαροι, which was altered by the copyist into καλύστριοι; nevertheless he himself hesitates in adopting this explanation, and very justly observes, that شكاري *shikari*, means properly a *hound*, from شكردن *shikardan*, to hunt; and that كلّه *kalla*, signifies the top of the head, rather than the head itself.

10. As to the unicorn described by Ctesias, (§. 25,) in a very circumstantial manner, but without the addition of its Indian name, I must beg leave to make it the subject of a few remarks. If there really is such an animal as a unicorn, resembling the stag or the horse, a notion which appears to be again entertained in modern times, we must look for it in Africa, the only country in which it has been reported to exist, by the concurrent testimony of all travellers, from Barthema down to Barrow. But the animal described by Ctesias, after the Persian manner of representing it, and which occurs frequently on the ruins of Persepolis, seems to me, in all its essential characteristics, to be no other than the Asiatic rhinoceros. To the latter will apply, 1. what Ctesias says of its wildness and strength, (§. 26. Compare Bruce's Travels, vol. v. p. 105,) which prevented its being ever taken alive; 2. its at first slow, but continually increasing pace; (Bruce also, p. 97, says that the rhinoceros sets off at a gentle trot, which after a few minutes

is increased to a rapid gallop, and which the animal keeps up for a long time, though a horse can easily overtake him;) 3. the circumstance of its flesh being unfit to eat (Ctesias, §. 26). It is true the Abyssinians, according to Bruce, eat the flesh of the elephant, as they do also of the rhinoceros, but it has a disagreeable musky flavour. The flesh, however, of an animal of the stag or horse kind (Ctesias calls it a *wild ass*) would not be *bitter*, as represented in the above paragraph. 4. A still more evident proof, in my opinion, of its being the rhinoceros, is the single horn, together with the property attributed to it of counteracting the effects of poison; for which purpose it is still the custom in Asia to make drinking cups of that material. The colour of this horn, according to Ctesias, is red at the point, black in the middle, and white at the base; which agrees very well with the account of Bruce, (p. 93,) who describes its exterior surface as of a reddish-brown. It is probable, also, that Ctesias may be describing the animal's horn after it had been formed into a drinking vessel, in which case, the variety of colour he notices might be produced by artificial means, and by the removal of the outer covering.[3]

The figure of an ass, with the size of a horse, which Ctesias attributes to his unicorn, agrees also with the size and unwieldy appearance of a rhinoceros. On the ruins of Persepolis, indeed, it is represented with a more slender shape, and more like a horse; this, however, is due to the imagination of the sculptor alone; and when we recollect that it was also a fabulous animal which he meant to portray, we shall have as little reason to expect a faithful adherence to natural history in this case, as we have in those of the martichora and the griffin. Ctesias further remarks, as a peculiarity worthy of attention, (§. 25,) that all asses, tame as well as wild, (among which last he reckons his unicorn,) and other solid-hoofed animals, have no huckle-bones,

[3] This conjecture is reduced almost to a certainty, by a passage in MANUEL PHILO *de animal. propriet.* cap. 37, which treats of the Indian onager and its horn, and is evidently borrowed from Ctesias. The author asks an Indian prince what the cup out of which he drank was made of, and which was ornamented with three rings, of a white, black, and red colour? Τί δή ποτ' ἐστὶν ὁ κρατὴρ ἐξ οὗ πίνεις; (καὶ γὰρ διαυγὴς καὶ προμήκης εὑρέθη, καὶ τρεῖς ἔχει ζωστῆρας ὡς λίθου φλέβας,) λευκόντι μέλανά τε καὶ τὸ χρῶμα πορφυροῦν. The reply is, that it was made of the horn of the ὄναγρος, or wild ass.

(ἀστραγάλους,) or gall in the liver; whereas the unicorn possesses both. He himself declares he had seen such a huckle-bone, which resembled that of an ox, but was as heavy as lead, and throughout of a bright red colour (ὥσπερ κινάβαρι, like cinnabar, or rather, like vermilion). He observes also, that the animal was hunted as much for the sake of these bones, as for its horn. The circumstance of the unicorn having a gall-bladder agrees perfectly well with the rhinoceros, which, as I am informed by M. Blumenbach, actually has one, and of a considerable size. Here then we discover an additional proof of the identity of these two animals. Ctesias merely notices the fact as remarkable, because he classes his unicorn with the *Solidunguli*, which, as he very justly observes, do not in fact possess a gall-bladder. What he says of the *astragalus* is so far correct and applicable to the rhinoceros, inasmuch as the latter certainly has huckle-bones, provided that be the true meaning of the Greek word. But how Ctesias, himself a physician, could possibly assert that solid-hoofed animals had no huckle-bones, which, on the contrary, they really have, just as much as the cloven-footed, and which are, moreover, common to all animals, quadrupeds as well as quadrumanous, not omitting the human subject itself—this we must confess is perfectly unaccountable. According to Blumenbach, there is nothing particular in the huckle-bone of a rhinoceros, either as regards colour or specific gravity. It is possible, therefore, that Ctesias may have seen one of these bones artificially stained with red, which he mistook for the natural colour; and as it was also one of the objects for which the animal was hunted, we can scarcely doubt its being applied to some sort of use, and consequently, that it was fashioned by the hand of art, and perhaps some addition made to its natural weight.

On the other hand, however, I must not omit to notice certain difficulties in the description of Ctesias, which seem to contend against my hypothesis, and point to some other animal than the one I have supposed. The first of these respects colour. According to Ctesias, the unicorn is white, with a red head, and blue or dark eyes; whereas the rhinoceros is all over of a yellowish or greyish brown, his flanks only present a slight tinge of flesh colour, while the eyes are dark brown.[4] We must not, however, examine Ctesias too rigorously on the subject of colours, for his martichora is also said to be of a bright red, and he describes the griffin to be black, with a red breast. In fact, I am strongly inclined to suspect that he took these colours from some painted representation of the animals in question. His unicorn, both as described by himself, and as it is represented on the ruins of Persepolis, has a solid hoof, and one horn on the forehead; neither of which is the case with the rhinoceros. But if we consider the Persians to have derived their knowledge of the animal merely from hearsay and exaggerated reports, this apparent difficulty will soon vanish; for having heard it described as strong and quick-footed, they naturally attributed to it a slender form, with a solid hoof, and placed the horn on the forehead as the most convenient situation. Besides, the hoof of the rhinoceros is not entirely cloven, like that of oxen and other animals, but only in part. For the same reason, the Arabs attribute to the *Kerkend* or rhinoceros a single hoof, and also speak of its horn as placed on the head or fore part of it. Even Marco Polo, (lib. iii. 15,) though certainly describing the rhinoceros of Asia, nevertheless observes, "in medio frontis gestat unum cornu." It is not improbable that the curvature of the horn, when viewed in front, may make it appear to be situated higher up than it really is.

The exaggerated statements of Ctesias relative to the strength and swiftness of this animal, are nothing compared to what the Arabian authors relate; according to whom, the *Kerkend* requires upwards of a hundred parasangs of land for his support, that he chases all other animals away from his neighbourhood, carries off elephants upon his horn, and so forth!

The observations already made appear to be confirmed by the Indian or Persian name of the unicorn, as preserved to us by Ælian, *De Natura Animalium*, xvi. 20.

"There is also," says this writer, "among them (the Indians) a one-horned animal, which they call *kartazonon*."[5]

[4] For these and several other particulars, I am indebted to the kindness of M. Blumenbach; and I have myself also seen a living specimen of the animal in this country.

[5] *Λέγεται δὲ καὶ ζῶον ἐν τούτοις εἶναι μονόκερων, καὶ ἀπ' αὐτῶν ὀνομάζεσθαι καρτάζωνον.*

From the description he gives of it, though somewhat incorrect, it is evident that the Indian rhinoceros is the animal meant, and that Ælian drew his account from good authorities. Bochart (*Hieroz.* i. p. 934) wanted to change the above appellation into καρκαζωνον, in order to make it correspond better with the modern term, which is *kerkeddan*, or *kerkendan*, (کرکدن کرکندن ;) he has omitted to notice another form, *karkadan*, کرکدان, which would have been still more applicable. But as the word in question occurs twice, the proposed change seems too hazardous, and the termination دن or دان, *den, dán*, is too remote from ζωνος, as the letter د *d* is usually expressed in Greek by a τ. Suppose, however, we take καρταζωνος without alteration, as a word compounded of کرک *kerk*, the ancient and still surviving Persian term in use, to signify a rhinoceros, and تازان *tázán*, currens, velox, irruens? *Tázán*[6] is the participle of تازیدن, to run, to fall upon; the whole expression, therefore, would designate the rhinoceros: or, if we reject the idea of ριν, "the nose," which is not implied in the word *kerk*, it would mean *fera velox*, "the swift beast;"[7] an appellation very suitable to the notions of strength and swiftness, popularly attributed to this animal. From the distinguished situation the unicorn occupies in the entrance of the palace of Persepolis, it might perhaps have been a symbol of strength and activity, as the martichora was of courage and wisdom.

With regard to the *winged unicorn*, I must confess the appellation appears to me inappropriate.[8] This fabulous animal is also noticed by Le Bruyn (tab. 158). It is, however, perfectly distinct from the unicorn, by the circumstance of its being represented with the head of a lion and the body of a griffin: the only thing it has in common with the former is the horn. It is consequently a monster of a peculiar kind, which the fanciful imagination of the sculptor

[6] The long â in Persian occasionally sounds something like the Greek ω.

[7] The true meaning of *Kerk* is lost. It also denotes a species of goat with red hair; a large kind of eagle, *avis magna quæ elephantem tollit*, (the *Roc* of the Arabian Nights,) and also *Hylactor* (see Cast. Lex. Hept.): the latter meaning is probably the same as *Molossus*. Perhaps the word may signify, generally, *bellua fera*, θηρ.

[8] [It has since been altered. HEEREN.]

has furnished with the head of a lion, the horn of a unicorn, and the figure of a griffin; it is in fact only another way of representing a griffin, and perhaps a more suitable designation for it would be, the *lion-headed griffin*.

12. A large tree, (proceeds Ctesias,) which distils an odoriferous oil, is called in the Indian language, κάρπιον, but in Greek, μυροῤῥόδα, i. e. "unguent-roses." (Ctes. §. 28.) This word seems to be compounded of کار *kâr*, faciens, and بوي *bui*, odor suavis; *karbui*, then, suave olens, expresses the Greek μυροῤῥόδα, not, indeed, literally, but yet as far as the sense is concerned. *Kâr*, the participle of *kerden*, forms several compound words, mostly, however, as an affix, though sometimes also as a præfix; for example, کار ساز *kâr sâz*, faciens concordiam. The expression بوي كردن *bui kerden*, is still generally applied to perfumes. Reland (p. 215) considers the tree in question to be the cinnamon, which is called in Persian قرفه *kirfah:* the Singhalese call it *koredhu*, whence *kirfah* and *karpion* have been derived. *Kirfah*, however, is properly an Arabic word, from the root قرف *karafa*, decorticavit, and denotes the peeled bark of the cinnamon tree, cassia, etc. Paulinus à S. Bartolomæo, (in his dissertation, *De Antiquitate et Affinitate Linguæ Zendicæ, Samscrdamicæ et Germanicæ*, Paduæ, 1798, 4to, p. 49,) remarks, that the Sanscrit name of the cinnamon tree, is *karuva*, of the bark, *karuvatoli*. The first of these words has certainly some sort of resemblance to Karpion, and may possibly be the very word Ctesias meant to express. The signification, however, of κάρπιον is not mentioned.

13. Lastly, Ctesias (§. 30) describes a certain kind of mineral spring, called by the Indians, βαλλάδη, which he interprets to mean ὠφελίμη, "useful" or "wholesome." With this I shall compare the Persian ولا or ولاد, *velâd* or *velâ*, "eminent," "strong," "mighty," though it appears to have formerly signified, "excellent;" as, according to Castell, the word is also applied to a sort of rich silk stuffs. Reland (p. 211) cites بلاد *belâd*, laudatus, because what is useful deserves praise. According to Father Paulino, *ballam*, in Sanscrit, means "water," and *nallada*, "good:" in this case, the word

βαλλάδη, would be properly Indian, though expressed in a very concise manner.[9]

In the Appendix to the *Excerpta* of Ctesias, (§. 32,) which is only found in the MS. of Munich, and probably does not belong to that writer, mention is made of an Ethiopian animal, under the name of κροκόττας, which is interpreted in Greek by κυνολύκος. According to the description, it should be the hyæna, but then the word is not Ethiopic, as might be supposed; for the proper name in that language is *Tekula*. I am almost inclined to look for κροκόττας in the Persian كرك which usually means a wolf, and كوت which signifies "lame," pedibus infirmus. "Lame wolf," would be no improper designation, as applied to the hyæna, for the Arabian naturalists always describe that animal with an infirm gait, for which reason he has the epithet of العرجا *Al-àrjâ*, or the "lame." (See Bruce's Travels, vol. v. p. 113.)

From the above comparisons, which are certainly not all of them far-fetched or strained, it would seem, that the words cited by Ctesias, as Indian, are in fact of Persian origin, or nearly related thereto. There are, besides, several Indian glosses to be found in Hesychius,[10] and other writers, to which the same observation will apply. One example from the former may suffice: Hesychius writes, Μαὶ, μέγα, Ἰνδοί; now μαὶ, being pronounced in later times like the word *may*, is evidently the Persian مه *mih*, which signifies "*great*." In Sanscrit, it is *mah*, or *mahe* [maha]. Here then we meet with a sound more nearly allied to the Persian than the Indian.

How are we to explain this phenomenon? can we suppose that Ctesias knowingly gave out these Persian words for Indian, or that he really mistook them for such? The last is the opinion of Reland, according to whom, (p. 209, 211, 219,) the Greeks and Romans, owing to their ignorance of

[9] *Balada*, in Sanscrit, would mean, "giving strength;" which might very well allude to the sanitary virtues of the spring, but whether such an epithet ever occurs is another question. Trans.

[10] They have already been in part collected and explained by Reland; but a great many still remain for future discussion. Some of them, however, are pure Indian, as for instance, ἀναγκης, ὄρνεόν τι Ἰνδικὸν, which, according to Father Paulino, is the Sanscrit for a "bird:" again, παταλα, Sanscrit, *pattala*, a "commercial town," etc.

the countries and languages, very often confounded the latter, and mistook Persian words for Indian. This may certainly apply very well to the Greeks of later times, but Ctesias, who resided so long in Persia, cannot but have been perfectly able to distinguish the language of that country from the Indian, while, on the other hand, it is impossible to conceive for a moment, that he seriously meant to deceive his readers. We may easily allow certain words not expressly mentioned as Indian, in the Excerpta, to be Persian names of Indian objects or productions; most of them, however, are accompanied with the remark, that they are Indian, though, nevertheless, they have a Persian sound, as in the case of σιπταχορα, καρπιον, etc. The more probable supposition is, that in the northern parts of India, which Ctesias is particularly describing, a dialect of the Persian was spoken; and perhaps we might infer as much from the ancient tradition which represented Bokhara and the countries on the Oxus, to have been colonized from Istakhar or Persepolis, that is, admitting the report to extend so far back. But without laying too much stress on this tradition, we must bear in mind that the Sanscrit, which is the parent source of all the Indian dialects, and was certainly at one time a living language, and, according to all appearances, current in Northern India, is most intimately connected with the Persian, both in matter and form, as Father Paulino has shown in the Treatise already alluded to. And when we reflect on the influence which emigration, the admixture of different tribes, and a variety of other circumstances, occurring through a space of so many hundred years, must unavoidably have exercised on the languages in question, we shall readily believe the affinity between them to have been still greater in ancient times.

This very resemblance, however, may possibly appear, to some of my readers, to interpose a serious objection to the truth of my comparisons; and certainly it may seem strange to look in the modern Persian for words quoted by a writer who lived upwards of two thousand years ago. In reply to this, I shall merely observe, that the Parsi dialect has, for the most part, undergone but little apparent change, and, notwithstanding the revolution of empires, and the overwhelming effect of Arabian dominion, religion, and litera-

2 B 2

ture, has, like its Occidental sister, the German, managed to preserve its radical words and primitive form. It has indeed introduced a number of Arabic terms, but its peculiar and altogether Western character has effectually secured it from essential change. Owing to this fortunate circumstance, we are enabled to detect in the modern language of Persia, most of the Persian words occurring in Herodotus and other ancient writers, when they have not entirely disappeared in the lapse of centuries.

APPENDIX V.

On the words Pasargada and Persepolis; by Professor Tychsen.

You desire to know, my dear Sir, first, whether the words *Pasargadæ* and *Persæ*, considered as the names of a people, are etymologically distinct, or whether they are synonymous? and, secondly, whether *Pasargada* and *Persepolis*, as names of places, have a different signification? To this question I have only a few observations to offer as a reply, though, at the same time, I am obliged to confess they are nothing more than conjectural. The explanation of ancient Persian words by the help of the modern language of Persia is very frequently uncertain, owing to our ignorance respecting the pronunciation; as, for example, whether we are to say, Pāsargādæ or Păsargădæ; and, in the next place, because the modern Persian, though really descended from the ancient, has nevertheless lost a great number of words, and undergone other considerable modifications, in the course of time. In many cases, therefore, we are reduced to the necessity of guessing at the signification of the word in question, when not pointed out by ancient documents.

Pasargadæ is evidently a compound term, formed of *pasar* and *gadæ*. Of both these words, several etymologies have been furnished from the Persian, of which I shall only notice the most probable.[1] At setting out, I take it for

[1] D'Herbelot (*Bibl. Orient.* voce *Pesser*) explains *Pesser-gheda*, or *Keda*, by "sons of the house;" and goes on to say, "there is no doubt that the word *Pasargades*, which signifies 'children of the house,' or princes of the blood royal of Persia, was corrupted by the Greek writers from *Pessergheda*." I must be allowed to doubt the correctness of this etymology: for although *Pesser* certainly does mean "son," yet the idea of "royal house," is not contained in the word *keda*; which does not signify "house," in the acceptation

granted that both *a*'s are short, because there is no word having the *a* long (ا) that will furnish any tolerable etymology.

To begin, then, with Gada; which I consider to be the same as the Persian *Kedeh* or *Kadeh*, (كده) signifying "place," "abode," etc., and often joined to substantives, in order to form a compound word; as, for example, *Atesh-Kedeh*, "the place of fire" or "fire-altar," *Mei-Kedeh*, "wine-house," etc.

Pasar may either be compared to the well-known Persian word بزرك *buzurk*, "great," "magnificent," "powerful;" in which case the final letter, being repeated in the second member of the compound, will suffer elision; or, still more probably, with برز *bezer*, "light," "splendour," "ray." In the first case, therefore, *buzurk-kedeh* would signify, "the place" or "abode of the great;" in the second, *bezer-kedeh* would be, "the abode" or "country of light."

Upon comparing the proper name *Persæ* with the last-mentioned word, we discover a very striking affinity of signification. According to Anquetil Du Perron, *Pares*, (پارس) in the Zend language, means, "pure," "brilliant," an appellation which, in a physical sense, applies very well to Fars, or Persia Proper, as enjoying an ever clear sky; and is equally appropriate in a religious point of view, as alluding to the introduction of Magianism, the religion of light and purity. Even in the modern Persian, the word *Parsa* (پارسا) means "pure," though it is more correctly employed in a moral sense, as denoting "holy," "pious." *Persæ*, therefore, as the name of a people, would signify "the inhabitants of *Pars*," or, according to the etymology just given, "the country of light;" and *Pasargadæ*, as a patronymic formed by the Greeks from Pasargada, would have precisely the same meaning, that is, provided we are right in our comparison.

With regard to the second question, viz. whether Pasar-

of "family," but solely in that of "abode," "habitation." Besides, *Pesserkeda* would more correctly mean "house of children;" to say nothing of the fact, that it was not the whole tribe of the Pasargades, but only a part of it, the family of the Achæmenides, which consisted of princes. D'Herbelot seems to have had in his mind the peculiar acceptation of the French word *maison*, *maison royale*.

gada and Persepolis, considered as names of places, are of different signification; we may easily answer it by what has gone before. *Pasar*, (Bezer,) and *Pares*, mean very nearly the same thing, and *Gada*, (Kedeh,) as we have just noticed, is synonymous with πόλις. The interpretation of ancient writers who explain *Pasargada* by *castra Persarum*, is so far correct, as *Pasar* agrees in sense with *Pars*, from which the proper name *Persæ* was derived.

In drawing the above comparisons, the Greek σ has been rendered by the Persian ز (*ze*,) not altogether in conformity, I must confess, with the general rule laid down for comparing languages, according to which the *sigma* of the Greeks should correspond with the Arabic *sin* (س). But the Greeks and Romans frequently expressed the ز of Persian words by an *s*; for instance, the name *Pyroses*, occurring in Ammian, (lib. xix. 3,) is undoubtedly the Persian فیروز *Firuz*, "victor," as Ammian himself explains it; the case is the same with Hormisdas, Isdegertes, etc. The liberty I have taken may therefore be justified by analogy; and the interchange of the letters *b* and *p* can present no difficulty whatever.

Supposing the Greeks to have written the word incorrectly, as they very often did, when translating a foreign term into their own language, we might bring *Pasargada* and *Persepolis* into still closer affinity with each other, merely by a slight transposition of the letter *r*, as *Parsagada;* the name would signify "place of the Persians," and be exactly equivalent to *Persepolis*. Reland (Diss. viii. *De Vet. Ling. Pers.* p. 213,) has already adopted this reading, which he found in Curtius, (v. 6,) who correctly writes *Persagada*. Explanations, however, which render it necessary to alter the original word, are for that very reason to be rejected, particularly in a case where it so often occurs as the one in question; and, besides, very little dependence is to be placed on the authority of a writer so comparatively modern as Curtius, who most likely wrote *Persagada*, purely and solely for the sake of etymology. I am of opinion, too, that after what has been already observed, the emendation of Reland is altogether unnecessary.[2]

[2] The word *Gada* may also be compared with the Persian *Tshadar*, which

The proposed change, however, is not so bold as that adopted by several modern geographers, who have written the word "*Pasagarda*," which has found its way even into our manuals, and is so spelled in the latest map of Persia. For this reading I can discover no other kind of authority than a fancied resemblance in termination to such words as *Tigranocerta*, *Artagicerta*, and others, compounded of the Aramæan *Carta*, which means "city." The comparison, however, is inadmissible, because, as the Persian language belongs to an essentially different family from the Aramæan dialects, it would be absurd to attempt illustrating the former by the help of the latter.

You yourself, my dear Sir, will be best able to judge, whether Pasargada and Persepolis, on account of this affinity between the two names, are to be considered as synonymous appellations of one and the same place, and how far our geographers are authorized in placing them nearly a whole degree apart from each other. You will perhaps find that the *Pasargadæ* of Herodotus are in fact the Persepolitans, whom that writer distinguishes from the other Persian tribes, on account of the reigning dynasty of the Achæmenides being descended from them; of which latter appellation I may remark, in passing, that it scarcely contains a single syllable common to that of the fabulous Jemshid.

signifies "tent," or "camp;" and thus Persagada would mean precisely "*Castra Persarum*." But we shall scarcely meet with an example of the hard sound *tsh* (tshim) being ever expressed by γ; to say nothing of the omission of the final letter *r*. Father Paulino compares the Indian *paser*, "puer," "a young man," and *cada*, "a plain," so that the whole word would signify "*the field of youths*."

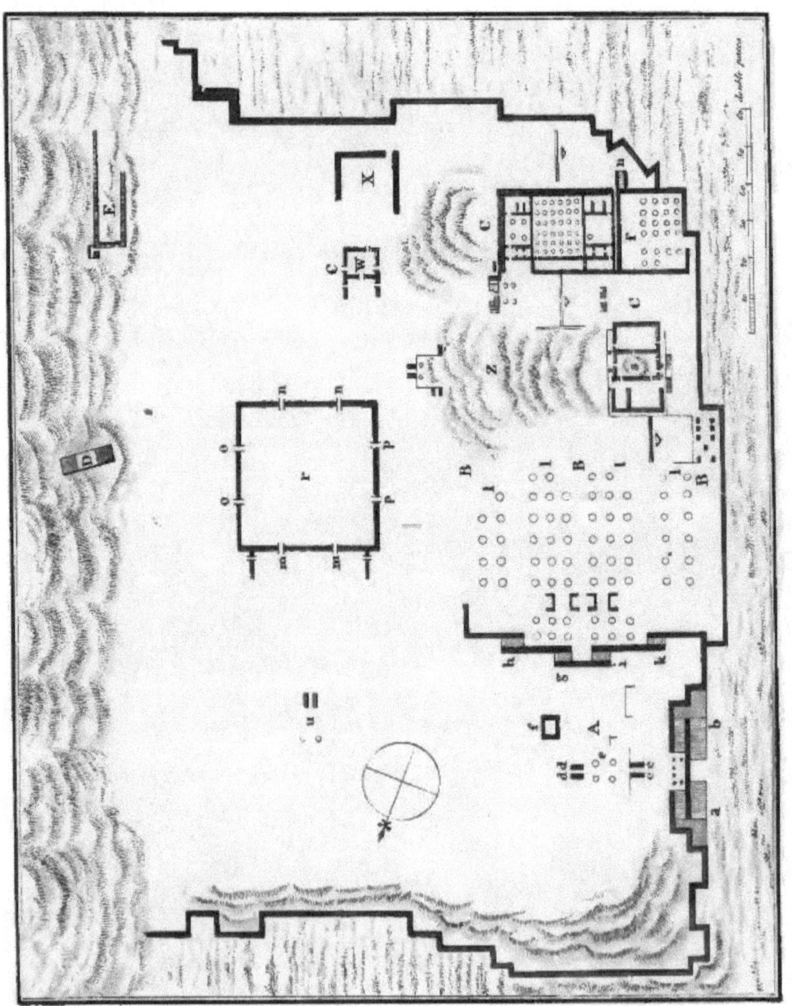

GROUND PLAN OF THE RUINS OF CHEHEL - MINAR OR PERSEPOLIS.

APPENDIX VI.

Some observations on Herder's Persepolis.[1]

In my treatise on Persepolis, I have purposely refrained altogether from alluding to Herder's publication on the same subject, because nothing would be gained by a repetition of what had been said before; without at the same time presuming to assert, that my own investigations have been of any considerable service to this branch of literature. We have each of us travelled by different roads; and it would not, therefore, be uninteresting to know how far these have conducted us to the same point.

Herder rests his illustrations on Eastern tradition, such as it is found in modern Asiatic writers, or as it has been orally communicated from one generation to another. Thus he supposes the buildings of Chihel Minar to be the palace of Jemshid, on the walls of which there is an allegorical representation of the actions and government of this king, without, however, seeking to establish, from the hypothesis, either that the edifice is really the work of Jemshid, or that it belongs to his age. Moreover, his commentary is confined to the building, an explanation of the tombs being reserved for some future period. I, on the contrary, have begun with the latter, and, agreeably to my plan, have not relied on tradition, or modern testimony, but simply and solely on the evidence of contemporary writers. This, I am ready to allow, has not led me to any such positive re-

[1] It has been announced, that in the new edition of Herder's works, his treatise on Persepolis would be corrected and enlarged. The author regrets his having been unable to consult this edition, though it is probable that Herder's principal notions continue the same.

sults as those of my predecessor; and I have been obliged to content myself with determining in general terms the date of the buildings, and the use for which they were probably intended. · Accordingly, I think I have succeeded in proving that they must be referred to the period of the Persian empire, and that the building itself, as the residence and place of sepulture of the Persian kings, was considered in the light of a sanctuary, and held to be the chief place in the kingdom.

Upon comparing these two results together, it will easily be perceived, that they are not in any degree opposed to each other. For when I maintain in general that the representations sculptured on the monuments of Chihel Minar are those of a happy reign and brilliant court, according to Eastern notions, I cannot but consider it very probable that the ideal picture given of Jemshid's reign in the Zendavesta, formed their ground-work; and the rather as they so frequently afford traces of Zoroaster's religion. But I could not bring forward this opinion without infringing the severe rules of criticism which I had imposed on myself.

Supplement.

The further illustrations of Persepolis promised by Herder, did not appear till after his death, and the publication of the second edition of my work; they will be found in his first volume, which is devoted to philosophy and history, under the title of Persepolitan letters addressed to several learned men; one of them being particularly addressed to myself. Whoever is acquainted with my labours, will soon perceive that the greatest part of these letters, even where I am not mentioned by name, are written against me, and that not unfrequently with a degree of harshness which might appear surprising in a writer who talks of urbanity in every page, if we were not prepared for this by his earlier polemical writings. I first defended myself against his representations in the *Intelligenzblatt der Allgem. Litter. Zeitung*, 1806, No. 17; and afterwards more at large in a treatise which I read in the year 1808 to the Göttingen Society of Sciences, (*Eruditorum conamina ad explicanda urbis Persepolis monumenta censuræ subjecta,)* and which was only published in an abridged form, *(Göttinger Ge-*

lehrte Anzeiger, 1809, No. 4,) as it did not seem proper to be included in the general collection of commentaries, which ought to have something higher for its object than the disputes of the learned. If the aggressions of which I complain were not made in a periodical paper, I should rest satisfied with what I have so often professed, that if my works cannot defend themselves, they do not merit any protection from me. But as the allegations in question are placed at the head of Herder's works, they will not be so easily consigned to oblivion as the other polemical writings; and under these circumstances, I consider myself bound to offer something in reply.

In my opinion, a monument of antiquity is to be regarded as the public property of succeeding ages, and every one is at liberty to exercise his ingenuity in explaining it, so far as it is involved in obscurity. Consequently each individual may have a way of his own, and whatever rank he holds in the list of illustrators, his claim to originality is as good as that of the very first, whether or not he attains to the same results.

Such is the relation in which I stand with respect to Herder. Throughout the whole course of my researches, I have nothing in common with him; I have followed a path of my own, and have drawn my information from other sources than his; my right to my own work is therefore incontestable. The duty also which I owed him as my predecessor, has been fulfilled by explaining in the last appendix the plan of his commentary and my own, without contradicting him. Even supposing that I carried the interpretation no further than he had done himself, the merit of having confirmed those results by a critical examination would be due to me; that is, so far as any merit will be ascribed to such inquiries. Was I, in this case, liable to any charge of plagiarism from Herder, and had he any reason to say that he would not be deprived of the fruit of his researches? Who wished to deprive him of any part of his merit?

But does the interpretation, as Herder represents, remain where he left it? The public are in a condition to judge; I fear no comparison, and will confine myself to the following observation: Herder, in his Persepolis, has given only a general explanation; he says that the palace of Jemshid was the palace of the Persian government, on the walls of which the king and his court are represented. This is also my opinion, but have I gone no further than this general assertion, which occurs to the mind naturally of itself? Have I not entered into details in my interpretation, which is indeed its peculiar character? Moreover, as Herder has not even once alluded to the tombs, or to the figures represented on them, should not my explanation of the latter, and the proofs by which I have ascertained the personages to whom they belong, and consequently the general epoch at which they were built, be considered as belonging entirely to myself? Is this not to advance the question beyond the point where Herder left it? I have here intentionally omitted to notice the inscriptions, as it is my purpose to return to them hereafter.

But I am again reproached, (p. 191, 192,) for not having gone sufficiently into details. I ought to have described the nations represented on the great relief one by one, and have illustrated them by a comparison with the list of satrapies in Herodotus. It will readily be believed, that a writer who has devoted several months to an investigation of Persepolis, with Herodotus constantly before him, has not left this undone. It has, however, led me to conclude that no certain result is to be derived from this course; on which account I have omitted to mention it. The attempt has been renewed in the present edition, but without my having reason to congratulate myself on its greater success.

What Herder is the least able to pardon me, is the use I have made of contemporary Greek writers, in order to the illustration of Persepolis. "As they have not mentioned Persepolis by name, we ought not to take them for our authority, particularly in fixing the age of the building; the edifice itself must inform us of this" (p. 189). But does not Ctesias describe the tombs, Xenophon the court and body-guard, and Diodorus (from later sources) the palace? Whence can we obtain purer and more certain intelligence than the accounts of contemporary writers? Perhaps the traditions which Herder follows? This assertion is a very singular one, and serves to show into what absurdities the love of contradiction will sometimes bring a man. For it has never yet come into the mind of any one, to maintain seriously, that popular traditions, after the lapse of two thousand years, have more weight than the accounts of contemporary authors. Are we then, according to this system, to receive confidently all that the Orientals are pleased to advance concerning Solomon and Alexander the Great? Besides this, a curious circumstance occurs with respect to these Persian traditions. According to Herder himself, (p. 213,) the Persian tradition relative to Jemshid originated in the monuments of Persepolis. Thus the tradition was formed from the monuments, and, conversely, the monuments are to be explained by the tradition. This is criticism indeed, with a vengeance!

It appeared probable to me that the arts amongst the Persians, and particularly that of architecture, may have had a Bactrian origin. At the same time I have said, as clearly as I could, that I considered Bactria as the eastern part of the Median kingdom, with which, according to the Zendavesta, it was incorporated; so that this expression can mean nothing more than that the Persians borrowed their arts from the Medes, as they did their religion, and civilization in general. Herder, on the contrary, derives their architecture successively from the Egyptians, (p. 145,) which he retracts in another place (p. 153); then from the Greeks, then from the Babylonians, though he afterwards says it was not Babylonian (p. 189); and lastly from the Medes: "it was," says he, "an Egyptico-Grecian art, regulated after the Medo-Persian manner" (p. 167). Is this intelligible? And how can we answer a writer who so frequently contradicts himself?

After this, (p. 158,) it is objected to me, that I have named Persepolis the residence of the Persian kings after their death. Is not, however, such an expression justifiable, when I have proved, as Herder himself cannot deny, that the kings were buried here; that, agreeably to the Persian custom, the servants of the dead kings attended them hither, where they were obliged to remain; and that this place was by no means the usual residence of the sovereigns, but that they went to it at certain seasons only, for the performance of certain sacred rites? Have I ever called it a Necropolis, a city of the dead, (or rather a mere cemetery,) as Herder imputes to me? Have I not, on the contrary, said expressly that it was considered by the Persians as the capital of their empire, *caput regni?*

I had advanced a conjecture that the name of Persepolis is a translation of Pasargada, and that they may both have had originally the same signification, although the language of a later period distinguished between them. A greater Orientalist, who understands the Persian language, which Herder did not, has confirmed my notion by etymological proofs. (See above, Appendix V.) But Herder informs me that the word Pasargada signified assembly, camp of the Persians; and that every camp gave rise to a Pasargada (p. 156, 159). The first of these notions I published myself, and before him. Could then Herder have forgotten in the warmth of his zeal, what he had previously read in my own work? With regard to the second, I acknowledge that wherever the Persians encamped, there was a Persian camp; though I deny that every such place bore afterwards the name of Pasargada. I am acquainted with only one Pasargada, and Herder has failed to prove that there were more places of the same name.

If there is any one merit which I have endeavoured, as far as possible, to communicate to my writings, and especially to the present work, it is that of the utmost perspicuity. My experience, however, has brought me to the conclusion, that though it may be possible enough to secure my being understood by the generally educated reader; an attempt to satisfy the critical scholar is but labour in vain. My conjecture respecting the original identity of Persepolis and Pasargada has been the motive for inducing an esteemed French writer, Sainte-Croix, (*Examen critique des historiens d'Alexandre-le-Grand*, p. 892,) to accuse me of having denied the existence of Persepolis. And this I am accused of, who have actually been engaged in illustrating the monuments of this very Persepolis! Another writer, St. Julien de Ruet, (*Tableau du commerce des anciens,* vol. ii. p. 525,) who follows Sainte-Croix, absolutely complains, and with every appearance of sincerity, of my defending such paradoxical assertions!

Another objection of Herder's is drawn from my explanation of the fabulous animals. I have taken my illustrations from Ctesias, who has described them exactly as they are on the reliefs, or only with such variations as may evidently be included in the circle of this species of mythology. If this be the case, and the Indica of Ctesias contain only such traditions of Eastern Asia as had found their way to the Persians; what can be excepted against this method of interpretation? It seems obviously a better proceeding than to borrow our lights from Ferdousi, who confessedly used the traditions which had been formed from the monuments of Persepolis. Herder himself has been unable to deny that the griffin and unicorn appear exactly the same on these monuments as Ctesias has described them; and with respect to the wonderful animal with a human head, I have said that I consider it to be the same as the *martichora* of Ctesias, which, as a quadruped with a human head, agrees with it in its essential character; though, at the same time, I have not overlooked the differences which exist in the minor details. According to Ctesias, the term martichora signifies *destroyer of men.* Hence I have explained this animal as being the symbol of strength and military courage; and I considered it a very appropriate emblem for placing before the gates of a palace, which was the central point of an empire gained by conquest. Is not all this in strict keeping? Is it not consistent? Moreover, the etymological explanation of Ctesias has been also confirmed by M. Tychsen, from the Persian, who adds, that at this day the Persians are accustomed to name a hero and great warrior, *merdemkhor.* If this does not at the same time confirm my own explanation, I am ignorant what does.

With respect to the figures of the kings engaged in single combat with the fabulous animals, I said, that these probably represented the king as a bold and successful hunter; that this appeared to me the simplest and most suitable interpretation, because it is conformable to the spirit of the East, where hunting is considered as an exercise preparatory to war, where the great hunter shares the glory of a hero; and because Darius is thus distinguished in the inscription reported by Strabo. This I advanced, as what appeared to me the most probable supposition, without, however, rejecting Herder's idea, that these animals were the representations of subjugated nations and kingdoms. But here also I am in the wrong. It would be impossible to understand how a writer who thinks he has caught the spirit of the East more than all others, who has in all probability read the Cyropædia, as well as the Travels of Chardin and Bernier, can deny that hunting is here regarded in the light which I have stated, were it not to be accounted for by the spirit of contradiction. Moreover, I said in a former part of my work, that I considered my conjecture only as the most probable which has been offered. Accordingly I have now changed it for another, without adopting that of Herder (vol. i. p. 186).

For the attempt which has been made to clear up the inscriptions, the public are not indebted to me, but to M. Grotefend. The readers will be the best judges, whether this interpretation continues where Herder left it. No objection of any importance against M. Grotefend's method has hitherto come to my knowledge: on the contrary, the Orientalists of Germany and France have received it with approbation. In his Persepolis, Herder has left this subject untouched. In his Persepolitan letters, he begins by expressing a high admiration of the method of interpretation followed by the late M. Tychsen, of Rostock. But, unfortunately for him, this impartial scholar retracted his own, after he became acquainted with that of M. Grotefend. I forbear all further observations on the subject, as they will naturally occur to the reader of themselves.

In this reply I have confined myself to the monuments of Persepolis. What Herder says of the age of Zoroaster, whom he makes contemporary with Darius, and of the Persian religion, would furnish matter for long discussion. But both our writings lie before the public, and I have no desire to repeat what has been said of me. It is indeed no agreeable task to engage in literary polemics with a man whose deserved reputation I have no wish to lessen; nor should I have been willing to disturb him if he had not first begun this dispute.

APPENDIX VII.

Additions to page 448 of the first volume. On the most ancient Navigation of the Persian Gulf.

In my inquiries into the commerce of the Phœnicians and Babylonians, I have, as I think, sufficiently proved, that these people navigated the Persian Gulf, and that they maintained by its means a considerable traffic with India, either directly, or through the intervention of other nations. Some publications which have since come into my hands have given me occasion to subjoin the following remarks on the subject.

I have already shown that the Phœnicians possessed some colonies in the Persian Gulf, amongst which I reckon the Bahrein islands, named Tyrus and Aradus, after two of their largest cities. A modern traveller, Dr. Seetzen, (see his Letter in Zach's Monthly Correspondence for Sept. 1813,) has remarked, as I had indeed myself, that there were traces of Phœnician appellations in the names of several places in the Persian Gulf; from which Dr. Seetzen concludes, that the Phœnicians had several colonies in the islands and on the neighbouring shores; and this conclusion he employs in explaining the journey to Ophir. According to him, the length of the voyage may be easily accounted for, by the supposition, that the Phœnician ships sailed along the coast from one colony to another, for the purpose of traffic, before they returned to the place from whence they set out. Moreover, Edrisi expressly mentions an Ophir in the region of Bahrein, (there is another in the country of Omân,) beyond which, he says, there is a place named El-Harrah, which would seem to be the ancient Gerrha. All this is extremely probable. As soon as the Phœnicians participated in the trade of the Persian Gulf, they could not dispense with colonies in this; and necessity obliged them

VOL. II. 2 C

to found several on the two shores and in the islands. At the same time this confirms my opinion respecting Ophir, and that it did not imply any one single place, but generally the southern emporia of Arabia Felix, Africa, and perhaps India, so far as the ancients were acquainted with it. This explanation is favoured by analogy, as the appellations of distant places and countries are usually vague amongst all nations; and much perplexity has been introduced into ancient geography by attempts to ascertain them; as, for example, in the case of Thule. The explanation is also agreeable to history, as it discovers to us, why several Ophirs are found in those different countries, and at the same time enables us to account for the duration of the voyage, and the nature and variety of the merchandise. Lastly, it is agreeable to etymology, as Ophir in the Arabic language signifies, "rich countries." (See Tychsen, *De Commerciis Hebræorum, in Commentat. Soc. Gött.* vol. xvi. p. 164.) Thus, I consider Tarshish to be a general appellation for the countries with which the ancients were acquainted in remote parts of the West; for Spain in particular. The more recent opinion of Gosselin, with which Vincent concurs, (ii. p. 638,) urges that the expression, *ships of Tarshish*, should be rendered generally, ships of the sea, and this notion is favoured by Luther. But in the Second Book of Chronicles, (xix. 21,) there is express mention of ships going to Tarshish, ללכות תרשיש; which the interpretation in question would suppose to be interpolated. (Tychsen, l. c.) Should we explain the Hebrew Tarshish by the word *sea*, this will not affect the existence of the Phœnician Tartessus, as a colony in Spain, which is sufficiently known from the authority of Greek and Roman authors.

Besides the Phœnicians, the Babylonians or Chaldæans navigated the Persian Gulf. The arguments which have been already adduced appear to me sufficient to establish the fact; Dr. Vincent, however, has led me to remark the existence of other proof. (*Peripl.* ii. p. 356.) He supposes that the destruction of Tyre by Nebuchadnezzar had for its object the extension of Indian commerce to the Persian Gulf and Babylon, and from thence, through the empire of this king, to Damascus and Syria, by way of Palmyra. At the same time he quotes a fragment of Abydenus, (in Scaliger, *De Emendat. Temp.* Notæ ad Beros. p. xii.,) concerning the works designed by Nebuchadnezzar, near Babylon, according to which he made two canals, the Harmacales and Aracanus, constructed large sluices, confined the waters of the Tigris by a dam, and built the city of Tenedon, as a defence against the incursions of the Arabs. This city of Tenedon, above the mouth of the Pasitigris, was a considerable emporium; and as lately as the age of Nearchus afforded a market for Arabian and Indian productions.

APPENDIX VIII.

On the Voyages of the Phœnicians and Carthaginians to Britain, and their settlements on the coast.

In my disquisition upon the voyages of the Carthaginians to the Tin-islands, from not being aware of the existence of any others in the neighbourhood, I had identified the *Insulæ Œstrymnides* with the Scilly group, though, at the same time, I could not conceal from myself the difficulties connected with this hypothesis. A critical notice of my work, inserted in the Metropolitan Magazine for January, 1832, and for which I feel very much obliged to the writer, has since pointed out the inadmissibility of my assumption; and from a more accurate knowledge of the locality than I could pretend to, the Reviewer has been enabled to place the whole subject in a better light, and I am, therefore, anxious to submit his explanation to the reader. Before we proceed, however, I shall first of all endeavour to show how far we are justified in supposing the Phœnicians, and their colonists the Carthaginians, to have extended their voyages as far as Britain, and to have formed settlements on the coast: in doing this, we must be careful to make a due discrimination between what has real historical testimony for its basis, and that which depends on conjectural probability alone.

In the portion of my work relating to the Carthaginians, (see African Nations, Appendix vi.,) I have already cited the authority which, as connected with this question, must be looked upon as the first and most important, being no less than that of the Carthaginian commander Himilco, to whom the charge of the expedition destined for the British shores was intrusted; and though it comes to us through an indirect channel, we must still be content to receive it as entitled to our earliest consideration.

The Carthaginians fitted out two grand simultaneous expeditions for the purpose of planting colonies, and pushing their discoveries further: one of them, under Hanno, was destined for the western coasts of Africa; the other, under Himilco, for the corresponding shores of Europe. Both commanders had their respective adventures commemorated on a public monument, set up in one of the principal temples of Carthage. The account of Hanno's expedition has fortunately been preserved in a Greek translation, already noticed in the volume on the Carthaginians (App. vi.); where it was shown, that the account in question is not a detailed narrative of Hanno's adventures, or even an extract of any such narrative, as has been generally supposed, but, as the title itself proves, "a public memorial;" in fact, a mere inscription, such as the Carthaginians were accustomed to inscribe on public monuments in commemoration of some great national undertaking. What has been said of Hanno's voyage will also apply to that of Himilco. Unfortunately, however, but little information has come down to us respecting the latter; and that little is contained in the fragments of a poem by Avienus, entitled, "Ora Maritima;" which, as far as they relate to this subject, will be found in the Appendix above referred to.

These fragments supply us with the following data:—

1. The Phœnicians had, in very early times, extended their voyages from Gades along the coasts of Europe.

2. The Carthaginians did not merely follow in their wake; but had also founded a series of independent colonies beyond the pillars of Hercules, along the shores of Spain, from whence they sailed still further to the country where tin and lead were to be procured.

3. This was also the destination of Himilco's voyage:

but whether his expedition consisted of a single ship, or of a whole squadron, is uncertain; probably the latter was the case, as it is known to have been with respect to the undertaking of Hanno.

4. The extent of the voyage itself was the Insulæ Œstrymnides, which Himilco reached after a four months' sail.

5. These islands lay contiguous to the shores of Albion, so near, in fact, that the communication between them and the main-land was kept up by means of boats made of leather:[1] they were also within two days' sail of the "Holy Island," inhabited by the Hiberni.

6. The coasts of Albion, opposite to this island, were inhabited by a people whose chief occupation was commerce; for which purpose they traded thither in their canoes.

All this is clearly deducible from the passages cited in the above-mentioned Appendix; but still the original question recurs—which are the Insulæ Œstrymnides?

Unacquainted with the existence of any others, I had set them down as the Scilly Islands, to which the Reviewer objects, that such a determination is out of the question, they being nothing more than bare rocks, at too great a distance from the main-land, and situate in too stormy a sea to admit of being approached in canoes. On the other hand, the opinion of the Reviewer points to St. Michael's Mount, as the probable situation of the Œstrymnides, which is accessible from the main at ebb tide, and where also there are traces of other small islands, now submerged. I will, however, give the whole passage in the words of the writer himself:—"We are of opinion, that the present St. Michael's Mount is intended, which, at low water, is joined to the main-land, and where tin is found in two ways, in stream works, and by mining. The Scilly Isles are mere rocks: St. Michael's Mount, it is true, is not more of itself; but we know that

[1] Boats formed of wicker work, covered with oil-cloth or leather, are still in common use throughout Wales, and particularly on the Wye and Severn, where they are termed *Coracles;* they are not much bigger than a moderately sized basket, and are only made to hold one person, who also carries it about with him, and makes use of it, as occasion may require. The public papers, however, lately noticed an occurrence of shipwreck on the western coast of Ireland, from which it appears that boats of this description are also used on the open sea, and are large enough to accommodate upwards of half a dozen people, having been employed in the above instance to convey the survivors to land. TRANS.

there was other land, perhaps isolated also, in Mount's Bay, and since submerged. In those days we do not believe tin was found in mines, whence it is now taken in the state of ore: it was in all probability collected from the stream works, in the form which is denominated grain-tin. These stream works are horizontal excavations, open to the earth's surface, whence the tin is obtained by washing. These stream works do not require machinery to descend into them, or to drain them. Pickaxes of holm, boxwood, and hartshorns, have been often found in them, the instruments of a rude people and age. May not Œstrymnon in Avienus mean the Lizard? The bay and isles, Mount's Bay? Then is all accounted for."

With this explanation I fully concur, as the most probable that has yet been offered; for it not only removes the difficulty, but perfectly coincides also with the customs of the Carthaginians, whose usual plan it was to make choice of some small island contiguous to the shore, as an emporium for their merchandise, of which the Cerne islands, off the coast of Libya, are an instance. I take then St. Michael's Mount, with the islets formerly surrounding it, to be the Insulæ Œstrymnides; Mount's Bay to be the Sinus, and Cape Lizard the Promontory, mentioned by Avienus. These islands are situate on the coast of Cornwall, the native country of tin and lead. I do not see, however, why the means of obtaining the metal should be limited to merely trenching the soil, as in the case of the stream works above noticed. The Phœnicians possessed considerable skill in mining operations, which it is not likely they would have failed to exercise in the case before us. The only serious difficulty seems to consist in Ierna's being placed at a distance of only two days' sail from the spot; but perhaps it would be unreasonable to expect very minute accuracy in such fragments as those we have alluded to.

The above explanation agrees also with the account given by Diodorus, (i. p. 347,) who mentions, that "the inhabitants of the British continent were very skilful in obtaining the tin, which they afterwards conveyed to a small island, called Fetis, accessible from the shore, dryshod, when the tide is out:" this was the mart where the foreign merchants carried on their trade, and took in their cargoes.

We may receive it then as an historical fact, that the Phœnicians, and after them, the Carthaginians, extended their discoveries and their commerce from Gades to the shores of Britain, and indeed to the coast of Cornwall, as being the nearest, and at the same time the most abundant in the productions they particularly sought for. It is not expressly said that they also passed over into Ireland, nor in fact is it probable they did, because the articles they were in quest of could not be procured there. They were, however, acquainted with the island, and from their having denominated it "the holy," they must in consequence have attached to it certain ideas connected with religious worship. An intercourse between Britain and Ireland must also have existed, from the fact of its being known how many days the passage thither would require.

The next question is, whether the Phœnicians or Carthaginians ever established any permanent settlements on the coasts of Britain? We know that the colonies of the latter people extended a considerable way along the western shores of the Spanish peninsula, but how far they reached in this quarter we have no positive means of ascertaining. Certainly no account on which we can rely of their having founded colonies in Britain, has come down to us. That it was the general custom, however, of the Carthaginians to form such settlements may be inferred from the account of Hanno's expedition, and that Himilco's also had a similar object in view is very probable. Moreover, Diodorus and Strabo both expressly mention, that the natives of these islands became civilized through their commerce and intercourse with foreigners.[2] No Phœnician remains of any kind, that I am aware of, have hitherto been discovered in Britain. In Ireland, however, they have still a tradition, founded on the songs of their bards,[3] that a portion of the island was once in the possession of settlers who came from Spain, and were called Phenics; these might certainly have been Phœnicians, but they might also have been of Iberian descent. Nevertheless, the tradition is altogether too vague to carry any weight in a critical examination of the question.

[2] STRABO, p. 265. We must take care, however, not to confound his Insulæ Cassiterides, which can hardly be any other than the Scilly Isles, with our Insulæ Œstrymnides.

[3] See Turner's History of England in the Middle Ages, vol. i. p. 282.

APPENDIX IX.

On the Commerce of Palmyra and the neighbouring Cities.[1]

MY object in the present essay is to illustrate the commercial history of Palmyra and the neighbouring cities of Arabia Petræa, and the eastern parts of Syria, by means of ancient monuments and inscriptions, still found existing after the lapse of centuries; at the same time, I shall not omit to notice the corresponding statements of contemporary and other writers. Before we proceed, however, to a general discussion of the subject, it will be requisite to premise a few observations relative to the situation and history of Palmyra itself.

This celebrated city, whose ruins still attest its former importance, was situated in the heart of the Syrian desert,[2] though on an isolated spot well watered, and abounding with palm trees, from which latter, in fact, it derived its name. It was distant about four or five days' journey from Damascus, and about two or three from the Euphrates. The peculiarity of its situation is well described by Pliny;[3] "Palmyra," says he, "urbis nobilis situ, divitiis soli, et aquis amœnis, vasto undique ambitu arenis includit agros, ac velut terris exempta a rerum natura privata sorte, inter duo imperia summa Romanorum Parthorumque; et prima in discordia semper utrimque cura." Palmyra, however, went into decay, and its very name was almost forgotten, in consequence of the commercial routes of the caravans from Syria to the Euphrates being altered. It was only in the

[1] From a Latin dissertation by the author, entitled *Commercia urbis Palmyræ vicinarumque urbium, ex monumentis et inscriptionibus illustrata.*

[2] Lat. 34. Long. 38° 10′ from Greenwich.

[3] PLIN. *Hist. Nat.* vi. 21.

latter part of the seventeenth century that it again came into notice; and certain English merchants established at Aleppo having had their curiosity excited by the reports of the wandering Arabs, proceeded, in the year 1691, to explore its ruins, and brought home with them copies of some of the inscriptions, which were afterwards published in the Transactions of the Royal Society.[4] From this epoch the attention of antiquaries was generally directed to these interesting remains, until, in the year 1751, two English travellers, named Bouverie and Dawkins, well furnished with the necessary means, having undertaken a journey to the Levant, with the view of exploring the remains of antiquity to be found in that neighbourhood, determined at the same time to pay a visit to Palmyra, not merely for the purpose of supplying a general description of the ruins, but also of bringing home with them an accurate delineation of the particular buildings, together with copies of the inscriptions. In effecting the latter part of their intention, they were singularly fortunate in making choice of Mr. R. Wood, himself also an antiquarian, and an architect of very great taste. Under his superintendence was published the magnificent work entitled "The Ruins of Palmyra;"[5] as well as another of similar form and subject matter, being dedicated to the scarcely less surprising remains of the city of Heliopolis, or Baalbec, in Syria.

The origin of the city Palmyra, as we learn from the Jewish records, may be referred to the tenth century before the birth of Christ, it having been built, together with some other cities in Eastern Syria, by Solomon the son and successor of David. This is expressly mentioned in the book of Kings,[6] and in the Chronicles,[7] where we read, that "Solomon built Tadmor in the wilderness;" and, according to Josephus,[8] Tadmor is the same as Palmyra. "This city," says he, "was built and strongly fortified by Solomon, who called it Thadamor, as indeed the Syrians do to this day, but the Greeks call it Palmyra." We are not indeed told

[4] *Philos. Trans.* vol. 48. An explanation of them was attempted by ABRAHAM SELLER, in his *Antiquities and History of Palmyra.* Appendix. London, 1696.

[5] *The Ruins of Palmyra, otherwise Tadmor,* London, 1753. The splendid work of CASSAS, *Voyage pittoresque en Syrie,* etc., contains drawings of the buildings, but not of the inscriptions.

[6] 1 KINGS, ix. 18. [7] 2 CHRON. viii. 4. [8] *Ant. Jud.* viii. 6.

for what particular purpose Solomon built Palmyra, but as he is said to have surrounded it with very strong fortifications, it must have been intended as a fortress or garrison town to repress the incursions of the wild roving hordes of the desert, especially as the kingdom of Judæa, in consequence of the warlike expeditions of his father David, was extended as far as the banks of the Euphrates. After the time of Solomon, we find no mention of Palmyra in Jewish history, which is not much to be wondered at, considering the revolt of Syria from the Jews, upon the erection of an independent kingdom at Damascus. Some writers, indeed, are of opinion, that the city was taken and destroyed by Nebuchadnezzar,[9] though I have not been able to ascertain on what authority they found their opinion; it is, however, so far probable that Nebuchadnezzar may have taken Palmyra, as we know that in the course of repeated expeditions against the kings of Judæa and Damascus, he at length reduced the whole of Syria into his power. After the time of Cyrus, Palmyra, from the nature of its situation, was most likely subject to the Persians; but as long as their empire lasted, I can find no mention made of it; from whence we may rightly infer, that the city was not at that period of very great importance, even though it might have served the purposes of commerce. We are equally without information as to Palmyra during the military career of Alexander, both when he took possession of Syria, after the battle of Issus, and when he marched from Egypt to the Euphrates; because, in order to avoid the desert, he proceeded straight to that river, which he crossed at Thapsacus. After the death of Alexander, upon the foundation of the empire of the Seleucidæ, the condition of Palmyra seems to have been the same with that of Syria generally; at least, in the monumental inscriptions, of which we shall have soon occasion to speak, the method of computing time by the æra of the Seleucidæ universally prevails; but we look in vain for any account of the city itself during the reign of those monarchs.

We now come down to the time of the Romans; and here, at length, the name of Palmyra seems to have become

SELLER, *loc. cit.* p. 379.

known to the Western world. For when, upon the overthrow of Mithridates, and the expulsion of his ally Tigranes from Asia Minor and Syria, those countries were reduced to the form of Roman provinces, the city of Palmyra, in all apparent probability, underwent the same fate. It was possible, however, considering its isolated situation in the middle of a desert, that it might have continued free and independent; and that this is no unwarrantable supposition appears, among other circumstances, particularly from what is reported of the conduct of M. Antony in his expedition against Palmyra, and also from what we read in the historian Pliny. For when Antony, after the defeat of Brutus and Cassius, took possession of Syria, he despatched his cavalry to plunder Palmyra, by way of remunerating them for their services, objecting against the citizens the crime of siding alternately with the Romans and Parthians, on the confines of whose territories their town was situated. The design of Antony was indeed prevented, as the inhabitants, having obtained previous intelligence, abandoned the city, and transported all their valuable effects beyond the Euphrates, on the further bank of which river they posted a guard of archers to defend the passage, so that the detachment were obliged to return empty-handed, and without even coming to an engagement. But had the Palmyrenians been under the power of Rome, I can hardly understand how they could possibly fall under the accusation imputed to them by Antony. However the case may be, this at least is sufficiently evident, that the inhabitants at this period had already acquired a great reputation for wealth. The same may be inferred, I think, from the words of Pliny: "Palmyra, privata sorte utitur inter duo imperia summa, Romanorum Parthorumque, et prima in discordia utrimque cura:" for what else can the expression "privata sorte utitur" signify, as applied to a town situated between two powerful empires, than that it was subject to neither of them? and if, upon the breaking out of quarrels between the two powers, it was the first object of both to secure the alliance of such a city as Palmyra, is it not plain that the latter must have been independent, from the very circumstance of its being free to choose which party it would side with?

Palmyra, however, seems to have undergone considerable change soon after the time of Pliny: in fact, it had now reached a period which, if we may judge from existing remains, was by far the most flourishing and prosperous the city had yet seen. ' Its still surviving monuments almost all belong to the age of the Antonines, including the reign of Adrian, and extend downwards to its final decay under the emperor Aurelian. What was the particular condition of Palmyra under Trajan the contemporary writers have omitted to notice; but as we read of its being *restored*[10] by Adrian, who was his successor, it had probably experienced some reverses of fortune, either in consequence of the wars carried on in Mesopotamia, Syria, and Arabia, during the latter part of Trajan's reign, or from the earthquakes which at that time devastated Antioch and other neighbouring cities. From the remark of Stephanus, just alluded to, it appears, that Adrian not only restored Palmyra, but that he also called it, after his own name, Adrianopolis; an appellation, however, which subsequently grew into disuse. In the inscriptions the name of Adrian occurs twice.[11] From one of them we learn, that the emperor paid a visit to the city, and was received with great pomp and magnificence. The inscription itself is in honour of a certain Malech, also called Agrippa, who, on this occasion, when the town was filled with strangers, supplied the public baths with unguents at his own expense. The other inscription is found not in the city itself, but in a neighbouring Mohammedan mosque, and commemorates the piety of a certain Abilenus of Decapolis; who, in the year of the Seleucidæ 445, (A. D. 133,) had erected an oratory to the health of Adrian, and prepared a *pulvinar*, or *lectisternium*, on the occasion. If we inquire how it came to pass that the splendour of Palmyra increased to such a degree under the Antonines, we should recollect what was the peculiar situation of the Asiatic provinces during the reign of those princes. Upon Adrian's spontaneously restoring to the Parthians the provinces which had been taken from them by Trajan, the protracted war between that people and the Romans was followed by a tranquil state of affairs, which lasted all through the reign of

[10] STEPHAN. *de Urb. sub* Παλμυρα.

[11] *Ruins of Palmyra*, No. XX., and SELLER, No. xviii. p. 363.

Antoninus Pius, and consequently for upwards of forty years. That, during this long interval of peace, as was natural, the arts also of peace were cultivated, magnificent buildings erected, and an additional stimulus given to the commercial intercourse of Asia, particularly now that a free passage was allowed to merchants travelling through the Parthian territories, has already been shown in another place.[12] In the absence of almost all the contemporary historians, a sufficient degree of light is thrown upon the subject by the monumental inscriptions of Palmyra, for enabling us to understand how that, in common with the other cities of Syria, attained such an eminent degree of splendour, owing to the vast increase of wealth consequent upon commercial speculation.

With regard to the political condition of Palmyra at this period, it is evident from the inscriptions, that the Romans allowed her such a measure of civil liberty as the "urbes αὐτονομοι" enjoyed. We hear of public decrees being issued by the senate and people, though at the same time we meet with frequent mention of the Procurator of Augustus, who, under the title of Ducenarius, superintended the collection of the imperial revenue.[13]

As long as the Parthian empire lasted, Palmyra continued faithful to the Romans, whom she frequently assisted in their wars with the former power; and, as the inscriptions testify, gave a splendid reception to the emperors Alexander Severus and Gordian,[14] when they visited the city. About this time, however, a great revolution took place in Asia; the Parthian empire, under the Arsacides, being overthrown, and the Persian dynasty of the Sassanides, under Artaxerxes, being established in its room. The latter, who boasted their descent from the ancient kings of Persia, accordingly strove to recover the provinces formerly belonging to the Persians, but now in the possession of the

[12] See Appendix, *On the sources of Ptolemy's Geography*. Joh. Malala, in his *Chronicon*, gives a list of the public buildings erected by the Roman emperors in Syria; and among them, a temple at Heliopolis, by Antoninus Pius. What is surprising, however, the name of Palmyra is not even mentioned by this writer.

[13] *Ruins of Palmyra*, No. xv. xvi. xvii. These inscriptions, however, belong to the last ages of Palmyra; that is, to the time of Gallienus.

[14] Inscript. No. ix. Compare Jul. Capitolinus *in* Gord. iii. cap. 9.

Romans, which necessarily gave rise to new and frequent wars between the two nations. On this occasion, too, the Palmyrenians, we are informed, continued for some time to side with the Romans. Their forces were commanded by Odenatus, a bold and successful general, of noble birth, and the husband of Zenobia; who, having entered into a league with Balista, the præfectus prætorii, defeated the Persian king Sapor, who had invaded the Roman provinces, drove him beyond the Euphrates, took possession of his capital, Ctesiphon, and restored the wavering power of Rome in the East.[15] In return for these services, he was associated by Gallienus in the empire, under the title of Augustus. Upon the assassination, however, of Odenatus by his kinsman Mæonius, A. D. 260, the whole face of affairs was completely changed: his widow Zenobia, a woman of masculine spirit, who administered the government in the name of her sons, neglected the interest of Rome to make an alliance with the Persians; and, with the view of founding an independent kingdom for herself, carried arms over a wide extent of country, invaded Egypt and the provinces of Asia Minor, and affected the haughty title of "Queen of the East."[7] Her success, however, was not of long duration; for Aurelian, having restored tranquillity in the West, proclaimed war against Zenobia, routed her at Emesa, besieged Palmyra, whither she had fled after the battle, and, upon her attempting to escape, took her prisoner and carried her to Rome to adorn his triumph. The consequences of this defeat were ruinous to Palmyra; the citizens having again revolted, Aurelian came back and took the place by storm, slew the inhabitants, according to his own declaration in a letter to the senate,[17] and finally razed the city to the ground, A. D. 273. There is no occasion to enlarge upon this part of our subject, as it will be found at length in the contemporary Roman historians.

With respect to the commerce of Palmyra, we shall be best able to explain its nature by referring to that of Asia in general. This has already been done in a preceding part of this work, where I have proved the commerce in

[15] Trebellius Pollio *in* Odenato, *Script. Hist. Aug.* vol. ii.
[16] Trebellius Pollio *in* Zenobia.
[17] Flavius Vopiscus *in* Aureliano, *Script. Hist. Aug.* vol. ii.

question to have been carried on by land rather than by sea, though in fact the latter kind was not wanting. The peculiar nature of Asiatic land-commerce is such that it cannot be engaged in by a single individual, or by a few only, but requires the co-operation of a numerous body of merchants travelling in company, who form what is termed a *caravan*. The length of the journey, and the savage disposition of the wild roving hordes, who subsist by plunder, would effectually deter a small unarmed band of individuals from making the attempt. Accordingly, it was usual for a numerous and well-armed body of merchants to assemble together, who elected one of their number as leader of the whole caravan. Their merchandise was transported on camels; but as neither men nor beasts of burden could possibly accomplish the whole journey without stopping, it became necessary to select certain halting-places, for rest and refreshment. Such of these places as offered favourable opportunities in point of situation for the establishment of fairs and markets, became in process of time themselves emporia of considerable trade, and, under fortunate circumstances, soon grew to such a pitch of wealth and prosperity, as to vie with the most splendid cities of the East. Such was Palmyra. Being situated on the confines of the Roman and Parthian empires, its very situation rendered it singularly adapted for all the purposes of intermediate commerce, or, as we should term it, "a carrying-trade." This species of commerce, more than any other, is calculated to insure abundant profits, as the goods that have been purchased from one set of traders are not retailed to another, but at a considerable advance upon the prime cost. A similar observation is made by Appian, who says, "Palmyreni, mercatores sunt, qui merces ab Arabibus ac Parthis coemtas, Romanis iterum vendunt."[18] How extremely profitable this kind of trade was to the Palmyrenians has been already noticed by Pliny, where he speaks of the Arabians:[19] "gentes," says he, "quæ hæc agunt, in universum sunt ditissimæ, ut apud quas maximæ Romanorum ac Parthorum opes subsistant, vendentibus quæ capiunt, nihil autem invicem redimentibus." The latter part of this remark will generally apply

[18] APPIAN, *De Bellis Civilibus*, lib. v.

[19] PLIN. *Hist. Nat.* vi. 31.

also to the commercial intercourse of modern Europe with China.

The situation, therefore, of Palmyra in the heart of the Syrian desert, made it necessary that the commercial routes leading thither should be traversed, not by single traders, but by a whole society of merchants, sharing the danger in common. A safe passage through the territories of the wild Arabs was only to be purchased by money, or secured by force of arms. The tribes inhabiting the district now called Nejed were famous, even in the remotest times, for the number and superiority of their camels, with which they supplied the Palmyrenians, who would otherwise have been utterly unable to accomplish their long commercial journeys.

The passage, however, through the countries inhabited by the wandering Arabs was attended with very considerable expense:—"Mirum enim," says Pliny, "ex innumeris illorum populis, pars magna in commerciis aut latrociniis."[20] During the prosperous ages of Palmyra, this expense was occasionally defrayed by private citizens or magistrates, to whom, in consequence, public honours were decreed either by the senate and people of the city, or by the caravans of merchants themselves. These honours consisted in erecting a statue, accompanied with an inscription,[21] commemorative of the liberality and public spirit of the individual concerned; and it is owing to the fortunate preservation of certain of these inscriptions, that we are enabled in any measure to illustrate the commerce of Palmyra. In prosecuting this subject, we shall therefore, first of all, inquire into the particular articles in which Palmyrenian commerce consisted; secondly, into its nature, and method of carrying on; and thirdly, we shall examine the several routes along which it passed.

With respect to the merchandise itself, we have already ascertained it to have consisted for the most part of Arabian and Indian productions; what these were may be easily

[20] Plin. loc. cit.

[21] In Wood's *Palmyra*, these inscriptions are twenty-three in number, of which thirteen are in Palmyrenian character and dialect, with the addition of the Greek interpretation, (explained by Eichhorn, in *Comment. Rec. Soc. Gött.* vol. vi.,) and the rest in Greek alone. Three of the latter are here inserted, the fourth or last has been already interpreted by Eichhorn, in the work just quoted.

gathered from Herodotus, Strabo, and other writers. From Arabia was procured frankincense, myrrh, and other aromatics; and from India also, articles of perfumery, pearls, precious stones, together with cotton and silk stuffs of various kinds; all accurately enumerated by the author of the Periplus. At Palmyra were to be had silken garments of a very expensive kind, and remarkable both for their extreme delicacy of texture as well as brilliance of colour, (these were conveyed to Rome, where, however, they were at first prohibited,[22]) purple vests of Indian manufacture, embroidered with gold and precious stones, and other articles of commerce, too numerous to mention.

I shall now proceed to notice those inscriptions which serve to throw some light on the character of Palmyrenian commerce. These are four in number, three being written in Greek only, and the last in the dialect of Palmyra, with a Greek translation subjoined. I shall here present them to the reader as they occur in Mr. Wood's work, together with a translation in Latin, remarking beforehand, that I do not intend to trouble him with the niceties of verbal criticism, which would be foreign to my purpose; as all that I wish to deduce from them has reference exclusively to commercial subjects.

I.

(*Ruins of Palmyra*, No. XVIII. In the court of the great temple.)

Ἡ *βουλὴ καὶ ὁ δῆμος Σεπτίμιον τὸν κράτιστον ἐπίτροπον Σεβάστου Δουχενάριον - - - [ελ]εοδότην τῆς μητροκολωνείας, καὶ ἀνακομίσαντα τὰς συνοδίας ἐξ ἰδίων καὶ μαρτυρηθέντα ὑπὸ τῶν ἀρχεμπόρων, καὶ λαμπρῶς στρατηγήσαντα καὶ ἀγορονομήσαντα τῆς αὐτῆς μητροκολονείας, καὶ πλεῖστα οἴκοθεν ἀναλώσαντα, καὶ ἀρέσαντα τῇτε αὐτῇ βουλῇ καὶ τῷ δήμῳ καὶ νυνεὶ λαμπρῶς συμποσίαρχον τῶν τοῦ Διὸς Βήλου ἱερῶν τειμῆς ἕνεκεν ἐτ - - - Ξανδικῷ.*

"Senatus Populusque (*Palmyrenus*) Septimium optimum Procuratorem Ducenarium Augusti, qui oleum curavit donandum metropoli coloniæ, quique suo sumptu commeatum mercatoribus iter commune facientibus præbuit; et a negotiorum præsidibus amplum testimonium adeptus est;

[22] Flavius Vopiscus *in* Aureliano, cap. 29, 45.

fortiter et cum laude militantem, et ædilem ejusdem metropoleos coloniæ, plurimas etiam opes domi impendentem; ideoque placentem idem Senatui Populoque; nunc magnifice symposiarchum agentem in sacrificiis Jovis Beli honoris ergo *(coluit) anno - - mense Xandico.*"

The Septimius mentioned in the above inscription, called also Orodes, was the Ducenarius or Procurator of the emperor, and at the same time, ἀγρόνομος, or *ædile* of the city of Palmyra. He is commended on many accounts.

First. Because he made the city a present of oil; for there can be no doubt, that the letters ελ are to be supplied, as Seller has correctly observed.[23] It is easy to conceive, that the consumption of oil must have been very great, not only for the purposes of daily use, but also for the public baths, particularly when we consider the numerous population of the city. Such a present, therefore, must have been very acceptable to the Palmyrenians, as oil could not be procured except at a vast expense, owing to the peculiar situation of Palmyra.

Secondly. Because he entertained or provisioned the company of travelling merchants at his own expense. The inscription therefore alludes to the caravans, whom Septimius Orodes furnished with provisions for their journey.

Thirdly. This grateful attestation was made to Septimius by the prefects or head-men of the merchants (τοῖς ἀρχεμπόροις); whence we may conclude, that at Palmyra the merchants constituted a particular rank or assembly of individuals, who had their own presiding officers; of whom, however, nothing further is known.

Fourthly. This Orodes, it appears, was also the *Symposiarch*, upon occasion of festivals and sacrifices being held in honour of Jupiter Belus, or the Sun, who was the tutelar divinity of the city, as well as of its merchants. He is said to have discharged this office in a splendid manner, as having taken upon himself the whole management of the sacrifices, together with the sumptuous banquets which usually succeeded. We learn, therefore, from the above inscription, that the care of superintending sacred and commercial matters was vested in the same person, which also supplies us with an additional proof, that among the Palmyrenians, as

[23] SELLER, in the Appendix, p. 323.

well as the other nations of the East, an intimate connexion subsisted between religion and commerce.

For all these services, the senate and people of Palmyra awarded to Septimius Orodes the honour of a public inscription, and no doubt also a statue, set up in the court of the principal temple, commemorating his munificent liberality to his native town.

II.

(*Ruins of Palmyra*, No. X. In the long portico.)

Ἰούλιον Αὐρήλιον Ζεβαίδαν Μοκίμου τοῦ Ζεβαίδου Ασθορουβαιδα οἱ σὺν αὐτῷ κατελθόντες εἰς Ὀλογεσιάδα ἐμπορείαν ἔστησαν ἀρέσαντα αὐτοῖς τειμῆς χάριν Ξάνδικῷ του ΗΝΦ ἔτους.

"Julium Aurelium Zebidam Mozimi F. Zebidæ nepotem mercatores qui cum illo descenderunt ad Vologesiæ mercatum constituerunt Asthorubaida, virum ipsis gratissimum honoris gratia, *a.* 558. *Sel.* (*Chr.* 246.)

1. Here again we meet with a company of merchants, under the conduct of Aurelius Zebida, coming down from Palmyra to Vologesia, a town situate on the Euphrates, in order to attend the markets held there.

2. These merchants, it seems, elected Zebida to the office of Astorubaida. The latter appellation must of course be interpreted from the Palmyrenian dialect, and not from the Greek. According to Prof. Ewald; "It is of Semitic origin, the latter part of the compound being evidently the Arabic, بيدا, *Baida*, i. e. desertum; with respect to ασθερου, supposing the letter θ to represent ת, it might stand for אִסְתָּרוּ, tutela; so that the whole word would mean *præsidium deserti;* but it seems more likely to come from אִשְׁטָרוּ, (in Hebrew, שׁוֹטֵר,) which makes the whole equivalent to *præfectus deserti.*" Which of these two interpretations be the more probable I leave my readers to judge, though I certainly prefer the last mentioned, so that Astorubaida would be a kind of honorary title conferred upon the leader of a caravan, after a prosperous journey, similar to that of Imperator, with which the Roman legions saluted their general. In fact, it is a title not merely given by acclamation, but commemorated on a public monument, which could hardly have been done without public authority.

2 D 2

3. This inscription was set up, possibly together with a statue, by the company of merchants, (not by the senate and people,) because Zebaida had discharged his office of conductor with great credit. The date of the inscription coincides with the year 246, A. D., and consequently with the reign of the emperor Philip. As to Zebaida himself, it is not altogether improbable, that he was the same person as Zaba, or Zabda, who is mentioned among the generals of Zenobia, in the time of Aurelian, twenty-five years afterwards,[24] in which case he must have been a young man when he was appointed Astorubaida; but in a question of so much uncertainty, I dare not venture to be positive.

III.

(*Ruins of Palmyra*, No. V., in the court of the temple.)

Νέσῃ 'Αλλάτου τοῦ Νέση τοῦ 'Αλλάτου συνοδιάρχην οἱ συναναβάντες μετ' αὐτοῦ ἔμποροι ἀπὸ Φοράθου καὶ 'Ολογασιάδος τειμῆς καὶ εὐχαριστείας ἕνεκεν ἔτους ΓΝΥ μηνὸς Ξανδικοῦ.

"Nesæ, Allati F. Nesæ N. Synodiarchæ, mercatores qui cum eo descenderunt ab Euphrate et Vologesia, honoris et gratitudinis causa (hanc statuam posuerunt) a. 453, (Chr. 141.)"

This inscription is almost of similar import with the preceding one. We learn from it,

1. That it was set up, and perhaps together with a statue, in the court of the temple, in honour of a certain Nesa, the son of Allatus, of whom nothing more is known.

2. That this was done by the company of merchants to whom Nesa had served the office of *Synodiarch*, or conductor.

3. That this company also had returned to Palmyra from the Euphrates, and the city of Vologesia.

4. That this occurred in the year 141, A. D., and consequently under the reign of Antoninus Pius.

And lastly, from the circumstance of the inscription being set up in the court of the temple itself, we derive another proof of the connexion between commerce and religion.

IV.

(*Ruins of Palmyra*, No. XIII. This inscription is found

[24] Zosimus, i. 50, 51. F. Vopiscus in Aureliano, cap. 25.

in the long portico, and is written both in Greek and in the Palmyrenian dialect. The Greek translation is imperfect, but the Palmyrenian is preserved entire, and has been interpreted by Eichhorn (loc. cit.) in Hebrew and Latin. It is short indeed, but remarkable, from being set up in honour of a Jew.)

Ἡ Βουλ[ὴ] καὶ ὁ Δῆμος Ἰ]ούλιον Αὐρήλιο[ν ---- αθον Μάλη ἀρχέμπορον ἀνακομίσαν[τα ----] συνοδίαν προῖκα ἐξ ἰδίων τειμῆς χάριν ἔτους Θξψ.

Hæc est statua Julii Aurelii Schalmalath, filii Malæ, Hebræi, ducis societatis peregrinatorum, quam in ejus honorem erexit S. P. Q. P. quod adduceret talem societatem. Gratis solebat itinera facere. A. 569, (Chr. 258.)

1. This monument it appears was erected in honour of a certain Schalmalath, who is expressly said to have been a Jew. It follows therefore, that Jews[25] also exercised the mercantile profession at Palmyra, were in the habit of making journeys, and held in so much respect as to have public honours paid them.

2. This Schalmalath had served the office of ἀρχέμπορος, or conductor of the caravan, which he brought safe to Palmyra, and indeed at his own private expense. The addition of "gratis solebat itinera facere," leads us to infer that he had often exhibited such proofs of liberality before, and thus have laid repeated claims to the gratitude of the city.

3. The statue and inscription were erected to him, not by the merchants themselves, but by the senate and people of Palmyra, which is an additional proof of their high regard for individuals who had deserved well of the merchants when on a commercial expedition. Nor is it surprising that public honours should be awarded them in consequence, when we consider that the welfare of the state absolutely depended on the safe arrival of the caravans.

It is, I think, sufficiently evident, from what has been advanced on this subject, that the commercial interests of Palmyra were supposed to be under the special protection of the gods, that is, of the tutelar divinity of the city, viz. the Sun. This is confirmed by the character of the places

[25] What a vast concourse of strangers there was in Palmyra may be gathered from the list of captive nations which adorned the triumph of Aurelian, given by Flav. Vopiscus, c. 33. He mentions the Blemmyes, Axumitans, natives of Arabia Felix, Indians, Bactrians, Iberians, Saracens, Persians, besides others from the North.

where the inscriptions are found. The temple dedicated to the Sun stood in the middle of a spacious area or court, forming a square, and of such extent, that a whole encampment of Bedouin Arabs is contained in the enclosure. This was surrounded with double peristyle, each consisting of about a hundred pillars, behind which was a series of apartments. The entrance was through a grand and highly ornamented portico; immediately upon entering were seen two large tanks or reservoirs, eight feet deep, and furnished with steps to go down into the water; the whole court being paved with marble.[26] Its modern appellation among the Arabs is, "the court of Camels," which leads us in a moment to suspect, that its original destination was precisely similar. It has, in fact, all the appearance of an Eastern caravanserai; its form is square; the portico, with the adjoining apartments, seem intended for the convenience of travellers; the tanks supplied an abundance of water, while the spacious court afforded plenty of room for the beasts of burden, and the merchandise they conveyed.

It is here too, as we have already seen, that the statues with inscriptions were erected in honour of those individuals who had conducted the caravans at their own expense. In the neighbourhood was another stupendous portico, upwards of four thousand feet long, itself also ornamented with inscriptions and statues in honour of particular merchants. When we take all this into consideration, are we not authorized in supposing this court of the temple to have been originally a kind of public inn, (the erection of such places in the East being always regarded in the light of a religious obligation,) destined for the reception of the merchants and their camels? May not the long portico, secured as it was from the scorching rays of the sun, have been a kind of bazâr or exchange, where the merchants exposed their commodities for sale, and at the same time assembled for the transaction of business? We must, it is true, be content to leave this for mere conjecture; but that the place in question was in some way or other subservient to the purposes of commerce, is plain enough from the inscriptions themselves.

As to the enormous wealth of the Palmyrenian merchants,

[26] Compare for this and what follows, the concise description of CASSAS, attached to his Views of Palmyra.

it will be sufficient to quote what Flavius Vopiscus says of Firmus, a native of Seleucia, and the ally and friend of Zenobia, who arrogated to himself the title of prince, but was afterwards overthrown by Aurelian:—"De hujus divitiis multa dicuntur. Nam et vitreis quadraturis domum induxisse perhibetur, et tantum habuisse de chartis, ut publice sæpe diceret exercitum se alere posse papyro et glutino. Idem et cum Blemmyis (Nubiæ populo supra Ægyptum) societatem maximam tenuit, et cum Saracenis (Arabibus); naves quoque negotiatorias ad Indos sæpe misit. Ipse quoque habuisse dicitur duos dentes elephanti, pedum denûm, ex quibus Aurelianus ipse sellam constituerat facere."[27]—It is well known that the inhabitants of Sidon understood the art of manufacturing glass; which however was not employed for windows, or for making cups and other articles of domestic use, but solely for the luxurious purpose of overlaying the walls of their houses, etc.

It now remains for us to say something of the particular routes by which the Palmyrenian merchants travelled in their commercial expeditions. I consider this part of our subject of very great importance, as involving not merely the conveyance of merchandise, but also the propagation of religious opinions, laws, and national civilization in general. As far as Palmyra is concerned, I shall rest my deductions chiefly on the authority of Appian and Pliny, before quoted, and which proves the Palmyrenians to have had in their hands the intermediate commerce, or carrying trade, between the countries of the East and the whole Western world. The language of these writers is alone sufficient to show, that the commercial routes in question were directed partly towards the South, partly towards the East, and partly towards the West.

Those routes which had a southern direction, led, in the one case, into Arabia, in the other to Egypt. That the Arabian trade was of very great importance, and perhaps the most considerable of all, I consider to be evident from what has gone before. With regard to the particular route which it traversed, some light is thrown on the subject by a passage in Pliny (Hist. Nat. vi. 32). "Nabatæi, Arabiæ

[27] FLAV. VOPISCUS *in* FIRMO, cap. 3.

populus, oppidum includunt *Petram* nomine in convalle, paulo minus duorum millium passuum amplitudine, circumdatum montibus inaccessis. Huc convenit utrimque *bivium* eorum qui et Syria (al. Syriæ) Palmyram petiere, et eorum qui ab Gaza venerunt." As to the situation of Petra, there can no longer be any doubt that it is the same as the modern *Carrak*. It has been seen and described by Burckhardt;[28] and a ground plan and views of the ruins are given by Laborde. The place is strongly fortified by nature, and is distant about thirteen geographical miles south of the Dead Sea. An extremely narrow defile between lofty mountains, more like a sheep-walk than a regular path, leads to a plain of moderate extent, shut in on all sides by precipitous rocks, in the middle of which stands the city of Petra, still remarkable for its remains of ancient buildings. In the time of Alexander, and consequently therefore under the Persian dynasty, Petra was the emporium for the aromatics which the Nabatheans brought thither from Arabia Felix. Antigonus formed the design of plundering this opulent city; and with that view sent his son Demetrius, who carried off from Petra five hundred talents of silver, together with a large quantity of frankincense; he was however eventually defeated in his enterprise, for the Nabatheans pursuing after him, succeeded in recovering the stolen booty.[29]

From the words of Pliny, whichever reading we choose to prefer, one thing at least is certain, that at Petra the commercial road parted in two directions, one leading to the left, towards Gaza and the shores of Syria; the other to the right, towards Palmyra. We have already shown from Strabo,[30] that the road to Arabia Felix, that is, the region of Hadramaut, the native country of frankincense, occupied seventy days' journey from Petra; though it is not likely the Palmyrenian merchants proceeded further than the last-named place, which was the market for the productions of Arabia.

That Palmyra maintained a commercial intercourse with Egypt, that is, with Alexandria, may be inferred from the vicinity of these cities, as well as the example of Firmus quoted above. If, as he is reported to have done, he kept

[28] *Travels in Syria and the Holy Land*, p. 422.
[29] This story is related by Diodorus, ii. p. 390.
[30] Strab. p. 1113: see the chapter on the *Phœnicians*.

up a close correspondence with the Blemmyans, a people of Nubia, who traded at Meroe in the interior of Africa, it is evident that a part of this commerce also was in the hands of the merchants of Palmyra. Moreover, we learn of Firmus, that he had a share in the Indian trade, and by sea too; according to Strabo,[31] the grand emporium for the latter was the port of Myos Hormos in Egypt, situate on the Arabian Gulf, from whence also Firmus must have despatched his ships to the Indian markets; for, to the best of our knowledge, the Persian Gulf, in the time of the Parthian empire, was not open to the trade with India. However this may be, it is quite certain that the Palmyrenians, in addition to their commerce by land, exercised also a sea trade with India.

Further: that the routes leading from Palmyra towards the east were also frequented by her merchants might be inferred from the situation of that city itself, as being the intermediate point of the carrying trade between the East and the Western world. The inscriptions, however, are conclusive of the fact. From them we learn, that one of these routes was directed towards the Euphrates, and consequently to Babylonia; which I have already shown to have been, in very ancient times, a celebrated commercial country.[32] The city, indeed, from which it derived its own name, was no longer in existence when Palmyra flourished, as we are informed by Strabo and Pliny. The latter has these words:—"Babylon, Chaldaicarum gentium caput, diu summam claritatem obtinuit in toto orbe. Nunc ad solitudinem rediit, exhausta vicinitate Seleuciæ, ob id conditæ a (Seleuco) Nicatore intra nonagesimum lapidem, ad Tigrin. Ferunt ei plebis urbanæ DC. M. esse. Invicem ad hanc exhauriendam Ctesiphontem, quod nunc caput est regnorum juxta tertium ab ea lapidem condidere Parthi. Et postquam nihil proficiebatur, nuper Vologesus rex aliud oppidum *Vologesocertam* in vicinio condidit."[33] Now if the treasures of Parthia were exhausted by the Arabian trade, as the same writer asserts to have been the case, there can be no doubt that the cities just mentioned were the principal emporia for it.

We learn however from the inscriptions, that the Palmyrenian caravans did not actually proceed as far as the great

[31] Strab. p. 179. [32] See the *Babylonians*. [33] *Hist. Nat.* vi. 30.

cities, but stopped short in the town of Vologesia, which Pliny calls Vologesocerta. It is, in fact, the peculiar nature of Asiatic commercial intercourse, that the merchants travelling in company do not go at once to the royal cities, but halt at some station in the neighbourhood, where they expose their goods for sale, and which, from that circumstance, and from being much frequented by the inhabitants and general traders, becomes itself a town of considerable importance; from hence to the capital the road is easy and secure, and individual merchants may proceed thither without danger. Thus the caravans for Constantinople stop short at Brussa, and those for Cairo in the town of Girgeh. In the same manner, the inscriptions inform us that the merchants of Palmyra halted at Vologesia; which was situate on the Euphrates, near Babylon, and only a day's journey or two from Ctesiphon. Vologesia was built by Vologesus, the first of that name, and a contemporary of Nero, a little before Pliny's time, as he himself reports.[34] The inscription already noticed shows, that markets or fairs (ἐμπορεῖα) were held here for the sale of merchandise brought by the caravans. From hence the merchants could proceed to Seleucia and Ctesiphon with perfect security, and without the risk of being plundered; whereas from Palmyra, through the middle of the desert, they were obliged to travel in numerous companies, and well armed. There appear to have been certain stations on this route, the names of which, otherwise unknown, are mentioned by Ptolemy.[35] In the time of Strabo, when Vologesia was not yet built, the Syrian merchants turned off towards the north, and passed the Euphrates at Anthemusias, in order to escape the oppressive exactions of the petty Arabian princes.[36] The merchants of Palmyra, who frequented the royal cities and commercial towns of the Parthian empire, brought home with them the productions of India, and even, as appears likely, of China itself, the original country of silk; these they disposed of to the traders of the Roman world. We have already shown in another place, that Babylonia and its various cities were, from the most ancient times, the common emporia of Eastern commerce. But as the limits of the Parthian empire were

[34] PLIN. *Hist. Nat.* loc. cit.

[35] PTOL. v. 15: for instance, Avoria, Adacha, and others.

[36] STRAB. p. 1084.

contiguous to India, it was very easy for the inhabitants of the former to hold a commercial intercourse with the Indians; though it does not, indeed, appear that the Palmyrenians themselves ever proceeded as far as India, by land; the extreme limit of their mercantile expeditions being the city of Vologesia.

Lastly: the commercial routes of Palmyra were directed towards the cities of Syria and the Phœnician ports. The particular stations on the line are not, in fact, mentioned by any writer of antiquity; but we have sufficient evidence in the splendid ruins of temples and other buildings still found at Emesa, (Homs,) and Heliopolis (Baalbec). The predominant worship in these places, as at Palmyra, was that of the sun; and they were both situated on the direct road from the latter city to the shores of the Mediterranean; so there can be no doubt of their having been stations for the caravans of Palmyra.

The accounts of recent travellers, particularly Seetzen and Burckhardt, speak also of magnificent ruins, scarcely less remarkable than those of Palmyra, existing in the eastern part of Palestine, beyond the Jordan and the Dead Sea, formerly called Decapolis. The principal of these remains are found at the ancient Gerasa, Gadara, and Philadelphia. The ruins of Gerasa, named Jerash by the Arabs, have been described by Burckhardt,[37] and consist of a temple and portico, together with an amphitheatre: those of Gadara and Philadelphia are said to be little inferior. If we ask how these cities, on the very margin of the desert, arrived at such a pitch of splendour, opulence, and luxury, the same causes may be alleged as contributed to the elevation of Palmyra. They were all situate on the direct road which led from Petra, the principal emporium of Arabian commerce, to Damascus and Palmyra; they flourished in the same age, their architectural remains exhibit the same character, and the name of Antoninus occurs at least once in all three.[38] But as we do not find in these ancient cities any inscriptions similar to those of Palmyra, I forbear to enlarge upon them in this place, having confined myself throughout to such evidence only as depended on the express testimony either of ancient writers or of the monuments themselves.

[37] *Travels in Syria*, p. 252.

[38] BURCKHARDT, loc. cit. The words Μαρκου Αυρ - - - - ν, occur on a fragment of stone.

APPENDIX X.

On the latest additions to Sanscrit Literature.

In the preface to The Indians I have given a complete list of the works connected with Sanscrit which had appeared in Europe up to 1824, (the date of the last edition of this work in Germany,) and from which most of my information on the subject had been derived. During the seven years' interval which has elapsed since that time, Sanscrit literature has received some very considerable and important additions, chiefly, too, by the labours of my own countrymen; and in order to show how far the opinions I then advanced have been confirmed, or otherwise, it will be necessary for me to enter upon a brief review of those works which have subsequently made their appearance, as well through the medium of translations as in impressions of the original text. They are as follows:—

Rigvedæ Specimen. Edidit Fridericus Rosen. Londini, 1830. All that we had hitherto known of the Vedas was contained in the valuable essay of Mr. Colebrooke, inserted in the eighth volume of the Asiatic Researches. In the above work, we are now, for the first time, presented with a specimen of the text itself. The only copy, I believe, of these sacred writings, viz. the one that Polier brought to Europe, has been lying many years unnoticed in the British Museum. Professor Rosen has now commenced drawing it from obscurity; and although his specimen is but of limited extent, it is nevertheless sufficiently ample to give us an insight into the language, the poetry, and, to a certain degree, the contents also of the Vedas. It consists of seven hymns, selected from the first of the four Vedas.

Of the two great epic poems, the first part of the Ramayana has been published by Schlegel: *Ramayana, id est, Carmen epicum de Ramæ rebus gestis poetæ antiquissimi Valmicis opus.* Vol. i. pars 1, 1829. It contains the text of the first, and a considerable portion of the second book, out of the seven which complete the entire poem.

The other great epic, the Mahabharat, is also gradually coming to light. In addition to the episode of Nalus, which had already appeared, we now possess the *Diluvium cum tribus aliis Mahabharati episodiis præstantissimis*, primus edidit Franciscus Bopp, 1829. This publication, besides the episode of the Deluge, so interesting to compare with the narrative of Moses, contains also the mythic history of Savitri, the rape of Draupadi, and the return of Arjuna to Indra's heaven, of which last, however, only the latter half has yet been published.

Schlegel and Lassen have also conjointly edited, in the original Sanscrit, the celebrated collection of fables contained in the Hitopadesa, under the title of, *Hitopadesa, id est, institutio salutaris*, curâ A. W. von Schlegel et Chr. Lassen, 1830.

Almost immediately after this, the Sacontala came out, together with the episode of the Mahabharat, on which it is founded, described as, *La reconnaissance de Sacontala, drame Sanscrit et Pracrit de Calidasa, publiée pour la première fois en original*, par A. L. Chézy. Paris, 1830.

And further we may notice, *Nalodaya, Sanscriticum carmen Calidasæ adscriptum*, edidit Ferd. Benary, 1830. The Nalodaya is a later attempt upon the episode of Nalus in the Mahabharat, and is also attributed by the Hindus to Calidasa.

When to these are added Haughton's *Institutes of Menu*, London, 1827, and Wilson's *Theatre of the Hindus*, consisting wholly of translations, I believe we shall not have omitted any work of particular importance. With the assistance of the above publications, it is evident that we are much better qualified to pronounce with certainty upon the poetic literature and history of the Hindus, than we could possibly have done in 1828. Let us now, then, examine how far the principles I then laid down are confirmed by the information that has thus subsequently come to light. These principles were the following:—

1. The classic poetry of the Hindus, when considered with regard to its relative antiquity, may be classed under three different eras; the most ancient of which is that of the Vedas; the second, that of the great epic poems; and the third, that of the dramatic writings; so far, we had assigned the right characteristics to each of them: a fourth kind, which comes in later, (since the birth of Christ,) cannot properly be said to belong to the classic ages.

2. The epic poem was the fountain-head of the arts and sciences, and the source from whence most of the other kinds of poetry took their rise.

3. It was also the true source of the Hindu national theology, while the Vedas, on the other hand, were merely an embodied representation of the objects of natural religion.

The determination of the respective eras of Sanscrit poetry could then only be effected by means of historic testimony; but now, we are in possession of the most valuable and authentic evidence, which, however, to be made available, requires a critical acquaintance with the language itself. I shall therefore refer to the following passages from an article inserted in the *Göttingen gelehtre Anzeiger*, by Professor Ewald, in order that it may be seen how far my classification met the approval of one of the most profound Sanscrit scholars of the present day. "The specimens from the Vedas," he observes, "are sufficient for enabling us to trace a variety of style between those ancient writings, and the other specimens of Hindu literature which come nearest to them in point of antiquity. This would prove that an interval of many centuries must have elapsed between the composition of the Vedas and the Ramayana: we see how the Sanscrit of the former has been softened and smoothed down in the epic poems, to almost as great a degree as the language of Homer, when deprived of its native freedom by the hands of the Grecian dramatists. The metre also of the Vedas betrays evident marks of a similar distinction, far removed as it is from the formality and unalterable rules to which the epic slokas are subject." An equal modification of style may likewise be discovered, upon comparing the epic and dramatic writers. The language of the Sacontala is the purest Sanscrit. Sir William Jones's translation, however well it may generally serve to represent its poetical beauties, is nevertheless very far from always conveying the true sense, or even elegance, of the original. At the same time, we perceive that, while the Sanscrit is exactly the same all over India, the popular idiom of the Pracrit, on the other hand, is divided into two distinct dialects, of which the higher one, spoken by the female characters of the play, differs but little from the Sanscrit, except in its broader pronunciation; the second, which is put into the mouths of the lower classes, differs in a very material degree. The precise periods of time that must have intervened between the respective writers of the Vedas, the two epic poems, and the Sacontala, cannot now with any certainty be determined, from the want of accurate chronological data. We may, however, from a comparison of the different eras of our own national poetry, be able to form some conjectures with respect to those of the Sanscrit; and, indeed, whoever will take the trouble to compare the Vedas, the Ramayana, and the Sacontala, with Luther's Psalms and Church Hymns, Klopstock's Messiah, and Schiller's Maid of Orleans, would easily find himself induced to carry the parallel much further.

That the epic poetry of India was the fountain-head of the arts as well as the source of the dramatic and lyric species, has been already demonstrated, from the representations on the Hindu monuments, drawn from thence; and the argument is further strengthened by the account given of the colossal reliefs at Mavalipuram and Ellora, inserted in the last volume of the *Transactions of the Royal Asiatic Society of Great Britain.* With respect to the dramatic poetry of the Hindus being founded on their great epic poems, we are in possession of new and decisive evidence in Chézy's edition of the Sacontala, in conjunction with the episode of the Mahabharat, from whence the dramatist has borrowed his materials. "And though," as Professor Ewald observes, "we might be inclined to assign a more recent date to the episode of Sacontala than to the rest of the Mahabharat, still it is by no means less certain that the latter poem must have been composed some centuries before the time of Calidasa, the author of the drama."

And lastly, it is now also evident, from the above-mentioned specimens of the Vedas, that they cannot be looked upon as the source of the present mythology of the Hindus. "At that early period," remarks the same distinguished critic, "a complete revolution must have taken place in the philosophical notions of the people, which shows itself still more clearly in their religion and mythology than in the language itself. The hymns of the Vedas are addressed to the dawn of day, the sun, fire, and rain, etc.: the descriptions of such deities are merely personifications, in which there is not the slightest exhibition of heroic adventure. Of the infinitely rich and perfectly mythological characters of the epic poems, (such as Siva, Krishna, etc.,) not the slightest vestige is discoverable; while at a later period the simple divinities of the Vedas shrink quite into the back-ground."

Thus, what Herodotus said of his countrymen may with equal propriety be applied to the Hindus, viz. that their mythology owed its existence to the epic poets; and the fact that the æsthetic and religious systems of India may be dated from the Ramayana and the Mahabharat, in the same manner as Greece derived hers from the Iliad and Odyssey, will no longer admit of a doubt.

APPENDIX XI.

On the Commerce of Ceylon.[1]

When the British first took possession of Ceylon, and began to extend their researches into the interior of that interesting island, they soon met with the most convincing proofs that its former condition must have been very different from what they now saw. They beheld with astonishment the stupendous remains of ancient civilization, not merely

[1] From a Latin Dissertation by the author, entitled "De Ceylone Insula per viginti fere sæcula communi terrarum mariumque Australium Emporio;" read before the Göttingen Society in 1831.

temples and other edifices, but, what is more extraordinary, tanks of such amazing extent as to deserve rather the name of lakes, being intended for the purposes of irrigation, and not formed by nature, but constructed by art, and the whole faced with hewn stone. Upon examining these striking relics of former prosperity, still existing after the lapse of ages, the question very naturally arose, to what period is their erection to be referred? That a considerable portion of the general history of India itself must depend on that of Ceylon, is certain, not only from the remains just alluded to, but also from the express testimony of ancient writers. The worship of Buddha, concerning the rise and progress of which we at present know so little, still flourishes in Ceylon; and however foreign this may appear to the question before us, it is hardly necessary to remark that religion has at all times exerted no small influence on the fortunes of commerce.

We must first however premise a few observations on the nature, situation, and productions of this island, in order thereby to illustrate the peculiarities of its commercial history. That the Taprobane[2] of the ancients is synonymous with the Ceylon of the moderns, and the Selan-Div[3] of the Hindus, it would be superfluous to show; for in this point the geographers are all agreed; though at the same time I willingly allow that the accounts of ancient authors may sometimes be applied to other islands. In fact, it is generally the case with all distant countries and islands, to be called by vague and indefinite appellations, in proof of which we need only mention the name of India itself as employed by Europeans.

Ceylon is by far the largest island of India on this side the Ganges: its circumference having been ascertained by modern travellers to amount to a hundred and twenty geo-

[2] Onesicritus is recorded as the first author who mentions Ceylon under the title of Taprobane, and its variety of names in the East, as well as in Europe, is one of the extraordinary circumstances that attend it. See the list given in VINCENT's *Periplus of the Erythræan Sea*, p. 493. Taprobane has been ingeniously derived from *Tap*, an island, and *Raban*, or *Ravan*, (for *b* and *v* are indifferently pronounced,) a former king of the island, conquered by Rama, *Asiatic Res.* vol. v. p. 39. TRANSL.]

[3] [Selandiv, or Serendib, was corrupted by the Arabs from Singhala-dwipa, which is the true Sanscrit name, meaning the island of Singhala, or the "lion-raced," in allusion to a former king of Ceylon, fabulously reported to have sprung from a lion. See *Asiatic Res.* vol. vii. p. 48. TRANSL.]

graphical miles. Some ancient writers indeed have assigned it a much greater extent, a mistake which may very possibly have arisen from confounding Ceylon with the Ultra-Gangetic peninsula, or from placing too much confidence in the fabulous reports of certain navigators of the age of Ptolemy. On the other hand the companions of Alexander, and among them Onesicritus, have indicated its real size with sufficient accuracy when they put it down at five thousand stadia.[4] In either case it is reasonable to suppose that the circumference of the island has always continued the same, particularly as there is nothing to show that it has lost by the encroachment of the ocean. The more plausible opinion, however, that it was formerly joined to the continent, is evidently disproved by the oldest Hindu poems now extant, which uniformly represent Lanka, or Ceylon, as detached from the main-land, and only joined to it by a bridge.

The interior of Ceylon is occupied by mountans covered with impenetrable forests, the highest of which is the one now commonly called Adam's peak, in the southern part of the island. The shores are generally level, and on the northern side form an extensive and continuous plain. Its central position between the east coast of Africa, Arabia, and India on either side the Ganges, as far as the shores of China, seems to have been destined by nature for Ceylon's becoming the grand emporium of the South; while its ample and secure harbours afford unusual facilities to navigation.[5] It is separated from the continent by a narrow frith, abounding in shoals, but intersected by channels sufficiently wide and deep to admit the passage of a moderately-sized vessel.

The northern part of the island, already alluded to, and extending from Trincomalee on the east, as far as Aripa and Manaar on the west, requires to be examined somewhat

[4] Strabo, xv. p. 1012. [According to Strabo, Onesicritus did not mention whether it is in length, breadth, or circumference. In all probability he meant the latter, because, at eight stadia to the mile, this amounts to six hundred and twenty-five miles; which is not very far from the truth, for in Rennell's map the length is two hundred and eighty miles, the breadth one hundred and fifty, and the circumference six hundred and sixty. To make amends, however, for accuracy in this point, he adds that it lies twenty days' sail from the continent. Transl.]

[5] The harbour of Trincomalee is said to be the best in India.

more in detail. Manaar[6] is a small island, separated from the larger one of Aripa by a narrow channel. The sea is here full of shoals as far as Tuttocarin on the opposite continent, and was celebrated even in the remotest antiquity for its fisheries of pearl-oysters, and a species of shell called chank,[7] which is used by way of ornament, and in certain religious ceremonies. It is not therefore surprising that this portion of the island, as being most adapted to the purposes of navigation and commerce, as well as the cultivation of rice, should consequently have been more crowded with inhabitants than the other parts, a circumstance which is confirmed by the remains that still exist. It is in this neighbourhood we meet with the ruins of the once flourishing cities of Mantotti and Condromalee; and, according to the testimony of Knox,[8] the banks of the river Aripa, which flows into the bay of the same name, are covered with fragments of pillars and ruined buildings. At Mantotti is seen an immense artificial reservoir, called by the natives Cattocarle, or The Giant's Tank, of capacity sufficiently ample for the irrigation of land producing upwards of forty million pounds of rice.[9] The number of Roman coins also found

[6] [Manaar in the Tamul language signifies a sandy river, applied here to the shallowness of the strait. *Asiatic Res.* vol. v. p. 395. Transl.]

[7] *Voluta gravis* of Linnæus. [Specified as the *Murex Tritonis* by M. Bournouf. The chank shells, which are of a spiral form, are chiefly exported to Bengal, where they are sawed into rings of various sizes, and worn on the arms, legs, fingers, and toes of the Hindus, both male and female. They are likewise used entire to sound as a horn at funerals, and are employed for other purposes in religious ceremonies. A chank opening to the right hand is highly valued, and being rarely found always sells for its weight in gold. Thousands of these shells are also buried with the bodies of opulent and distinguished persons in Bengal, which is the cause of the great and constant demand for them. Transl.]

[8] Robert Knox, *Historical Relation of the Isle of Ceylon*, vol. iv. chap. 10.

[9] Sir Alexander Johnston, in a Memoir read before the Royal Asiatic Society of Great Britian, i. 3. p. 347. Compare the account of Ant. Bertolacci, (formerly comptroller-general of the customs,) in his excellent work, *A View of the Agricultural, Commercial, and Financial Interest of Ceylon.* London, 1817, p. 131. [The circumference of this tank is nearly eighteen miles, and the dam laid across the Aripa river to divert the stream into it, is constructed with stones of seven and eight feet in length, by four in breadth, and from two to three feet thick. The length of the dam itself is six hundred feet, its breadth in some parts sixty, never less than forty, and its height from eight to twelve. Not less surprising are the works constructed round the lake of Candeley, about sixteen miles from Trincomalee. This lake or tank, which is nearly fifteen miles in circumference, is embanked in several places, with a wall of huge stones, each from twelve to fourteen feet long, and of proportionable breadth and thickness. That part of this majestic work particularly deserves attention, where, by a parapet of nearly one hundred and

here, particularly of the age of the Antonines, is another proof of the active and flourishing state of commerce in Ceylon in former times.

Having thus premised, it will now be requisite to say something of the method in which I purpose to conduct the present inquiry; confining myself throughout to such facts as are derived from sources purely historical and worthy of credit; to notice mythological and fabulous reports, would be altogether foreign to my design. We shall commence, therefore, with the epoch at which the most certain and ample testimony relative to the commerce of Ceylon was consigned to writing: we shall then ascend into more remote periods, in order to show the corresponding antiquity of the commerce in question; the next step will be to return to the point of setting out, and so descend into the middle ages as far as their termination; in pursuing which course, I hope to establish on satisfactory grounds the truth of the proposition already stated in the commencement of this Essay, viz. "that Ceylon continued to be the common emporium of Southern commerce for upwards of two thousand years."

Our first epoch, then, will be nearly the middle of the sixth century after the birth of Jesus Christ. In this period, that is to say, about A. D. 560, and in the reign of the emperor Justin II., a merchant named Cosmas, who afterwards became a monk, travelled for commercial purposes as far as Adule, at that time a celebrated port, belonging to the king of Axume in Ethiopia, and situate near to Arkeeko. Here he met with a certain acquaintance by the name of Sopater, just then on his return from Ceylon, which he had visited in the capacity of a merchant. It was from the report of this voyager that Cosmas drew his account of Ceylon and its commerce as it then existed, and which he has inserted in his *Typographia Christiana*, a work of unquestionable veracity. And as all I propose to advance in the present discussion will be founded on this account of Cosmas, I shall make no apology for transcribing the whole passage from the version of Montfaucon,[10] as follows :—

fifty feet in breadth at the base, and thirty at the summit, two hills are made to join in order to encompass and keep in the waters of the lake. BERTOLACCI, etc. p. 14. TRANSL.]

[10] *Montefalconii Collectio nova Patrum*, tom. ii. pp. 333—338.

"Taprobane is a large island in the Indian Ocean, called by the Hindus *Silediva*, where the precious stone termed hyacinth[11] is found; and it is situated above the pepper country (περαιτέρω τῆς χώρας τοῦ πεπέρεως). A great number of small islands, closely adjoining, surround it; each of which contains fresh-water springs, and abounds with cocoa-nuts (ἀργελλίοις).[12] According to the inhabitants, the large island is nine hundred miles in length, and as many in breadth. It is governed by two kings, who are always in a state of mutual hostility; one of them possesses the mountainous region producing the hyacinth-stone, and the other, the remaining portion of the island, in which are the commercial towns and harbours, and which is, therefore, most frequented by the neighbouring people. There is also a church of Christians from Persia, under the inspection of a presbyter ordained in the latter country, together with a deacon, and other ecclesiastical officers.[13] The native inhabitants, with their respective kings, profess a different religion. Numerous temples are to be seen in the island, and in one of them particularly there is said to be a hyacinth of great brilliance and uncommon size, being almost as large as the cone of a pine-tree (στρόβιλος); this stone is placed in an elevated and conspicuous situation within the sacred edifice; and, when illumined by the rays of the sun, reflects a light which may be seen a considerable distance, forming altogether a most curious and extraordinary spectacle.

"A great number of vessels from all parts of India, Persia, and Ethiopia, are in the habit of trafficking with Ceylon, so conveniently situated as it is with regard to those countries, while the island itself has also a numerous fleet of ships belonging to its own merchants. From the interior countries of the East, (τῶν ἐνδοτέρων,) that is to say, from Sina, (Τζίνιτζας,) and other mercantile places, she procures silk, aloes, cloves, and tzandana, (τζανδάναν,) with other articles of commerce peculiar to those regions: these, in her turn, she transmits to more distant countries; to Male, where the

11 [The ruby of Ceylon is proverbial. Paolino. PLIN. xxxvii. 41. TR.]

12 [*Narikela* is the Sanscrit, and *nargil* the Persian name for the cocoa-palm tree. TRANSL.]

13 [These Christians were Nestorians, whose *catholicos* resided at Ctesiphon, and afterwards at Mosul; in fact, they were the same as the Malabar Christians of St. Thomè. TRANSL.]

pepper grows; to Calliana, a place of great trade, from whence the return cargo consists of native brass, (χάλκος,) sesasum-wood,[14] and other articles adapted for clothing (σησάμινα ξύλα καὶ ἕτερα ἱμάτια); further, she transports them to Sindus, the country of musk, or castoreum, and spikenard; and also to Persia, Homerite, and Adule; from all these parts Ceylon receives an exchange of merchandise, which, together with her own produce, she forwards into the interior of India. Sinde, moreover, is the commencement of the last-named country; for the river Indus divides it from Persia. The principal trading towns of India are, Sindus, Orrhota, Calliana, Sibor, Parti, Mangaruth, Salopatana, Nalopatana, and Pudapatana, the last five being included under the province of Male; about five days and nights' journey further (from Male) is Silediva, or Taprobana. Still further, on the continent, is Mavallo, which produces a peculiar kind of shell-fish; and Caber, which affords the alabandanum.[15] Next to this is the country where cloves grow; and, lastly, Sina, whence silk is procured; beyond this there is no other region, the ocean forming the boundary of Sina to the east.

"The island of Silediva, therefore, being situated almost in the middle of India, and producing the precious stone called hyacinth, receives merchandise from all other countries, and supplies them in its turn; it is consequently itself a place of very great mercantile resort. This I was told both by Sopater himself, and his fellow-travellers, who had sailed from Adule to the same island."

Thus far the account which Cosmas has handed down of Ceylon, according to the relation of Sopater. It is evident, therefore, that, about the middle of the sixth century after the birth of Christ, this island was the common centre, as it were, of the commercial transactions which took place between the countries of the South, from the eastern shores of Africa as far as China. Nor can there be any doubt of the nature and character of this trading intercourse; for it

[14] [It is uncertain what this article can be; but it is also mentioned in the Periplus, and may possibly be a corrupt reading in both. Transl.]

[15] [Vossius reads ἀλαῖς ἀδινόν, which seems unintelligible; but he informs us it means nutmegs of Banda. We are, however, at present on the coast of Coromandel. Hoffman says, all *merces barbaricæ* are so called, as also toys and trifles. Transl.]

is equally clear that Ceylon was the intermediate point, where the merchandise of many different countries was collected together, and a mutual interchange of their respective productions negotiated; it follows, therefore, that the kind of trade here carried on was one of exchange, or, in other words, a carrying trade, notwithstanding the island also had its own exports, consisting in articles of native produce. We further learn, from the passage above quoted, that Ceylon was at this time inhabited by two distinct races, and governed by two different princes. The mountainous, or interior part of the island, which produced the precious stones and cinnamon, was subject to one of them; and the coast, with its harbours and commercial towns, came under the dominion of another or more, who, as it appears, were continually at war with the former. This circumstance may be explained by supposing the maritime districts to have been in the possession of a race of foreigners, who had established themselves in the island with a view to commerce, and were of a different origin from the native inhabitants. That these strangers were Persians must be inferred from the words of the author; at the same time we may reasonably comprehend under that denomination, not only Persians properly so called, but also, on account of the trade carried on with them, the inhabitants of the countries immediately bordering on the Persian Gulf. These foreigners seem to have constituted a single colony of Christians, noticed by Sopater more particularly, because that traveller had himself embraced the same faith. It is, however, extremely probable that natives of other countries, Arabia or Malabar for instance, had also settled in the island at the same time with the former.

Among the various kinds of commerce carried on with foreign nations, particular mention is made of that with the Ethiopians at the port of Adule. For at this time flourished the kingdom of the Axumitæ, to whom the productions of India were indispensable, being exchanged for the gold with which the country abounded. We further meet with the Homeritæ, inhabiting the shores of Arabia Felix, in whose country was the harbour of Aden, situate beyond the straits of Babelmandel, and therefore easily accessible to ships sailing direct from India, without a change of wind being necessary. Next to these, the Persians are mentioned, that is, natives of the Persian Gulf, together with the Mediterranean provinces of Persia itself.

The most important trade, however, of Ceylon, was that carried on with the continent of India, comprising the western coast of the peninsula, from the mouths of the Indus as far as the land of Malabar, where pepper grows. We here meet with the name of Sinde, an appellation still in use to denote the countries situate on the lower part of the Indus. The fact of musk being noticed as an article of importation from this quarter, necessarily leads us to infer the existence of a corresponding commercial intercourse with Thibet and the Himalaya mountains, which is the native country of the drug in question. On the shores of India, several ports are mentioned by name; as Orrhota, now called Surat; Calliana, the modern Callian, near Bombay; Sibor, which is uncertain; and Male, still preserved in Malabar. This latter is the native country of pepper, and was, in the time of Cosmas, so remarkable for its extensive trade, as to contain no less than five ports, to be sought for in the modern provinces of Cochin and Travancore, and whose names all ending in *patan*, evidently betray their Indian origin. Mavallo, which comes next in the enumeration, from whence the shell-fish termed *chanks* are procured, I take to be Manaar; the only mistake committed by Cosmas is, that he places it on the continent, whereas, in fact, it is a small island. On the eastern or Coromandel coast, we look in vain for the famous city of Mavalipuram, cut out of the solid rock; an omission which is the more surprising, because Caber, or Cabera, immediately follows, in which every body will at once recognise the river Caveri with the town situate at its mouth, close to the modern Tranquebar. Alabandanum, occurring as one of its productions, would seem to specify a particular kind of precious stone.[16]

It is not, however, merely the produce of the Indian peninsula that we read to have been conveyed to Ceylon; but that also of countries and islands much more remotely situated. Of this kind are the spices, and silk, imported from Tzinitza, or China. That the Sunda islands were al-

[16] [Reported by Mons. Dutens to be something between an amethyst and a ruby. TRANSL.]

ready well known many ages before the time of Cosmas, we shall have occasion to show hereafter, from Ptolemy. It seems most likely, therefore, that voyages between these several places were made by the Chinese, in the same kind of vessels which they now use, called *junks*. This indeed may be inferred from the express words of Cosmas, when he mentions the importation of "aloes, spices, and tzandana, from Tzinitza, and other distant regions." As to *tzandana*, it seems to be identical with the modern sandal-wood; and all writers are unanimous in considering silk as the peculiar and exclusive produce of China and the neighbouring countries alone.

It may appear strange that so few of the indigenous productions of Ceylon itself are mentioned; that is to say, only precious stones and pearls, without a single allusion to cinnamon and ivory, with which the island abounds. This apparent inconsistency, however, is removed, when we come to consider the very nature of Singhalese commerce, and at the same time serves to show the vast extent and importance of the latter. For, as we have already seen, the trade of Ceylon consisted for the most part in the exchange of foreign goods, brought thither in great quantities from distant regions; in comparison with which the sole produce of the island itself, would seem very trifling and insignificant. Besides, cinnamon grew only in the interior, and not in the northern parts of the island, to which alone Sopater's visit was confined; and we must also recollect, that at this early period, gardens appropriated to the cultivation of cinnamon were not yet in existence.[17] The same peculiarity, however, is observable in the commercial history of the Phœnicians, Venetians, and Dutch, as long as they continued in succession to monopolize the trade of the whole world. For the productions mentioned as peculiar and indigenous to either people, are precisely those of native manufacture; whereas, on the other hand, nothing of the kind appears to have been yet extant among the inhabitants of Ceylon. With regard to silk manufactures, which at this time flourished in high perfection on the Indian continent, we shall show presently that the art was not introduced into Ceylon

[17] [See this argument further examined in VINCENT's *Periplus*, etc., p. 511, sq. TRANSL.]

till a much later period; though to be sure the island was already a most extensive market for silk goods of foreign manufacture.

What has been advanced, therefore, up to the present stage of our inquiry, may be considered as amounting to an absolute proof of the fact, that Ceylon, especially the northern part of it, was, in the sixth century of our era, the common mart of Australian commerce. Now, if we ascend from this epoch into more remote times, the reader surely will not require a description of the island always as circumstantial as that of Cosmas; which, indeed, would be altogether unnecessary for the purpose of insuring credit to our relation; for the nature and extent of Singhalese commerce being once ascertained, we shall have less occasion for particular proof in the sequel.

Setting out then from the middle of the sixth century, and passing over an interval of four hundred years, let us go back to the second century after Christ; that is, to the age of Ptolemy the geographer. Here also we meet with indications equally certain, though more concise than those exhibited by Cosmas. In Ptolemy's work on geography,[18] there is a whole chapter dedicated to Ceylon, (called by the natives Salice,) which contains such an accurate description of the island, as may justly excite our admiration. The particular sources from which this writer derived his geographical information, namely, the reports of contemporary navigators and merchants, have already been pointed out in a separate treatise.[19] Ptolemy, however, seems to have been acquainted not only with the shores of the island and its harbours; but even in some degree with the interior also, though less accurately than the former. His description of Ceylon commences with the northern part, proceeding westward as far as the southern promontory, and from thence to the eastern shores and the interior of the island. He remarks, that it was formerly called Palæsimundi, (which we shall presently see confirmed by Pliny,) but in his own time Salice, and the natives Salæ[20] (whence Selan and Ceylon);

[18] Ptolem. *Geogr.* lib. vii. cap. 4. [19] See Appendix XII.

[20] [There is a particular caste on the island at this day, called Salé, or Challe, and Challias; they are labourers, manufacturers of stuffs, and cinnamon-peelers, and are settled in the southern districts of the island, where

that the productions for which it was celebrated were rice, honey, ginger, precious stones, viz. beryl and the hyacinth; gold and silver; elephants and tigers; but what is astonishing, not one word about cinnamon here either! In the first place, therefore, he mentions rice, which grows only in the northern part of the island, where lakes have been dug for watering the lands. The precious stones and metals are found in the interior alone; and ivory, in the southern part, where the geographer places the elephant-pastures. On either coast of the island four ports are noticed, and twelve cities; particularly on the northern side, where was the commercial town of Modutti, (recognisable in Mandotti,) and also that of Talacori. In the interior are six cities, among which Amurogrammum, the residence of the court, and the capital Maagrammum,[21] are specified. This account of Ptolemy will derive some illustration from comparing it with the narratives of modern travellers. Among these the most remarkable, and at the same time the earliest, is Robert Knox, a native of Scotland, who, in the year 1657, was shipwrecked on the coast of Ceylon, and detained in the island nearly twenty years in captivity; until at length he fortunately contrived to escape to the Dutch settlements on the shore, from whence he returned to Europe. This extraordinary man was possessed of every qualification which would be required in a traveller who sits down to describe distant countries; the utmost degree of historical credit, and an attentive eye to every thing worthy of remark; add to this, a perfect acquaintance with the language of the natives, so that it is not greatly to be wondered that the contents of later itineraries are scarcely more than a supplement to the description of Knox. He had himself seen the monuments of antiquity still extant in the island; and had diligently inquired into their former names, most of which he committed to writing; and upon comparing his account with that of Ptolemy, some of them appear to be still in common use. The geographer, for instance, calls the principal river in the island by the name of Ganges, in which we are at no loss to

they form the principal part of the population in the neighbourhood of Point de Galle. *Asiatic Res.* vol. vii. p. 431.. Transl.]

[21] [Maha-grammam, i. e. the great city. There is a town in the south-eastern part of the island still called Mahagam, or Mahagram. Transl.]

recognise Mavela Gonga,[22] which flows into the ocean near Trincomalee. The mountain called by Ptolemy, Malea, under which were the elephant-pastures, extending as far as the sea, still bears the name of Malell among the natives;[23] but among Europeans, that of Adam's Peak. It is situated in the southern part of the island, and is a place of distinguished resort for pilgrims from all quarters. The name of the royal city Amurogrammam, appears to survive in the Amuroburro of Knox, in which, according to the tradition of the inhabitants, ninety kings formerly reigned, who erected many temples, and had divine honours paid to them in consequence.[24] The word *gramma*, which often occurs in the island, would seem properly to imply, not only a city, but its surrounding territory as well; for thus Knox also observes, that Amuroburro is the name of a city together with the neighbouring country.[25] This town was situated

[22] [Maha-bali-ganga, i. e. the great river of Bali. TRANSL.]

[23] KNOX, *Description of Ceylon*, vol. i. p. 4.

[24] Ibid. vol. i. p. 44.

[25] Ibid. vol. iv. p. 323. [In order to appreciate the author's derivation of Amuroburro from Amurogrammam, it may be necessary to observe, that the Indian terminations *grammam, burro*, or *pura* and *gore*, are nearly synonymous; and mean in either case a village or town. A paper, containing some remarks upon Anarajahpura, or Anaradhepura, (evidently the Amuroburro of Knox,) and Mehentélé, in the island of Ceylon, by Captain Chapman, R. E., was read before the Asiatic Society of London, at their general meeting on the 21st July, 1832. This officer visited Anarajahpura in 1828, and was induced to lay his notes before the Society in consequence of finding the oral traditions collected by him on the spot, to agree in a remarkable manner with the accounts contained in the Ceylonese Histories, entitled Mahavansi, Rajavali, and Rajaratnacari; translations of which, prepared under the auspices of Sir A. Johnston, are now in course of publication. The city of Anaradhepura is situated in the district of Neura Wanny, in the interior of Ceylon, about 8° 15′ N. lat. and 80° 35′ E. long. According to the native records it continued to maintain its rank and importance for the long period of fifteen hundred years. The only traces now remaining of magnificent buildings, once said to have existed within its limits, are nine temples still held in great reverence, and ruined tanks and groups of columns scattered about for several miles. Captain C. devotes a section to each of these temples, which he subsequently illustrates by copious extracts from the histories above named. From Anaradhepura the captain and his party proceeded to Mehentélé, about twelve miles north-east of the former place, the road to which was, for some distance, along a beautiful lake, formed by an artificial embankment, upwards of two miles in length, of great thickness, and in many places thirty feet in height. The large *daghope*, or hill-temple, at Mehentélé, is said to be a hundred and twenty cubits high, and is approached by a flight of two hundred steps. After describing the other antiquities of Mehentélé, and illustrating them by extracts from the sacred histories, Captain C. concludes with a disquisition respecting the antiquity of Anaradhepura; the foundation of which, from various authorities, he places at 470 B. C.; thus assigning to these interesting remains, the remote antiquity of two thousand three hundred years. TRANSL.]

on the northern side of an extensive plain, the largest in the island, in which were artificial lakes upwards of a mile in circuit, for irrigating the rice plantations.[26] And in fine, the Modutti of Ptolemy, which he describes as a commercial city, is called Mantotti by the present inhabitants; in its neighbourhood is the Giant's Tank, destined for the same purpose as the above-mentioned lakes.

According to Ptolemy, various nations inhabited the island, called indeed by the common name of Salæ, but otherwise of different races; he begins his enumeration with those on the western side, and then proceeds to those on the east. Their unknown names appear to indicate a Malabar origin; which, although I must leave for others to decide, it is no less certain that the condition of the island in the age of Ptolemy, was precisely similar to that described by Cosmas; in other words, that the shore was occupied by foreigners, who possessed the harbours and commercial towns, while the interior was left to the aboriginal inhabitants.

Ptolemy adds, that *before*, or to the west of Ceylon, lay a multitude of smaller islands, in number amounting to one thousand three hundred and seventy-eight, nineteen of which he mentions by name.[27] That this must be understood of the Maldives, no one who is acquainted with their situation, can possibly doubt. For they are not so properly single islands, as a congeries of smaller ones, called Atollons, being eighteen or nineteen in number, and defended by a belt of coral reefs against the violence of the ocean; while each of them contains a multitude of sandy islets, separated only by narrow channels. It is evident, therefore, that the islands alluded to by Ptolemy, must be these very Atollons; and the vast number assigned to them is itself a proof that they were not merely accessible, but also frequently visited by navigators.

But further, the Sunda islands, as they are now called, to the eastward of Ceylon, were by no means unknown to Ptolemy. He mentions particularly Jabadia, the most fertile of all, and which is no other than Java (Javan-Dwipa); the capital town he represents to be Argentea, on the northern side of the island and upon the site of the modern Ban-

[26] JOHNSTON, loc. cit. p. 546.

[27] PTOL. vii. 4. s. fin.

tam, which is at no great distance from the Dutch settlement of Batavia. The very name of Sunda, however, may be found in Ptolemy; for he notices three islands in this situation called Sinde. Three others are likewise mentioned under the name of Sabadib, in which we again meet with the Hindu termination *dib*, or more correctly *dwipa*, signifying an island: the inhabitants are stigmatized by him as cannibals, an epithet which has been abundantly confirmed by the testimony of modern travellers. The fact, hitherto conceived too horrible to be true, has at length been established beyond the possibility of a doubt by the researches of Mr. Anderson,[28] who visited the Battas inhabiting the interior of Sumatra and the adjacent islands, and found those people in the common habit of feeding on human flesh, though in other respects possessing a high degree of civilization, and by no means unacquainted with the refinements of life.[29] Ptolemy mentions several other islands, which it would be hazardous, perhaps, to attempt defining with individual accuracy; but as Java, particularly the northern part, was well known to him, we can hardly suppose him to have been ignorant of the celebrated passage called the straits of Sunda, between that island and Sumatra. That the Java sea was navigated, is evident from Ptolemy's mentioning a peculiar kind of vessel in use among these islands, the planks of which were fastened by bolts of wood instead of iron, in perfect agreement with the description of Pliny.[30] When we add to this, his account of India beyond the Ganges, together with the Golden Chersonesus, now called the peninsula of Malacca, and Serica, with its various cities and ports, it will be impossible to doubt, that in the age of Ptolemy these countries were accessible to navigators, and that Ceylon was the common mart for the trade of them all.

From Ptolemy let us now proceed to Arrian, the author of a work entitled, the Circumnavigation of the Erythræan,

[28] ANDERSON'S *Mission to the East Coast of Sumatra, in the year* 1823.

[29] [See also, *Life and Public Services of Sir Stamford Raffles*, 4to, p. 425. In a letter to Mr. Marsden, the historian of Sumatra, Sir Stamford gives a detailed account of this extraordinary and revolting practice, from which it appears, upon the most unimpeachable testimony, that the Battas are cannibals both upon principle and system, and that criminals and prisoners are not only eaten according to the law of the land, but that the same law even permits their being mangled and eaten alive! TRANSL.]

[30] PLIN. *Hist. Nat.* vi. 26.

or India Sea, certainly prior in time to the geographer, though it is doubtful whether he flourished in the reign of Nero, or under the Antonines. The excellent account of Indian commerce preserved to us in the Periplus of this writer, is too well known to require illustration in this place, at the same time that it is equally worthy of credit, as the author himself visited India as a merchant, and therefore describes what came under his own immediate observation. In this work we are presented with an accurate description of the Malabar coast, together with a distinct notice of its different ports, and the particular kind of trade for which they were severally remarkable. Hence we gather the flourishing state of commerce on the southern part of the peninsula, in Cochin and Travancore, the native country of the pepper-plant, and in the close neighbourhood of Ceylon itself. To this latter island, indeed, our author never went; which is much to be regretted, though what he has written concerning it is well worth an attentive examination.[31] In his time, it appears, the former name of the island, Taprobane, had been changed to Palæsimundum; that the northern part was best cultivated; that distant voyages were often made from thence in large vessels; and that the island abounded with pearls and precious stones, fine linen, and tortoise-shell. In this brief notice, the first point which requires discussion is the origin of the name of Palæsimundum;[32] and here, fortunately, we may borrow some light from Pliny.[33] In fact, the historian informs us that Palæsimundum was a very large city, containing upwards of two hundred thousand inhabitants. It seems, therefore, to have been the capital of the island, being much frequented by merchants and seafaring men, so that possibly the name of

[31] ARRIAN, *Peripl. M. Erythræi*, ed. Stuckii, sub fine. It is, however, quite evident, both from the testimony of Arrian, and in a later age, that of Ibn Batuta, a celebrated traveller of the fourteenth century, that much of what is here advanced respecting the commerce of Ceylon may with equal justice be applied to the opposite coast of Malabar. He mentions several very flourishing places of trade in Malabar, filled with opulent Mohammedan merchants, and frequented by vessels from China. See *Travels of Ibn Batuta*, chap. xviii., *translated from an Arabic MS.* London, 1829.

[32] [With respect to the derivation of this word, the late Mr. Hamilton considered *Simuntu* as expressing the utmost boundary, or extremity; in this case, *Palisimuntu*, or *Palæsimundu*, would signify the limit of the expedition of Bali, the Indian Hercules, as he has been called.]

[33] *Hist. Nat.* vi. 24.

the town may have been applied to designate the whole island, just as in our time Batavia is often put for Java collectively. Ptolemy, indeed, does not mention the city by name; but he speaks of the promontory of Anarismundum, which Salmasius long ago suspected to mean the same thing.[34] The city in question was situated on the northern side of the island; and by some has been sought for in the modern Jafnapatam. It is more probable, however, according to the account of Pliny, which we shall presently refer to, that its site must be looked for on the bay of Trincomalee, which is, besides, the finest harbour in all India. Large vessels are also mentioned, adapted for making long voyages, and distinct from those formed out of a single piece of timber. Though Arrian, therefore, could not furnish us with such a correct description of Ceylon as those who had actually been there, it is nevertheless sufficiently evident from his account, that the northern part of the island was then in the highest state of cultivation, and the seat of a most extensive trade, not only with western countries, but also with the East as far as the mouths of the Ganges, including the Golden Chersonesus, or Malacca, and the neighbouring islands, even to the remotest province of China.

Let us now proceed to the examination of Pliny.[35] The accounts furnished by this author are of two kinds, which ought to be carefully distinguished from one another: the first belongs to his own age, or at least that of the Cæsars; the second comprises what he copied from older writers. We learn, however, both from himself and Strabo, that in his time, as well as during the Cæsars, who immediately preceded him, a very large trade was carried on with India through the Arabian Gulf. From the time, indeed, that Egypt was reduced to a Roman province, navigation took such extraordinary strides, that not only single vessels, but whole fleets, yearly set sail to the different ports of India, and were freighted back with a return cargo of native produce, in exchange for specie. What Pliny relates of Ceylon, was borrowed from the accounts of the ambassadors who had been sent from that island to Rome, in the time of the emperor Claudius. This embassy was occasioned by

[34] SALMAS. *ad Solin.* p. 684. [35] *Hist. Nat.* vi. 24.

the following circumstance: a freedman of Annius Plocamus, who farmed the customs on the Red, or Indian Sea, happened, as he was coasting about Arabia, to be blown away by the north wind, and carried to the port of Hippuri in Ceylon, where he was kindly received and hospitably entertained by the king of the country for the space of six months. At his suggestion the king was induced to send an embassy to Cæsar, consisting of four persons, under the direction of their chief, Rachia (in which latter appellation we immediately recognise the Hindu Rajah, and therefore an honorary title, and not a proper name, particularly as the individual himself is called a chief, or prince, *princeps)*. These ambassadors reported that there were upwards of five hundred towns in this island; that Palæsimundu, with its adjoining harbour, was the most magnificent of all, and contained the royal palace, together with a population of two hundred thousand souls. That in the same neighbourhood was the lake Megisba, three hundred and seventy-five miles in circumference, from which two rivers flowed, one to the north, the other, called Palæsimundum, close to the town of that name, and emptying itself into the sea by three mouths. From this account it is evident, first, that the freedman above mentioned must have been carried to Ceylon by the Etesian wind, or, in other words, by the north-east monsoon; that he landed on the northern side, where, as we have before observed, those lakes are found, and, in short, at the harbour of Hippuri, the precise locality of which I cannot venture to determine. In the second place, it is equally clear that the island must have been in a very flourishing state, to contain no less than five hundred cities, of which it appears that Palæsimundum, with its port, was the chief. All these particulars coincide with the bay on which Trincomalee is situated; the largest river in the island, by name Gonga or Ganges, flows into it; the harbour is the most convenient in the whole island; even the remains of the ancient city are still to be found; and if I may be allowed to conjecture, its very name is discoverable. In a map of Ceylon, edited by Bertolacci,[36] there is a place laid down on the northern mouth of the river, by the name of

[36] BERTOLACCI, *View of the Agricultural and Commercial Interests of Ceylon.* London, 1817.

Pontjemolli, which might easily be corrupted, by Greek enunciation, into Palæsimundum.[37] Be this as it may, however, it is quite evident that Ceylon was at this time possessed of a very extensive commerce; for we learn that the father of Rachia himself undertook a voyage to Serica, on a commercial speculation. We shall omit the rest of Pliny's account, in which, if we sometimes discover truth mingled with fable, (admitting the latter to have come from the ambassadors,) there will be no great reason for surprise, as it was this writer's especial aim to collect wonderful stories; for he closes his account with, "the rest is according to the report of our navigators." There is no occasion, then, to dwell any further on this part of our subject, my design being merely to show that the condition of Ceylon, as far as relates to commerce, was the same in the age of Claudius, and consequently at the commencement of our era, as we have already proved it to have been in the time of Ptolemy and Cosmas.

From the period of the Cæsars, let us now go back to more remote times, that is, to the age of the Ptolemies and Alexander the Great. In the three centuries which intervene, we meet with presumptive evidence of the splendour of Ceylon; though the accounts of writers respecting the island itself are less frequent and less circumstantial. In the first place, but few of those accounts have come down to us; and secondly, the commercial intercourse between Ceylon and the Western world was more seldom, and took a circuitous route. It is altogether erroneous to suppose, as is very often the case, that under the Ptolemies, annual voyages were in the habit of being made between Egypt and India; because there would obviously be no occasion to go to the latter country, for what was to be obtained much nearer home, in the abundant and well-supplied markets of Arabia Felix. Besides, we have the decisive testimony of Strabo, to the point, that although he saw in the harbour of Myos Hormos as many as one hundred and twenty ships of burden destined for India, yet he never heard of more than

[37] [Making every possible allowance for the liberties taken by the Greek writers, in accommodating foreign sounds to their own pronunciation, it will still be very difficult for the author to persuade any one of the probability of the derivation given in the text. Besides, the name Pontjemolli may be comparatively modern. Transl.]

one or two vessels at most having undertaken this voyage during the reign of the Ptolemies.[38] In fact, the Egyptians were not yet acquainted with the periodical winds, blowing every six months from an opposite quarter, called monsoons; which, according to Arrian, were not discovered till some ages after, by Hippalus,[39] when Egypt had already become a Roman province: there is no doubt, however, that the Arabians had made use of them long before. All that has come down to us of the age of Ptolemy, is the account of a voyage said to have been made by one Iambulus, which is either a fabrication, or at least mixed up with fable; it is quoted by Diodorus.[40]

The accounts, therefore, of Ceylon, which were current among the Alexandrines in the age of the Ptolemies, did not come from eye-witnesses who had themselves visited the island, but only from the report of Alexander's followers, Nearchus and Onesicritus, and after them, from Megasthenes and Daimachus, who were sent as ambassadors by the Seleucidæ to the Indian court of Palibothra, and from whom Eratosthenes, Agatharchides, and subsequently Strabo and Pliny, borrowed their accounts of Ceylon. All these writers, therefore, relate, not what they had actually seen, but what they had gathered by hearsay, in the distant countries bordering on the Ganges; and, of course, they contain much that appears fabulous.

Let us see, then, what Alexander, in his expedition to India, heard reported of the island of Ceylon. That its reputation was very great, even at this early period, is attested by Strabo and Pliny.[41] The latter has these words, "Taprobane was for a long time considered to be a second world, and went by the appellation of Antichthones. It was discovered to be an island during the expedition of Alexander the Great. Onesicritus, the admiral of his fleet, says, that it produces larger elephants than India. According to Megasthenes it is divided by a river, and the inhabitants are called Palæogoni,[42] and abound much more with gold and large pearls than the Indians. Eratosthenes makes it seven thousand stadia in length, and five thousand in breadth. It has

[38] STRABO, xi. p. 179. [39] ARRIAN, *Peripl. M. Eryth.* sub fine.
[40] DIODORUS, i. p. 167. [41] PLIN. et STRABO, in loc. cit.
[42] [That is, probably, the descendants of Bali? TRANSL.]

2 F 2

no cities, but only villages, of which there are reckoned upwards of seven hundred. Its beginning is in the Eastern Ocean, and was formerly supposed to be twenty days' sail distant from the kingdom of the Prasii; but it being afterwards found that the natives commonly made the passage in vessels of very slight build, like those used on the Nile, the distance was reduced to seven days' sail. The intermediate ocean is here and there shoaly, but with occasional channels so deep that no anchor can reach the bottom. For this reason the vessels, which are generally of about three thousand amphoræ burden, are built sharp fore and aft, in order to avoid the necessity of going about, in the narrows. The natives only put to sea during three months of the year, and wait a hundred days after the summer, and as many after the winter solstice, before they venture out."

The expression which Pliny himself makes use of in quoting these remarks, viz. "that he borrowed them from ancient writers," is a sufficient proof that they belong to the age of Alexander and his successors.[43] Strabo likewise refers to the same authority, and in enumerating the various articles of merchandise, particularly tortoise-shell and ivory, exported from Ceylon into India, affords convincing testimony that the island was at that time the seat of a widely-extended commerce. No further evidence therefore is required to show, that upwards of three hundred years before Christ, and consequently nine hundred before the time of Cosmas, the island of Ceylon, and above all, the northern part, together with the channel which divides it from the Indian continent, was the seat of a very active and opulent trade.

But if Ceylon had already acquired such a distinguished name as a commercial emporium in the time of Alexander, we are fully justified in concluding that its celebrity extends much further back, and reaches even the epoch of Persian dominion. This, indeed, is corroborated by the Journal of Nearchus, who commanded the fleet of the Macedonian conqueror. We are informed, that as this officer was entering the Persian Gulf on his return from India, the promontory of Maketa, now called Muskat,[44] was pointed out

[43] STRABO, XV. p. 1012.

[44] [The author must surely be mistaken; for in all our maps, this promontory is now called Cape Mussendon, whereas Muskat, the ancient Moscha Portus, is at least seventy leagues further to the east. TRANSL.]

to him as the principal mart for cinnamon (which is a native of Ceylon) and other Indian productions, which were transported from thence into Assyria, i. e. Babylonia. The same writer also notices the pearl-fisheries of India. There can be no reasonable doubt, therefore, that the produce of Ceylon found its way to the markets of Arabia, Babylonia, and Persia, as early as the time of the Persian empire.

There is no occasion to carry the subject any further back, to the voyages of the Phœnicians and Jews under Solomon; this has been already done in another treatise; and besides, the name of Ceylon does not occur in that early period. Lest I should therefore advance what is doubtful and uncertain, in the place of what is clear and authentic, I shall rest satisfied with having endeavoured to show, that five centuries before Christ Ceylon was already noted for her trade and navigation.

Let us now, then, retrace our steps to the time of Cosmas and Sopater, the epoch from which we set out, preparatory to establishing the correspondent activity of Singhalese commerce in the middle ages. Here it will, perhaps, be objected, that we must necessarily grope our way in the dark; for, excepting the accounts of two Arabian travellers, published by Renaudot, we have no information relative to India or Ceylon, prior to the invasion of the Mongols in the eleventh century. The objection is certainly valid, as far as India is concerned; but with respect to Ceylon, considerable light has been thrown on the subject by a memoir of Sir Alexander Johnston, lately read before the Asiatic Society of London.[45] Sir Alexander was for seven years one of the judges of the supreme court of Ceylon, and visited every part of the island, particularly the northern coast, which is now almost deserted, with the view of supplying government with data in their projected restoration of its ancient commerce. Hence he was led to investigate the nature and form of Singhalese trade in earlier times; and for this purpose he applied himself not so much to the native Hindus as to the Mohammedan merchants and priests still residing in the island, whose fathers had themselves been engaged in this very commerce. We have, therefore, not

[45] *Transactions of the Royal Asiatic Society of Great Britain and Ireland*, vol. i. part iii. p. 537—543; from which the following is taken.

the fabulous reports of the natives to guide our inquiry, but the authentic evidence of men who still cherished a recollection of former prosperity. Their accounts comprise the interval of time which elapsed since the Mohammedan merchants first visited the island; and upon comparing them with the narrative of Cosmas before quoted, every one must be satisfied of their correctness and veracity. We find, in short, the account of Cosmas and Sopater repeated in almost the same words.

From them it appears that the first Mohammedans who established themselves in the island, were Arabs of the family of Hashem; who, in order to escape from the tyrannical oppression of the Caliph Abdolmelic, withdrew about the end of the sixth century, from the Euphrates to the coast of Malabar and the Concan, and subsequently into Ceylon; so that these emigrations were a consequence of the disputes between the Abassidæ and the Hashemites. In Ceylon they founded eight colonies, at Trincomalee, Jafnapatam, Mantotte and Manaar, Cudramalle, Putlam, and then at Columbo, Barberin, and Point de Galle. The most celebrated of these, however, were Manaar and Mantotte, on account of their proximity to the narrow channel dividing Ceylon from the continent; their commanding the passage through; and also on account of the pearl-fisheries in their neighbourhood.[46] The whole trade, therefore, passed from the hands of the Arabs and Malabarians, who had formerly possessed it, into those of the Mohammedans; and was carried on with Egypt, Arabia, Persia, and Hindustan, on one side, and with the Ultra-Gangetic countries, the peninsula of Malacca, and the adjacent Archipelago as far as China, on the other. It was in this part of the island that the Chinese merchants, who had left their own country with a cargo of silk goods, and bartered them on the voyage for aloes, nutmegs, and articles of perfumery, sold the latter to traders from Arabia and Persia; so that Ceylon became the centre of an exchange commerce between the productions of the East and those of the Western world. The Singhalese merchants were, even at that time, persons of considerable wealth; but the most flourishing period of their commercial pros-

[46] The ruins of Mantotte are still to be seen, near the Giant's Tank, called Cattocarli. SIR A. JOHNSTON, p. 546, not. 2.

perity, was the interval between the tenth and twelfth centuries. Their ample warehouses, extending from Manaar to Mantotte, were then filled with the most valuable productions of Ceylon and the neighbouring countries; such as rice from Trincomalee; purple dye from Jafna; shells and pearls from Cudramalle; areca-nuts and betel leaf from Putlam; cinnamon and precious stones from Columbo; cocoa-nut oil from Barberin; and ivory from Point de Galle: all this, however, was nothing compared to the merchandise procured from foreign countries. Moreover, these spirited merchants contrived to maintain their influence in the straits as well as on shore, by stationing armed vessels in the roadstead to defend the channels, by which alone the harbour could be approached. They also took care that the artificial lakes or tanks, of which there are said to have been upwards of six hundred, built for the purpose of irrigating the rice plantations, should be always kept in efficient repair; the adjacent country was therefore in a most excellent state of cultivation, and thickly populated. Sir Alexander Johnston also informs us, that about this time a number of silk weavers were first introduced into Ceylon, from India; to whom the king of the island granted unusual privileges, and allowed them to have their own laws and courts of justice.

In this manner did commerce flourish in the hands of the Mohammedan merchants of Ceylon, till the beginning of the sixteenth century. From that period, however, it gradually declined, in consequence of the great change brought about in navigation by the discovery of a passage to India round the Cape of Good Hope; when the straits between Ceylon and the continent were no longer frequented by vessels, and the Portuguese, followed by the Dutch, successively established themselves in the island. Nevertheless, it is still said to contain near seventy thousand Mohammedans, dispersed abroad in the various ports and towns on the coast.

I shall now draw these observations to a close, though much still remains worthy of closer investigation; particularly when we are furnished with some more accurate descriptions of the northern part of the island, and the ancient monuments there found. What has hitherto been advanced, however, may be considered sufficient to establish the truth of our proposition, that Ceylon, for the space of about two thousand years, continued to be the common emporium of Southern commerce; and that, consequently, commercial history in general, but particularly with reference to India, is mainly dependent on that of Ceylon. We have also alluded to the peculiar nature of this commerce, which was carried on by foreign colonists, who had made settlements on the coast, while the native inhabitants, confining themselves to the interior of the island, abstained altogether from maritime occupations. And, further, it has been shown that these foreigners were of various countries; being either Arabians, Persians, or Hindus from the coast of Malabar,[47] whose descendants are still found on the island.

APPENDIX XII.

On the sources of Ptolemy's Geography.[1]

THE question relative to the authorities consulted by Ptolemy, in drawing up his Geography, was first mooted by the late Dr. Brehmer of Lubeck, and by that lamented scholar answered in a novel manner.[2] Before his time, it had been usual to assume the fact of their being purely Grecian;

[47] KNOX, p. 323, expressly declares, that the natives of Malabar extraction are altogether different from the Singhalese; both as regards their physical appearance, their language, and their habits of life. The same writer mentions having seen a town in Ceylon, exclusively inhabited by Malabarians; but subject to the king of the island. Compare BERTOLACCI, p. 39, sq., who carefully enumerates the different races of inhabitants.

[1] From an essay laid before the Royal Society of Göttingen, July 17, 1824, *De fontibus Geographicorum Ptolemæi, tabularumque iis annexarum; num ii Græcæ an vero Tyriæ originis fuerint?* and which may also be considered as a supplement to the extracts from the author's other treatises, presented to the same Society, and which are found in his *Historical Works*, vol. iii. The essay itself appeared in the *Comment. Rec. Soc. Götting.* vol. vi.

[2] In his *Entdeckungen aus dem Alterthum*, Th. i. ii. Lubeck, 1822.

Brehmer, on the contrary, maintained that Ptolemy's work itself, as well as the accompanying charts, usually attributed to a certain Agathodæmon, who is said to have lived at Alexandria in the fifth century, were in reality derived from Phœnician or Tyrian sources. In other words, that Ptolemy, or, more properly speaking, his predecessor, Marinus of Tyre, who lived but a short time before him, and whose work he only corrected, must have founded his geographical descriptions and maps on an ancient Tyrian Atlas, representing in several plates or tables, probably as many as are contained in Ptolemy's work, namely, twenty-six, the whole world as known to the Tyrians. That this ancient Atlas was the fruit of the commercial voyages and travels of the Phœnicians, which naturally led to the construction of geographical charts; and, indeed, rendered such an undertaking indispensably necessary. And, that the above-mentioned work, therefore, together with the accompanying maps, might properly be considered as exhibiting the commercial geography of the Phœnicians: a new ray of light would thereby be thrown on the subject itself, and at the same time upon remote antiquity in general; while the geographical knowledge and extensive commerce of that enterprising people would emerge at once from the obscurity in which they have so long been enveloped.

Before we proceed to examine the ground-work of this hypothesis, it will be necessary to premise a few words respecting Ptolemy's Geography, and the accompanying charts. In the first of the eight books which compose the whole work, the author informs us of the origin and object of his present undertaking, and lays down some rules for the construction of maps. The six following contain little more than a bare nomenclature of towns, mountains, and rivers; always, however, with the addition of their longitude and latitude, according to the three climates of the world, and the several countries they respectively contain. The eighth and last book comprises a catalogue of three hundred and fifty towns, together with the length of the day in each, for the purpose of determining its latitude, and the distance either east or west of Alexandria, with regard to time, for its longitude. According to the report of Ptolemy himself, he was led to undertake this work by the example of his immediate predecessor, the above-mentioned Marinus of Tyre, who must have lived about the commencement of the second century, as Ptolemy flourished in the middle of the same period. This Marinus had published three successively improved editions of his Geography; the two first being furnished with maps, which he was only prevented from adding to the third by death. Ptolemy bears witness to the great care bestowed upon this work: in fact, Marinus had made use of every available source in the accounts of travellers, whether ancient or modern, in order to improve his Atlas (πίναξ γεωγραφικὸς). The maps, however, belonging to the second edition were no longer applicable to the third, which had been so much improved; and the followers of Marinus would have been led into a great many mistakes, had they attempted so to apply them: moreover, there was still room for considerable improvement in the text of the third edition itself. In consequence, Ptolemy determined to undertake the labour of correcting Marinus where it should be necessary, adopting, however, the general substance of his work, and subjoining to the last book some instructions on the method of drawing geographical charts.[3] This will serve to explain the relation in which Ptolemy's work stands to that of Marinus: with the exception of some improvement in the details, and the addition of the first and eighth books, which undoubtedly belong to the former writer, the remaining portions of the work are the sole and exclusive property of Marinus alone.

Some good manuscripts of this work, particularly one in the Imperial Library at Vienna, and another in that of St. Mark at Venice, are furnished with a series of ancient maps, twenty-six in number, of which ten are devoted to Europe, four to Africa, and the remaining twelve to Asia. These maps are, in the MSS. themselves, attributed to a certain Agathodæmon; for at the end we read the following subscription: Ἀγαθοδαίμων μηχανικὸς Ἀλεξανδρεὺς ὑπετύπωσε. He was, therefore, an artist of Alexandria: but this comprehends all that we certainly know of him. The common opinion, that he lived in the fifth century, rests upon the bare assumption of his being the same individual as the grammarian named

[3] Ptol. *Geogr.* i. cap. 6, 17.

Agathodæmon, to whom some epistles written by Isidore of Pelusium are still extant. This supposition, however, is not only without foundation, but is even extremely improbable, from the unlikely circumstance that an artist should be at the same time also a grammarian. On the other hand, he might very possibly have been contemporary with Ptolemy, and have assisted him in the construction of his charts. Several passages[4] plainly intimate Ptolemy's own intention of adding maps to his work. In the modern editions of the Geography, these maps have not always remained without alteration, though copied in the first instance from the originals themselves. The first edition accompanied with the charts is that of Rome, in the year 1478;[5] these charts were copied in that of 1490. The second edition is that of Ulm, in 1482, which was furnished with maps by the care of Nicholas Donis, a Benedictine of the monastery of Reichenbach. It is a mistake to suppose, as is commonly done, that all the maps in our editions belong to this editor; for he had no share in either of the two which were issued at Rome. The nature and extent of the alterations made in the charts appended to these editions, can only be determined by a more accurate comparison of them with the originals. The Roman editors appear to have altered least: they have not introduced new names, but only supplied them in certain cases by a reference to Ptolemy himself; they do not even seem to have made any improvement in the geographical outline of countries which were incorrectly laid down.

We must, however, leave it to the future editor of Ptolemy to furnish a more accurate notice of these variations. In the mean time, we shall proceed to examine the arguments advanced by Brehmer in support of his hypothesis.

The first is grounded on the "declarations of Ptolemy himself."[6] The author here alludes to the passage where it is said, "that Marinus had met with several accounts of

[4] Particularly lib. i. cap. 19.

[5] An earlier one of 1475, the *editio princeps*, is without maps: as to the edition purporting to be of the year 1462, Fabricius and others have already shown that date to be spurious. All the old editions exhibit the Latin version, often altered and improved, of Jacobus Angelus. The first edition in the original Greek was that of Erasmus, printed at Basil in the year 1533, by Frobenius.

[6] BREHMER, *Entdeckungen*, i. 25.

earlier travellers; that he had carefully perused the writings of almost all his predecessors on this subject, and had made such corrections as they or himself deemed necessary. "This," says Brehmer, "is evident from the improvements in the successive editions of the Atlas (πίνακος γεωγραφικοῦ)."[7] But the last-mentioned work is, in fact, that of Marinus alone, which he several times edited and corrected according to the former editions. The passage consequently makes nothing for Brehmer; on the contrary, it rather militates against him, for it expressly mentions the accounts of preceding travellers, both ancient, indeed, and modern, as the sources from which the work was composed, but without any allusion to an ancient Tyrian Atlas being consulted for that purpose.

The next argument advanced by Brehmer is drawn from the "impossibility of constructing without a model, and with no other assistance than mere catalogues of names, and other data furnished by Ptolemy, a series of charts, so exact and conformable to nature as the ones in question."[8] This opinion, however, is formed only from an inspection of the charts as they appear in the printed editions; for the author never examined the manuscripts themselves, and therefore we are unable to judge of its correctness. But, independent of this, we are ready to allow, that no such ancient charts, supposing them to be as exact as the author mentions, could possibly have been designed without the help of some previous sketch. There is little doubt that charts of countries were in existence before the time of Marinus, and they might very likely have been made use of by him: indeed, we should not be at all surprised to find that the Phœnicians had attempted the construction of a general map of the known world, and even particular delineations of different countries. We learn from Herodotus,[9] that their neighbours and commercial allies, the Greeks of Asia Minor, possessed such maps; and if we do not find it expressly mentioned that the Phœnicians had theirs also, this circumstance ought to form no solid objection; because, where is it possible now to look for proofs in support of our opinion? The geographical attempts just alluded to might have been im-

[7] Ptol. i. cap. 6. [8] *Entdeckungen*, i. 37. [9] Herodotus, v. cap. 49.

proved from time to time, and thus have served as models to Marinus in constructing his own charts, which were nevertheless very imperfect, notwithstanding the improvements he made on the labours of his predecessors. Marinus, who was a native of Tyre, and undoubtedly had it in his power to consult the literary treasures of Alexandria, would easily find in the latter place all the requisite materials for his undertaking. But that at such an early period a complete and original Atlas should have been immediately formed, in consequence of the mercantile connexions of Tyre in the most ancient time, is, to say the least of it, an unnecessary assumption.

"Further," argues Brehmer, "many of the names occurring in Ptolemy's work evidently betray their Phœnician origin." It is certainly true, that many names in ancient geography come from the Phœnicians; but does it therefore follow, that they were all taken from a very ancient and original Atlas? And, as they must already have been a long time in use, might not the Greeks have adopted them in their own nomenclatures and charts?

The most important argument, however, advanced by Brehmer, still remains to be considered. He appeals to the extent of Ptolemy's geographical knowledge as compared with that of his predecessors, for instance, Eratosthenes and Strabo;[10] and, indeed, the difference between them on that score is sufficiently striking. Eratosthenes lived and wrote at Alexandria, and was himself superintendent of the famous library; we may therefore reasonably conclude that its ample resources were at his perfect disposal. Strabo, notwithstanding his temporary residence at Alexandria likewise, and the same facility of consulting its literary stores, nevertheless closely follows in the steps of Eratosthenes, and copies his descriptions of distant countries and regions; so that with some few exceptions, which have already been discussed in another treatise,[11] he has not much advanced the science of geography. The northern parts of Asia were entirely unknown to him; as a proof of which, he represents the Caspian Sea as a bay of the ocean; and his

[10] Brehmer, *Entdeckungen*, i. p. 24.

[11] *Commentationes de fontibus Strabonis*, in Comment. Rec. Soc. Götting. vol. v.

knowledge of India was extremely confined. Two or three cities in India, on this side the Ganges, comprehend the whole of his acquaintance with that part of the world; his notice of Ceylon is limited to a few traditional reports; of the Ultra-Gangetic peninsula he was perfectly ignorant. The little more that he knew of Arabia was chiefly derived from the verbal accounts of Ælius Gallus, the lieutenant whom he conversed with in Egypt. Of Æthiopia, the parts adjacent to the coast are almost all that he describes; while his knowledge of Libya extends no further than Ammonium. That he was completely ignorant of northern Europe from the Elbe to the Caspian, is his own honest confession. How very different does the case stand with regard to Ptolemy! In the Eastern part of the world, the continent of India now emerges from its obscurity: and though incorrectly laid down, yet enough is said of it to evince Ptolemy's knowledge of the coast, and the maritime towns, and even the interior of the country. Of Ceylon alone he notices upwards of twenty towns and harbours; and he is the first geographer who mentions the peninsula beyond the Ganges. His description of Arabia, comprising the interior as well as the coast, enumerates a large list of names. No less remarkable is his knowledge of the northern parts of the world; he was acquainted with the peninsula of Jutland and its inhabitants, if not also with Norway and Sweden. The Germanic nations, and even those inhabiting the modern countries of Poland and Lithuania,[12] as far as the Baltic, were well known to him. The Caspian Sea is no longer represented as a gulf of the ocean, for the existence of vast tracts of country to the north of that lake was now fully ascertained.

Hence, therefore, arises the question, whether during the interval of time which elapsed between Strabo and Marinus, and again between Marinus and Ptolemy, that is, during the first hundred and fifty years of our era, the science of geography had made sufficient progress to enable us to account for its extraordinary subsequent development, as exhibited in the works of latter writers? The scantiness of

[12] The names of these latter nations, frequently corrupt in the original, have been corrected and put in order, by the late M. Gatterer, in his third essay, *An Populorum Letticorum Origines liceat a Sarmatis repetere?* See *Comment. Soc. Götting.* vol. xii. p. 210, etc. The essay is accompanied with an improved map of Lithuania, after Ptolemy.

our authorities, particularly for the last half of the above period, including the reign of the Antonines, will not indeed permit us to return a positive answer to this question. Thus much, however, is certain, that war as well as commerce, by sea and land, most powerfully contributed thereto.

Among the causes, then, most favourable to the progress of geography, we may reckon, first, the wars which were carried on in the time of Augustus against the Germans of the north-west, as well as the confederation under Marbodus, in the opposite quarter; the history of which had already furnished Strabo with his account of Germany.[13] After Augustus and Tiberius, we may instance the wars in Britain, which commenced under Claudius, and lasted till Domitian; and were followed, not only by the subjection of the southern parts of the island, but also by the circumnavigation of the northern coast by Agricola, as we learn from Tacitus. Next to these were the wars under Nero against the Parthians; and, after the conquest of Mauritania, the almost incessant frontier war with the nations inhabiting the interior of Libya, the Garamantes and others, as far as the Great Desert. Under Domitian began the wars on the Danube against the Daci, so gloriously terminated by Trajan; who reduced Dacia itself into a Roman province. The Asiatic campaigns also of the same emperor, against the Parthians and the Arabians, must have greatly furthered the interests of geographical science. Add to these the wars in Ptolemy's own age, against the Marcomanni, which extended a considerable distance north of the Danube.

But still more influential was the operation of commerce in the improvement of geography. The late M. Gatterer has already shown, that it was owing to this cause the countries extending from the Danube to the Baltic first became known.[14] But more especially does the observation apply to the southern parts of the world, which, during this interval, progressively came to light. The conquest of Egypt by the Romans, laid the foundation of an improvement in geographical science; for we are told by Pliny, that from the time of their entering the country, a regular and spirited commercial intercourse was opened between Egypt and In-

[13] See my historical treatises. [14] GATTERER, loc. cit.

dia. Some kind of connexion, indeed, between the two countries, appears to have subsisted under the Ptolemies; but only through the medium of Arabia. Now, however, whole fleets of merchantmen set sail with the monsoons every year from Myos Hormos on the Arabian Gulf, to the ports of India and Ceylon;[15] from which latter island an embassy was sent to Rome as early as the reign of Claudius;[16] and in consequence, the Indian Ocean with the countries situate on its coast, and the neighbouring islands, became generally better known.

It is, however, certain, that during this period, especially the latter part of it under the Antonines, and therefore in the age of Ptolemy, the interior countries of Southern Asia, that is, Arabia and India, were no less explored by means of caravans, than the coasts were by sea voyages. This particularly holds good with regard to the reign of Antoninus Pius. But owing to some strange fatality, it has happened that the reign of this prince, the most excellent perhaps that ever sat on a throne, is precisely that of which we have the fewest memorials extant, from the almost complete destruction of the contemporary historians. It is nevertheless easy to show that this period must have been extremely favourable to the progress of general commerce, and consequently therefore of geography. At the commencement of his reign, Adrian made peace with the Parthians, and even restored to them the territories conquered by his predecessors; the consequence was, that for the space of forty years, under him and Antoninus Pius, the interior of Asia enjoyed almost perfect tranquillity. The happy effects which this moderation produced, are sufficiently demonstrable, in the absence of history, from the ruins discovered in those countries, not only at Palmyra, which has been explored long since, but also within these few years at Gerasa and Petra on the Syro-Arabian frontier, and also at other places. The style of architecture, as well as the number of inscriptions found in these ancient cities, prove beyond a doubt that their most flourishing period belongs to the age of the Antonines. From what other sources, indeed, could they have derived their opulence, situated as they were in a barren country,

[15] PLIN. *Hist. Nat.* vi. 24. [16] Ibid. vi. 26.

and even in the heart of deserts, except from the Indo-Arabian commerce, the high roads of which at that time, and long after, passed through those places? Although the evidence furnished by these data is sufficient generally to show that in the hundred years previous to Marinus and Ptolemy, wars, commerce, and travel had greatly contributed to the extension of geographical knowledge; yet we must not omit to include the active co-operation of professed writers on the science. The work of the elder Pliny will serve to confirm our position; what an abundance of geographical information do we not meet with in his first six books, upon comparing them with Strabo! We read of geometrical surveys carried on as early as the time of Augustus, under the superintendence of his son-in-law Agrippa;[17] and partially in the countries above Egypt, under Nero.[18] But what especially deserves our consideration in treating of this period, are the written accounts of land and sea voyages *(peripli)*. The only work of the latter kind now extant, is the celebrated Periplus of the Erythræan Sea, by Arrian; evidently the composition of a merchant who traded to the shores of the Indian peninsula, and a fair specimen of the manner in which these voyages were written. That such accounts of travels were of frequent occurrence, may be inferred from Ptolemy himself, who observes that Marinus borrowed his materials from similar authorities.[19] The successively improved editions of his work on geography are another proof of the fact; for how otherwise could Marinus obtain additional and more correct information on the subject, except by consulting the accounts of recent travellers? We have, indeed, the express testimony of Ptolemy on this point, for he mentions the names of certain writers whom Marinus had thus made use of.[20] These were, for the maritime countries of the Indian seas, Diogenes, Theophilus, an Alexander of Macedon, Dioscurius, and "many others:"[21] for the interior of Libya, Septimus Flaccus, and Julius Maternus:[22] and for the route to Serica, Titianus of Macedon, also called Maës,[23] the son of a merchant who had sent his commercial agent into that country. The narratives of all these travellers were consulted by Marinus. And if we

[17] Plin. iii. 3. [18] Ibid. vi. 35. [19] Ptol. i. 6. [20] Ibid. i. 9, 14.
[21] Ibid. i. 14, ἐξ ἄλλων πολλῶν. [22] Ibid. i. 8. [23] Ibid. i. 11.

inquire further, upon what Ptolemy founded his corrections of the Tyrian geographer, he himself informs us that it was the perusal of the latest itineraries.[24] With regard to the determinations of latitude and longitude, and particularly what is reported in the eighth book of the duration of the longest day, together with the distance of places from Alexandria according to time, we cannot, indeed, pretend that all this was the fruit of actual observation: but only, for the most part, the result of calculations made from the several distances laid down by the travellers above mentioned.

There is, therefore, no occasion for us to have recourse to the hypothesis of an ancient Tyrian Atlas in order to explain the improved state of geographical science, as exemplified in the works of Marinus and Ptolemy: on the other hand it is evident from the preceding remarks, that the countries and seas which they describe had been actually visited and explored by contemporary travellers; and such authorities might just as likely have been consulted by the writers in question, as any original Phœnician work. We have not indeed attempted to show from what sources Ptolemy borrowed all the particular details of his geography, or the accompanying charts. Such an inquiry presupposes a critical examination of the text, and a collation of the best manuscripts, together with a correct and scrupulously faithful copy of the ancient charts; and even then we could scarcely hope, considering the total loss of all the writings before noticed, to ascertain the precise authorities in every instance which Ptolemy consulted.

APPENDIX XIII.

On the Commercial Routes of Ancient Asia.

In the chart of Asia appended to this work, I have endeavoured for the first time to point out with critical ac-

[24] Ptol. i. 19.

curacy, the ancient commercial routes of Asia, as well by land as by sea. And, although a particular account of them has already been given in the course of the work itself, yet perhaps a general view of these routes, together with the authorities on which I formed my conclusions, will not be unacceptable to the reader, particularly as he will then be enabled to judge how far they are correct, or only probable. I shall also subjoin a review, before promised, (vol. i. p. 357, note,) of the commercial routes laid down by Dr. Brehmer in his map of Asia.

LAND-ROUTES.

I. ROUTES OF THE ARABICO-PHŒNICIAN CARAVANS.

Their direction is towards Petra in northern Arabia, and from thence to Phœnicia.

1. Route from Arabia Felix to Petra: attested by Strabo, (p. 1113,) who points out its direction, as well as the number of days' journey. (See vol. i. p. 356.)

2. Route from Arabia Felix to Gerra: also ascertained from Strabo (loc. cit.) by his mentioning the number of days' journey. The town of Leuke Kome[1] through which it passed, according to Seetzen, (Monatl. Corresp. Jan. 1813, p. 75,) was so called from the whiteness of its cliffs. I have made this route to commence from Mariaba, or Saba, as the capital town; the passages, however, already quoted from Ezekiel and the other prophets, evidently show that there was a commercial intercourse with all parts of the country.

3. Route from Gerra to Tyre; not positively mentioned, but there can be no doubt of its existence, particularly as on one hand, Gerra is represented as an opulent town, (see vol. ii. p. 433,) and on the other, its land commerce is expressly noticed by Agatharchides (Geogr. Min. i. 60, and Strabo, p. 1110); the prophets also, Ezekiel, xxvii. 15, and Isaiah, xxi. 13, allude to its connexion with Tyre, that is, if we assume, as is generally supposed, their Dedan to be one of the neighbouring islands in the Persian Gulf, pro-

[1] [It is not easy to see why this route should pass through Leuke Kome, such direction being less circuitous in the case of the first-mentioned route, from Arabia Felix to Petra. TRANSL.]

bably one of the Bahrein islands. (See vol. i. p. 434.) With regard to the direction of the route from Gerra to Tyre, we have no certain information. I have made it pass directly through the middle of the great Arabian desert, and perhaps I am justified in so doing by the passage above quoted from Isaiah. The modern route is from Hedjaz through the fertile plain of Nedjed, due west to Mecca, or the ancient Macoraba. According to Seetzen (Monatl. Corresp. Sept. 1813, p. 244,) it occupies the caravan thirty days, and passes through several villages, whereas the route to Medina is all desert. In this case the route would here join that of Yemen, and consequently, though longer, would be less dangerous.

4. The route to Egypt, particularly Memphis, (see vol. i. p. 361,) requires no explanation, as the commercial intercourse between that country and Phœnicia admits of no doubt whatever.

5. The route by which the Phœnicians traded with Armenia and the Caucasus, (see vol. i. p. 368,) is no where determined. But as these countries were well peopled and civilized, there was in all probability no general route, individual merchants being at liberty to choose their own way.

II. ROUTES OF THE BABYLONICO-PERSIAN CARAVANS.

A. *Routes leading to Western Asia.*

1. Route from Lydia to Susa in Persia: there can be no doubt of its existence, as Herodotus (v. 52) mentions both the direction and the number of stations. (See vol. i. p. 426.) Some mistake, however, seems to have crept into the text, for the whole amount of stations is said to be a hundred and eleven, whereas eighty-four only are specified. Whether this be owing to the inadvertence of Herodotus himself, or his transcriber, it is impossible to say.

2. Route from Babylon to Phœnicia: no where positively laid down, and perhaps there were several. We have two reasons, however, for presuming it to have passed through Palmyra. In the first place, because that was the most obvious direction, otherwise the caravan would have been obliged to make a large circuit to the north, or else have to

cross an extensive desert entirely without water; and on the other hand, we know Palmyra to have been a very ancient city, and that from its position it could scarcely have had any other original destination, than to serve as a resting-place to the caravans. (See vol. i. p. 366.) The route then led to Thapsacus, an important commercial town on the Euphrates, which it crossed at Circesium, and subsequently took a southerly direction through the Median wall to Babylon.

3. Route from Babylon to Syria; precisely determined by Strabo, p. 1084. This was exclusively a caravan-route, for none but a large body of merchants could undertake such a journey, as it passed directly through the heart of the Mesopotamian desert, and was infested by roving hordes of robbers, who levied a toll on all passengers. It traversed Syria, as far as Anthemusias, where it crossed the Euphrates; from hence it proceeded through Bambyca to Edessa; and afterwards, at a distance of three days' journey from the river, it passed through the steppes inhabited by the Scenites, or nomads, and where were some cisterns of water, to the town of Scene on the frontiers of Babylon, and about eighteen schœns, or seventy-five miles, distant from Seleucia on the Tigris. This route was probably frequented by the Phœnicians; but as Strabo quotes no authorities on the point, it is impossible to ascertain how long it had been in use; no doubt, however, it was from very early times.

B. *Routes leading to Eastern Asia.*

1. Route from Babylon and Susa to India: may be considered as forming but one single route, as the road between the two cities was much frequented, and the intermediate countries well peopled, and in a high state of civilization. (Arrian, iii. 16; see vol. i. 419.) From hence, however, the route to the countries situate on the Indus, could not take a direction full east without having to pass through the great desert between Persis and Media; it therefore proceeded due north of the desert, through the latter country, and was consequently, for the former part of its course, identical with the royal road, mentioned by Herodotus, on the left bank of the Tigris, leading into Asia Minor. Near

the Median frontier it joined the direct route to India, the principal stations of which have been enumerated by Strabo and Pliny. Now, as both these writers derived their information from earlier sources, Strabo from Eratosthenes, and Pliny from the companions of Alexander, that is, from Beton and Diognetus, who were attached to the royal army in the capacity of geographers, (βηματισταὶ, *itinerum dimensores*,) we cannot therefore doubt either the direction or the antiquity of the route before us. It is, nevertheless, frequently difficult to assign the exact position of certain places, owing to the corruption of the numbers in the MSS. and the very defective state of our modern charts of these countries. The reader may, however, advantageously consult Mannert, vol. v. part ii.

On leaving Mesopotamia, the route went directly east, in about 36° N. lat. to Ecbatana, the capital of Media, (Ptol. i. 22,) and from thence by Rages to the Caspian Gates (Πύλαι Κάσπιαι). Every thing that came from Western Asia to the east, must necessarily pass through these gates, because on the north the way was blocked up by the Hyrcanian mountains and their barbarous inhabitants, while towards the south began the desert. It is, therefore, important to ascertain the position of this pass. Its exact situation will be found in the Caspian mountains, which at this point divide Media from Aria, in 35° N. lat. and 52° E. long. (Compare Mannert, vi. ii. 175, with Rennell's chart.) According to Pliny, (vi. 17,) it was a very narrow defile, about eight Roman miles in length, cut through the rocks.

From the Caspian pass, the high road led by the following places: Hecatompylos in Parthia, Alexandria in Aria, Prophthasia in the country of the Drangi, Arachotus and Ortospana, to the Indus. With regard to these stations, the account of Eratosthenes, as preserved by Strabo, (p. 782—1053,) agrees perfectly with that of Beton and Diognetus in Pliny (vi. 17, 21); though they occasionally differ as to their respective distances; and therefore it is not always easy to determine their real position. As far as concerns the whole length of the route from the Caspian pass to the Indus, the difference between the two is not material, as may be seen in the following comparison of the several distances mentioned by both writers :—

	PLINY.	STRABO.		
	R. Miles.	*Stadia.*		*R. Miles.*
Hecatompylos	133.	1960	=	245.
Alexandria in Aria	566.	4530	=	566¼.
Prophthasia	199.	1600	=	200.
Arachotus	515.	4120	=	515.
Ortospana	250.	2000	=	250.
Alexandria	50.			
Peucela on the Indus	227.	1000	=	125.
	1940.	15210		1901¼.
Geographical miles,	388.			380.

This variation is too trifling to affect the general accuracy of the account; though not much stress is to be laid on this circumstance; for even Pliny has already observed, that the manuscripts of his time varied in their determination of places, as we still find to be the case in the modern copies. (See Salmas. Exercit. in Plin. p. 556.) Moreover, the sum total of 380 geogr. miles appears too much; for, as these places are laid down in our present maps, the distance scarcely exceeds 300. Our geographical knowledge, however, of this part of the world is not yet sufficiently accurate to enable us to determine every one of the admeasurements with correctness.

The first station is Hecatompylos, the capital of Parthia; its situation, however, cannot be precisely ascertained, owing to our uncertainty respecting the distances. Its name, signifying "a hundred gates," is evidently Greek, and according to Polybius, (x. 28,) was derived from the circumstance of a hundred roads meeting in that place. It must, therefore, have been an important mart for the carrying trade.

The second principal station is Alexandria in Aria, as far as which, Strabo expressly informs us, the route was one and the same all the way, but that her' it separated into two branches, one of which led to Bactria, and the other, with a southerly direction, into India. It would be desirable to ascertain the position of this town with sufficient accuracy; all that we have to guide us, however, is the bare information, that Alexandria was situate 566 miles to the east of Hecatompylos, and on the banks of the river Arius, (Plin. vi. 23,) which flowed into a lake of the same name (now called Zere). We must, therefore, look for it on the north or north-east of this lake; and, indeed, as Strabo describes the route to be perfectly straight as far as this place, and almost under the same parallel as the Caspian passes, we may possibly identify it with the ancient capital Artacoana, or the modern Herat. From hence the route proceeded with a southerly inclination to Prophthasia, in the country of the Drangi, which is either the present Zarang, or at least in its neighbourhood; and as both our authors agree in making its distance from Alexandria amount to nearly 200 miles, we shall be less liable to commit serious error, in assigning its probable situation. The next stage we come to is the town of Arachotus, in the country of the same name, which seems to be preserved in the modern appellation of Arocage; nevertheless, its real position cannot exactly be determined; nor, without a better knowledge than we now possess of the country itself and its inhabitants, will it be easy to explain why the road up to this place should make such a sharp turn to the south. This sudden inclination, however, ceases after passing Arachotus, where the road again winds to the north, in its course towards Ortospana and Alexandria. The latter town, from its situation at the foot of that mountain range, was also called Alexandria ad Paropamisum; and was formerly supposed to be the same with the modern Kandahar; but the researches of modern geographers have concurred to make it probable that Ortospana itself is the ancient Alexandria, distant about fifty miles south of Kandahar. (See Mannert, vol. v. part ii. p. 85.) It was an important commercial town, on account of the route from Bactria terminating there, and its being a place where three roads met (ἡ ἐκ Βάκτρων τρίοδος). From hence the Indian route proceeded across the river Choes, to Peucela and Taxila, where it was usual to pass the Indus.

III. ROUTES TO BACTRIA AND SAMARCAND.

1. Route from Western Asia to Bactria: the same as the Indian route as far as Alexandria in Aria, at which place it turned off into Bactria, a distance of 3000, or, according to another reading, 2870 stadia (about 375 or 358 English miles respectively); and from thence it proceeded 5000

stadia (or 625 miles) further to the borders of Central Asia, or Great Tartary, inhabited by the Issedones and Massagetæ. (Strabo, p. 782.)

2. Route from Bactria to India; considered by Strabo (p. 1053) merely as a continuation of the preceding, so that it might also be frequented by merchants who had come from Media, by way of the Caspian pass as far as Alexandria in Aria, and wished to avoid the more circuitous southern route. From Bactria the road went southwards over the mountains of Paropamisus, and at Ortospana formed a junction with the other Indian route, from which circumstance that place was called the Bactrian Trivium. We may understand this appellation to mean, that in addition to the two roads leading to India and Bactria, there was also a third, which led to the southern parts of the Indus. (See vol. i. p. 424.) This, however, is nothing more than a conjecture, and even without having recourse to such a supposition, we can easily imagine how a real *trivium* might have been formed at Ortospana, when we consider that place as the central point where the three roads to India, Bactria, and Western Asia, met together.

3. Route from Bactria to Little Bucharia and Serica: authenticated by a passage in Ctesias, where he speaks of Indian caravans from Little Thibet (already quoted and explained in vol. i. p. 425). The same passage also confirms in the most satisfactory manner the existence of a trading intercourse between the neighbouring inhabitants of Bactria and Upper India, and justifies my insertion of a corresponding commercial route in the map. This route joined the one from India, and the principal station for both was in the neighbourhood of the Stone Tower, mentioned above, p. 290, of this volume. With respect to the route from Serica to the Ganges, I have only been able to trace it by conjectural evidence.

C. *Commercial Route through Central Asia.*

This route, which proceeded from the Greek establishments on the Black Sea, over the Ural mountains to the country of the Argippæans, or Calmucks of Great Tartary, is founded on the accounts of Herodotus, and particularly a passage in his fourth book, (c. 24,) which has been sufficiently explained in this volume, p. 22, 23. In the map I have continued this route beyond the frontier of the Issedones, as we have already shown that extensive and highly commercial nation to have been in the immediate neighbourhood of the Seres; with whom an active trading intercourse was always maintained. That an exchange of the merchandise as well of Eastern as of Southern Asia, might very well take place in the country of the Issedones, will be evident enough when we consider that nation to have extended from Serica on the east, to the Jaxartes on the south, where, as we have seen from Strabo, the caravan-route from India terminated. Besides, how could Herodotus have acquired any tolerable knowledge of the various nomad tribes inhabiting Sogdiana, unless some kind of commercial intercourse had existed between them?

SEA VOYAGES.

The navigation of the Asiatic seas in former times, as far as we are able to ascertain its character, was confined to the Arabian and Persian Gulfs, and the Indian Ocean. The doubts which have been raised as to the practicability of these voyages, fall to the ground when we consider the various circumstances concurring to render them easy; in the first place, the voyages themselves were almost wholly along the coast, or, at all events, there was no occasion to get out of sight of land; and secondly, the distances were moderate; add to this the peculiar facilities afforded by the monsoons. The direction of these periodical winds, in that part of the Indian Sea now under consideration, is south-west in summer, and north-east in winter; the same order, but slightly varied, obtains also in the Arabian and Persian Gulfs, where they blow alternately from the north in summer, and from the south during a part of the winter. A single glance at the map will be sufficient to show how extremely favourable this peculiarity must have been to voyages made to and from the Indian peninsula, at different seasons of the year. The particular routes by sea are laid down on the map, and are as follow: 1. From the Arabian Gulf. 2. From Arabia Felix to India. 3. From the Persian Gulf also to India. To what has been already advanced in the body of this work, I have now only to add, that the general destination of these voyages was the Indian port of Barygaza, (Baroach,) which still continued to be the principal one in the time of the Periplus. Besides this, Pattala also, situate in the Delta of the Indus, appears to have been from the earliest times a place of considerable importance; and is represented as such in the expedition of Alexander. The further navigation from this port to Taprobane or Ceylon, as well as the eastern coast of the peninsula to the mouth of the Ganges, was very probably close along shore, and therefore need not have been specified on the map. The passage across the Bay of Bengal to Chryse, is given from the accounts contained in the Periplus.

Though, for reasons already mentioned in the foregoing appendix, we do not feel ourselves authorized in assigning such a remote antiquity to the commercial routes laid down by Brehmer, after the determinations of Ptolemy, as that scholar attached to them; it will nevertheless be as well to furnish the reader with a comparative sketch of my own map, and that which Brehmer has subjoined to the first volume of his work. These routes, both in their general course and destination, are the same with those which have been heretofore pointed out, after other authorities, in my earlier maps; only their number has been augmented, and the direction of particular routes occasionally varied; which was a natural consequence of Brehmer's founding his conclusions exclusively on Ptolemy. I shall here present them in the same order as my own.

1. Commercial routes of Arabia. Brehmer agrees with me in making Yemen, Gerra, and Petra, the principal marts of the Arabian land-trade; and in connecting them together by routes, similar to those of my own map. He mentions, however, some other routes traversing the interior of Arabia to certain towns called by Ptolemy, Carman, Itala, Thumna, and Macpha, of which I can meet with no precise information in the authorities I have consulted.

2. Babylonian routes to Arabia and Phœnicia; represented by Brehmer as running due east from Petra to Babylon, Teredon, and Gerra, and in a northerly direction from Petra to Palmyra, Thapsacus, and Trapezus on the Black

Sea; and again, from Babylon to Gerra. No direct route from Tyre and the other Phœnician cities is specified.

3. Babylonian routes to Eastern Asia. That which went from Babylon and Susa through Ecbatana and the Caspian passes, as well as the one leading to Aria, Ortospana, etc., corresponds generally with my own. On the other hand, Brehmer introduces another commercial route through Carmania to Gedrosia, of which I have not been able to discover any indication.

4. The route through Central Asia, he represents as leading from the city Tanais, across the narrow strip of land between the Caspian and Aral Seas, to Maracanda and Bactria.

5. Indian commercial routes; from Bactria to Taxila; from Ortospana to Taxila; from Ortospana to Pattala; and subsequently from Pattala to Barygaza and Soana on the Ganges; from Taxila to Delhi; from Bucephala on the Hydaspes, to Uzene, Tagara, Plutana, and Masalia (Masulipatam on the Coromandel coast).

6. Routes to Serica; one from Bactria, by Tashkend, to the Stone Tower; another from Taxila due north to the same place; and a third from the Ganges, also in a northerly direction to the same tower: of this last-mentioned route, however, only a portion can be ascertained.

7. The sea voyages from the Arabian and Persian Gulfs, the former from Yemen and the latter from the Bahrein islands, as laid down by Brehmer, correspond with those in my own chart. He has not, indeed, specified any particular route to the peninsula beyond the Ganges; but has merely pointed out the place of departure for vessels trading to Chryse.

THE END.

JOHN CHILDS AND SON, BUNGAY.

INDEX

TO

VOL. I.

VOL. II. 2 H

INDEX

TO

VOL. II.

Zeitfracht Medien GmbH
Ferdinand-Jühlke-Straße 7
99095 Erfurt, Deutschland
produktsicherheit@kolibri360.de